THE
Picture
Bible

Script by Iva Hoth

Illustrations by Andre Le Blanc

Chariot Victor Publishing

A Division of Cook Communications

Chariot Victor Publishing
A division of Cook Communications, Colorado Springs, Colorado 80918
Cook Communications, Paris, Ontario
Kingsway Communications, Eastbourne, England

THE PICTURE BIBLE
© 1978, 1998 by David C. Cook Publishing Co.

Bible editors: C. Elvan Olmstead, Ph.D., and Jim Townsend, Ph.D.
Revisions editor: Jeannie Harmon
Art Director: Andrea Boven
Designer: Paz Design Group
Interior Text Revisions: Cheryl Ogletree

The maps shown on pp. 12, 544, and 664 were developed
for Bible-in-Life Sunday School Curriculum

First hardcover printing, 1979
First paperback printing, 1981
Printed in the United States of America

LC 79—67013

ISBN: 0-78143-057-7 Deluxe Hardcover
ISBN: 0-78143-055-0 Storybook Hardcover
ISBN: 0-78143-058-5 Paperback

Table of Contents

WHEN MOSES SEES THE ISRAELITES WORSHIPING AN IDOL, HIS ANGER CAUSES HIM TO THROW DOWN THE STONE TABLETS.

▲ EXODUS 32 (page 157)

ABRAHAM IS WILLING TO OFFER EVEN HIS BELOVED SON, BECAUSE OF HIS LOVE FOR GOD.

▲ GENESIS 22 (page 65)

1ST CHINESE DICTIONARY		1ST OLYMPICS	ALEXANDER	ROME FALLS		COLUMBUS	TODAY	
2000 B.C.	1500 B.C.	1000 B.C.	500 B.C.	0	500 A.D.	1000 A.D.	1500 A.D.	2000 A.D.

BEFORE RECORDED TIME

THE FUTURE ▶

ABRAHAM   MOSES   DAVID ELIJAH ESTHER   JESUS BORN

B I B L E   H I G H L I G H T S   I N   T I M E

▲ JUDGES 6—7 (page 218)

1ST CHINESE DICTIONARY | 1ST OLYMPICS | ALEXANDER | ROME FALLS | COLUMBUS | TODAY
2000 B.C. | 1500 B.C. | 1000 B.C. | 500 B.C. | 0 | 500 A.D. | 1000 A.D. | 1500 A.D. | 2000 A.D.

BEFORE RECORDED TIME

THE FUTURE ▶

ABRAHAM   MOSES   DAVID ELIJAH ESTHER   JESUS BORN

B I B L E   H I G H L I G H T S   I N   T I M E

▲ **RUTH 2 (page 247)**

BECAUSE THE LORD IS MY SHEPHERD, I HAVE EVERYTHING I NEED.

▲ **1 SAMUEL 17 (page 281)**

1ST CHINESE DICTIONARY   1ST OLYMPICS ALEXANDER   ROME FALLS   COLUMBUS   TODAY
        2000 B.C.   1500 B.C.   1000 B.C.   500 B.C.   0   500 A.D.   1000 A.D.   1500 A.D.   2000 A.D.
BEFORE   THE
RECORDED TIME   FUTURE
        ABRAHAM   MOSES   DAVID ELIJAH ESTHER JESUS BORN
        B I B L E   H I G H L I G H T S   I N   T I M E

▲ **1 SAMUEL 15 (page 272)**

▲ **ESTHER 7 (page 475)**

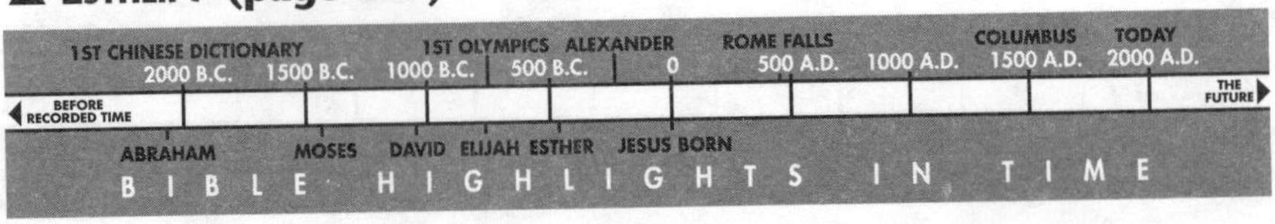

NEW TESTAMENT STORIES

▲ **DANIEL (page 521)**

1ST CHINESE DICTIONARY   1ST OLYMPICS ALEXANDER   ROME FALLS   COLUMBUS   TODAY
    2000 B.C.   1500 B.C.   1000 B.C.   500 B.C.   0   500 A.D.   1000 A.D.   1500 A.D.   2000 A.D.
◀ BEFORE
RECORDED TIME   THE
                                                                                                              FUTURE ▶
    ABRAHAM   MOSES   DAVID ELIJAH ESTHER   JESUS BORN
        B I B L E   H I G H L I G H T S   I N   T I M E

AND SO I AM GIVING A NEW COMMANDMENT TO YOU NOW--LOVE EACH OTHER JUST AS MUCH AS I LOVE YOU.

▲ **JOHN 13 (page 637)**

AND WHEN THE CROWD THAT CAME TO SEE THE CRUCIFIXION SAW THAT JESUS WAS DEAD, THEY WENT HOME IN DEEP SORROW.

I HAD HOPED THAT HE WAS THE ONE WHO WOULD DELIVER US FROM THE ROMANS.

▲ **LUKE (page 656)**

1ST CHINESE DICTIONARY			1ST OLYMPICS	ALEXANDER		ROME FALLS			COLUMBUS	TODAY	
	2000 B.C.	1500 B.C.	1000 B.C.	500 B.C.	0	500 A.D.	1000 A.D.	1500 A.D.	2000 A.D.		
BEFORE RECORDED TIME											THE FUTURE
	ABRAHAM	MOSES	DAVID	ELIJAH	ESTHER	JESUS BORN					

B I B L E   H I G H L I G H T S   I N   T I M E

▲ ACTS 9 (page 721)

Did You Know?

The Bible is filled with many exciting stories. Sometimes it is hard to keep everything in perspective. We have provided additional "Did You Know?" fact pages to help you better understand the people and events found in God's Word.

STORIES FROM THE
Old Testament

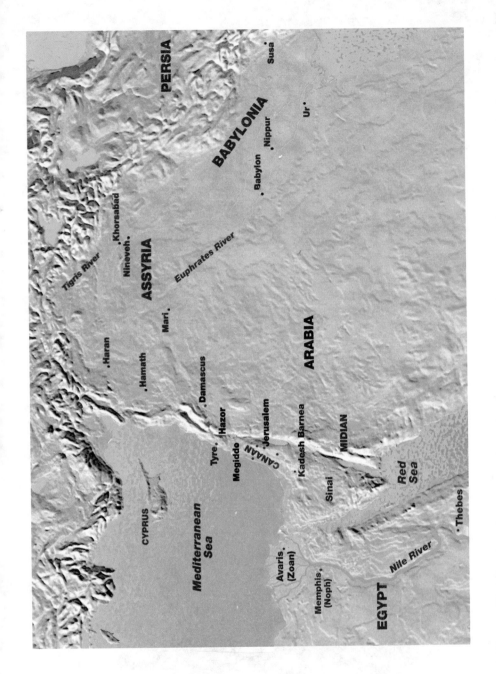

PERSIA

Susa

BABYLONIA

Ur

Nippur

Babylon

Khorsabad

Nineveh

ASSYRIA

Tigris River

Euphrates River

Mari

ARABIA

Haran

Hamath

Damascus

Hazor

Jerusalem

CANAAN

Kadesh Barnea

MIDIAN

Tyre

Megiddo

Sinai

Red Sea

CYPRUS

Mediterranean Sea

Thebes

Avaris (Zoan)

Memphis (Noph)

Nile River

EGYPT

Old Testament
World

In the Beginning

IN THE
BEGINNING

1st DAY

there was darkness—darkness and silence.
God created heaven and earth. His Spirit moved
through the darkness and across the waters. God
said, "Let there be light": and there was light.
How beautiful the light was! Then God divided the
light from the darkness and called the light Day
and the darkness Night.

2nd DAY

God made the sky.
In the sky He placed clouds
to hold the moisture.
And the sky was called Heaven.

3rd DAY

Then God gathered together the waters under the sky. He called these "seas" and He named the dry land "earth." On the land He made grass and flowers, and trees, and in each was the seed to replenish itself. The fruitful earth was to become a place of beauty.

4th DAY

To light the earth, God made the sun to shine by day, and the moon to shine by night ... The days, the years, and the seasons were also set by God. Then He made the stars and placed them in the heavens.

5th DAY

God looked upon the land and seas and said: "Let the waters abound with living creatures" —and the seas and rivers became alive with whales and fish....

"Let there be birds"—and the open sky above the earth was filled with winged creatures.

"Be fruitful and multiply," God said as He blessed the living creatures of the sea and sky.

6th DAY Then God said, "Let the earth bring forth living creatures"... and animals of all kinds filled the earth. So the waters, the sky, and the earth were filled with life. To have dominion over all these things, God created the first man, Adam, and the first woman, Eve. They were the greatest of all God's creations, for He gave them a mind to choose between good and evil, and a soul that would live forever.

And on the seventh day God rested ...

God took Adam and Eve to the garden of Eden and showed them the beauty and fruitfulness of it. And God commanded: Of every tree you may eat freely ... but of the tree of knowledge of good and evil you may not eat, for in the day that you eat it, you will surely die....

God's Wonderful Creation

Before time, space, or the world existed, there was God. Nothing existed before God. And He created all that exists. His plan is perfect.

Here are some interesting facts about God's creation:

▶ God created day different from night. A day is the time it takes for a planet to spin around once.

▶ The largest tree can grow higher than 367 feet and wider than 20 feet across.

▶ About 71% of the Earth is covered by water.

▶ There are 4600 species of mammals—the largest is the blue whale. Adam gave animals names.

▶ A human child has about 200 bones which stop growing when he or she is 25 years old.

▶ God placed the Sun 93 million miles from Earth to perfectly heat and light our world. It is the closest star to us.

▶ The Earth is 24,859 miles around at the Equator.

▶ God made things in perfect balance!

▶ God put a blanket of air around the Earth to protect us from the heat and cold of space.

People are God's greatest creation.

17

Did You Know?

Adam and Eve

Adam and Eve are unique in many ways. No one lives before them to teach them how things should be done. God is their teacher.

Here are other ways that they are unique:

▶ Adam is the first man; Eve is the first woman.

▶ Adam is first to name the animals.

▶ They are the first parents. Their sons are Cain, Abel, and Seth.

▶ Adam is made from the dust of the earth; Eve is made from Adam's rib.

▶ Adam and Eve take care of the Garden of Eden.

▶ They are the first people to sin against God. They have to leave the beautiful garden.

Read about Adam and Eve on pp. 6-14 of your Picture Bible.

Temptation in the Garden
FROM GENESIS 3

BUT ADAM AND EVE KNOW THEY HAVE DISOBEYED GOD. THEN THEY HEAR HIS VOICE CALLING THEM.

I'M AFRAID!

QUICK—LET'S HIDE!

IN THE STILLNESS OF THE GARDEN THEY HEAR GOD ASK: "HAVE YOU EATEN THE FRUIT THAT I TOLD YOU NOT TO EAT?"

EVE GAVE ME SOME FRUIT—AND I ATE IT.

THE SERPENT TEMPTED ME!

"BECAUSE YOU DISOBEYED ME," GOD SAID, "YOU MUST LEAVE THIS BEAUTIFUL GARDEN AND WORK HARD FOR YOUR LIVING."

LOOK! A FLAMING SWORD GUARDS THE ENTRANCE— WE CAN NEVER GO BACK.

WHERE CAN WE GO? WHAT CAN WE DO?

Jealous Brothers

FROM GENESIS 4:1–8

OUTSIDE THE GARDEN OF EDEN THE LAND IS BARREN, HOT AND DRY. WEARY, ALONE AND FRIGHTENED, ADAM AND EVE SEARCH UNTIL THEY FIND A PLACE TO MAKE A HOME.

REMEMBER HOW BEAUTIFUL EDEN WAS? IF ONLY...

YES, IF ONLY WE HAD OBEYED GOD. WE MUST MAKE CERTAIN THAT WE TEACH OUR CHILDREN SO THAT THEY DON'T MAKE THE MISTAKE WE DID!

SO ADAM TEACHES THEIR SONS, CAIN AND ABEL, ABOUT GOD.

HE MADE THE EARTH AND EVERYTHING WE HAVE.

I LIKE TO THINK OF GOD GIVING ME MY LITTLE LAMB.

23

24

The Verdict

FROM GENESIS 4:8–26; 5; 6:1–8

IN A LONELY PASTURE, CAIN KILLED HIS BROTHER, ABEL. CAIN IS SURE NOBODY SAW THE MURDER. BUT SUDDENLY THE KILLER IS AFRAID. DID SOMEONE SEE HIM? WHO?

HE LOOKS AROUND...AND THEN HE HEARS THE VOICE OF GOD ASKING: "WHERE IS ABEL, YOUR BROTHER?"

I–I DON'T KNOW. AM I MY BROTHER'S KEEPER?

GOD KNOWS I HAVE KILLED ABEL!

TERRIFIED, CAIN HEARS GOD'S VERDICT—AS PUNISHMENT FOR MURDERING ABEL, CAIN MUST LEAVE HOME AND FOREVER BE A FUGITIVE.

OH, GOD! PLEASE! THIS PUNISHMENT IS MORE THAN I CAN TAKE!

BUT GOD'S SENTENCE WAS CARRIED OUT. CAIN FLED TO A LAND CALLED NOD. THERE HE MARRIED AND BUILT THE FIRST CITY, WHICH HE NAMED FOR HIS SON, ENOCH.

ADAM AND EVE ARE HEARTBROKEN BY THE LOSS OF THEIR TWO SONS.

OUR HOUSE IS SO EMPTY AND STILL. OH, ADAM, WILL WE ALWAYS BE ALONE LIKE THIS?

WE BROUGHT THIS TRAGEDY ON OURSELVES, EVE—AND SO DID CAIN. BUT GOD HAS BEEN GOOD TO US. LET'S ASK HIM TO HELP US NOW...

IN TIME, A THIRD SON IS BORN TO THEM.

WE'LL CALL HIM SETH.

AND WE'LL TEACH HIM TO OBEY GOD THE WAY ABEL DID.

AGAIN ADAM AND EVE'S PRAYERS ARE ANSWERED, FOR SETH LEARNS TO OBEY GOD. TWO OF HIS DESCENDANTS ARE ENOCH WHO "WALKED WITH GOD" AND METHUSELAH WHO DIED AT THE AGE OF 969—THE OLDEST MAN WHO EVER LIVED.

26

BUT, AS GENERATIONS PASS, PEOPLE AGAIN TURN AWAY FROM GOD...

THEY LIE, CHEAT, MURDER...

THEY WORSHIP THE SUN AND THE MOON AND THE STARS... AND BOW DOWN BEFORE IDOLS.

BUT THERE IS ONE MAN, NOAH, WHO LOOKS UPON THIS SINFULNESS WITH FEAR.

HOW LONG WILL GOD ALLOW THIS WICKEDNESS TO CONTINUE?

When the Rains Came

FROM GENESIS 6:7–22; 7:1–10

YOUR WICKEDNESS CANNOT CONTINUE! TURN AWAY FROM YOUR IDOL WORSHIP! RETURN TO GOD WHO CREATED US AND GAVE US ALL THAT WE HAVE!

LISTEN TO NOAH! HE THINKS HE'S BETTER THAN ANYONE ELSE!

WHAT'S HIS GOODNESS DONE FOR HIM?

BUT NOAH REMAINS TRUE TO GOD. AND ONE DAY GOD SPEAKS TO HIM: "THE EARTH IS FILLED WITH VIOLENCE ...I WILL DESTROY THOSE WHOM I HAVE CREATED. MAKE AN ARK, FOR I WILL SURELY BRING A FLOOD OF WATERS UPON THE EARTH."

NOAH OBEYS—AND SETS TO WORK BUILDING AN ARK ACCORDING TO THE DIRECTIONS GIVEN HIM BY GOD.

POOR NOAH, HE THINKS HE CAN FLOAT A BOAT ON DRY LAND.

WHAT WILL HE THINK OF NEXT?

WHEN THE ARK IS COMPLETED, GOD DIRECTS NOAH AND HIS FAMILY TO ENTER... AND TO TAKE WITH THEM SEVEN PAIRS OF EACH KIND OF ANIMAL AND BIRD THAT IS GOOD TO EAT, AND ONE PAIR OF EACH KIND NOT USED FOR FOOD.

The Great Flood

FROM GENESIS 7:16–24; 8; 9; 11

LOOK! THE GREAT DOOR OF NOAH'S ARK IS CLOSING!

YES...IT'S BEING SHUT BY A GREAT INVISIBLE HAND!

THE RAINS POUR DOWN STEADILY FOR FORTY DAYS AND FORTY NIGHTS.

WATER FLOWS OVER THE LAND AND RISES ABOVE THE MOUNTAIN-TOPS. ALL THE EARTH IS COVERED... ONLY NOAH'S GREAT ARK SURVIVES. THE FLOOD DESTROYS ALL THAT IS EVIL.

AT LAST THE WATER LEVEL DROPS AND THE ARK RESTS ON THE TOP OF THE MOUNTAINS OF ARARAT.

I WILL SEND OUT A DOVE; IF IT DOES NOT COME BACK WE WILL KNOW IT HAS FOUND LAND.

BUT THE DOVE RETURNS!

NOAH SENDS OUT A DOVE AGAIN, AND IT RETURNS.

AN OLIVE BRANCH! THAT MEANS SOME LAND MUST BE DRY AGAIN.

SEVEN DAYS LATER, NOAH SENDS OUT A DOVE A THIRD TIME. IT DOES NOT RETURN BECAUSE IT HAS FOUND A PLACE TO NEST.

SO, A LITTLE OVER A YEAR AFTER THE FLOOD BEGAN, NOAH STEPS ON DRY LAND ONCE MORE. HE, HIS FAMILY AND THE ANIMALS IN THE ARK ARE THE ONLY CREATURES ON EARTH.

HOW GOOD IT IS TO WALK ON THE GROUND AGAIN!

YES—TO FEEL GRASS UNDER YOUR FEET AND WARM SUNSHINE ON YOUR FACE.

ALL THAT WAS EVIL HAS BEEN DESTROYED. THROUGH US, GOD IS GIVING MANKIND A NEW START. WE MUST OBEY GOD—AND TEACH ALL WHO FOLLOW US TO DO SO.

AS SOON AS NOAH LEAVES THE ARK, HE BUILDS AN ALTAR. HERE HE THANKS GOD FOR HIS CARE AND ASKS GOD'S GUIDANCE IN HELPING NOAH AND HIS FAMILY TO MAKE A NEW START. THEN GOD MAKES A PROMISE TO NOAH AND TO ALL HIS CHILDREN, FOREVER...

34

Noah—Man of Righteousness

▶ **Read about Noah on pp. 27-34.**

In contrast to the sinful people, God sees only one person on earth who stands out as righteous—Noah. He tries to please God when everyone else chooses to turn away. Here are some interesting facts about Noah:

▶ Noah is 480 years old when God tells him He will destroy the world with water.

▶ Noah preaches for 120 years without one person responding to his message!

▶ Noah is 600 years old when the flood begins.

▶ After the Flood, Noah becomes a farmer.

▶ Noah has a wife, three sons—Shem, Ham, and Japheth, and their wives. These people help Noah build the ark.

▶ There are nine generations from Adam to Noah.

God tells Noah exactly how to build the ark.

After the Flood, Noah offers thanks to God, and God promises never again to destroy the world by water.

Did You Know? **The Ark and the Flood**

Here are some interesting facts:

▶ The Bible tells us that the sources of the Flood are: 1) upheavals in the oceans, probably due to earthquakes and volcanoes, and 2) rain falling for 40 days and 40 nights.

▶ God tells Noah to take two of all the clean animals and seven of every unclean animal. Clean animals are those that chew their cud and have a split hoof, like a cow or sheep.

▶ Noah and the animals are on the ark one year and ten days.

▶ The ark lands in the Ararat mountain range in Turkey. The exact mountain of the landing is not known.

▶ The Flood is the biggest catastrophe ever experienced by the earth and its inhabitants.

▶ The ark is 450 feet long (longer than a football field), 75 feet wide, and 45 feet high. It has three decks.

▶ Only eight people—Noah and his family—are saved . . . in the whole world!

The Tower that Crumbled
FROM GENESIS 11

A TOWER THAT WILL REACH TO HEAVEN — HOW BEAUTIFUL IT IS!

IT CAN BE SEEN FOR MILES. IN TIME OF DANGER WE WILL RALLY OUR FORCES AROUND IT. NO ONE IS GOING TO CONQUER AND SCATTER US! WITH THIS TOWER, WE'LL BE INVINCIBLE!

BUT GOD IS DISPLEASED WITH THE PEOPLE'S DESIRE FOR FAME AND POWER. TO STOP THEIR WORK ON THE TOWER, HE CAUSES THE PEOPLE TO SPEAK IN DIFFERENT LANGUAGES.

WHAT KIND OF TALK IS THAT? HOW CAN I WORK WITH A MAN I CAN'T UNDERSTAND?

BECAUSE THEY CANNOT UNDERSTAND ONE ANOTHER, THE BUILDERS ARE CONFUSED. THEY STOP WORKING ON THE TOWER. ONE BY ONE, THE FAMILIES WHO SPEAK THE SAME LANGUAGE MOVE AWAY. THE GIANT TOWER, CALLED BABEL, BEGINS TO CRUMBLE...

SOME OF THE FAMILIES MOVE DOWN THE EUPHRATES RIVER —AND THERE BUILD THE GREAT TRADING CITY OF UR. OTHERS PITCH THEIR TENTS ON THE PLAINS BEYOND. THE BIBLE TRACES THE GENERATIONS FROM NOAH'S SON, SHEM, TO A TRIBAL CHIEFTAIN NAMED TERAH WHO LIVES OUTSIDE UR.

ONE DAY IN TERAH'S CAMP THERE IS GREAT EXCITEMENT—EVERYONE IS GETTING READY FOR A TRIP TO UR.

MAY WE TRADE OUR WOOL FOR ANYTHING WE WANT, FATHER?

YES, ABRAHAM. BUT FIRST YOU MUST HELP ME LOAD OUR SUPPLIES.

LOOK! GREEN BEANS AND MELONS!

WE'LL TRADE SOME OF OUR SUPPLIES FOR FRESH VEGETABLES. THEN YOU, HARAN AND NAHOR MAY GO INTO THE CITY.

A THROW STICK FOR YOUR BAG OF WOOL.

IT'S A DEAL!

IMAGINE THROWING A STICK THAT WILL COME BACK TO YOU.

WHAT IS THAT TOWER?

IT IS A TEMPLE TO THE MOON-GOD.

BACK HOME, ABRAHAM THINKS OFTEN ABOUT HIS VISIT TO UR. AND AS HE GROWS OLDER HE WONDERS ABOUT THE TEMPLE OF THE MOON-GOD.

ONE EVENING ABRAHAM TALKS TO SARAH, THE MOST BEAUTIFUL GIRL IN HIS FATHER'S CAMP.

IT'S ONLY THE MOON, SARAH, NOT SOMETHING TO WORSHIP.

ABRAHAM—BE CAREFUL. MANY PEOPLE HERE WORSHIP THE MOON-GOD. THEY MIGHT HEAR YOU AND DO YOU HARM.

WOULD YOU CARE, SARAH?

YES, ABRAHAM. EVERYONE EXPECTS YOU TO BE HEAD OF OUR TRIBE, SOMEDAY.

SARAH, I LOVE YOU AND WANT YOU TO BE MY WIFE. BUT IT'S ONLY FAIR THAT YOU SHOULD KNOW I DO NOT BELIEVE IN THE MOON-GOD. THERE IS ONLY ONE GOD—THE GOD WHO MADE THE MOON, THE STARS, THE SUN— EVEN US!

I LOVE YOU, ABRAHAM. BUT GIVE ME TIME TO THINK...

A FEW DAYS LATER, A CARAVAN STOPS AT TERAH'S CAMP.

MAY WE CAMP HERE WHILE WE SELL OUR GOODS IN UR?

YOU ARE WELCOME. MY SON, ABRAHAM, WILL SHOW YOUR MEN WHERE TO WATER YOUR CAMELS.

SO YOU COME FROM CANAAN. DO THE PEOPLE THERE WORSHIP THE MOON-GOD, UR?

NO, THEY HAVE THEIR OWN GODS, CALLED BAALS.

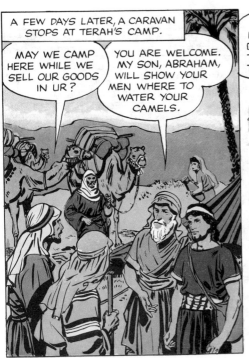

BAAL! THE MOON-GOD! EVERYONE HAS A DIFFERENT GOD. ABRAHAM, I BELIEVE AS YOU DO—THERE IS ONLY ONE GOD.

DO YOU, SARAH? THEN WE'LL BOTH TRUST IN GOD—NO MATTER WHAT HAPPENS.

IT IS A FESTIVE DAY FOR ALL OF THE TRIBE WHEN ABRAHAM AND SARAH ARE MARRIED. DURING THE CEREMONY SARAH PRAYS TO GOD, ASKING FOR COURAGE TO STAND BY HER HUSBAND— FOR THEY ARE TWO AGAINST MANY WHO BELIEVE IN OTHER GODS.

ONE NIGHT, SEVERAL WEEKS LATER, SARAH WAKENS TO FIND ABRAHAM GONE...

ABRAHAM! ABRAHAM!

The Journey Begins

FROM GENESIS 11

OH, ABRAHAM! ARE YOU ALL RIGHT? I WAS FRIGHTENED WHEN I FOUND YOU GONE.

SARAH, TONIGHT FATHER TERAH TOLD US WE ARE LEAVING UR AND MOVING NORTH. GOD PROMISED TO MAKE A GREAT NATION OF MY PEOPLE IF I WILL FOLLOW HIM. MAYBE THIS IS THE WAY I CAN LEAD OUR PEOPLE FROM THE WORSHIP OF FALSE GODS.

STRANGE...AT ONE TIME I WOULD HAVE BEEN AFRAID TO LEAVE UR. BUT NOW I'M EAGER TO GO.

NEXT MORNING—EARLY—TERAH DIRECTS THE WORK OF BREAKING CAMP...

LOT, NOW THAT YOUR FATHER IS DEAD, YOU WILL TAKE HIS PLACE AS HEAD OF YOUR FAMILY. WORK WITH YOUR UNCLES, ABRAHAM AND NAHOR.

AT LAST THE GREAT DAY ARRIVES. THE FLOCKS... DONKEYS LADEN WITH SUPPLIES...THE FAMILIES...ALL FORM A GREAT CARAVAN THAT PUSHES NORTH ALONG THE EUPHRATES RIVER.

I WONDER WHAT LIES AHEAD, ABRAHAM.

HAVE NO FEAR, SARAH, GOD WILL GUIDE US.

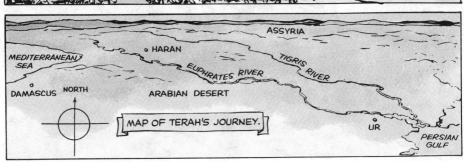

ASSYRIA

HARAN

MEDITERRANEAN SEA

EUPHRATES RIVER

TIGRIS RIVER

DAMASCUS   NORTH

ARABIAN DESERT

MAP OF TERAH'S JOURNEY.

UR

PERSIAN GULF

AFTER A FEW DAYS OUT ABRAHAM CALLS A MEETING OF NAHOR AND LOT.

IT WILL BE COOLER FOR THE FLOCKS IF WE REST BY DAY AND TRAVEL AT NIGHT.

BUT WHAT ABOUT WILD ANIMALS?

I'M TRUSTING THE ONE TRUE GOD TO PROTECT US.

I AGREE WITH UNCLE ABRAHAM.

Into the Unknown

FROM GENESIS 11

I'LL PAY 700 PIECES OF SILVER FOR YOUR CAMELS.

SOLD. HERE, SCRIBE, FIX UP A BILL OF SALE!

ABRAHAM WEIGHS OUT THE SILVER. SOON HE IS RAISING HIS OWN HERDS AND FLOCKS.

ALL GOES WELL IN TERAH'S CAMP UNTIL ONE DAY WORD SPREADS THROUGHOUT THE TENTS—TERAH IS ILL!

THIS IS THE TIME TO TELL YOUR FATHER ABOUT ABRAHAM'S GOD —BEFORE ABRAHAM BECOMES CHIEF!

NO, MY FATHER IS TOO ILL.

THAT NIGHT TERAH, THE OLD CHIEFTAIN, DIES. GRIEF-STRICKEN, HIS SONS LEAVE THE TENT OF THEIR FATHER...

OH, ABRAHAM!

44

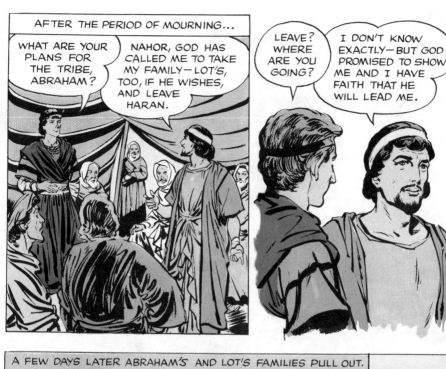

45

A Big Lie
FROM GENESIS 12:1–15

MILE AFTER MILE ABRAHAM'S GREAT CARAVAN TRAVELS ON—STOPPING AT WATER HOLES TO REST AND WATER THE FLOCKS.

I KEEP WONDERING— WHAT IF WE'RE ATTACKED, OR THE PASTURES DRY UP, OR...

WE'RE NOT COWARDS, MAN! THERE ARE DANGERS SURE, BUT ABRAHAM OUR LEADER, HAS FAITH IN GOD. I'M LEARNING TO HAVE FAITH, TOO!

AT LAST THE CARAVAN REACHES CANAAN. THE PEOPLE THERE ARE FRIENDLY...

SO THE WEARY TRAVELERS MAKE CAMP ON A HIGH HILL. ABRAHAM BUILDS AN ALTAR AND GIVES THANKS TO GOD.

SOON THE TENTS ARE TAKEN DOWN AGAIN, CLOTHING PACKED, AND THE ANIMALS ROUNDED UP FOR THE MOVE SOUTH.

ABRAHAM, YOU ARE WORRIED. IS SOMETHING WRONG?

YES, SARAH, I'M AFRAID YOU ARE SO BEAUTIFUL THAT SOME MAN IN EGYPT MAY KILL ME SO HE CAN MARRY YOU. WHEN WE REACH EGYPT WE MUST NOT LET THE PEOPLE KNOW YOU ARE MY WIFE.

KILL YOU! OH, ABRAHAM, I'LL DO ANYTHING YOU ASK!

IN EGYPT WHILE ABRAHAM AND LOT INQUIRE ABOUT PASTURE LAND...

WHAT A BEAUTIFUL WOMAN!

WHO ARE YOU?

I'M ABRAHAM'S SISTER.

TAKE HER TO PHARAOH —HE WILL REWARD YOU FOR BRINGING SUCH A BEAUTIFUL WOMAN TO HIS COURT.

PHARAOH'S COURT! WILL I NEVER SEE ABRAHAM AGAIN?

Raiders of Sodom

FROM GENESIS 12:16–20; 13; 14:1–13

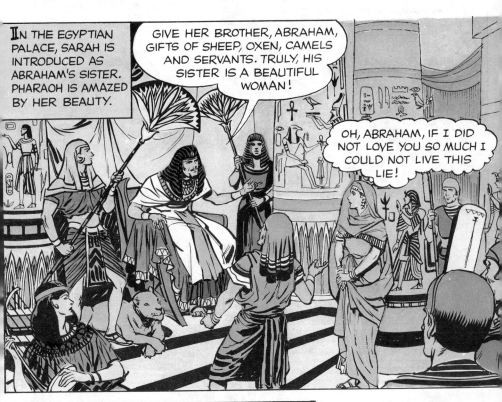

IN THE EGYPTIAN PALACE, SARAH IS INTRODUCED AS ABRAHAM'S SISTER. PHARAOH IS AMAZED BY HER BEAUTY.

GIVE HER BROTHER, ABRAHAM, GIFTS OF SHEEP, OXEN, CAMELS AND SERVANTS. TRULY, HIS SISTER IS A BEAUTIFUL WOMAN!

OH, ABRAHAM, IF I DID NOT LOVE YOU SO MUCH I COULD NOT LIVE THIS LIE!

BUT SARAH'S PRESENCE IN PHARAOH'S COURT BRINGS TROUBLE. A PLAGUE BREAKS OUT...

THIS SICKNESS CAME UPON US AT THE TIME THE FOREIGN WOMAN WAS BROUGHT HERE. I HAVE LEARNED SHE IS REALLY ABRAHAM'S WIFE—NOT HIS SISTER. GET RID OF HER!

WHEN PHARAOH LEARNS THE TRUTH ABOUT SARAH, HE CALLS FOR HIS SOLDIERS.

BRING ABRAHAM AND SARAH TO ME—NOW!

ABRAHAM! WHY DIDN'T YOU TELL ME THE TRUTH ABOUT YOUR WIFE? TAKE HER—AND GO YOUR WAY—AT ONCE!

PHARAOH'S ORDERS ARE CARRIED OUT AT ONCE, AND ABRAHAM LEAVES EGYPT.

OH, SARAH, FORGIVE ME. ALL THIS LONG JOURNEY FROM UR I TRUSTED GOD, AND HE PROTECTED US. WHEN I BECAME AFRAID AND DID NOT SEEK GOD'S HELP, I WAS A COWARD.

I FORGIVE YOU, ABRAHAM, AND I'M SURE GOD FORGIVES YOU, TOO. SEE, GOD HAS PROTECTED US EVEN WHEN WE FORGOT TO TRUST HIM.

ON THE LONG WAY BACK TO CANAAN, ABRAHAM HAS TIME TO THINK ABOUT GOD'S GUIDANCE...AND THE GREAT TRIBAL CHIEFTAIN RETURNS WITH RENEWED FAITH TO THE LAND GOD PROMISED HIM.

ABRAHAM AND LOT PROSPER—THEIR FLOCKS INCREASE. BUT THEIR HERDSMEN BEGIN TO QUARREL.

MAKE WAY FOR LOT'S SHEEP!

NO! ABRAHAM IS THE CHIEF— HIS FLOCKS COME FIRST!

WHEN ABRAHAM HEARS OF THE QUARRELS, HE TALKS OVER HIS NEXT MOVE WITH SARAH—

THIS TIME, SARAH, I'LL MEET THE PROBLEM AS I THINK GOD WOULD WANT ME TO.

THEN YOUR PLAN CANNOT FAIL.

THE NEXT DAY...

COME WITH ME, LOT. WE MUST DECIDE WHAT TO DO WITH OUR FLOCKS.

WHY SHOULD WE CLIMB A HILL TO DO IT?

THERE MUST BE NO MORE QUARRELING AMONG OUR PEOPLE. WE WILL SEPARATE— CHOOSE WHERE YOU WOULD LIKE TO GO AND I WILL TAKE WHAT IS LEFT.

I'LL TAKE THE VALLEY—NEAR THE CITY OF SODOM!

A Stranger's Prophecy

FROM GENESIS 15—18; 19:1-10

"LOOK TOWARD HEAVEN, AND COUNT THE STARS, IF THOU BE ABLE TO NUMBER THEM:..SO SHALL THE NUMBER OF THY DESCENDANTS BE."

LATER, WHEN SARAH COMES TO HIM WITH A PLAN, HE LISTENS...

BY THE CUSTOM OF OUR PEOPLE I CAN GIVE YOU HAGAR, MY HANDMAID, AS A WIFE THAT SHE MIGHT HAVE A SON FOR ME.

GOD HAS PROMISED ME AN HEIR— PERHAPS THIS IS RIGHT...

HAGAR HAS A SON, AND HE IS THE PRIDE OF ABRAHAM'S HEART.

MY ISHMAEL IS A PROUD AND DARING ONE!

REMEMBER, HAGAR, HE IS **MY** SON! I ADOPTED HIM!

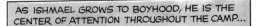
AS ISHMAEL GROWS TO BOYHOOD, HE IS THE CENTER OF ATTENTION THROUGHOUT THE CAMP...

...AND THE SOURCE OF TROUBLE BETWEEN HAGAR AND SARAH.

SOME DAY MY SON WILL RULE THIS WHOLE TRIBE!

HAGAR GETS MORE SURE OF HERSELF EVERY DAY!

ABRAHAM WORRIES ABOUT THE TROUBLE IN HIS CAMP. ONE DAY WHILE HE IS RESTING AT NOON TIME AND THINKING ABOUT ISHMAEL, HAGAR AND SARAH, HE LOOKS UP...

THREE STRANGERS APPROACH HIS CAMP. ABRAHAM GREETS THEM AND INVITES THEM TO REST AND EAT WITH HIM.

WHILE THEY ARE EATING, ONE OF THE STRANGERS GIVES ABRAHAM SURPRISING NEWS!

YOUR WIFE, SARAH, WILL HAVE A SON.

WHO ARE THESE STRANGERS TO BRING FALSE HOPE TO ABRAHAM? I AM TOO OLD TO HAVE CHILDREN!

AND HOW WOULD THIS AFFECT HAGAR?

IF SARAH HAS A SON, WHAT WILL HAPPEN TO ISHMAEL —AND ME!

WHEN THE STRANGERS LEAVE, ABRAHAM WALKS A WAY WITH THEM.

THAT CITY OF SODOM IS SO WICKED THAT GOD MAY HAVE TO DESTROY IT.

THIS IS A MESSENGER FROM GOD! THEY ARE TALKING ABOUT THE PLACE LOT LIVES!

ABRAHAM PRAYS FOR SODOM, AND GOD PROMISES THAT THE CITY WILL BE SAVED IF THERE ARE TEN GOOD MEN IN IT.

MEANTIME TWO OF THE STRANGERS HAVE REACHED SODOM. ABRAHAM'S NEPHEW, LOT, WELCOMES THEM.

THERE'S SOMETHING STRANGE ABOUT THOSE TWO MEN.

YOU ARE STRANGERS HERE. COME, STAY AT MY HOME.

YES. LOOK—THEY'RE GOING TO LOT'S HOUSE. LET'S FOLLOW THEM.

THEY LOOK AS IF THEY'LL CAUSE TROUBLE. LET'S RUN THEM OUT OF TOWN

LATER THAT NIGHT, A SUSPICIOUS CROWD SURROUNDS LOT'S HOUSE...

THOSE STRANGERS— BRING 'EM OUT!

NO! THEY ARE GUESTS IN MY HOUSE!

IT WILL BE WORSE FOR YOU, LOT, IF YOU DON'T SEND THEM OUT.

BUT, JUST AS THE MOB REACHES OUT FOR LOT, THE TWO STRANGERS PULL HIM INSIDE AND LOCK THE DOOR!

BREAK DOWN THE DOOR!

LET'S GET THEM!

Lost in the Desert

FROM GENESIS 19:11–30; 21:1–16

OUTSIDE LOT'S HOUSE IN SODOM, THE MOB GOES WILD. RIOTERS HOWL FOR REVENGE AGAINST LOT AND THE STRANGERS WHO RESCUED HIM.

COME ON— WE'LL BREAK DOWN THE DOOR!

AS THE MEN PUSH AGAINST LOT'S DOOR, THE ANGELS STRIKE THE RIOTERS BLIND.

HELP! I CAN'T SEE!

MY EYES— WHO HIT ME?

INSIDE LOT'S HOUSE...

RUN FOR YOUR LIVES! THE LORD HAS SENT US TO DESTROY THIS WICKED CITY!

MY FAMILY— I MUST SAVE THEM!

BUT LOT'S SONS-IN-LAW ONLY LAUGH WHEN HE TRIES TO WARN THEM. THEY REFUSE TO LEAVE THE DOOMED CITY, SO, EARLY THE NEXT MORNING, THE TWO ANGELS LEAD LOT, HIS WIFE AND THEIR TWO DAUGHTERS AWAY. SUDDENLY ALL SODOM BURSTS INTO FLAME!

DON'T LOOK BACK AT THE CITY— OR YOU WILL ALSO DIE!

I DON'T CARE WHAT GOD SAYS—I WANT TO GO BACK!

LOT'S WIFE STOPS...LOOKS BACK LONGINGLY...AND IS TURNED INTO A PILLAR OF SALT...SO ONLY LOT AND HIS TWO DAUGHTERS ESCAPE GOD'S PUNISHMENT.

NEXT MORNING, ABRAHAM GOES TO THE HILLTOP TO WORSHIP—AND SEES THE SMOULDERING RUINS OF THE WICKED CITY...

AS SURELY AS NIGHT FOLLOWS DAY, DESTRUCTION FOLLOWS SIN. O GOD, HELP ME TO LEAD MY PEOPLE IN THE PATHS OF RIGHTEOUSNESS!

EAGER TO LEAVE THE RUINS OF SODOM, ABRAHAM MOVES TO BEER-SHEBA, NEAR THE DESERT. HERE, SARAH'S SON IS BORN.

ABRAHAM HAS NAMED HIS SECOND SON, ISAAC.

WHAT WILL BECOME OF ISHMAEL, HIS FIRST SON? HE MIGHT HAVE BEEN OUR RULER AFTER ABRAHAM, BUT NOW THE BABY, ISAAC, WILL RULE OUR PEOPLE.

I'M AFRAID THERE WILL BE TROUBLE.

SARAH AND HAGAR BECOME MORE JEALOUS DAY BY DAY. THEN AT THE BABY ISAAC'S FIRST FEAST...

SEE HOW CLUMSY LITTLE ISAAC IS!

ISHMAEL! BE QUIET!

SARAH IS ANGRY! WHAT WILL SHE DO?

HAGAR'S SON CAN'T MAKE FUN OF MINE! ABRAHAM, YOU MUST SEND ISHMAEL AND HAGAR AWAY, BEFORE THEY CAUSE TROUBLE IN THE TRIBE.

NIGHT AFTER NIGHT, ABRAHAM SEEKS GOD'S ANSWER TO HIS PROBLEM. FINALLY, HE KNOWS WHAT HE MUST DO.

EARLY ONE MORNING...

BECAUSE OF SARAH'S JEALOUSY, IT IS BETTER THAT YOU AND ISHMAEL LEAVE. HAVE NO FEAR, GOD WILL WATCH OVER YOU.

DAY AFTER DAY, THEY WANDER THROUGH THE BURNING SAND. ONE FEAR POUNDS IN HAGAR'S MIND.

WILL THE WATER HOLD OUT TILL WE FIND AN OASIS?

AT LAST THE DREADED MOMENT COMES...

THERE'S NO MORE WATER, MOTHER! I'M DYING OF THIRST!

I KNOW, SON. SO AM I. LIE DOWN IN THE SHADE OF THE BUSH.

O GOD, LET ME NOT SEE THE DEATH OF MY CHILD!

Test of Faith

FROM GENESIS 21:17–21; 22:1–10

DEAD TIRED AND CHOKING WITH THIRST, HAGAR TURNS HER BACK ON HER SON, ISHMAEL... SHE CANNOT WATCH HIM DYING. SUDDENLY SHE HEARS A VOICE. IT'S GOD SAYING: "LIFT UP THE LAD, FOR I WILL MAKE HIM A GREAT NATION".

HAGAR STARTS TOWARD HER SON... AND SEES A SPRING NEARBY.

WATER! WE WILL NOT DIE! O ISHMAEL, GOD HAS SAVED US!

DRINK, MY SON, GOD IS WITH US. WE NEED NEVER BE AFRAID AGAIN!

KNOWING GOD IS WITH THEM, HAGAR AND ISHMAEL CONTINUE THEIR JOURNEY TO A PLACE IN THE WILDERNESS WHERE THEY BUILD A HOME. YEARS PASS—ISHMAEL MARRIES AN EGYPTIAN GIRL AND BECOMES THE HEAD OF A GREAT DESERT TRIBE.

IN ABRAHAM'S CAMP, THE YEARS PASS SWIFTLY, TOO. YOUNG ISAAC PROVES HIMSELF A WORTHY SON OF THE TRIBE'S GREAT LEADER.

HE STOLE MY STAFF!

IF YOU TOOK HIS STAFF, RETURN IT. AND YOU, EBER, REMEMBER THAT WE DON'T SETTLE QUARRELS WITH OUR FISTS.

THE WHOLE CAMP WONDERS AS ABRAHAM AND ISAAC SET OUT...

61

Abraham— Man of Faith

Many times Abraham demonstrates his faith in God by doing exactly what God asks him to do without question. Here are some examples:

▶ **God asks Abraham to leave his home and go to an unknown land.** *Abraham leaves with his whole family and goes almost 600 miles to Haran (page 41).*

▶ **Abraham wants an heir. God promises him as many descendants as there are stars.** *He believes God, even though it doesn't happen right away. At age 100, God gives Abraham Isaac. (page 51).*

There are 8,000 stars visible from earth. But at any one time, we can only see about 2,000.

▶ **God asks Abraham to sacrifice his son.** *Abraham prepares to do that, but God supplies a ram at the last minute (page 62).*

Abraham lives 175 years. Isaac lives 180 years.

Abraham is thought of as the father of the Hebrews.

Did You Know?

A Bride Is Chosen

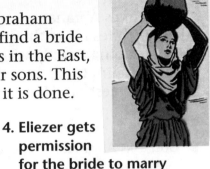

On pp. 67-71, we read about Abraham sending his servant, Eliezer, to find a bride for his son, Isaac. In Bible times in the East, parents select the bride for their sons. This story helps us understand how it is done.

1. Abraham sends Eliezer to select a bride and meet her family.

2. Eliezer meets with Rebekah's brother, the family's representative.

3. Eliezer is offered food but refuses to eat until the negotiation is complete.

4. Eliezer gets permission for the bride to marry and then a dowry amount is set. He gives many gifts to Rebekah's family, showing Abraham's great wealth.

• • • • • • • • • • • • • • • • • •

A dowry is a gift given to the bride's father to make up for the loss of his daughter's help.

• • • • • • • • • • • • • • • • • •

5. The marriage agreement is sealed by everyone eating food together.

• • • • • • • • • • • • • • • • • •

Some gifts are given to the bride. Rebekah's father gives her a nurse and maids to attend her.

• • • • • • • • • • • • • • • • • •

6. The bride goes to meet her husband and they are married.

The bride becomes part of the groom's family in Old Testament times.

Secret Mission to Haran

FROM GENESIS 22:11–18; 23:1–2,
19–20; 24:1–10

SUDDENLY, ABRAHAM HEARS THE VOICE OF GOD: "DON'T PUT YOUR HAND UPON THE BOY... FOR NOW I KNOW THAT YOU FEAR GOD."

AS ABRAHAM LOOKS JOYFULLY AT ISAAC, HE NOTICES A RAM IN A NEARBY THICKET.

A RAM FOR THE SACRIFICE! O GOD, MY GOD, I THANK YOU!

QUICKLY ABRAHAM RELEASES ISAAC AND PUTS THE RAM IN HIS PLACE ON THE ALTAR.

FATHER, YOU GAVE ME TO GOD—AND HE GAVE ME BACK TO YOU.

YES, MY SON, IT WAS A TEST OF FAITH. O ISAAC, NEVER DOUBT THE WISDOM AND LOVE OF GOD!

WITH JOYOUS HEARTS, ABRAHAM AND ISAAC GIVE THANKS TO GOD. AND ABRAHAM HEARS GOD'S PROMISE: "THROUGH YOU, ALL NATIONS OF THE EARTH SHALL BE BLESSED."

ON THE WAY HOME, ISAAC WALKS AHEAD—AND ALONE. THROUGH HIS MIND FLASH SCENES OF THE DAY. HE CAN STILL FEEL THE ROPES THAT TIED HIM ON THE ALTAR...SEE HIS FATHER'S DAGGER...FEEL THE JOY OF KNOWING HE WOULD NOT BE KILLED.

SARAH RUSHES OUT OF THE CAMP TO GREET THEM.

ISAAC, MY SON, WHAT HAPPENED? YOU LEFT HERE A BOY—YOU HAVE RETURNED A MAN— LIKE YOUR FATHER, STRONG, TALL, WISE.

FROM MY FATHER I LEARNED THE COST OF FAITH... AND FROM GOD, THE REWARD.

IN THE YEARS THAT FOLLOW, THE TRIBE OF ABRAHAM PROSPERS. THEN ONE DAY, SAD NEWS SPREADS THROUGHOUT THE CAMP...SARAH IS VERY SICK.

ONE EVENING, ABRAHAM APPEARS AT THE DOOR OF HIS TENT... THE CAMP GROWS QUIET... AND LIKE A MAN IN A DREAM, HE TELLS HIS PEOPLE, SARAH, HIS WIFE, IS DEAD.

SARAH IS BURIED IN A CAVE AT MACHPELAH, AND THE WHOLE TRIBE MOURNS HER DEATH.

ISAAC IS GOING ALONE INTO THE WILDERNESS TO MOURN FOR HIS MOTHER.

IT IS WELL. HE MUST CONQUER HIS GRIEF.

ONE DAY, ABRAHAM CALLS HIS MOST TRUSTED SERVANT TO HIM.

BEFORE I DIE, I WANT TO SEE MY SON HAPPILY MARRIED— TO A WOMAN OF MY OWN PEOPLE. GO TO HARAN AND BRING BACK A WIFE FOR ISAAC.

ABRAHAM'S SERVANT GATHERS A LONG CARAVAN. HE LEADS IT ACROSS THE DESERT AND FINALLY REACHES THE CITY OF HARAN, WHERE ABRAHAM'S RELATIVES LIVE.

WHAT A BIG CITY! HOW WILL I EVER FIND THE RIGHT WIFE FOR THE MAN WHO WILL ONE DAY BE CHIEF OF OUR TRIBE?

A Bride for Isaac

FROM GENESIS 24:11–67; 25:7–8

WHEN THE GIRL HAS FINISHED WATERING THE CAMELS, THE SERVANT GIVES HER EARRINGS AND GOLD BRACELETS.

REBEKAH RUNS TO TELL HER FAMILY. WHEN SHE SHOWS THE PRESENTS, LABAN, HER BROTHER, GOES OUT TO MEET ABRAHAM'S SERVANT.

WHAT IS YOUR NAME? DO YOU THINK THERE IS ROOM FOR ME TO STAY IN YOUR FATHER'S HOUSE?

HOW BEAUTIFUL THESE PRESENTS ARE! MY NAME IS REBEKAH, AND WE HAVE ROOM FOR YOU IN OUR HOUSE. WAIT...

COME! MY FATHER HAS ROOM FOR YOU AND YOUR CARAVAN.

ABRAHAM'S SERVANT TELLS WHO HE IS AND EXPLAINS THAT GOD HAS CHOSEN REBEKAH TO BE THE BRIDE OF ISAAC, SON AND HEIR OF ABRAHAM, HER GREAT UNCLE.

EARLY THE NEXT MORNING, THE CARAVAN GETS READY TO RETURN TO ABRAHAM'S CAMP. REBEKAH SAYS GOOD-BY TO HER FAMILY AND THE CARAVAN BEGINS ITS LONG JOURNEY.

TAKE REBEKAH TO BE THE WIFE OF MY UNCLE'S SON— AS THE LORD HAS SPOKEN.

69

DAYS LATER, THE CARAVAN NEARS ABRAHAM'S CAMP. REBEKAH WONDERS...

WHAT WILL ISAAC BE LIKE? TALL AND STRONG LIKE A CHIEF'S SON? I WONDER IF HE WILL LOVE ME...

WHO IS THE MAN COMING TO MEET US?

IT IS ISAAC!

HE IS HANDSOME!

IS THIS WOMAN TO BE MY WIFE?

WHEN ISAAC SEES REBEKAH, HE FALLS IN LOVE WITH HER AT ONCE AND TAKES HER TO HIS FATHER FOR HIS BLESSING.

MAY GOD WHO HAS GUIDED ME, GUIDE YOU, MY CHILDREN. SERVE HIM ALWAYS.

THE WHOLE CAMP REJOICES WHEN ISAAC AND REBEKAH ARE MARRIED. "LONG LIFE AND HAPPINESS," SHOUT THE PEOPLE WHO KNOW THAT SOMEDAY ISAAC WILL BE THEIR CHIEFTAIN.

YEARS LATER, THEY REJOICE AGAIN, WHEN TWIN SONS, JACOB AND ESAU, ARE BORN TO ISAAC AND REBEKAH.

MORE YEARS PASS AND ABRAHAM GROWS OLDER. HE BECOMES FEEBLE AND FINALLY TOO SICK TO MOVE. THE END IS NEAR AND THE PEOPLE DREAD THE NEWS ISAAC BRINGS ONE DAY...

MY FATHER IS DEAD!

OUR SORROW IS GREAT...

YES, BUT WE SALUTE YOU, ISAAC, OUR NEW CHIEF!

IN HIS FIRST MOMENTS AS CHIEF OF THE TRIBE, ISAAC THINKS OF HIS BROTHER...

TAKE THE NEWS OF MY FATHER'S DEATH TO HIS FIRST SON, ISHMAEL.

ISHMAEL! WHAT IF HE TAKES REVENGE ON ISAAC?

TRADERS FROM THE WILDERNESS SAY ISHMAEL IS A MIGHTY HUNTER— HIS ARROWS NEVER MISS!

ISAAC WOULD BE NO MATCH FOR SUCH A ONE!

The Scheming Brother

FROM GENESIS 25:9–33

THE WHOLE TRIBE MOURNS THE DEATH OF ITS GREAT LEADER, ABRAHAM. THROUGHOUT THE CAMP THERE IS A STIR OF UNEASINESS. BEHIND ISAAC'S BACK MEN WHISPER, "WILL ISHMAEL COME?" ONE DAY, A GREAT CLOUD OF DUST RISES IN THE DISTANCE...

IT'S ISHMAEL! WITH A BAND OF RIDERS!

BREATHLESSLY, THE WHOLE CAMP LOOKS ON AS ISAAC GOES OUT TO MEET HIS BROTHER.

ISHMAEL—MY BROTHER!

THAT SAME DAY THE TRIBE OF ABRAHAM JOURNEYS TO THE BURIAL CAVE OF MACHPELAH—TO PLACE THE BODY OF ITS GREAT CHIEFTAIN BESIDE HIS WIFE, SARAH. BUT IN THE MIDST OF THEIR GRIEF, THE PEOPLE ANXIOUSLY WATCH ISHMAEL...

BUT ISHMAEL, LIKE ISAAC, HAS KNOWN THE LOVING CARE OF GOD. THE OLDER BROTHER HAS NO THOUGHTS OF REVENGE.

IS IT WELL WITH YOU AND YOUR PEOPLE, ISHMAEL?

I HAVE TWELVE SONS. MY TRIBE IS POWERFUL. THE SONS OF ABRAHAM WILL LIVE IN PEACE, MY BROTHER.

TIME AND AGAIN GOD HAD TESTED ABRAHAM'S FAITH... AND BY FAITH ABRAHAM HAD OBEYED, TIME AND AGAIN, TOO, GOD HAD PROMISED TO MAKE ABRAHAM THE FOUNDER OF GREAT NATIONS...AND THROUGH HIS SONS THE PROMISE WAS FULFILLED.

UNDER ISAAC'S PEACEFUL LEADERSHIP, THE TRIBE CONTINUES TO GROW. THE PEOPLE ARE LOYAL, EVEN WHEN ISAAC MOVES THEM FROM PLACE TO PLACE TO AVOID WAR WITH NEIGHBORING TRIBES OVER WATER HOLES THAT ARE RIGHTFULLY HIS. BUT ISAAC FAILS TO SEE THE CONFLICT BETWEEN HIS OWN SONS.

WHICH ONE WILL RULE OUR TRIBE AFTER ISAAC?

ESAU—IT IS HIS BIRTHRIGHT BECAUSE HE WAS BORN FIRST.

WHEN ESAU RETURNS WITH FOOD, ISAAC PRAISES HIM.

ESAU IS A MIGHTY HUNTER.

MY TIME WILL COME —AND SOON!

JACOB BIDES HIS TIME... ONE MORNING, DURING A HOT SPELL, ESAU SETS OUT FOR A HUNTING TRIP...THIS IS THE CHANCE JACOB HAS BEEN WAITING FOR.

GAME WILL BE AT THE WATER HOLE, MILES AWAY. HE'LL BE TIRED AND HUNGRY AFTER THE LONG DAY'S HUNT. I'LL BE READY FOR HIM.

TOWARD SUNDOWN JACOB WAITS FOR HIS BROTHER OUTSIDE CAMP.

HERE HE COMES— AND WITHOUT ANY GAME!

CAMP WITH ITS FOOD IS ONLY A SHORT DISTANCE AWAY, BUT ESAU IS SO HUNGRY HE CANNOT WAIT...

I'M STARVED... GIVE ME SOME OF THE STEW.

WILL YOU TRADE YOUR BIRTHRIGHT FOR IT?

Cry of Revenge

FROM GENESIS 25:32–34; 26; 27:1–41

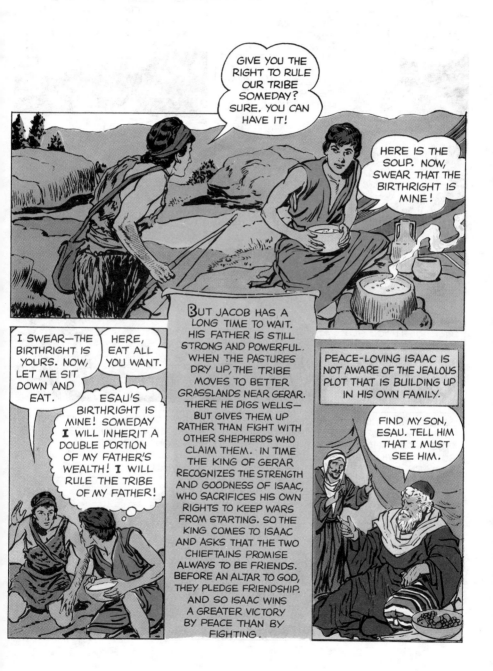

ISAAC HAS GROWN OLD. HIS EYESIGHT IS FAILING. NOW HE DECIDES IT IS TIME TO GIVE HIS ELDEST SON THE BLESSING WHICH WILL INCLUDE RULING THE TRIBE.

YOU CALLED ME, FATHER?

YES, ESAU. I AM OLD AND TIRED—AND I DON'T KNOW HOW SOON I SHALL DIE. BRING ME SOME CHOICE VENISON AND I WILL GIVE YOU THE BLESSING THAT SEALS YOUR BIRTHRIGHT.

THE NEWS REBEKAH OVERHEARS SENDS HER RUNNING THROUGH THE CAMP...

FIND JACOB! TELL HIM TO COME TO HIS MOTHER'S TENT— AT ONCE! HURRY!

LISTEN, JACOB! YOUR FATHER IS GETTING READY TO GIVE ESAU THE BLESSING. YOU MUST GET THAT BLESSING, OR THE BIRTHRIGHT YOU GOT FROM ESAU MEANS NOTHING.

BUT WHAT CAN I DO?

BEFORE YOU AND YOUR BROTHER WERE BORN, THE LORD SPOKE TO ME AND SAID: "THE ELDER SHALL SERVE THE YOUNGER." BUT ESAU WILL SERVE YOU ONLY IF YOU ARE CHIEF OF THE TRIBE.

MY SKIN IS SMOOTH, BUT ESAU IS HAIRY. FATHER WILL TOUCH ME AND KNOW I AM NOT ESAU. WHAT CAN WE DO?

I HAVE THOUGHT OF THAT, TOO. HERE, PUT ON ESAU'S ROBE—THESE SKINS ON YOUR ARMS AND NECK WILL MAKE YOU FEEL LIKE ESAU.

BUT WHAT IF...

GOD GIVE YOU THE FATNESS OF THE EARTH ...LET PEOPLE SERVE YOU... AND NATIONS BOW DOWN TO YOU... BE MASTER OVER YOUR BROTHERS... CURSED BE EVERYONE WHO CURSES YOU, AND BLESSED BE EVERYONE WHO BLESSES YOU.

NO SOONER IS THE BLESSING GIVEN, THAN JACOB RUSHES OUT OF HIS FATHER'S TENT.

MOTHER! THE BLESSING IS MINE! BUT WHAT WILL ESAU SAY?

NO MATTER WHAT ESAU SAYS, THE BLESSING IS YOURS. NOT EVEN YOUR FATHER CAN TAKE IT BACK NOW!

BUT WHILE JACOB AND HIS MOTHER ARE REJOICING, ESAU RETURNS.

ESAU PREPARES THE MEAT AND TAKES A LARGE TRAY OF IT TO HIS FATHER.

MY FATHER, EAT THE FOOD I HAVE BROUGHT YOU AND BLESS ME.

WHO ARE YOU?

WHO AM I?... WHY, I AM YOUR SON — YOUR FIRST-BORN SON, ESAU. YOU TOLD ME TO BRING YOU THIS VENISON SO THAT YOU COULD GIVE ME YOUR BLESSING.

I HAVE BEEN DECEIVED! I HAVE GIVEN THE BLESSING TO ANOTHER!

OH, FATHER, BLESS ME ALSO! PLEASE BLESS ME!

I CAN'T — YOUR BROTHER HAS TAKEN YOUR BLESSING!

BUT, FATHER, HAVE YOU NO OTHER BLESSING FOR ME?

ONLY THIS, MY SON. BY THY SWORD SHALT THOU LIVE AND SERVE THY BROTHER... BUT THE TIME WILL COME WHEN YOU WILL BREAK HIS YOKE FROM YOUR NECK.

TREMBLING WITH RAGE, ESAU LEAVES HIS FATHER'S TENT...

I'LL KILL JACOB FOR THIS!

A New Start

FROM GENESIS 27:42–46; 28; 29:1–25

WITH ESAU'S THREAT TO KILL JACOB RINGING IN HER EARS, THE SERVANT GIRL RUNS TO REBEKAH'S TENT.

ESAU IS GOING TO KILL JACOB!

ESAU IS UPSET—TELL NO ONE WHAT YOU HAVE HEARD. FIND JACOB AND TELL HIM TO COME TO ME— AT ONCE!

YOU MUST GO AWAY UNTIL YOUR BROTHER'S ANGER COOLS. GO TO MY BROTHER, LABAN, IN HARAN. I WILL SEND FOR YOU WHEN IT IS SAFE TO RETURN.

WHAT WILL I TELL MY FATHER?

ONCE AGAIN, REBEKAH PAVES THE WAY FOR HER FAVORITE SON.

ISAAC, ESAU'S WIVES ARE A GREAT TROUBLE TO ME. LIFE WILL NOT BE WORTH LIVING FOR ME IF JACOB MARRIES A WOMAN OF THIS COUNTRY. IF ONLY HE COULD MARRY A GIRL FROM MY PEOPLE—REMEMBER HOW YOUR FATHER'S SERVANT FOUND ME AT MY FATHER'S HOUSE IN HARAN AND BROUGHT ME TO YOU?

ISAAC'S THOUGHTS GO BACK OVER THE YEARS TO THE DAY HE FIRST SAW REBEKAH. HE ALSO KNOWS THERE WILL BE TROUBLE BETWEEN HIS SONS. HE SENDS FOR JACOB.

ASHAMED, BUT FRIGHTENED BY ESAU'S ANGER, JACOB COMES TO HIS FATHER.

GO TO THY MOTHER'S BROTHER, LABAN, AND FIND A WIFE FROM AMONG HIS FAMILY. GOD BLESS YOU, MY SON.

A FEW HOURS LATER—AT THE EDGE OF CAMP...

GOOD-BY, MY SON. I'LL SEND WORD WHEN IT IS SAFE TO RETURN.

MY FATHER IS OLD—I MAY NEVER SEE HIM AGAIN. ESAU WANTS TO KILL ME. OH, MOTHER, YOU ARE THE ONLY ONE I WILL BE ABLE TO COME BACK TO!

ONE PUNISHMENT FOR THEIR DECEIT IS THAT REBEKAH AND JACOB NEVER SEE EACH OTHER AGAIN.

TRAVELING FARTHER AND FARTHER FROM HIS FAMILY AND FRIENDS, JACOB IS TORTURED BY LONELINESS. HE ESPECIALLY MISSES HIS MOTHER, WHO HAS ALWAYS PROTECTED AND ADVISED HIM. HE IS HAUNTED BY THE MEMORY OF HOW HE TRICKED HIS FATHER AND BROTHER.

AS NIGHT APPROACHES...

IT'S GETTING DARK...I'LL HAVE TO STOP HERE TONIGHT.

JACOB SOON FALLS ASLEEP... AND HE DREAMS OF A SHINING LADDER, REACHING UP TO HEAVEN. ON THE LADDER ARE ANGELS, GOING UP AND DOWN AS IF BRINGING HELP FROM GOD. AND JACOB HEARS GOD SPEAK TO HIM, PROMISING TO TAKE CARE OF HIM AND BRING HIM SAFELY HOME AGAIN.

THE NEXT MORNING JACOB AWAKENS, STILL AWED BY THE DREAM HE HAD.

SURELY GOD IS IN THIS PLACE—AND THIS IS THE GATE OF HEAVEN.

JACOB REALIZES THE WRONG HE HAS DONE. BUT HE KNOWS THAT GOD WILL HELP HIM IF HE OBEYS HIM. QUICKLY HE TURNS A STONE ON END FOR AN ALTAR AND WORSHIPS GOD. HE CALLS THE PLACE BETH-EL, WHICH MEANS "THE HOUSE OF GOD."

IF GOD WILL GO WITH ME, I'LL BE GOD'S MAN.

JACOB GOES ON HIS WAY A STRONGER, NOBLER YOUNG MAN SO HE IS EAGER TO PUT BEHIND HIM THE DISHONESTY OF HIS PAST AND GIVE EVIDENCE OF GOD'S LOVE AND CARE.

SHEPHERDS AROUND A WELL. MAYBE THEY CAN HELP ME FIND MY UNCLE LABAN.

CAN YOU DIRECT ME TO THE CHIEFTAIN, LABAN?

LABAN? WHY, YES. THAT FLOCK OF SHEEP IS HIS. THAT'S HIS DAUGHTER, RACHEL, WITH THEM!

WHAT A BEAUTIFUL GIRL!

QUICKLY HE ROLLS THE STONE FROM THE WELL AND HELPS RACHEL WATER THE SHEEP. WHEN HE TELLS WHO HE IS, SHE RUNS TO TELL HER FATHER.

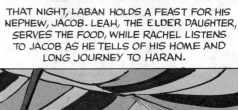

THAT NIGHT, LABAN HOLDS A FEAST FOR HIS NEPHEW, JACOB. LEAH, THE ELDER DAUGHTER, SERVES THE FOOD, WHILE RACHEL LISTENS TO JACOB AS HE TELLS OF HIS HOME AND LONG JOURNEY TO HARAN.

A MONTH LATER, LABAN MAKES A BARGAIN WITH JACOB.

WHAT KIND OF WAGES DO YOU WANT TO WORK FOR ME?

I LOVE RACHEL. I WILL SERVE YOU SEVEN YEARS IF I CAN MARRY HER!

LABAN AGREES. FOR SEVEN YEARS JACOB TAKES CARE OF LABAN'S FLOCKS, AND BECAUSE HE LOVES RACHEL, THE YEARS SEEM BUT A FEW SWIFT DAYS. THEN AFTER SEVEN YEARS, JACOB CLAIMS HIS BRIDE...

I HAVE WORKED SEVEN YEARS FOR YOU, LABAN. NOW GIVE ME RACHEL FOR MY WIFE.

YOU HAVE SERVED ME WELL, JACOB. I'LL ARRANGE THE WEDDING FEAST AT ONCE.

THERE IS MUCH REJOICING, AND AT THE END OF THE WEDDING FEAST, LABAN BRINGS HIS DAUGHTER TO JACOB.

HERE IS YOUR BRIDE, JACOB.

RACHEL, MY DEAR! I HAVE WAITED SEVEN YEARS FOR THIS MOMENT.

BUT, TOO LATE, JACOB DISCOVERS THAT HE HAS BEEN TRICKED!

YOU GAVE ME LEAH— NOT RACHEL—FOR MY WIFE!

Bargain in the Desert

FROM GENESIS 29:26—32:6

SO JACOB MARRIES RACHEL AND BEGINS HIS SECOND SEVEN YEARS OF WORK FOR LABAN. UNDER JACOB'S CARE THE FLOCKS CONTINUE TO INCREASE. AT THE END OF THE SEVEN YEARS JACOB THREATENS TO LEAVE, BUT LABAN MAKES ANOTHER BARGAIN: JACOB CAN HAVE ALL OF THE SPECKLED OR SPOTTED ANIMALS. SO, JACOB STAYS; AND IN A FEW YEARS HIS FLOCKS OUTNUMBER LABAN'S. LABAN BECOMES ANGRY...

ONE DAY JACOB CALLS HIS WIVES TO HIM.

I CAN SEE THAT TROUBLE IS RISING IN THE TRIBE. IT IS BETTER IF WE LEAVE WHILE YOUR FATHER IS AWAY. HELP ME PACK, AND WE WILL GO AT ONCE.

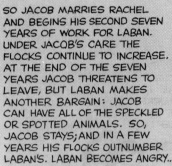

THE CAMEL TRAIN IS QUICKLY PACKED, THE FLOCKS HERDED TOGETHER; SOON THE CARAVAN IS ON ITS WAY.

LABAN MAY FOLLOW— KEEP WATCH AND TELL ME IF YOU SEE HIM COMING.

AS THEY TRAVEL, JACOB GUARDS THE CAMEL ON WHICH HIS BELOVED RACHEL AND HER ONLY SON, JOSEPH, ARE RIDING. LEAH AND JACOB'S OTHER TEN SONS WATCH WITH JEALOUS EYES. WITHOUT REALIZING IT, JACOB IS SOWING SEEDS OF TROUBLE FOR THE SON HE LOVES THE BEST...

SEVERAL DAYS AFTER LEAVING LABAN...

LOOK—RIDERS! LABAN AND HIS MEN. QUICK—TELL JACOB!

JACOB IS READY WHEN HIS FATHER-IN-LAW ARRIVES.

JACOB, WHY DID YOU LEAVE WITHOUT GIVING ME A CHANCE TO SAY GOOD-BY?

I WAS AFRAID YOU MIGHT HAVE KEPT YOUR DAUGHTERS FROM GOING.

I HAVE ENOUGH MEN SO I COULD TAKE REVENGE ON YOU. BUT THE GOD OF YOUR FATHERS HAS TOLD ME NOT TO HARM YOU.

SO LABAN AND JACOB SET UP A HEAP OF STONES AS A MARKER AND MAKE AN AGREEMENT NEVER TO HARM EACH OTHER.

THE LORD WATCH BETWEEN ME AND THEE, WHEN WE ARE ABSENT ONE FROM ANOTHER.

THE NEXT MORNING LABAN RIDES AWAY.

EAGERLY JACOB CONTINUES HIS JOURNEY HOME. ON THE WAY HE HAS A WONDERFUL VISION...

AN ARMY OF ANGELS! THE HOSTS OF GOD ARE CAMPED BESIDE ME!

HE IS COMFORTED BY THE ANGELS—BUT AS HE NEARS HIS HOME COUNTRY, HE BEGINS TO WORRY ABOUT HIS BROTHER, ESAU, WHO ONCE PLANNED TO MURDER HIM.

RIDE AHEAD—SEARCH OUT ESAU. TELL HIM I AM RETURNING HOME WITH MY FAMILY AND FLOCKS. TELL HIM I HOPE HE WILL FORGIVE ME.

JACOB WAITS ANXIOUSLY FOR THE RIDERS TO COME BACK. HE REMEMBERS THE TIME WHEN HE LIED TO HIS FATHER AND STOLE HIS BROTHER'S BLESSING...WHEN ESAU THREATENED TO KILL HIM...

FINALLY THE SCOUTS RETURN...

WE SAW ESAU! HE'S COMING TO MEET YOU— WITH 400 MEN!

Journey to Hebron

FROM GENESIS 32:7—33; 35:1–20

JACOB IS FRIGHTENED...
BUT HE IS ALSO SHREWD. HE DIVIDES HIS CARAVAN
INTO TWO SECTIONS, AND SENDS SERVANTS AHEAD
WITH PRESENTS FOR ESAU.

IF ESAU ATTACKS ONE GROUP, THE OTHER CAN ESCAPE.

THAT NIGHT JACOB PRAYS—CONFESSING HIS SINS, ADMITTING HIS FEAR, AND ASKING GOD'S HELP. BUT STILL HE CANNOT SLEEP.

MY FAMILY WOULD BE SAFER ON THE OTHER SIDE OF THE RIVER.

SO, IN THE MIDDLE OF THE NIGHT, HE MOVES HIS FAMILY...

YOU WILL BE SAFER ON THE OTHER SIDE, RACHEL.

I WISH YOU WOULD STAY WITH US.

BUT JACOB NEEDS TO BE ALONE... AND LATER THAT NIGHT AS HE PRAYS, HE FEELS HIMSELF WRESTLING WITH A MYSTERIOUS STRANGER. IT IS A FIERCE STRUGGLE, BUT JACOB DOES NOT GIVE UP UNTIL THE STRANGER BLESSES HIM: "THY NAME SHALL BE CALLED NO MORE JACOB, BUT ISRAEL: FOR AS A PRINCE HAST THOU POWER WITH GOD."

THE NEXT MORNING JACOB FINDS HIMSELF LAME FROM WRESTLING WITH THE ANGEL. BUT JACOB IS HAPPY...FOR HE KNOWS HIS EVIL NATURE HAS BEEN CONQUERED AND THAT HE HAS BEEN BLESSED BY GOD. JACOB GOES CONFIDENTLY TO MEET HIS BROTHER.

JACOB, MY BROTHER! I AM HAPPY TO SEE YOU AGAIN!

ESAU! HOW GLAD I AM. YOU DO NOT HATE ME ANY MORE!

PROUDLY JACOB PRESENTS HIS FAMILY...

AND THIS IS MY WIFE, RACHEL, AND MY SON, JOSEPH.

IT IS GOOD TO SEE MY BROTHER'S FAMILY. GOD HAS BLESSED YOU MUCH.

AFTER FEASTING TOGETHER, THE BROTHERS SAY GOOD-BY. JACOB HEADS TOWARD HIS FATHER'S HOME IN HEBRON.

FAREWELL, AND GREET MY FATHER FOR ME.

I WILL TELL HIM ALL IS WELL WITH YOU. GOOD-BY, AND GOD BLESS YOU, ESAU.

SOME TIME LATER ON THE WAY, JACOB STOPS AT BETH-EL.

THIS STONE, RACHEL, MARKS THE PLACE WHERE I SAW ANGELS COMING TO ME FROM HEAVEN, AND WHERE GOD PROMISED TO TAKE CARE OF ME. HE HAS, RACHEL...MORE THAN I DESERVE.

GOD HAS BEEN GOOD TO US, JACOB. AND I PRAY THAT HE WILL TAKE CARE OF OUR SON, JOSEPH— AND THE CHILD WHO IS SOON TO BE BORN.

FARTHER ALONG ON THE JOURNEY— NOT FAR FROM BETHLEHEM— RACHEL'S CHILD IS BORN...

IT'S A BOY, BUT OH, MY MASTER, YOUR WIFE, RACHEL, IS DEAD!

JACOB BURIES HIS BELOVED WIFE, RACHEL. THEN HE AND HIS FAMILY CONTINUE SADLY ON THEIR JOURNEY...STOPPING NOW AND THEN TO REST AND FEED THE FLOCKS. AS THEY TRAVEL ON, JACOB WONDERS...

RACHEL AND MY MOTHER ARE DEAD. WILL I GET TO MY FATHER WHILE HE IS STILL ALIVE?

Into the Pit

FROM GENESIS 35:27–29; 37:1–26

JACOB'S HAND TREMBLES AS HE SHADES HIS EYES AND LOOKS TOWARD THE DISTANT CITY OF HEBRON.

IS THAT WHERE MY GRANDFATHER, ISAAC, LIVES?

YES, JOSEPH. I PRAY WE ARE NOT TOO LATE... HE IS VERY OLD.

JACOB'S PRAYERS ARE ANSWERED. AT THE SIGHT OF HIS BLIND AND AGED FATHER, HE FALLS TO HIS KNEES.

O FATHER, I AM YOUR SON, JACOB— THANK GOD, I AM WITH YOU AGAIN.

JACOB, MY SON! I HAVE PRAYED FOR YOUR RETURN. DO YOU HAVE CHILDREN NOW?

PROUDLY JACOB PRESENTS HIS 12 SONS TO THEIR GRANDFATHER, ISAAC.

FATHER, THESE ARE JOSEPH AND BENJAMIN, THE SONS OF MY BELOVED RACHEL.

BE STRONG, MY CHILDREN, AND OBEY GOD ALWAYS.

Wrestling with a Stranger

▶ Read about Jacob on pp. 72-120.

IF GOD WILL GO WITH ME, I'LL BE GOD'S MAN.

Jacob is a deceiver. He tricks his brother out of the birthright and deceives his father out of the family blessing. Esau is so angry he threatens to kill Jacob. But two things happened to change Jacob:

▶ Jacob dreams of a ladder to heaven with angels going up and down. The Lord promises him the ground where he is sleeping, many children, and that He will be with Jacob whereever he goes. Jacob calls the place Bethel, meaning "house of God." (See p. 82.)

Did You Know?

▶ Jacob wrestles all night with a stranger. Needing to have God's blessing as he faces angry Esau, Jacob refuses to let the stranger go. When morning comes, God changes Jacob's name to Israel, and he becomes the father of the Israelite nation. (See p. 90.)

▶ Jacob has twelve sons for whom the twelve tribes of Israel are named.

Did You Know?

God Turns Bad into Good . . .

▶ **Read about Joseph on pp. 97-122.**

Sometimes circumstances seem bad when actually they are opportunities for God to show us His power and love. Joseph faces several things that seem bad, but God turns them around for good.

▶ **Joseph is sold as a slave by his brothers. . . .**
> He becomes the manager of Potiphar's household. Potiphar is captain of the king's guard (p. 97).

▶ **Joseph is falsely accused and thrown into prison. . . .**
> He finds favor and is put in charge of all the prisoners (p. 100).

▶ **Even though Joseph is in prison, he is called before Pharaoh to interpret a dream. . . .**
> Pharaoh makes him ruler over all of Egypt (p. 103).

▶ **The brothers who hated Joseph now come to him for food. . . .**
> Joseph forgives them and gives them all the food they need (p. 113).

Joseph stays true to God.

94

WHEN ISAAC DIES, JACOB TAKES OVER AS HEAD OF THE TRIBE. WORD IS SENT TO ESAU, WHO COMES TO HELP JACOB BURY THEIR FATHER. AS SOON AS ESAU LEAVES, JACOB CALLS HIS SONS TO HIM...

THERE IS NOT ENOUGH PASTURE LAND FOR ALL OF OUR FLOCKS. WE WILL TAKE SOME OF THEM TO SHECHEM.

MAY I GO WITH MY BROTHERS TO TEND THE FLOCKS?

NO, JOSEPH, STAY HERE WITH ME. I HAVE SOMETHING FOR YOU.

SEE HOW FATHER FAVORS JOSEPH!

HE ALWAYS HAS! NOW HE MAY TRAIN HIM TO RULE THE TRIBE.

I'LL NEVER TAKE ORDERS FROM JOSEPH!

WHEN THE OLDER SONS ARE GONE...

HERE, MASTER JOSEPH, IS THE COAT YOUR FATHER HAD MADE FOR YOU.

FOR ME! WHY IT'S JUST LIKE A CHIEFTAIN'S ROBE!

WHEN THE OLDER SONS RETURN, THEY ARE JEALOUS OF JOSEPH'S COAT. THEN HE TELLS THEM ABOUT HIS DREAMS...

STILL LATER JOSEPH HAS ANOTHER DREAM...

I DREAMED THE SUN AND MOON AND STARS BOWED TO ME.

WHAT? SHALL YOUR PARENTS AND BROTHERS SERVE YOU?

LAST NIGHT I DREAMED WE WERE BINDING SHEAVES, AND ALL OF YOUR SHEAVES BOWED DOWN TO MINE.

BOW DOWN TO HIM? **NEVER!**

JACOB SOON FORGETS HIS OWN ANGER TOWARD JOSEPH, BUT THE SECOND DREAM WHIPS THE OLDER BROTHERS' HATRED INTO A BURNING RAGE.

SEVERAL DAYS LATER THE BROTHERS ARE TENDING THE SHEEP SOME DISTANCE FROM CAMP, AND JACOB SENDS JOSEPH TO SEE HOW THEY ARE GETTING ALONG.

HERE COMES THE DREAMER.

I'VE HAD ENOUGH OF HIS TALK. LET'S GET RID OF HIM!

Slave Train to Egypt

FROM GENESIS 37:27–36; 39:1–20

THROWN INTO A DEEP PIT BY HIS JEALOUS BROTHERS, JOSEPH WAITS HELPLESSLY WHILE THEY DECIDE HIS FATE.

SEE THAT CARAVAN COMING? WE COULD SELL THEM JOSEPH AS A SLAVE. THAT WOULD GET RID OF HIM!

SO THE BROTHERS PULL JOSEPH OUT OF THE PIT AND DRAG HIM TO THE CARAVAN.

THE BOY IS OUR SLAVE. WHAT WILL YOU GIVE US FOR HIM?

HE'S A HANDSOME ONE—SHOULD BRING A GOOD PRICE IN EGYPT.

HE LOOKS SOFT—I'LL GIVE YOU 20 SHEKELS.

BUT I'MMM—

KEEP STILL, SLAVE!

IT'S A DEAL— TAKE HIM!

THE CARAVAN IS WELL OUT OF SIGHT BY THE TIME REUBEN RETURNS...

WHERE IS JOSEPH? WHAT HAVE YOU DONE TO HIM?

WE SOLD HIM TO SOME TRADERS. THEIR CARAVAN IS GOING TO EGYPT. HERE'S YOUR SHARE OF THE MONEY.

SOLD HIM? OH, NO! WHAT WILL YOU TELL FATHER?

WE'LL SMEAR JOSEPH'S COAT WITH GOAT'S BLOOD AND LET FATHER THINK HE WAS KILLED BY A LION.

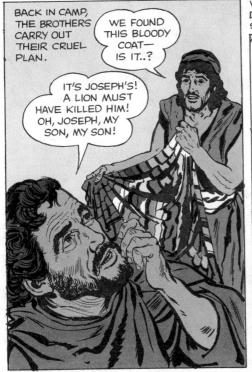

BACK IN CAMP, THE BROTHERS CARRY OUT THEIR CRUEL PLAN.

WE FOUND THIS BLOODY COAT— IS IT..?

IT'S JOSEPH'S! A LION MUST HAVE KILLED HIM! OH, JOSEPH, MY SON, MY SON!

WHILE JACOB IS STILL MOURNING THE DEATH OF HIS BELOVED SON, JOSEPH IS SOLD AGAIN AS A SLAVE IN EGYPT.

LOOK— THIS BOY IS STRONG AND HANDSOME. HE'D MAKE A FINE SLAVE, EVEN IN THE KING'S PALACE. HOW MUCH AM I BID?

THIRTY SHEKELS!

I AM A SLAVE! O GOD, PLEASE HELP ME!

AND SO, JACOB'S FAVORITE SON BECOMES THE SLAVE OF POTIPHAR, CAPTAIN OF THE KING'S GUARD. BUT JOSEPH DOES NOT BEG FOR PITY. HE PUTS HIS TRUST IN GOD AND HOLDS HIS HEAD UP PROUDLY.

GOOD SLAVE FOR THIRTY SHEKELS!

HE DOESN'T HAVE THE MANNER OF A SERVANT. TELL ME MORE ABOUT HIM.

SOME TRADERS BROUGHT HIM DOWN FROM CANAAN. HE'S STRONG— INTELLIGENT, TOO!

AND HANDSOME! IN THE RIGHT CLOTHES, HE'D PASS FOR A PRINCE!

YEARS PASS, AND POTIPHAR MAKES JOSEPH MANAGER OF ALL OF HIS PROPERTY.

THINGS ARE BETTER WITH JOSEPH IN CHARGE.

HE PRAYS EVERY DAY, ASKING HIS GOD TO HELP HIM.

BUT JOSEPH'S SUCCESS ALSO LEADS TO TROUBLE. POTIPHAR'S WIFE FALLS IN LOVE WITH THE HANDSOME, YOUNG SLAVE. ONE DAY WHILE POTIPHAR IS AWAY...

JOSEPH, COME, SIT BESIDE ME. TELL ME WHERE YOU CAME FROM AND WHY YOU ARE IN EGYPT.

THANK YOU, BUT I HAVE WORK TO FINISH BEFORE POTIPHAR RETURNS.

MUST YOU ALWAYS THINK OF POTIPHAR?

HE IS MY MASTER— I WILL NOT BE UNTRUE TO HIM OR DISOBEY MY GOD.

NO MAN CAN SCORN ME—AND LIVE!

SHE BIDES HER TIME...WHEN POTIPHAR RETURNS SHE GREETS HIM WITH TEARS IN HER EYES, AND A LIE ON HER LIPS.

YOUR HEBREW SLAVE TRIED TO KISS ME! I SCREAMED AND HE LEFT...BUT HE DROPPED HIS ROBE. HERE— SEE IT!

I'LL THROW HIM IN PRISON FOR THIS!

BEFORE THE SUN SETS THAT DAY, JOSEPH IS CHAINED AND THROWN INTO THE KING'S PRISON.

HO— WHAT A HANDSOME PRISONER WE HAVE WITH US!

WHEN HE'S BEEN HERE AS LONG AS I HAVE, HE'LL FORGET WHAT IT'S LIKE TO WEAR SUCH FINE, CLEAN CLOTHES.

The King's Dream

FROM GENESIS 39:21–23; 40—42:1–6

FALSELY ACCUSED, JOSEPH FACES HIS FIRST NIGHT IN PRISON. BUT HE IS NOT AFRAID, AND HE IS NOT ALONE BECAUSE GOD IS WITH HIM. JOSEPH PRAYS... AS HE HAS DONE EVERY OTHER NIGHT IN HIS LIFE.

WHAT GOD CAN SAVE HIM NOW?

LEAVE HIM ALONE! HE IS BRAVER THAN THE REST OF US.

ONE LONG, HOT DAY FOLLOWS ANOTHER. THE PRISONERS QUARREL OVER FOOD—WATER—THE BEST PLACE TO SLEEP. ONE DAY A FIGHT BREAKS OUT...

STOP IT! FIGHTING WON'T HELP US.

EVEN IN PRISON GOD IS WITH JOSEPH. WHEN THE KEEPER OF THE JAIL LEARNS JOSEPH IS A LEADER, HE PUTS JOSEPH IN CHARGE OF THE OTHER PRISONERS.

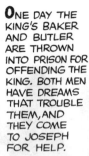

ONE DAY THE KING'S BAKER AND BUTLER ARE THROWN INTO PRISON FOR OFFENDING THE KING. BOTH MEN HAVE DREAMS THAT TROUBLE THEM, AND THEY COME TO JOSEPH FOR HELP.

WHAT DO YOU THINK MY DREAM MEANT?

IN THREE DAYS YOU WILL BE THE KING'S BUTLER AGAIN. WHEN THAT TIME COMES, PLEASE SAY A GOOD WORD FOR ME.

NOW TELL ME WHAT MY DREAM MEANS.

I'M SORRY, BUT THE DREAM SHOWS YOU WILL BE HANGED, IN JUST THREE DAYS.

JOSEPH'S WORDS COME TRUE. THREE DAYS LATER, ONE MAN DIES, AND THE OTHER RETURNS TO SERVE THE KING. BUT HE FORGETS HIS PROMISE. TWO YEARS GO BY...

YOU CALLED, O KING?

YES. IS THERE NO ONE IN MY WHOLE KINGDOM WHO CAN TELL ME WHAT MY DREAM MEANS? I MUST FIND OUT...

O KING, I KNOW A HEBREW PRISONER WHO CAN TELL THE MEANING OF DREAMS. HE TOLD MINE!

BRING HIM TO ME—AT ONCE!

THE BUTLER WASTES NO TIME IN HAVING JOSEPH RELEASED FROM PRISON. HE KNEELS BEFORE THE PHARAOH OF EGYPT.

IS IT TRUE YOU CAN TELL THE MEANING OF DREAMS?

NOT I—BUT MY GOD GIVES THE ANSWER, O PHARAOH. TELL ME YOUR DREAM.

I SAW SEVEN FAT COWS COME OUT OF THE NILE RIVER. AFTER THEM CAME SEVEN LEAN COWS THAT ATE THE FAT ONES.

GOD IS WARNING YOU THAT THERE WILL BE SEVEN YEARS OF GOOD CROPS FOLLOWED BY SEVEN YEARS OF FAMINE.

LET PHARAOH APPOINT A WISE OFFICER TO STORE GRAIN DURING THE SEVEN GOOD YEARS. THEN THERE WILL BE FOOD FOR ALL DURING THE SEVEN YEARS OF FAMINE.

WHO IS WISER THAN YOU, SINCE GOD IS WITH YOU?

PHARAOH QUICKLY SUMMONS THE OFFICERS OF HIS COURT. AS THEY WATCH, HE PUTS HIS OWN RING ON JOSEPH'S FINGER.

I HAVE PUT YOU IN CHARGE OF ALL EGYPT. ONLY I, PHARAOH, WILL BE GREATER THAN YOU!

FROM THE THRONE ROOM, JOSEPH GOES TO HIS OWN ROOM AND KNEELS IN PRAYER, THANKING GOD FOR PROTECTION AND GUIDANCE.

JOSEPH ORDERS THE PEOPLE TO START PREPARING FOR THE FAMINE. HE BECOMES FAMOUS, AND ALL REJOICE WHEN HE MARRIES THE BEAUTIFUL DAUGHTER OF THE PRIEST OF ON.

I AM PROUD TO BE YOUR WIFE, JOSEPH. YOU HAVE DONE SO MUCH FOR OUR PEOPLE.

THERE IS MORE TO BE DONE, MY DEAR. THE YEARS OF PLENTY WILL PASS QUICKLY.

ALL TOO SOON, THE FAMINE BEGINS. AS IT CONTINUES, PEOPLE FROM OTHER COUNTRIES COME TO EGYPT SEEKING FOOD. ONE DAY TRIBESMEN FROM CANAAN ENTER JOSEPH'S CITY...

IN ORDER TO BUY GRAIN, THEY APPEAR BEFORE THE GOVERNOR OF EGYPT. THEY BOW BEFORE HIM...

MY BROTHERS! THEY DO NOT RECOGNIZE ME AFTER ALL THESE YEARS!

Trouble in Egypt

FROM GENESIS 42:6–38

THE GRAIN SACKS FILLED, THE BROTHERS LEAVE EGYPT AT ONCE. THAT NIGHT AS THEY SET UP CAMP...

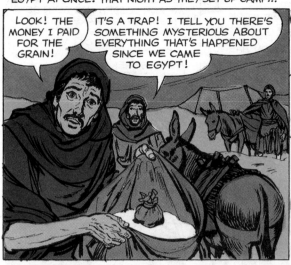

LOOK! THE MONEY I PAID FOR THE GRAIN!

IT'S A TRAP! I TELL YOU THERE'S SOMETHING MYSTERIOUS ABOUT EVERYTHING THAT'S HAPPENED SINCE WE CAME TO EGYPT!

I'D NEVER GO BACK EXCEPT—

EXCEPT THAT WE LEFT SIMEON THERE IN PRISON. AND BENJAMIN IS THE ONLY ONE WHO CAN SET HIM FREE.

WHO KNOWS— MAYBE NEXT TIME WE COME THE GOVERNOR WILL KEEP BENJAMIN— OR ONE OF US!

FOR DAYS, AS THE CARAVAN TRAVELS NORTHEAST THE BROTHERS WORRY ABOUT WHAT THEIR FATHER WILL SAY.

BACK HOME, THEY PROUDLY SHOW THEIR FATHER HOW MUCH GRAIN THEY HAVE BROUGHT...

LOOK— THE MONEY IS IN MY SACK, TOO!

AND MINE!

WHAT IS THIS? MONEY IN YOUR GRAIN SACKS— AND WHERE IS SIMEON?

IN—IN PRISON IN EGYPT, AND...

SIMEON IN PRISON? WHY? SPEAK UP. WHAT HAPPENED?

THE WHOLE TRIP WAS VERY STRANGE, FATHER. THE GOVERNOR SAID WE WERE SPIES. HE PUT US ALL IN PRISON, THEN HE RELEASED ALL OF US BUT SIMEON. SIMEON HAS TO STAY THERE—UNTIL WE TAKE BENJAMIN TO EGYPT.

BENJAMIN TO EGYPT? NEVER! MY SON JOSEPH HAS BEEN DEAD THESE MANY YEARS—NOW SIMEON IS LOST TO ME. I WILL NOT PART WITH BENJAMIN.

BUT FATHER—WHAT ABOUT SIMEON?

YES, WHAT ABOUT SIMEON? AND WHAT ABOUT **US** IF THE GRAIN RUNS OUT AND WE HAVE TO GO TO EGYPT AGAIN? WE CAN'T GO WITHOUT BENJAMIN!

THE GRAIN IS USED SPARINGLY, BUT ONE DAY JACOB'S HUNGRY TRIBE HAS TO FACE THE TRUTH...

THE GRAIN IS ALMOST GONE—WHAT SHALL WE DO?

The Stolen Cup
FROM GENESIS 43:1—44:12

JACOB, THE OLD CHIEFTAIN, FACES A HARD DECISION...

BUT WHY SHOULD THE GOVERNOR OF EGYPT HOLD SIMEON IN PRISON UNTIL HE SEES BENJAMIN? WHAT DOES HE WANT WITH MY YOUNGEST SON?

NOBODY KNOWS. BUT IF I DON'T GO, SIMEON WILL DIE IN PRISON—AND WE WILL STARVE. I MUST GO, FATHER—I MUST!

BENJAMIN IS RIGHT.

THEN—GO. TAKE DOUBLE THE AMOUNT OF MONEY FOR GRAIN—TAKE GIFTS TO THE GOVERNOR. AND MAY GOD BE MERCIFUL TO US!

DAYS LATER, JACOB'S SONS LEAD THEIR PACK ANIMALS THROUGH THE GATES OF THE EGYPTIAN CITY.

DON'T WORRY, BENJAMIN, WE'LL DO EVERYTHING WE CAN TO PROTECT YOU.

I AM NOT AFRAID—GOD WILL TAKE CARE OF US HERE JUST AS HE DOES IN OUR FIELDS AT HOME.

BUT EVEN AS THEY WONDER, THE GOVERNOR HAS THE BROTHERS SERVED — GIVING THE LARGEST PORTION TO BENJAMIN. IT IS A SIGN OF GREAT HONOR.

DO YOU SEE THAT?

AT LEAST BENJAMIN IS SAFE!

THE BANQUET ENDS; THE NEXT MORNING THE BROTHERS BUY THEIR GRAIN AND LEAVE. BUT THEY ARE HARDLY OUT OF THE CITY BEFORE A CHARIOT OVERTAKES THEM.

STOP! ONE OF YOU HAS STOLEN MY MASTER'S SILVER CUP!

YOUR MASTER'S CUP? WE ARE INNOCENT! SEARCH US IF YOU WILL.

IF THE CUP IS FOUND, THE MAN IN WHOSE SACK IT IS HIDDEN SHALL BECOME MY MASTER'S SLAVE!

ONE BY ONE THE SACKS ARE SEARCHED... AT LAST THE OFFICER OPENS BENJAMIN'S...

THE CUP!

Joseph's Secret

FROM GENESIS 44:13—45:26

THE ONE IN WHOSE BAG THE CUP WAS FOUND SHALL BE MY SERVANT— THE REST OF YOU MAY RETURN TO YOUR FATHER.

IF BENJAMIN DOES NOT RETURN HOME, OUR FATHER WILL DIE OF GRIEF. LET ME BE YOUR SLAVE INSTEAD OF BENJAMIN.

FOR A MOMENT THERE IS SILENCE. THEN THE GOVERNOR TURNS TO HIS GUARDS.

GO! LEAVE ME ALONE WITH THESE MEN.

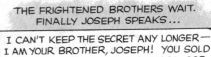

THE FRIGHTENED BROTHERS WAIT. FINALLY JOSEPH SPEAKS...

I CAN'T KEEP THE SECRET ANY LONGER— I AM YOUR BROTHER, JOSEPH! YOU SOLD ME AS A SLAVE MANY YEARS AGO. GOD HAS BLESSED ME RICHLY...NOW WE ARE TOGETHER AGAIN.

115

WHEN PHARAOH HEARS THE NEWS, HE CALLS FOR JOSEPH...

GIVE YOUR BROTHERS WAGONS SO THEY CAN BRING THEIR FAMILIES AND YOUR FATHER TO LIVE IN EGYPT.

LOADED WITH SUPPLIES AND GIFTS THE HAPPY CARAVAN SETS OUT FOR HOME. WHEN THEY APPROACH JACOB'S CAMP, SOME OF THE BROTHERS RUN AHEAD TO TELL THE GOOD NEWS.

FATHER! FATHER! WE HAVE NEWS!

JOSEPH IS ALIVE! HE'S THE GOVERNOR OF ALL EGYPT!

JACOB RISES TO GREET HIS SONS...BUT WHEN HE HEARS JOSEPH'S NAME HE SINKS BACK...

JOSEPH ALIVE? I CAN'T BELIEVE IT!

South into Egypt

FROM GENESIS 45:27–28; 47;
48; 50:1–15

BUT, FATHER, WE ALL _SAW_ HIM! AND HE WANTS YOU TO COME TO EGYPT TO SEE HIM.

LOOK! THE WAGONS LOADED WITH FOOD AND GIFTS FROM JOSEPH—FOR YOU!

JOSEPH—THE SON OF MY BELOVED RACHEL—IS ALIVE! O GOD, I THANK THEE, I THANK THEE!

THE EXCITING NEWS SPREADS QUICKLY THROUGHOUT THE CAMP. SOON THE TRIBE OF JACOB BEGINS MOVING SOUTH TOWARD EGYPT. ON THE WAY JACOB STOPS TO WORSHIP AT A PLACE WHERE HE HAD WORSHIPED AS A BOY.

THAT NIGHT GOD SPEAKS TO HIM IN A VISION: "FEAR NOT TO GO DOWN INTO EGYPT, FOR I WILL GO WITH THEE."

DOWN IN EGYPT, JOSEPH AND HIS FAMILY WAIT ANXIOUSLY!

IS MY GRANDFATHER RICH AND POWERFUL LIKE PHARAOH?

NOT LIKE PHARAOH, MY SON, BUT HE IS THE CHIEF OF A TRIBE.

WHEN I WAS JUST A YOUNG BOY HE GAVE ME A BEAUTIFUL COAT OF MANY COLORS.

DO YOU STILL HAVE THE COAT?

IT WAS TAKEN FROM ME BEFORE I CAME TO EGYPT MANY YEARS AGO...

FOR A MOMENT JOSEPH RELIVES THE TIME WHEN HIS BROTHERS SOLD HIM AS A SLAVE. SUDDENLY A MESSENGER INTERRUPTS HIS MEMORIES...

EXCELLENCY, YOUR FATHER AND BROTHERS ARE CAMPED IN GOSHEN!

JOSEPH HURRIES TO HIS CHARIOT AND RACES TOWARD HIS FATHER'S CAMP.

FATHER! O, MY FATHER!

MY SON! GOD HAS ANSWERED MY PRAYERS.

BACK IN THE CITY, JOSEPH PROUDLY PRESENTS HIS FATHER TO PHARAOH, WHO GIVES JACOB THE BEST PASTURE LAND IN ALL EGYPT.

MAY GOD BLESS YOU FOR YOUR KINDNESS TO US.

FOR SEVENTEEN YEARS JACOB AND HIS SONS LIVE HAPPILY IN EGYPT. THEN ONE DAY A MESSENGER BRINGS SAD NEWS TO JOSEPH...

SIR, YOUR FATHER IS VERY ILL. HE WANTS YOU AND YOUR SONS TO COME— RIGHT AWAY!

THEY HURRY TO JACOB'S BEDSIDE.

BRING YOUR SONS TO ME SO I CAN BLESS THEM BEFORE I DIE.

MAY GOD, WHO HAS GUIDED ME ALL MY LIFE, BLESS MY GRANDSONS.

BECAUSE OF THE WICKEDNESS OF HIS OLDER SONS, JACOB GIVES THE FAMILY BIRTHRIGHT TO JOSEPH AND HIS SONS.

THEN JACOB CALLS ALL OF HIS SONS TO HIM AND BLESSES THEM. JACOB DIES AND HIS SONS CARRY THE OLD CHIEFTAIN'S BODY BACK TO HIS HOMELAND OF CANAAN.

AFTER JACOB'S FUNERAL, JOSEPH WALKS AWAY FROM THE CAMP ALONE. HIS BROTHERS WATCH HIM SUSPICIOUSLY...

JOSEPH WAS GOOD TO US WHILE OUR FATHER LIVED, BUT NOW...

HE MAY GET EVEN. THERE'S ONLY ONE THING TO DO...

Death Sentence

FROM GENESIS 50:15–26;
EXODUS 1:1—2:1–2

FOLLOWING THE BURIAL OF THEIR FATHER, JOSEPH AND HIS BROTHERS GO BACK TO EGYPT. BUT THE BROTHERS ARE AFRAID THAT JOSEPH MAY NOW TAKE REVENGE FOR THE EVIL THEY DID TO HIM.

WE HAVE ONLY ONE COURSE TO TAKE—BUT LET'S WAIT UNTIL WE REACH EGYPT.

YES, OUR FAMILIES ARE THERE.

IN EGYPT THE BROTHERS WASTE NO TIME...

TAKE THIS MESSAGE TO OUR BROTHER, JOSEPH.

JOSEPH WEEPS WHEN HE HEARS THE WORDS OF THE MESSENGER.

BRING MY BROTHERS TO ME—IS IT POSSIBLE THAT EVEN YET THEY HAVE NOT LEARNED THAT I HAVE FORGIVEN THEM?

OUR MESSAGE CONTAINED THE WORDS OF OUR FATHER—ASKING YOU TO FORGIVE US. WE WILL WORK FOR YOU AS SERVANTS IF YOU DEMAND IT, BUT PRAY DO NOT HARM US OR OUR FAMILIES.

DO NOT BE AFRAID. YOU DID EVIL, BUT GOD USED IT FOR GOOD.

FOR YEARS THE SONS OF JACOB LIVE HAPPILY IN EGYPT.

GOD HAS BEEN GOOD TO US—MORE THAN WE DESERVE.

AS LONG AS I LIVE I WILL THANK GOD AND SEEK HIS FORGIVENESS.

WHEN JOSEPH IS VERY OLD HE CALLS HIS RELATIVES TO HIM.

GOD WILL BRING YOU OUT OF THIS LAND UNTO THE LAND WHICH HE GAVE TO ABRAHAM, TO ISAAC, AND TO JACOB. WHEN YOU RETURN, TAKE MY BODY WITH YOU, FOR I WOULD BE BURIED IN THE LAND OF MY FATHERS.

SOON AFTERWARD, JOSEPH DIES.

ALL EGYPT MOURNS JOSEPH'S DEATH. BUT AS NEW RULERS COME TO THE THRONE...

THE NEW KING DOES NOT LIKE US HEBREWS. HE HAS FORGOTTEN THAT IT WAS OUR ANCESTOR JOSEPH WHO SAVED EGYPT FROM FAMINE.

THIS COULD MEAN TROUBLE FOR US.

FROM HIS ROYAL YACHT ON THE NILE, THE KING FROWNS AS HE WATCHES THE HEBREW SHEPHERDS WITH THEIR RICH FLOCKS.

THERE ARE TOO MANY HEBREWS IN EGYPT! IN CASE OF WAR THEY MIGHT TURN AGAINST US. HOW CAN WE KEEP THEM FROM CAUSING TROUBLE?

NEXT DAY THE KING INSPECTS A NEW BUILDING PROJECT.

WE NEED WORKMEN. THOUSANDS MORE THAN WE HAVE.

I HAVE IT! THE HEBREWS WILL WORK AS SLAVES. IT WILL SAVE US MONEY AND THEY WON'T BE ABLE TO CAUSE TROUBLE.

SO FROM DAYLIGHT TO DARK HEBREW MEN AND BOYS ARE DRIVEN FROM THEIR HOMES AND FORCED TO WORK UNDER WHIP-CRACKING SLAVE DRIVERS.

BUT THE HEBREWS ARE STRONG.

WE WORK THEM HARDER EVERY DAY, BUT THERE ARE MORE HEBREWS THAN BEFORE. THE KING WILL NOT BE HAPPY ABOUT THIS...

WHEN THE KING HEARS THE REPORT...

I'LL TAKE CARE OF THE SLAVES! THROW EVERY HEBREW BOY BABY IN THE RIVER!

THE CRUEL ORDER IS CARRIED OUT. HEBREW MOTHERS AND FATHERS RISK THEIR LIVES TO PROTECT THEIR SONS...BUT THE KING'S MEN NEVER GIVE UP THEIR SEARCH.

NIGHT AFTER NIGHT ONE HEBREW FATHER HURRIES HOME FROM WORK—AFRAID THAT THE SOLDIERS HAVE VISITED HIS HOME.

O GOD, HELP ME SAVE OUR BOY FROM THE EGYPTIANS.

Cry of a Slave

FROM EXODUS 2:3–11

THERE'S MIRIAM! A SIGN THAT MY LITTLE SON IS STILL SAFE.

QUICKLY THE FATHER ENTERS THE HOUSE—AND BOLTS THE DOOR.

SURELY GOD IS WITH US— OUR BABY IS THREE MONTHS OLD AND STILL PHARAOH'S SOLDIERS HAVE NOT FOUND HIM.

GOD WILL HELP ME FIND A WAY TO SAVE OUR SON!

NEXT DAY THE MOTHER SETS ABOUT PREPARING A LITTLE BASKET.

KEEP WATCH, MIRIAM, I'M ALMOST FINISHED.

THEN, CAREFULLY AVOIDING THE EGYPTIAN SOLDIERS, SHE TAKES THE BASKET AND HER TINY SON TO THE RIVER.

BROTHER'S BASKET FLOATS LIKE A LITTLE BOAT!

KEEP WATCH OVER HIM, MIRIAM. OH, MY SON, IT TEARS MY HEART TO SEND YOU AWAY. MAY GOD WATCH OVER YOU AND PROTECT YOU ALWAYS...

MIRIAM HIDES IN THE BULRUSHES AND WATCHES...

THE PRINCESS! WILL SHE SEE THE BABY'S BASKET?

LOOK—WHAT A STRANGE LITTLE BASKET! I WONDER WHAT'S INSIDE IT?

THE MAID BRINGS THE BASKET TO THE PRINCESS, WHO OPENS IT.

A HEBREW BABY! LISTEN TO HIM CRY! WE MUST FIND SOMEBODY TO FEED AND CARE FOR THE CHILD.

AT THIS POINT MIRIAM STEPS FORTH...

SHALL I FIND A HEBREW NURSE FOR THE BABY?

YES—BRING HER TO ME AS SOON AS YOU CAN.

MOTHER! COME AT ONCE! THE PRINCESS HAS FOUND OUR BABY— AND SHE WANTS A HEBREW NURSE FOR HIM.

GOD HAS ANSWERED MY PRAYER, MIRIAM. MY SON WILL BE SAFE WITH THE PRINCESS.

AT THE RIVER'S EDGE—

TAKE THIS BABY, AND CARE FOR HIM. IF ANYONE QUESTIONS YOU, SEND WORD TO ME AT ONCE.

SO THE HEBREW BABY IS RETURNED TO HIS OWN HOME —BUT NOW UNDER THE PROTECTION OF THE KING'S DAUGHTER. THAT NIGHT THE MOTHER, FATHER, MIRIAM AND YOUNG AARON KNEEL AND PRAY...

O GOD, WE THANK THEE FOR SAVING OUR LITTLE SON. HELP US TO TRAIN HIM TO SERVE THEE!

THE LITTLE BOY LIVES IN HIS HOME UNTIL HE IS ABOUT FOUR YEARS OLD. THEN HIS MOTHER TAKES HIM TO THE PALACE TO LIVE WITH THE PRINCESS WHO HAS ADOPTED HIM.

HE WILL BE _MY_ SON. HIS NAME WILL BE MOSES BECAUSE THAT IS LIKE THE WORD THAT MEANS "TO DRAW OUT", AND I DREW HIM OUT OF THE WATER.

YEARS PASS, AND THE BOY MOSES LIVES THE LIFE OF A YOUNG PRINCE IN PHARAOH'S PALACE. HE LEARNS TO WRITE AND READ. LATER HE GOES TO COLLEGE. ONE DAY HE DRIVES THROUGH THE CITY...

...TO A PLACE WHERE HEBREW SLAVES ARE WORKING. AS HE WATCHES THE SLAVES TOIL, HE IS STARTLED BY A MAN'S SCREAM...

The Fiery Bush

FROM EXODUS 2:11—3:4

Moses jumps from his chariot to investigate...and finds an Egyptian guard beating a Hebrew slave.

In sudden anger Moses strikes out hard—

LOOK! HE KILLED THE GUARD!

THE NEXT DAY MOSES RETURNS. WHEN HE SEES TWO HEBREWS FIGHTING, HE TRIES TO STOP THEM.

WHY DO YOU FIGHT AMONG YOURSELVES?

WHO MADE YOU A JUDGE OVER US? ARE YOU GOING TO KILL ME AS YOU DID THAT EGYPTIAN?

IF PHARAOH HEARS OF THIS HE WILL ACCUSE ME OF BEING A TRAITOR. THERE IS ONLY ONE THING FOR ME TO DO, AND I MUST DO IT NOW...

LATER THAT DAY IN THE PALACE...

PRINCE MOSES KILLED AN EGYPTIAN GUARD FOR BEATING A HEBREW SLAVE!

FIND THE TRAITOR—AND KILL HIM!

BUT PHARAOH'S ORDERS ARE TOO LATE...MOSES HAS A HEAD START ON THE SOLDIERS WHO CHASE HIM. HE ESCAPES— AND AFTER LONG, HARD RIDING REACHES THE LAND OF MIDIAN.

ONE EVENING HE RESTS BY A WELL.

GET AWAY FROM HERE UNTIL WE WATER OUR SHEEP!

NO— WE WERE HERE FIRST. YOU LEAVE US ALONE!

STAND BACK—THE GIRLS WERE HERE FIRST!

THE COWARDLY SHEPHERDS RETREAT—AND MOSES HELPS THE GIRLS WATER THEIR FLOCKS.

WHEN THE GIRLS RETURN TO THEIR CAMP ONE OF THEM TELLS THEIR FATHER WHAT HAPPENED AT THE WELL

WHERE IS THIS MAN? FIND HIM AND INVITE HIM TO EAT WITH US.

I AM ZIPPORAH. MY FATHER, JETHRO, INVITES YOU TO EAT WITH US.

MOSES ACCEPTS THE INVITATION—AND THAT NIGHT AFTER SUPPER...

I NEED A SHEPHERD—WHY DON'T YOU STAY WITH US?

THANK YOU, I WILL.

THIS WILL BE A GOOD PLACE TO HIDE FROM PHARAOH.

131

MOSES STAYS WEEKS AND THEN MONTHS. HE MARRIES ZIPPORAH AND IN TIME THEY HAVE TWO SONS.

GERSHOM HANDLES HIS SLING VERY WELL.

HE WILL MAKE A GOOD SHEPHERD— LIKE HIS FATHER.

YEAR AFTER YEAR THE FLOCKS OF JETHRO INCREASE. BUT ONE YEAR THE GRASSES DRY UP AND MOSES LEADS HIS SHEEP TO PASTURES NEAR THE MOUNTAIN OF SINAI.

BUT MOSES CANNOT FORGET THE HEBREW PEOPLE IN EGYPT.

I WONDER IF PHARAOH IS STILL ALIVE... AND WHAT HAS BECOME OF MY SISTER MIRIAM AND MY BROTHER AARON?

HE WONDERS, TOO, ABOUT THE HEBREW SLAVES STILL STRUGGLING UNDER THE WHIPS OF EGYPTIAN RULERS. ONE DAY HE LOOKS UP TO SEE A STRANGE SIGHT ON MOUNT SINAI.

A BUSH ON FIRE— YET IT IS NOT DESTROYED!

HE STEPS CLOSER—THEN STOPS. A VOICE FROM THE FIERY BUSH CALLS OUT **"MOSES!"**

132

Pharaoh's Revenge

FROM EXODUS 3:4—5:21

HERE AM I!

ONCE AGAIN MOSES STARTS TOWARD THE BUSH, BUT THE SAME VOICE WARNS HIM: "DO NOT COME NEARER... TAKE OFF YOUR SHOES, FOR THE GROUND ON WHICH YOU STAND IS HOLY GROUND."

THE VOICE CONTINUES: "I AM THE GOD OF YOUR FATHERS...GO DOWN TO EGYPT, TELL PHARAOH TO SET THE HEBREWS FREE."

WHO AM I TO SPEAK TO THE PHARAOH OF EGYPT?

MOSES IS AFRAID—AFRAID OF THE PHARAOH OF EGYPT, AFRAID HE CANNOT SPEAK PROPERLY— AFRAID THE HEBREW PEOPLE WILL NOT BELIEVE HIM. BUT GOD ASSURES HIM: "GO— YOUR BROTHER AARON WILL SPEAK FOR YOU. I WILL BE WITH YOU."

MOSES OBEYS. HE RETURNS TO CAMP AND TELLS HIS FATHER-IN-LAW WHAT GOD HAS CALLED HIM TO DO.

GO IN PEACE. GOD WILL STRENGTHEN YOU, AS HE HAS PROMISED.

AND SO MOSES SETS OUT FOR EGYPT WITH HIS WIFE AND SONS.

MEANTIME...IN THE SLAVE HUTS OF EGYPT, THE HEBREWS ARE ASKING GOD TO HELP THEM.

WHILE AARON, THE BROTHER OF MOSES, IS PRAYING, GOD SPEAKS TO HIM: "GO INTO THE WILDERNESS TO MEET YOUR BROTHER."

AARON IS SURPRISED AT THE STRANGE COMMAND. BUT, LIKE MOSES, HE OBEYS. SOON HE IS ALONE IN THE WILDERNESS.

MOSES HAS BEEN GONE FROM EGYPT FOR MANY YEARS. WILL HE KNOW ME? DOES HE KNOW I'M COMING? I WONDER WHAT GOD WANTS US TO DO?

AARON'S QUESTIONS ARE SOON ANSWERED. HE MEETS HIS BROTHER AT MOUNT SINAI.

MOSES!

AARON—I HAVE BEEN WATCHING FOR YOU!

HOW DID YOU KNOW I WAS COMING?

GOD TOLD ME YOU WOULD COME —TO HELP ME.

QUICKLY, MOSES EXPLAINS THAT GOD HAS CALLED THEM TO LEAD THE HEBREWS OUT OF SLAVERY IN EGYPT.

Moses, God's Leader

Moses is a great man of God—prophet, leader, and lawgiver to God's people, the Israelites. Because Moses is God's spokesman, God entrusts him with special information that he explains to the people.

▶ **The Tabernacle:** God gives Moses instructions to build a tent for worshiping Him in the wilderness. It becomes the center of the Israelite camp and reminds them that worshiping God is very important (p. 163).

▶ **The Law:** God gives Moses laws to teach His people how to live. The Ten Commandments are part of this Law (p. 157).

▶ **The Priesthood:** God instructs Moses to separate Aaron's family for priestly service. They perform special duties in the tabernacle that no one else is allowed to do.

Moses writes the first five books of the Bible. These books are referred to as the Pentateuch.

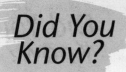

Did You Know?

Countdown to Freedom

▶ Turn to pp. 137-143 in your Picture Bible for the story.

God uses plagues to convince Pharaoh to let the Israelites leave Egypt. But because they are his slaves, Pharaoh doesn't want to let them go. God finally steps in with plague number ten and Pharaoh is convinced that God is serious. He lets the Israelites go.

The plague countdown:
1. **Water to blood**
2. **Frogs**
3. **Lice**
4. **Flies**
5. **Diseased cattle**
6. **Boils on people and animals**
7. **Hail**
8. **Locusts**
9. **Darkness for three days**
10. **Death of the firstborn son**

▶ The Egyptians worship the Nile River. When the water turns to blood, all of the fish die and the river stinks.

A locust is a grasshopper that travels in destructive swarms and devours vegetation.

▶ The plague of lice could also include gnats, maggots, sand flies, and fleas.

▶ The death angel passes over the Hebrew homes where blood is brushed on the frame of the front door. Jews today still celebrate this deliverance as Passover.

Plague of Death

FROM EXODUS 5:22—11:5

WHEN MOSES AND AARON DEMAND THE RELEASE OF THE HEBREW SLAVES, PHARAOH IS FURIOUS—AND MAKES THE SLAVES WORK HARDER THAN BEFORE. IN ANGER THEY TURN AGAINST MOSES. MOSES SEEKS GOD'S HELP AND IS TOLD TO VISIT PHARAOH AGAIN.

SHOW ME HOW POWERFUL YOUR GOD IS.

WHEN THIS ROD STRIKES THE GROUND, IT WILL BECOME A SERPENT.

AARON'S WORDS COME TRUE, BUT PHARAOH ONLY LAUGHS.

YOU ARE CLEVER, BUT MY MAGICIANS CAN DO THE SAME THING.

PHARAOH CALLS FOR HIS OWN MAGICIANS. THEY TOO THROW DOWN THEIR RODS—WHICH BECOME SERPENTS.

SEE?

BUT WHILE PHARAOH WATCHES, THE SERPENT OF AARON DEVOURS THE SERPENTS OF THE EGYPTIAN MAGICIANS. PHARAOH IS STUNNED... BUT HE REFUSES TO ADMIT THAT MOSES' GOD IS MORE POWERFUL THAN THE GODS OF EGYPT.

AGAIN MOSES SEEKS GOD'S HELP... AND AGAIN GOD TELLS HIM WHAT TO DO. IN THE MORNING MOSES AND AARON MEET PHARAOH ON THE BANK OF THE RIVER NILE.

WHAT ARE *YOU* DOING HERE?

BECAUSE YOU WILL NOT LET THE HEBREWS GO, THE RIVER WILL BE TURNED TO BLOOD.

AT MOSES' COMMAND, AARON STRIKES THE WATER WITH HIS ROD AND THE WATER TURNS RED.

I DON'T DARE BATHE IN THAT BLOODY STREAM!

WHEN WOMEN COME TO WASH THEIR CLOTHES IN THE RIVER, THEY ARE TURNED BACK. MEN HAVE TO DIG WELLS TO GET DRINKING WATER. FINALLY THE RIVER IS CLEAR AGAIN, BUT STILL PHARAOH WILL NOT LISTEN TO MOSES' PLEA. AND SO GOD SENDS A DIFFERENT PLAGUE...

IN THE STREETS OF THE CITY...

FROGS—MILLIONS OF THEM... EVERY-WHERE!

AND IN THE EGYPTIAN HOMES...

EE-EEK! A FROG IN MY BREAD DOUGH!

EVEN IN THE PALACE...

FROGS IN MY BED! I CAN'T STAND THIS—SEND FOR MOSES AND AARON.

ASK YOUR GOD TO TAKE AWAY THE FROGS, AND I WILL LET THE HEBREWS GO.

IT SHALL BE AS YOU SAY.

BUT WHEN THE FROGS ARE GONE, PHARAOH BREAKS HIS PROMISE. SO STILL ANOTHER PLAGUE DESCENDS ON EGYPT...

FIRST THERE COMES A PLAGUE OF LICE—LATER GREAT SWARMS OF BITING FLIES FILL THE AIR...

ONCE AGAIN PHARAOH PROMISES TO FREE THE HEBREWS. BUT WHEN THE FLIES DISAPPEAR, HE BREAKS HIS WORD. THEN DISEASE BREAKS OUT AMONG THE CATTLE, AND PHARAOH AND HIS PEOPLE SUFFER FROM PAINFUL BOILS.

FATHER, WERE THE SLAVE DRIVERS CRUEL TODAY?

THEY ARE ALWAYS CRUEL, SON, BUT RIGHT NOW THEY ARE SUFFERING FROM TERRIBLE BOILS WHILE WE ARE STRONG AND HEALTHY.

STILL PHARAOH KEEPS THE HEBREWS IN EGYPT. SO A TERRIBLE STORM STRIKES...

HAILSTONES AS BIG AS MY FIST!

THROUGHOUT THE LAND, THE EGYPTIAN FARMERS WATCH THE STORM WITH TERROR.

OUR CROPS ARE RUINED...

...BUT NO HAIL FALLS ON THE LAND WHERE THE HEBREWS LIVE.

LATER, MILLIONS OF LOCUSTS SWARM THROUGH THE LAND. AFTER A STRONG WIND BLOWS THEM AWAY, THE DAY BECOMES AS DARK AS NIGHT.

IT'S SO DARK—I'M AFRAID.

WILL THESE TERRIBLE TROUBLES NEVER CEASE?

AFTER THREE DAYS OF DARKNESS PHARAOH CALLS FOR MOSES AND AARON.

I'LL LET YOUR PEOPLE GO—BUT YOUR SHEEP AND CATTLE MUST REMAIN IN EGYPT.

NO!· NOT A HOOF SHALL BE LEFT BEHIND.

THEN THEY SHALL STAY! AND YOU—GET OUT OF HERE. IF I SEE YOUR FACE AGAIN, YOU'LL DIE!

QUICKLY MOSES CALLS FOR A MEETING OF THE HEBREW LEADERS.

GOD HAS TOLD ME THAT THE ANGEL OF DEATH WILL CROSS EGYPT—TAKING THE FIRST-BORN OF EVERY FAMILY...

FIRST-BORN OF *EVERY* FAMILY?

WAIT!· WE WILL BE SAVED— IF WE OBEY GOD!

141

Trapped

FROM EXODUS 11:6—14:12

142

THIS DOUGH·HAS NO YEAST—WE'LL HAVE TO EAT FLAT BREAD CAKES.

BE READY FOR THE SIGNAL TO MARCH!

...AND AT MIDNIGHT THE ANGEL OF DEATH STRIKES ALL EGYPT.

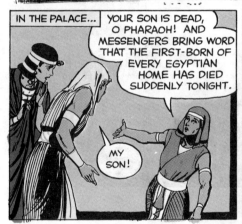

IN THE PALACE...

YOUR SON IS DEAD, O PHARAOH! AND MESSENGERS BRING WORD THAT THE FIRST-BORN OF EVERY EGYPTIAN HOME HAS DIED SUDDENLY TONIGHT.

MY SON!

SUMMON MOSES AND AARON— AT ONCE!

IT'S TOO LATE—TOO LATE! MY SON IS DEAD.

THIS TIME PHARAOH DOES NOT BARGAIN ABOUT CATTLE OR SHEEP.

TAKE YOUR PEOPLE— TAKE YOUR CATTLE AND GET OUT OF EGYPT. SERVE YOUR GOD AS YOU HAVE SAID.

THE ORDER TO MARCH IS GIVEN...IMMEDIATELY THE SLAVES RUSH OUT FROM THEIR SLAVE HUTS, AND MEET AT A CAMP IN THE COUNTRY.

WE'RE FREE! WE'RE FREE!

THANK GOD, MY CHILDREN WILL NOT BE SLAVES IN EGYPT!

THE NEXT DAY THE GREAT EXODUS FROM EGYPT IS ON ITS WAY. JOYFULLY THE HEBREWS MARCH TOWARD THE LAND GOD HAS PROMISED THEM WILL BE THEIR HOME. THEY ARE GUIDED BY A BRIGHT CLOUD BY DAY...

AND A PILLAR OF FIRE BY NIGHT.

BUT IN THEIR RUSH FOR FREEDOM THEY DO NOT FORGET TO TAKE WITH THEM THE BODY OF THEIR GREAT LEADER, JOSEPH.

HE WAS A GREAT MAN IN EGYPT, BUT HE ASKED TO BE BURIED IN HIS HOMELAND.

AFTER SEVERAL DAYS OF TRAVEL, THEY REACH THE RED SEA...

THE SEA IS IN FRONT OF US AND THE MOUNTAINS ALL AROUND.

WHAT WILL WE DO NOW? WHERE CAN WE GO?

145

Crossing the Sea

From Exodus 14:10—16:10

PHARAOH AND HIS ARMY LOOK AT THE HEBREWS CAMPED BESIDE THE RED SEA.

TRAPPED—JUST AS I SAID!

GOOD! THEY'LL SOON SEE WHO IS MIGHTIER—PHARAOH OR THE GOD THEY WORSHIP!

AS MOSES SPEAKS THE CLOUD THAT LEADS THEM MOVES TO THE BACK OF THE CAMP.

LOOK! THE CLOUD IS HIDING US FROM THE EGYPTIANS!

AT THE SAME TIME IN THE HEBREW CAMP...

I'D RATHER SERVE THE EGYPTIANS THAN DIE THIS WAY!

FEAR NOT, STAND STILL, AND SEE THE SALVATION OF THE LORD. THE EGYPTIANS WHOM YOU SEE TODAY, YOU SHALL SEE NO MORE.

THEN MOSES HOLDS OUT HIS HAND, AS GOD HAD TOLD HIM. A STRONG EAST WIND BLOWS ALL NIGHT AND ROLLS BACK THE WATERS OF THE SEA...

AWED BY THE SIGHT, THE HEBREWS RUSH JOYFULLY ACROSS THE PATH IN THE SEA.

PHARAOH CHARGES, BUT THE HEBREW CAMP IS EMPTY! THE EGYPTIANS RACE OUT ACROSS THE SEA FLOOR, BUT SAND CLOGS THEIR CHARIOT WHEELS...

IN TERROR THEY TRY TO TURN BACK... BUT THE WIND DIES, AND THE WATERS RETURN. ALL OF PHARAOH'S MEN ARE CAUGHT IN THE RUSHING SEA.

SAFE ON THE OTHER SIDE, THE HEBREWS LOOK BACK...

GOD HAS SAVED US!

I'LL NEVER AGAIN DOUBT THAT MOSES WAS SENT BY GOD TO SAVE US FROM THE EGYPTIANS.

JOYFULLY THE HEBREWS CELEBRATE GOD'S DELIVERANCE. THE TRIBES DESCENDED FROM JACOB (ISRAEL) ARE A FREE PEOPLE—READY TO FORM A NEW NATION. MIRIAM, MOSES' SISTER, LEADS THE WOMEN'S CHORUS SINGING PRAISES TO GOD.

THE LORD IS MY STRENGTH AND SONG: HE IS MY SALVATION.

SING TO THE ♪ LORD. ♫

FROM THE RED SEA, THE ISRAELITES MARCH ACROSS THE DESERT. BUT AFTER DAYS OF TRAVEL THEY FORGET WHAT GOD HAS DONE FOR THEM. AND THEY BEGIN TO COMPLAIN...

I'M THIRSTY.

THREE DAYS AND NO WATER IN SIGHT.

AT LAST THEY FIND A SPRING, BUT...

IT'S BITTER! WE CAN'T DRINK THIS!

WE'LL ALL DIE OF THIRST!

MOSES PRAYS TO GOD FOR HELP—AND GOD POINTS OUT A TREE. MOSES THROWS IT INTO THE SPRING.

NOW TASTE THE WATER AND KNOW THE POWER OF GOD!

IT'S PURE NOW.

...GOD HAS SAVED US AGAIN. NOW I _KNOW_ THAT GOD IS GUIDING MOSES!

WITH RENEWED FAITH, THE PEOPLE CONTINUE THEIR JOURNEY. AS THEY TRAVEL ACROSS THE HOT SANDS THEIR THOUGHTS ARE OF THE HOMELAND GOD HAS PROMISED THEM. THEY DREAM OF GREEN FIELDS...FRESH STREAMS...GREAT FLOCKS.

BUT THERE IS NO FOOD IN THE DESERT. THE PEOPLE GROW HUNGRY...THEY FORGET THAT GOD CARED FOR THEM WHEN THEY WERE THIRSTY...ANGRILY THEY GO TO MOSES AND AARON...

LOOK—OUR FOOD IS GONE. HOW CAN WE FEED OUR CHILDREN?

HAVE YOU BROUGHT US OUT HERE IN THE WILDERNESS TO STARVE US TO DEATH?

BY EVENING YOU WILL KNOW WHO BROUGHT YOU HERE!

149

Attacked!

FROM EXODUS 16:11–17

THAT EVENING GREAT FLOCKS OF QUAIL DROP INTO THE CAMP.

BIRDS! THOUSANDS OF THEM!

FOOD—ENOUGH FOR EVERYONE!

MOSES WAS RIGHT. GOD SENT THE QUAIL TO FEED US. GOD IS LEADING US!

YES—ONLY GOD COULD SAVE US FROM STARVING. NEVER AGAIN WILL I DOUBT GOD'S POWER AND GUIDANCE.

EARLY THE NEXT MORNING THE PEOPLE ARE SURPRISED TO FIND A STRANGE WHITISH COVERING ON THE GROUND.

WHAT IS IT? IT LOOKS LIKE FROST!

IT IS MANNA—FOOD THAT GOD HAS SENT YOU.

HOW GOOD GOD IS TO US—

GATHER WHAT YOU NEED FOR THIS DAY ONLY.

HOW CAN I BE SURE THERE WILL BE MORE TOMORROW? I'D BETTER COLLECT ALL I CAN!

SEE—I'LL PUT THIS EXTRA ASIDE FOR TOMORROW. NO MATTER WHAT HAPPENS TO THE OTHERS, _WE_ WILL NOT GO HUNGRY.

BUT THE NEXT MORNING...

UGH! IT HAS SPOILED!

I SEE NOW— MOSES WARNED US. WE MUST HAVE FAITH THAT GOD WILL TAKE CARE OF US.

ON THE SIXTH DAY OF THE WEEK, THE PEOPLE GATHER FOOD FOR THAT DAY AND THE SABBATH. THE FOOD KEPT FOR THE SABBATH DOES NOT SPOIL...NEITHER DOES IT APPEAR ON THE GROUND ON THE SABBATH.

WITH RENEWED FAITH IN GOD, THE ISRAELITES CONTINLE THEIR JOURNEY. AS THEY TRAVEL TOWARD MOUNT SINAI, WHERE MOSES WAS CALLED BY GOD TO SET THEM FREE FROM SLAVERY, MOSES SENDS HIS WIFE AND TWO SONS ON AHEAD TO VISIT THEIR OLD HOME.

TELL YOUR FATHER, JETHRO, WHAT GOD HAS DONE FOR OUR PEOPLE!

FARTHER ON...WHILE THE ISRAELITES CAMP IN A PEACEFUL VALLEY...FIERCE TRIBESMEN WATCH FROM THE HILLS...

THIS WILL BE EASY—A SURPRISE ATTACK, AND THE CAMP IS OURS!

152

BUT THE ISRAELITE SENTINELS SEE THE DANGERS...

RAIDERS! PREPARE FOR AN ATTACK!

MOSES CALLS UP HIS FIGHTING MEN...

JOSHUA, CHOOSE OUR BEST SOLDIERS AND FIGHT OFF THOSE RAIDERS. I'LL STAND ON TOP OF THE HILL WITH THE ROD OF GOD IN MY HAND.

THE BATTLE RAGES ALL DAY...JOSHUA'S SOLDIERS KNOW THAT GOD HAS HELPED MOSES LEAD THEM; AS LONG AS THEY SEE MOSES WITH HIS ROD UPRAISED, THEY TRUST IN GOD AND HAVE THE COURAGE TO FIGHT BRAVELY...

BUT WHEN MOSES' WEARY ARMS DROP...

THE ISRAELITE SOLDIERS ARE AFRAID...AND RETREAT BEFORE THE SAVAGE ATTACK OF THE RAIDERS...

The Mountain Trembles

FROM EXODUS 17:12—19:20

THEN MOSES BUILDS AN ALTAR AND LEADS HIS PEOPLE IN A PRAYER OF THANKSGIVING TO GOD.

FRESH FROM THEIR FIRST MILITARY VICTORY, THE ISRAELITES EAGERLY PUSH ON.

ONLY A FEW WEEKS AGO WE WERE SLAVES IN EGYPT. NOW WE ARE FREE MEN— STRONG ENOUGH TO DEFEND OURSELVES!

WHEN WE GET TO THE PROMISED LAND— WE'LL BUILD A NATION—MIGHTIER THAN ALL EGYPT!

WHEN THEY REACH THE WILDERNESS OF MOUNT SINAI, MOSES SETS UP CAMP. ONE DAY A MESSENGER BRINGS HIM GOOD NEWS...

YOUR FATHER-IN-LAW, JETHRO, YOUR WIFE AND SONS ARE ON THEIR WAY TO SEE YOU.

PROUDLY, MOSES SHOWS JETHRO AROUND THE CAMP. AS THE DAYS GO BY, JETHRO MAKES SOME KEEN OBSERVATIONS...

THIS IS WRONG. I MUST SPEAK TO MOSES AT ONCE.

MOSES GOES OUT AT ONCE TO MEET THEM...

HOW GLAD I AM TO SEE YOU!

I HAVE BEEN HEARING THE WONDERFUL THINGS GOD HAS DONE FOR YOU AND YOUR PEOPLE.

MOSES, YOU CANNOT SERVE AS JUDGE TO ALL THESE PEOPLE. TEACH THEM WHAT THEY SHOULD DO...THEN APPOINT GOOD MEN TO HELP YOU JUDGE THEM.

MOSES TAKES HIS FATHER-IN-LAW'S ADVICE.

YOU WERE RIGHT...THIS GIVES ME MORE TIME TO TEACH MY PEOPLE ABOUT GOD.

SOON AFTER THIS MOSES GOES UP THE MOUNTAIN TO TALK WITH GOD. WHEN HE RETURNS, HE HAS NEWS FOR HIS PEOPLE.

PREPARE YOURSELVES... FOR ON THE THIRD DAY THE LORD WILL COME DOWN IN THE SIGHT OF ALL THE PEOPLE UPON MOUNT SINAI!

ON THE MORNING OF THE THIRD DAY THUNDER ROLLS ACROSS THE SKY... LIGHTNING FLASHES... THEN THE SOUND OF A TRUMPET FILLS THE AIR.

IT IS THE SIGNAL TO LEAVE CAMP!

STAY BESIDE ME. DO NOT GO BEYOND THE BOUNDS MOSES HAS SET FOR US.

MOSES SAYS IF WE EVEN TOUCH THE MOUNTAIN, WE WILL DIE!

Commandments of God

FROM EXODUS 20—32:19

WHILE THE PEOPLE OF ISRAEL STAND BEFORE MOUNT SINAI, GOD SPEAKS FROM THE MOUNTAIN AND GIVES THEM THE TEN COMMANDMENTS:

I AM THE LORD YOUR GOD...YOU MUST HAVE NO OTHER GODS BEFORE ME.
YOU MUST NOT MAKE ANY IDOLS.
YOU MUST NOT USE THE NAME OF THE LORD YOUR GOD WRONGLY.
REMEMBER THE SABBATH DAY, TO KEEP IT HOLY.
HONOR YOUR FATHER AND YOUR MOTHER.
YOU MUST NOT KILL.
YOU MUST NOT COMMIT ADULTERY.
YOU MUST NOT STEAL.
YOU MUST NOT BEAR FALSE WITNESS...
YOU MUST NOT COVET ... ANYTHING THAT IS YOUR NEIGHBOR'S.

159

Death to an Idol

FROM EXODUS 32:20—40:17

SHOCKED BY THE SIGHT OF MOSES BREAKING THE STONE TABLETS, THE PEOPLE STOP WORSHIPING THE GOLDEN CALF.

WHAT WILL MOSES DO TO US?

AARON, WHERE DID YOU GET THIS IDOL?

THE PEOPLE GAVE ME THEIR GOLD! I THREW IT INTO A FIRE, AND OUT CAME THIS GOLDEN CALF.

THROW IT BACK INTO THE FIRE!

162

BACK IN CAMP, THE PEOPLE PRAY FOR MOSES' SAFE RETURN. BUT WHEN THEY SEE HIM COMING DOWN THE MOUNTAIN, THEY ARE AFRAID...

IT'S MOSES! BUT LOOK AT HIS FACE—IT HAS A BRIGHTNESS LIKE THE SUNLIGHT!

THE GLORY OF HAVING BEEN WITH GOD SHINES ON MOSES' FACE. HE COVERS HIS FACE WITH A VEIL SO THAT THE PEOPLE WILL NOT BE FRIGHTENED.

COME—DO NOT BE AFRAID. GOD HAS FORGIVEN YOU.

AND HE HAS GIVEN ME PLANS FOR A TENT-HOUSE OF WORSHIP. BRING YOUR OFFERINGS AND WE WILL ALL WORK TOGETHER TO MAKE IT.

THE PEOPLE GLADLY BRING JEWELRY, CLOTH, SKINS, RARE METALS AND WOOD SO THAT GOD'S HOUSE WILL BE BEAUTIFUL.

The Tabernacle

FROM EXODUS 25—40:18–38;
LEVITICUS 1—10:2

AFTER MANY WEEKS OF CAREFUL, LOVING WORK THE HOUSE OF GOD, THE TABERNACLE, IS READY... JOYOUSLY THE PEOPLE WATCH AS MOSES CARRIES THE SACRED ARK CONTAINING THE TEN COMMANDMENTS INTO THE TABERNACLE. HE PLACES IT IN A SPECIAL ROOM CALLED THE HOLY OF HOLIES. THEN A CLOUD COVERS THE TABERNACLE AND THE GLORY OF THE LORD FILLS IT.

NOW THE ISRAELITES ARE NO LONGER A MOB OF FLEEING SLAVES. IN THE ONE YEAR SINCE THEY LEFT EGYPT, THEY HAVE BECOME A NATION WITH LAWS, JUDGES AND A PLACE OF WORSHIP.

Traveling with the Israelites

Did You Know?

With over two million people leaving Egypt, Moses has his hands full. Yet he proves to be an able leader with God's help. Here are some of the things that happen along the way:

▶ The Red Sea parts. The Israelites cross on dry land (p. 147).

▶ Bitter water is made sweet (p. 149).

▶ The Israelites run out of food. God provides manna (p. 151).

▶ God gives them victory over an attack by enemy raiders (p. 152).

When Moses is delayed, the Israelites worship a gold calf (p. 158).

Did You Know?

The Journey Continues . . .

▶ People complain about the manna. God sends quail (p. 170).

▶ Some people rebel against Moses. God sends an earthquake (p. 181).

▶ The Israelites have no water. Moses strikes the rock and water flows out (p. 183).

▶ Because of the Israelites' grumbling, God sends snakes. Many are bitten, but God provides help (p. 184).

▶ Many times Moses prays to God for the people, and God forgives them. But when they refuse to take Canaan, God makes them return to wander in the desert (p. 177).

Because the Israelites rebel against God, they have to roam for forty years before they enter the Promise Land.

Fire in Camp

FROM NUMBERS 10—11:2

EXCITEMENT SPREADS THROUGH THE CAMP AS THE PEOPLE TALK MORE AND MORE ABOUT THE PROMISED LAND TO WHICH GOD IS LEADING THEM. ONE DAY THE BLAST OF TWO GREAT SILVER TRUMPETS FILLS THE AIR...

THAT IS A SIGNAL FOR ALL OF THE PEOPLE TO COME TO THE TABERNACLE. SOMETHING IMPORTANT MUST BE HAPPENING.

THE PEOPLE DROP WHAT THEY ARE DOING, AND HURRY TO THE TABERNACLE.

DOES THIS MEAN WE ARE GOING TO MOVE?

I DON'T KNOW. WE'LL HAVE TO WAIT AND SEE. OUR ORDERS COME FROM GOD.

WHEN EVERYONE HAS GATHERED...

LOOK! THE CLOUD IS LIFTING!

THE SIGN HAS BEEN GIVEN! EAGERLY THE PEOPLE LINE UP FOR THE MARCH TOWARD THE PROMISED LAND! LEADING THEM IS THE SACRED ARK, CARRIED BY THE PRIESTS.

A Family Divided

FROM NUMBERS 11:2—12:10

WHEN FIRE BREAKS OUT IN THE ISRAELITE CAMP, THE PEOPLE QUICKLY FORGET THEIR COMPLAINT ABOUT FOOD AND TRY TO BEAT BACK THE FLAMES.

DID GOD SEND THE LIGHTNING TO BURN OUR TENTS?

MAYBE IT'S A WARNING FOR US TO STOP OUR GRUMBLING ABOUT THE FOOD HE HAS GIVEN US.

HELP US, MOSES! THE WHOLE CAMP WILL BE LOST!

ONLY GOD CAN HELP YOU NOW. I'LL PRAY FOR YOU.

AND AS MOSES PRAYS, THE FIRE GOES OUT.

170

AS THE QUAIL LAND ON THE DESERT, THE ISRAELITES PICK UP ALL THEY CAN CARRY.

MEAT! ALL WE CAN EAT!

LET'S STORE UP ALL WE CAN TO EAT LATER ON.

HOW MANY MORE BASKETS DO I HAVE TO GATHER?

GET AS MANY AS YOU CAN. AT LEAST WE'LL HAVE ALL WE NEED.

THE PEOPLE STUFF THEMSELVES UNTIL MANY ARE SICK.

IT SERVES ME RIGHT. I WAS TOO GREEDY.

SOON AFTER THIS, THE ORDER IS GIVEN TO CONTINUE THE JOURNEY. ONCE AGAIN, A CLOUD BY DAY AND A PILLAR OF FIRE BY NIGHT LEAD THE PEOPLE...TO A CAMP SITE CLOSER TO THEIR PROMISED HOMELAND.

NO SOONER IS CAMP SET UP THAN MOSES' OWN BROTHER AND SISTER TURN AGAINST HIM.

MOSES ACTS AS IF HE IS THE ONLY SPOKESMAN FOR GOD. HE SEEMS TO FORGET, AARON, THAT YOU ARE THE HIGH PRIEST.

YOU'RE RIGHT, MIRIAM. IT'S TIME WE HAVE A TALK WITH OUR BROTHER.

IN ANGER, THEY GO TO MOSES...

WE'RE TIRED OF HAVING YOU RUN EVERYTHING, MOSES. DO YOU THINK YOU ARE THE ONLY ONE WHO CAN SPEAK FOR GOD? DIDN'T GOD CALL AARON TO BE THE HIGH PRIEST? AND DON'T FORGET, I AM A PROPHETESS, TOO!

BEFORE MOSES CAN ANSWER, GOD CALLS THE THREE OF THEM TO THE TABERNACLE.

THEN GOD SPEAKS FROM A CLOUD, AND TELLS THEM THAT HE HAS CHOSEN MOSES TO LEAD THE PEOPLE OF ISRAEL. WHEN THE CLOUD DISAPPEARS, MIRIAM AND AARON GET THE SHOCK OF THEIR LIVES.

Spies Sent Out

FROM NUMBERS 12:11—14:10

IN A FIT OF JEALOUSY, MIRIAM AND AARON ACCUSE THEIR BROTHER, MOSES, OF ACTING AS IF HE WERE GOD'S ONLY SPOKESMAN. GOD ANSWERS THEIR ANGRY WORDS AND TELLS MIRIAM AND AARON THAT MOSES IS HIS CHOSEN LEADER. WHEN GOD FINISHES SPEAKING, MIRIAM DISCOVERS THAT SHE HAS LEPROSY—THE DISEASE MOST DREADED BY THE ISRAELITES.

OH! NO! WHY DID I SPEAK AGAINST MOSES? HELP ME! HELP ME!

WE WERE WRONG, MOSES. BUT DO NOT HOLD IT AGAINST US—PLEASE! CAN'T YOU HELP MIRIAM?

ONLY GOD CAN HEAL HER, AARON. BUT I WILL PRAY FOR OUR SISTER.

HEAL HER NOW, O GOD, I BEG OF THEE.

MIRIAM IS HEALED, BUT SHE IS BANISHED FROM THE CAMP FOR SEVEN DAYS.

ON THE SEVENTH DAY MIRIAM RETURNS, AND AARON, AS HIGH PRIEST, ACCEPTS HER BACK INTO THE CAMP.

I HAVE LEARNED MY LESSON, AARON.

SO HAVE I. LET US NEVER AGAIN DOUBT OR QUESTION GOD'S WISDOM.

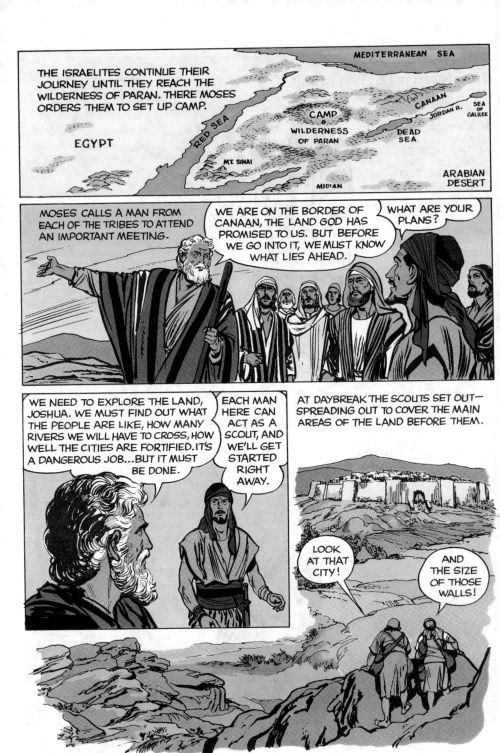

THE ISRAELITES CONTINUE THEIR JOURNEY UNTIL THEY REACH THE WILDERNESS OF PARAN. THERE MOSES ORDERS THEM TO SET UP CAMP.

MEDITERRANEAN SEA

EGYPT

RED SEA

MT. SINAI

MIDIAN

CAMP
WILDERNESS
OF PARAN

CANAAN

JORDAN R.

SEA OF GALILEE

DEAD SEA

ARABIAN DESERT

MOSES CALLS A MAN FROM EACH OF THE TRIBES TO ATTEND AN IMPORTANT MEETING.

WE ARE ON THE BORDER OF CANAAN, THE LAND GOD HAS PROMISED TO US. BUT BEFORE WE GO INTO IT, WE MUST KNOW WHAT LIES AHEAD.

WHAT ARE YOUR PLANS?

WE NEED TO EXPLORE THE LAND, JOSHUA. WE MUST FIND OUT WHAT THE PEOPLE ARE LIKE, HOW MANY RIVERS WE WILL HAVE TO CROSS, HOW WELL THE CITIES ARE FORTIFIED. IT'S A DANGEROUS JOB...BUT IT MUST BE DONE.

EACH MAN HERE CAN ACT AS A SCOUT, AND WE'LL GET STARTED RIGHT AWAY.

AT DAYBREAK THE SCOUTS SET OUT— SPREADING OUT TO COVER THE MAIN AREAS OF THE LAND BEFORE THEM.

LOOK AT THAT CITY!

AND THE SIZE OF THOSE WALLS!

175

Division in the Camp

FROM NUMBERS 14:10—16:5

JOSHUA PLEADS WITH THE PEOPLE TO HAVE COURAGE AND TAKE CANAAN, THE LAND GOD HAS PROMISED THEM. BUT THE PEOPLE ARE FRIGHTENED BY THE TEN COWARDLY SCOUTS WHO REPORT GIANTS AND FORTIFIED CITIES. ANGRILY THE PEOPLE TURN AGAINST JOSHUA AND HIS FELLOW SCOUT, CALEB.

STONE THEM!

DOWN WITH JOSHUA!

BUT SUDDENLY...

LOOK OVER THERE— THE TABERNACLE IS BURNING!

DON'T BE AFRAID— THE TABERNACLE IS **NOT** ON FIRE. IT GLOWS LIKE THAT BECAUSE GOD IS THERE TALKING TO MOSES.

O GOD, FORGIVE MY PEOPLE. DO NOT DESTROY THEM, EVEN THOUGH THEY HAVE DISOBEYED THEE.

MOSES COMES OUT OF THE TABERNACLE AND A HUSH FALLS OVER THE CROWD. HE RAISES HIS HAND...

BECAUSE YOU LACK FAITH TO ENTER THE PROMISED LAND, GOD HAS SAID YOU MUST TURN BACK TO THE WILDERNESS.

GO BACK TO THE WILDERNESS? NEVER!

YOU MEAN WE SHOULD GO INTO CANAAN ANYHOW?

WHO'S TO STOP US FROM TAKING CANAAN OURSELVES?

I'M WITH YOU!

YES— LET'S GO.

179

180

Serpents in the Wilderness

FROM NUMBERS 16:5—21:9, 21–35

KORAH AND SOME OF HIS FRIENDS LED A REVOLT AGAINST MOSES AND MOSES PROMISED THEM THAT ON THE FOLLOWING DAY GOD WOULD POINT OUT HIS CHOSEN LEADER. THE MOMENT HAS COME...

DEPART FROM KORAH AND THE MEN WHO WOULD LEAD YOU TO EVIL, LEST YOU LOSE YOUR LIVES. IF GOD HAS CHOSEN ME TO LEAD YOU, THE EARTH WILL OPEN AND SWALLOW THEM UP...

AS MOSES SPEAKS, THERE IS A GREAT EARTHQUAKE, AND THE TENTS OF KORAH AND HIS FOLLOWERS FALL INTO A DEEP CRACK IN THE EARTH

THE FRIGHTENED PEOPLE TURN ONCE AGAIN TO MOSES. AS GOD COMMANDED, MOSES LEADS THEM AWAY FROM THE PROMISED LAND... TO WANDER FOR YEARS IN THE WILDERNESS.

WHEN HARDSHIPS COME, THEY FORGET THAT IT WAS THEIR FEAR THAT KEPT THEM FROM TAKING THE GOOD LAND GOD HAD PROMISED THEM. AGAIN AND AGAIN THEY COMPLAIN...

NO WATER! NOW WHAT WILL I DO?

THE SPRING IS DRY! HOW CAN I COOK— OR WASH?

OUR TRIBAL LEADERS WILL TAKE THIS UP WITH MOSES!

WELL, MOSES, WHERE ARE WE GOING TO GET WATER?

DID YOU LEAD US OUT HERE TO DIE OF THIRST?

LET'S GO BACK TO EGYPT—AT LEAST WE HAD FOOD AND WATER THERE.

ONCE AGAIN, MOSES AND HIS BROTHER, AARON, TAKE THEIR PROBLEM TO GOD. AND GOD TELLS THEM EXACTLY WHAT TO DO.

183

BUT THE PEOPLE SOON FORGET GOD'S CARE... AND AGAIN THEY COMPLAIN...

THERE'S NOT ENOUGH WATER—I'M ALWAYS THIRSTY.

HAS NOT GOD ALWAYS GIVEN US WATER WHEN WE NEEDED IT?

YES, BUT—THE FOOD—I'M SICK OF THIS STUFF THAT MUST BE GATHERED EVERY DAY AND MADE INTO BREAD. I WANT FOOD LIKE WE HAD IN EGYPT—MELONS, FRUIT...

IN EGYPT YOU WERE BEATEN AND MADE TO WORK LIKE SLAVES. AND YOU CRIED FOR FREEDOM.

AND _YOU_ SAID GOD WOULD GIVE US FREEDOM! DO YOU CALL _THIS_ FREEDOM—WANDERING AROUND IN THE WILDERNESS?

SUDDENLY—AS PUNISHMENT FOR THEIR GRUMBLING—THE CAMP BECOMES ALIVE WITH POISONOUS SNAKES.

HELP! I'VE BEEN BITTEN!

184

185

I'M WELL! I'M WELL! I BELIEVED GOD WOULD HEAL US!

SO AM I!

ALL ARE HEALED WHO SHOW THEIR FAITH IN GOD BY OBEYING HIS COMMAND.

MOSES AND HIS PEOPLE CONTINUE THEIR JOURNEY—THIS TIME NO ONE COMPLAINS OR QUESTIONS MOSES' RIGHT TO LEAD. WHEN THEY REACH THE BORDER OF THE AMORITES MOSES SUMMONS TWO MESSENGERS.

GO—SPEAK TO KING SIHON. ASK IF WE MAY PASS THROUGH HIS LAND IN PEACE.

AT KING SIHON'S PALACE...

O KING, OUR LEADER, MOSES, ASKS IF WE MAY PASS THROUGH YOUR COUNTRY. WE WILL NOT DRINK FROM YOUR WELLS, OR—

NO! GET OUT AND STAY OUT—ALL OF YOU!

WHY SHOULD HE BE SO ANGRY?

I DON'T KNOW—BUT I'M SCARED. WHAT ARE WE GOING TO DO NOW?

187

AT DAYBREAK—KING SIHON STRIKES AND IS MET WITH A SURPRISE COUNTERATTACK FROM THE ISRAELITES.

THE AMORITES ARE DEFEATED IN A SWIFT BATTLE. THEN JOSHUA GOES ON TO TAKE THE ENEMY'S CAPITAL CITY OF HESHBON.

THE ISRAELITE SOLDIERS ARE EAGER TO PUSH ON, AFTER THIS VICTORY, BUT JOSHUA GOES TO MOSES FOR ADVICE.

SHALL WE MOVE NORTH INTO BASHAN? IT IS A POWERFUL COUNTRY WITH A GIANT FOR A KING.

SEND OUT SOME SCOUTS TO EXPLORE THE LAND FIRST, JOSHUA. THEN WE WILL DECIDE.

JOSHUA'S SCOUTS ARE DISCOVERED, AND A MESSENGER HURRIES TO TELL KING OG OF BASHAN.

O KING, I SAW SOME STRANGE MEN SPYING OUT OUR LAND.

THEY MUST BE THE ISRAELITES. THEY'VE JUST CONQUERED THE AMORITES, BUT **WE'LL** TEACH THEM A LESSON...

188

A New Leader

FROM NUMBERS 21:33—27:18;
DEUTERONOMY 34; JOSHUA 1

BOLDLY THE GIANT KING OG OF BASHAN SETS OUT TO TEACH THE ISRAELITES A LESSON IN WARFARE. BUT HE SOON FINDS HE IS NO MATCH FOR JOSHUA. OG'S ARMY IS BEATEN. HE TRIES TO ESCAPE...

AFTER HIM, MEN! CATCH HIM!

MEDITERRANEAN SEA

SEA OF GALILEE

BASHAN

CANAAN

JORDAN RIVER

RIVER JABBOK

PLAINS OF MOAB

AMORITES

AMMONITES

JERICHO •

RIVER ARNON

DEAD SEA

MOAB

BROOK ZERED

THE KING IS CAPTURED, AND THE ISRAELITES TAKE THE COUNTRY.

AFTER CONQUERING THE AMORITES AND BASHAN, THE ISRAELITES SET UP THEIR TENTS ON THE PLAINS OF MOAB.

189

OUR THREE TRIBES ARE READY TO SETTLE DOWN HERE AND BUILD OUR HOMES. DO WE HAVE YOUR PERMISSION?

YOU HELPED TO CONQUER THIS LAND, AND YOU MAY HAVE IT. BUT FIRST WE'LL NEED YOU TO HELP US CONQUER THE LAND THAT LIES AHEAD.

WE'LL HELP, MOSES.

YES, YOU CAN COUNT ON US.

FOR THE SECOND TIME THE ISRAELITES HAVE COME TO THE BORDER OF THE PROMISED LAND. THIS TIME THEY ARE NOT AFRAID. MEN TALK OF THE FLOCKS AND HERDS THEY WILL HAVE... AND WOMEN DREAM OF PEACEFUL HOMES IN THE LAND WHICH GOD HAS PROMISED THEM.

ONE DAY MOSES CALLS JOSHUA TO AN IMPORTANT MEETING...

GOD HAS TOLD ME THAT MY WORK HERE ON EARTH IS ALMOST FINISHED, JOSHUA. A NEW LEADER WILL TAKE OUR PEOPLE INTO THE PROMISED LAND.

A NEW LEADER? OH, NO, MOSES! WHO COULD EVER TAKE YOUR PLACE?

YOU— JOSHUA!

THE AGED LEADER CLIMBS MOUNT NEBO AND GAZES DOWN ON THE LAND GOD HAS PROMISED HIS PEOPLE —AND THERE—ALONE WITH GOD—HE DIES.

BACK IN CAMP JOSHUA PRAYS TO GOD FOR HELP, AND THE LORD ANSWERS: BE NOT AFRAID, FOR THE LORD THY GOD IS WITH THEE.

THE ISRAELITES MOURN THIRTY DAYS FOR MOSES. THEN, JOSHUA CALLS A MEETING.

THE CAMPAIGNS AHEAD WILL BE HARD AND DANGEROUS. BUT I'LL SEEK GOD'S GUIDANCE IN EVERYTHING WE DO.

AND WE WILL FOLLOW YOU AS WE DID MOSES!

THREE DAYS FROM NOW WE WILL CROSS THE JORDAN RIVER. THEN WE MUST CAPTURE THE CITY OF JERICHO—BUT FIRST WE NEED TO LEARN ALL WE CAN ABOUT IT.

ARE WE SURE WE CAN TAKE JERICHO?

YES! FORTY YEARS AGO OUR FATHERS TURNED BACK BECAUSE THEY WERE AFRAID. LET'S TRUST IN GOD—AND THE MAN HE HAS CHOSEN TO LEAD US!

THAT NIGHT AT THE RIVER'S EDGE...

YOU SCOUTS WILL BE IN DANGER EVERY MINUTE. BE CAREFUL, LEARN ALL YOU CAN, AND GET BACK SOON!

THE NEXT DAY—INSIDE THE CITY OF JERICHO...

THESE WALLS ARE THICK AND HIGH—AND WELL-FORTIFIED.

YES—AND THE SOLDIERS ARE WELL-ARMED.

LET'S ASK FOR LODGING AT THIS HOUSE.

THOSE STRANGERS LOOK SUSPICIOUS. I'D BETTER REPORT THEM TO THE CAPTAIN OF THE GUARD.

Crossing the Jordan

FROM JOSHUA 2:1—4:10

WHEN JOSHUA'S TWO SPIES ENTER JERICHO THEY AVOID THE PUBLIC INN AND SEEK LODGING IN THE HOUSE OF A WOMAN NAMED RAHAB.

WE ARE STRANGERS IN YOUR CITY—MAY WE HAVE A ROOM HERE FOR THE NIGHT?

YES—

THE KING'S SOLDIER IS SUSPICIOUS OF THESE MEN! I'LL FIND OUT WHAT BRINGS THEM HERE.

LATER...

DO YOU KNOW THAT YOU HAVE BEEN FOLLOWED?

FOLLOWED— BY WHOM?

I HEAR FOOTSTEPS— QUICK— I'LL HIDE YOU ON THE ROOF.

TWO MEN WERE SEEN STOPPING HERE. WHERE ARE THEY?

TWO MEN WERE HERE SEEKING A ROOM FOR THE NIGHT— BUT THEY LEFT JUST BEFORE THE GATES OF THE CITY WERE CLOSED! IF YOU HURRY YOU MAY FIND THEM...

THE SOLDIERS HAVE GONE— BUT THEY MAY HAVE LEFT SOMEONE TO WATCH THE HOUSE.

HOW CAN WE ESCAPE?

I KNOW THAT GOD WILL HELP YOU ISRAELITES TAKE JERICHO— IF I HELP YOU ESCAPE, WILL YOU PROTECT ME AND MY FAMILY WHEN THE CITY IS TAKEN?

THE SPIES PROMISE SAFETY TO RAHAB AND HER FAMILY.

HIDE OUT IN THE MOUNTAINS FOR THREE DAYS—AFTER THAT IT WILL BE SAFE FOR YOU TO CROSS THE RIVER TO YOUR OWN CAMP.

WHEN THE ATTACK COMES, KEEP YOUR FAMILY IN THE HOUSE ...AND TIE THIS RED ROPE IN YOUR WINDOW SO OUR MEN WILL KNOW WHERE YOU LIVE!

THE SPIES OBEY RAHAB—AND AFTER THREE DAYS, MAKE THEIR REPORT TO JOSHUA.

THE CITY IS WELL DEFENDED WITH TWO WALLS—EACH THIRTY FEET HIGH. THE OUTER WALL IS SIX FEET THICK AND THE INNER TWELVE.

BUT THE PEOPLE HAVE HEARD OF US AND THEY ARE AFRAID.

GOOD WORK, MEN. WE'LL GO AHEAD WITH OUR PLANS TO CROSS THE JORDAN AND TAKE JERICHO.

THE RIVER IS SWIFT AND WIDE— HOW CAN WE CROSS IT?

GOD HELPED OUR PEOPLE CROSS THE RED SEA. LET'S TRUST HIM TO HELP US NOW.

CARRY THE ARK OF THE LORD INTO THE RIVER!

AS THE PRIESTS OBEY, THE JORDAN SUDDENLY STOPS FLOWING!

STAND HERE WITH THE ARK UNTIL EVERYONE HAS CROSSED OVER.

FAR UPSTREAM THE WATERS OF THE JORDAN ARE HELD BACK WHILE THE GREAT MULTITUDE OF ISRAELITES CROSS OVER INTO THE LAND GOD HAS PROMISED THEM...

Siege of Jericho

FROM JOSHUA 4:1—6:20

As IF HELD BACK BY A GIANT HAND, THE WATERS OF THE JORDAN STOP FLOWING WHILE THE ISRAELITES CROSS OVER INTO THE PROMISED LAND. WHEN ALL HAVE CROSSED, JOSHUA ORDERS A MAN FROM EACH OF THE TRIBES TO BRING A LARGE STONE FROM THE RIVER BED.

CARRY THESE STONES TO CAMP. THEY WILL REMIND US OF HOW GOD STOPPED THE JORDAN SO THAT WE MIGHT CROSS OVER SAFELY.

THEN JOSHUA SETS UP 12 OTHER STONES IN THE MIDDLE OF THE JORDAN—AT THE PLACE WHERE THE PRIESTS HOLD THE ARK. AFTER THAT HE COMMANDS THE PRIESTS TO CARRY THE ARK ACROSS. WHEN THEY REACH THE BANK THE FLOOD WATERS OF THE JORDAN RUSH FORTH...

THE ISRAELITES SET UP THEIR FIRST CAMP AT GILGAL—AND HERE THEY CELEBRATE THEIR FIRST PASSOVER FEAST IN THE PROMISED LAND.

AND HERE, TOO, THEY FIND FRUIT AND GRAIN.

LOOK! FOOD— ENOUGH FOR EVERYONE!

THANK GOD— THIS IS TRULY A WONDERFUL LAND.

NOW THAT THE PEOPLE CAN FIND FOOD FOR THEMSELVES, GOD NO LONGER SENDS THE MANNA WHICH HE HAS FURNISHED THEM SINCE THEY LEFT EGYPT FORTY YEARS AGO.

WHILE THE REST OF THE CAMP IS ENJOYING THE NEW LAND, JOSHUA SCOUTS THE AREA IN PREPARATION FOR THE ATTACK ON JERICHO. SUDDENLY HE LOOKS UP AND SEES A MAN WITH A SWORD!

IS HE GOING TO TRY TO KILL ME?

BUT JOSHUA IS NO COWARD— BRAVELY HE FACES THE STRANGER.

ARE YOU FRIEND— OR ENEMY?

I AM THE CAPTAIN OF THE LORD'S ARMY!

198

WHAT IS IT YOU WANT TO TELL ME?

REMOVE YOUR SHOES—FOR THE PLACE WHERE YOU STAND IS HOLY GROUND.

JOSHUA OBEYS—

HERE IS WHAT YOU MUST DO TO TAKE THE CITY OF JERICHO—

WHEN THE ANGEL LEAVES, JOSHUA RETURNS TO CAMP AND CALLS THE PRIESTS TOGETHER.

I WANT THE ARK CARRIED AROUND THE WALLS OF JERICHO. SEVEN PRIESTS WITH TRUMPETS WILL MARCH AHEAD OF IT.

ONCE A DAY FOR SIX DAYS STRAIGHT JOSHUA MARCHES THE ISRAELITES AROUND THE CITY OF JERICHO. FROM HER HOUSE ON THE WALL RAHAB WATCHES ANXIOUSLY...

THE ISRAELITES GIVE NO SIGN OF ATTACK—YET THE CITY IS BREATHLESS WITH FEAR.

Attack that Failed

ONCE EACH DAY FOR SIX DAYS THE ISRAELITES HAVE MARCHED AROUND THE CITY OF JERICHO. NOW, ON THE SEVENTH DAY, JOSHUA ORDERS THEM TO MARCH AROUND SEVEN TIMES. THE PRIESTS BLOW THEIR TRUMPETS—THE MARCHERS SHOUT—AND THE WALLS OF THE MIGHTY CITY FALL FLAT.

JERICHO IS OURS!

BUT ONE SOLDIER, ACHAN, COVETS THE THINGS HE SEES.

WHY SHOULD I FIGHT FOR A CITY AND NOT TAKE SOME OF THE SPOIL? I'LL HIDE THESE, AND NO ONE WILL KNOW...

THAT NIGHT WHILE THE REST OF THE CAMP SLEEPS HE BURIES HIS STOLEN TREASURE.

THIS WILL HELP ME GET STARTED IN THIS NEW LAND.

FINALLY JERICHO IS SET ON FIRE... AND FROM A DISTANT HILLTOP JOSHUA AND HIS MEN WATCH.

SOON THERE WILL BE NOTHING LEFT OF A ONCE POWERFUL CITY.

IT WAS SO WICKED THAT IT HAD TO BE DESTROYED OR ITS EVIL WAYS WOULD HAVE SPREAD AMONG OUR PEOPLE.

THE NEXT DAY, JOSHUA CALLS SOME OF HIS SCOUTS TO HIM.

HERE LIES THE CITY OF AI—IT GUARDS THE APPROACH TO OUR FUTURE CAMPAIGNS. WE MUST FIND OUT HOW STRONG THE CITY IS BEFORE WE ATTACK IT.

WE'LL SCOUT IT OUT AS WE DID JERICHO.

203

204

Sin Brings Defeat

FROM JOSHUA 7:5—9:16

THE FRIGHTENED ISRAELITES RETURN FROM THEIR DEFEAT AT AI. JOSHUA AND THE WHOLE CAMP ARE STUNNED!

WHAT HAPPENED?

I DON'T KNOW—ALL OF A SUDDEN I WAS AFRAID—AND RAN.

T WAS AWFUL! THE SOLDIERS F AI CHASED S ALL THE WAY O THE STONE QUARRIES.

BUT WHY? WHY WERE YOU AFRAID? WHY DID YOU RUN?

THE SOLDIERS CANNOT ANSWER, SO JOSHUA SEEKS HELP FROM GOD.

O GOD, WHY DID THIS HAPPEN TO US? NOW OUR ENEMIES WILL DESTROY US.

GOD REPLIES THAT THE PEOPLE ARE BEING PUNISHED BECAUSE SOMEONE DISOBEYED HIM WHEN THEY TOOK JERICHO.

EARLY THE NEXT MORNING JOSHUA CALLS THE LEADERS OF THE TRIBES TO HIM.

SOMEONE DISOBEYED GOD'S ORDER AND KEPT PART OF THE SPOILS OF JERICHO FOR HIMSELF. THAT MAN MUST BE PUNISHED— OR WE WILL DIE AT THE HANDS OF THE ENEMY.

GOD POINTS OUT ACHAN AS THE GUILTY ONE.

IT IS TRUE—I SINNED AGAINST GOD AND MY PEOPLE.

NOW WE STAND RIGHT WITH GOD.

THAT SAME DAY JOSHUA CALLS HIS LEADERS TO HIM AGAIN.

TAKE THIRTY THOUSAND MEN AND HIDE THEM WEST OF AI. DO NOT ATTACK UNTIL I GIVE THE SIGNAL.

UNDER COVER OF DARKNESS THE ISRAELITES HIDE OUT AROUND AI.

WHAT IS JOSHUA'S PLAN?

I DON'T KNOW —BUT THIS TIME I'M NOT AFRAID. WITH GOD'S HELP WE WILL NOT FAIL.

206

EARLY THE NEXT MORNING, JOSHUA LEADS SOME OF HIS SOLDIERS AGAINST AI. REMEMBERING HOW THEY HAD CHASED THE ISRAELITES AWAY BEFORE, THE SOLDIERS OF AI RUSH OUT OF THE CITY GATE.

LET'S WIPE THEM OUT THIS TIME!

JOSHUA RAISES HIS SPEAR—IT IS THE SIGNAL FOR THE ISRAELITES IN AMBUSH. THEY RUSH IN AND SET FIRE TO THE CITY. THE SOLDIERS OF AI ARE CAUGHT IN A TRAP BETWEEN THE FORCES OF ISRAEL AND ARE QUICKLY DEFEATED.

208

Forced March

FROM JOSHUA 9:17—11:7

209

JOSHUA MARCHES HIS SOLDIERS ALL NIGHT— AND CATCHES THE ENEMY FORCES AROUND GIBEON BY SURPRISE.

DON'T LET A MAN ESCAPE!

FLEEING FROM THE ISRAELITES, THE ENEMY IS CAUGHT IN A TERRIBLE HAILSTORM.

JOSHUA IS AFRAID THE ENEMY WILL ESCAPE DURING THE NIGHT SO HE COMMANDS THE SUN AND MOON TO STAND STILL...

AND DAYLIGHT LASTS UNTIL JOSHUA WINS THE VICTORY. THE PEOPLE OF GIBEON ARE SAVED, BUT THE PRICE OF THEIR TRICK ALLIANCE IS THAT THEY MUST WORK AS SERVANTS FOR THE ISRAELITES.

UNDER JOSHUA THE ISRAELITES CONQUER ALL OF THE CITIES OF SOUTHERN CANAAN. THEN THEY GO BACK TO THEIR CAMP AT GILGAL.

PRAISE THE LORD. PEACE AT LAST!

Traitors to God

FROM JOSHUA 11:8—JUDGES 4:2

WHEN JOSHUA LEARNS THAT THE NORTHERN KINGS ARE FORMING A GREAT ARMY, HE MAKES A QUICK MARCH NORTH AND CATCHES THEM OFF GUARD. HIS LIGHTNING ATTACK THROWS THE ENEMY INTO PANIC.

WHAT HAPPENED?

WE'VE BEEN ATTACKED!

WE'RE SURROUNDED!

WITH QUICK, DECISIVE BLOWS, JOSHUA TAKES THE CAMP. SOME OF THE ENEMY TRY TO ESCAPE, BUT ISRAELITE SOLDIERS FOLLOW IN CLOSE PURSUIT. THE FIGHTING LASTS THROUGHOUT THE DAY, BUT BY NIGHTFALL THE ENEMY IS IN JOSHUA'S HANDS.

WHEN THE WAR IS OVER, THE ISRAELITES REJOICE AND GIVE THANKS TO GOD FOR THEIR VICTORIES. THEN JOSHUA CALLS THE LEADERS TO A SPECIAL MEETING.

WE HAVE WON MUCH OF THE LAND GOD PROMISED US; IT IS TIME FOR US TO DIVIDE IT AMONG THE TRIBES.

JOSHUA DIES, AND FOR A LONG TIME HIS LEADERS KEEP THEIR PLEDGE TO GOD. THEY BUILD UP STRONG CITIES AND JUDGES ARE CHOSEN TO RULE OVER THEM. BUT WHEN JOSHUA'S FRIENDS GROW OLD AND DIE, MANY OF THE ISRAELITES FORGET GOD...

AND BEGIN TO WORSHIP THE IDOLS OF THEIR NEIGHBORS...

AS A RESULT, THE ISRAELITES BECOME SO WEAK THAT THEY CANNOT DEFEND THEMSELVES AGAINST THE ATTACKS OF THEIR NEIGHBORS. TIME AND AGAIN ISRAELITE JUDGES LEAD THEIR PEOPLE BACK TO GOD AND VICTORY. BUT THE PEOPLE'S FAITH IS WEAK; WHEN THEY TURN AGAIN TO WORSHIP HEATHEN IDOLS THEY ARE INVADED BY KING JABIN'S RAIDERS...

Battle in the Storm

FROM JUDGES 4—5

AGAIN THE ISRAELITES FORGET ALL THAT GOD HAS DONE FOR THEM AND TURN TO WORSHIP THE IDOLS OF THEIR NEIGHBORS. SOON THEY BECOME SO WEAK AND AFRAID THEY CAN'T EVEN PROTECT THEIR OWN FIELDS FROM CANAANITE RAIDERS.

STOP! THAT'S MY GRAIN!

IT'S OURS NOW—SO, WHAT ARE YOU GOING TO DO ABOUT IT?

YEARS AGO OUR GREAT LEADER, JOSHUA, CONQUERED THE CANAANITES. NOW THEY ARE CONQUERING US!

WHAT'S THE MATTER WITH OUR LEADERS? WE'LL STARVE IF KING JABIN'S MEN KEEP STEALING OUR GRAIN.

ONE FIELD AFTER ANOTHER IS RAIDED UNTIL AT LAST THE FARMERS HAVE A MEETING.

SOMETHING MUST BE DONE—AT ONCE— TO STOP THOSE CANAANITES.

LET'S GO IN A BODY TO SEE DEBORAH.

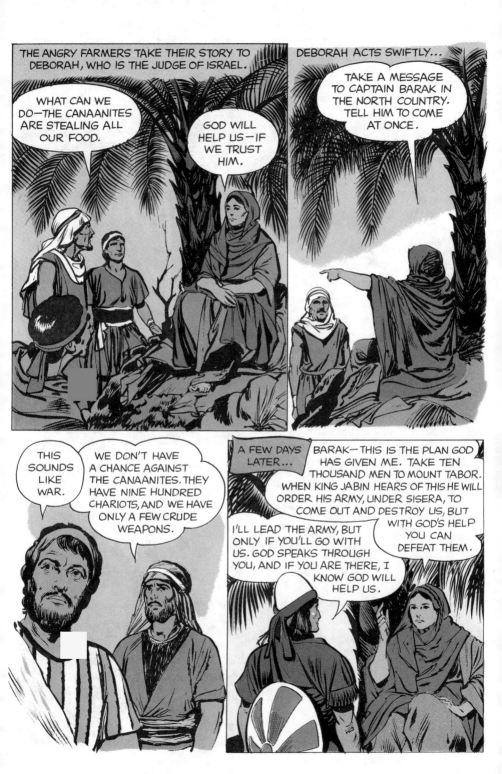

THE ANGRY FARMERS TAKE THEIR STORY TO DEBORAH, WHO IS THE JUDGE OF ISRAEL.

WHAT CAN WE DO—THE CANAANITES ARE STEALING ALL OUR FOOD.

GOD WILL HELP US—IF WE TRUST HIM.

DEBORAH ACTS SWIFTLY...

TAKE A MESSAGE TO CAPTAIN BARAK IN THE NORTH COUNTRY. TELL HIM TO COME AT ONCE.

THIS SOUNDS LIKE WAR.

WE DON'T HAVE A CHANCE AGAINST THE CANAANITES. THEY HAVE NINE HUNDRED CHARIOTS, AND WE HAVE ONLY A FEW CRUDE WEAPONS.

A FEW DAYS LATER...

BARAK—THIS IS THE PLAN GOD HAS GIVEN ME. TAKE TEN THOUSAND MEN TO MOUNT TABOR. WHEN KING JABIN HEARS OF THIS HE WILL ORDER HIS ARMY, UNDER SISERA, TO COME OUT AND DESTROY US, BUT WITH GOD'S HELP YOU CAN DEFEAT THEM.

I'LL LEAD THE ARMY, BUT ONLY IF YOU'LL GO WITH US. GOD SPEAKS THROUGH YOU, AND IF YOU ARE THERE, I KNOW GOD WILL HELP US.

215

I'LL GO, BUT BECAUSE YOU DID NOT HAVE THE FAITH TO LEAD BY YOUR-SELF, BARAK, YOU WILL NOT GET THE CREDIT FOR THE VICTORY. GOD WILL DELIVER JABIN'S GENERAL, SISERA, INTO THE HAND OF A WOMAN.

AFTER A QUICK MARCH, THE ISRAELITES REACH MOUNT TABOR. DEBORAH'S PROPHECY COMES TRUE—THE CANAANITE ARMY COMES TO MEET THEM.

HAVE FAITH—FOR THIS IS THE DAY THE LORD WILL DELIVER US!

DEBORAH GIVES THE SIGNAL...AND BARAK CHARGES DOWN THE MOUNTAIN AT THE HEAD OF HIS TROOPS. ABOVE THEM LIGHTNING FLASHES...

A CLOUDBURST TURNS THE PLAIN INTO A SEA OF MUD. THE IRON CHARIOTS OF THE CANAANITES SINK INTO THE MIRE. TRAPPED, THEY ARE AT THE MERCY OF THE ISRAELITES, WHO ATTACK WITH SPEED AND COURAGE.

THE CANAANITES RETREAT.

TO THE RIVER!

BUT THE KISHON RIVER IS ALREADY OVERFLOWING ITS BANKS... AND THE CANAANITES WHO TRY TO SWIM TO SAFETY SINK UNDER THE WEIGHT OF THEIR HEAVY ARMOR.

WHEN SISERA, GENERAL OF THE CANAANITE FORCES, SEES THAT THEY HAVE BEEN DEFEATED, HE TRIES TO ESCAPE TO A DISTANT CITY. ON THE WAY HE STOPS TO REST IN WHAT HE THINKS IS A FRIENDLY TENT. BUT THE WOMAN WHO LIVES THERE, NAMED JAEL, IS LOYAL TO ISRAEL AND KILLS SISERA WHILE HE IS ASLEEP.

WHEN DEBORAH LEARNS THAT THE CANAANITES HAVE BEEN DEFEATED, SHE SINGS A SONG OF VICTORY...

I WILL SING UNTO THE LORD; I WILL SING PRAISES TO THE LORD GOD OF ISRAEL.

THE PEOPLE REJOICE AND SING THEIR PRAISES, TOO. AND FOR FORTY YEARS THERE IS PEACE IN ISRAEL. FAMILIES WORK IN THEIR FIELDS AND HARVEST THEIR CROPS. BUT IN TIME THEY AGAIN FORGET GOD, AND FIND THEMSELVES IN MORE TROUBLE THAN EVER BEFORE.

Chosen by God

FROM JUDGES 6—7

IN THE YEARS OF PLENTY THAT FOLLOW DEBORAH'S VICTORY OVER THE CANAANITES, THE ISRAELITES AGAIN FORGET GOD. ONE BY ONE THEY JOIN THEIR NEIGHBORS IN WORSHIPING THE IDOL, BAAL. AT LAST ONLY A FEW MEN IN ALL ISRAEL REMEMBER THAT IT WAS GOD WHO HAD RESCUED THEM FROM THEIR ENEMIES.

ROVING BANDS OF DESERT TRIBESMEN BEGIN TO TERRORIZE THE ISRAELITE VILLAGES, AND RAID THE FIELDS.

RUN FOR YOUR LIVES!

IF THEY FIND WHERE I HID MY GRAIN, WE'LL STARVE.

WHEN THE RAID IS OVER...

IT'S GONE — MY GRAIN, IT'S GONE!

FOR SEVEN LONG YEARS THE ISRAELITES SUFFER AT THE HANDS OF THE DESERT TRIBESMEN. THEY HIDE OUT IN CAVES, THRESH THEIR GRAIN IN SECRET PLACES...BUT ALWAYS THE RAIDERS RETURN.

THEN EVEN MORE FRIGHTENING NEWS COMES...

THE MIDIANITES ARE COMING AGAIN. AND WITH THEM GREAT HORDES FROM THE EAST.

LIKE GRASSHOPPERS THE ENEMY SWARMS OVER THE ISRAELITE FIELDS...STEALING GRAIN, CATTLE, AND SHEEP.

ONE DAY A YOUNG ISRAELITE IS SECRETLY THRESHING HIS GRAIN WHEN A STRANGER APPEARS BEFORE HIM.

WHO ARE YOU? AND WHAT DO YOU WANT?

GOD HAS CHOSEN YOU, GIDEON, TO SAVE YOUR PEOPLE.

ME? I'M ONLY A POOR FARMER—HOW CAN I SAVE ISRAEL? GIVE ME A SIGN THAT YOU ARE THE ANGEL OF GOD.

GIDEON PREPARES SOME FOOD AND BRINGS IT TO THE STRANGER.

PUT THE FOOD ON THE ROCK.

THE STRANGER TOUCHES THE FOOD WITH HIS STAFF. INSTANTLY, A FIRE BURSTS FORTH AND CONSUMES IT.

I HAVE SEEN THE ANGEL OF THE LORD— FACE TO FACE!

WHEN THE ANGEL DISAPPEARS, GOD SPEAKS TO GIDEON AND TELLS HIM WHAT TO DO.

THAT NIGHT GIDEON AND HIS SERVANTS BREAK DOWN THE ALTAR OF BAAL.

AND WHEN THEY HAVE FINISHED, HE BUILDS AN ALTAR TO GOD.

BUT GIDEON IS STILL NOT SURE THAT HE HAS BEEN CALLED BY GOD. HE ASKS FOR A SIGN.

IF IN THE MORNING THIS WOOL IS WET WITH DEW AND THE GROUND IS DRY, THEN I'LL KNOW THAT I AM THE ONE CHOSEN BY GOD.

THE NEXT MORNING GIDEON HAS HIS SIGN...

THE GROUND IS DRY— BUT THERE'S ENOUGH DEW ON THIS WOOL TO FILL A WHOLE BOWL.

BUT GIDEON IS STILL AFRAID...

O GOD, GIVE ME ONE MORE SIGN. IF IN THE MORNING THE WOOL IS DRY AND THE GROUND IS WET, THEN I'LL KNOW.

THE NEXT MORNING...

THE WOOL IS DRY—AND THE GROUND IS WET! NOW I KNOW THAT I AM THE ONE CALLED TO SAVE MY PEOPLE!

221

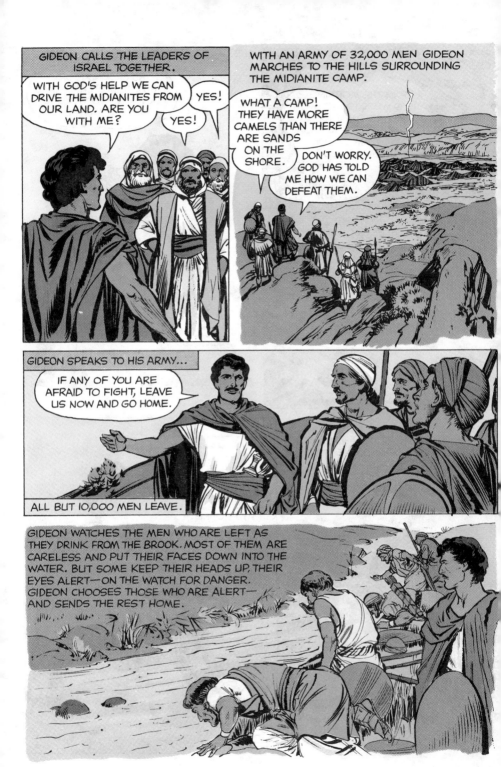

GIDEON CALLS THE LEADERS OF ISRAEL TOGETHER.

WITH GOD'S HELP WE CAN DRIVE THE MIDIANITES FROM OUR LAND. ARE YOU WITH ME?

YES!

YES!

WITH AN ARMY OF 32,000 MEN GIDEON MARCHES TO THE HILLS SURROUNDING THE MIDIANITE CAMP.

WHAT A CAMP! THEY HAVE MORE CAMELS THAN THERE ARE SANDS ON THE SHORE.

DON'T WORRY. GOD HAS TOLD ME HOW WE CAN DEFEAT THEM.

GIDEON SPEAKS TO HIS ARMY...

IF ANY OF YOU ARE AFRAID TO FIGHT, LEAVE US NOW AND GO HOME.

ALL BUT 10,000 MEN LEAVE.

GIDEON WATCHES THE MEN WHO ARE LEFT AS THEY DRINK FROM THE BROOK. MOST OF THEM ARE CARELESS AND PUT THEIR FACES DOWN INTO THE WATER. BUT SOME KEEP THEIR HEADS UP, THEIR EYES ALERT—ON THE WATCH FOR DANGER. GIDEON CHOOSES THOSE WHO ARE ALERT— AND SENDS THE REST HOME.

223

Philistine Raiders

FROM JUDGES 7:22–25; 8:28

THE STILLNESS OF THE NIGHT IS SUDDENLY BROKEN BY THE BLARE OF 300 TRUMPETS AND CRASH OF BROKEN PITCHERS. STARTLED FROM THEIR SLEEP, THE MIDIANITES RUSH OUT TO FIND THEIR CAMP ABLAZE WITH FLAMING TORCHES. IN THEIR PANIC THEY EVEN ATTACK ONE ANOTHER...BUT GIDEON AND HIS 300 ISRAELITES SURROUND THEM.

WE'VE BEEN ATTACKED!

WHERE'S MY SWORD— MY SHIELD?

THE MIDIANITES THINK THEY HAVE BEEN ATTACKED BY A GIANT ARMY...AND IN TERROR MANY TRY TO ESCAPE TO THE RIVER.

TAKE WORD TO THE TRIBE OF EPHRAIM TO HOLD THE FORDS OF THE JORDAN.

SOME OF THE MIDIANITES REACH THE JORDAN RIVER — BUT THEY ARE CAPTURED BY ISRAELITE SOLDIERS FROM EPHRAIM WAITING IN AMBUSH.

IN THE NORTH, GIDEON CHASES THE ENEMY ACROSS THE JORDAN...AND AT LAST ALL OF THE MIDIANITE FORCES ARE DEFEATED.

The Roller-Coaster Ride of the Israelites

The Book of Judges tells us about a rocky time in Israel's history. In fact, many people call this the roller-coaster period. When Joshua dies, the Israelites turn from God and fight with each other and their neighbors. When things get bad, they cry out to God and He sends a judge to straighten things out. When the judge dies, Israel forgets about God, and the whole cycle repeats. Israel goes up and down, just like a roller-coaster!

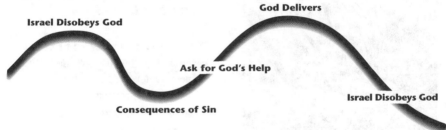

Israel Disobeys God

God Delivers

Ask for God's Help

Consequences of Sin

Israel Disobeys God

Here are interesting facts about some of the judges:

▶ **Ehud** (Judges 3:12-30) is a left-handed Benjamite who stabs the King of Moab with a dagger he has hidden under his clothes.

▶ **Shamgar** (Judges 3:31) slays 600 Philistines with a pointed stick used to urge oxen along.

Why was Israel weak? See p. 213.

▶ **Deborah** (Judges 4-5) was a prophetess and judge who urges Barak to attack the Canaanite army. God sends a cloudburst that immobilizes the enemies' 900 chariots of iron. Read the story on pp. 214-217.

Did You Know?

Who was the woman that killed the mighty Sisera? See p. 217.

▶ **Gideon** (Judges 6–8) defeats the 32,000-man Midianite army with 300 men. See pp. 219-224 for the details.

▶ **Jephthah** (Judges 10:6–12:7) makes a vow to God that if God gives him victory over his enemies, he will sacrifice the first thing that comes out of his house. Little does Jephthah realize that the sacrifice will be so great!

▶ **Samson's** (Judges 13–16) great strength allows him to kill 1,000 Philistines with the jawbone of a donkey and single-handedly carry the gates of a city to a nearby hill! Read his story on pp. 227-246.

• • • • • • • • • • • • • • • • • • •

Samson takes a Nazirite vow from birth. For anyone who takes this vow, it means:
• you can't eat grapes or drink wine.
• you can't cut your hair.
• you can't touch anything dead.

• • • • • • • • • • • • • • • • • • •

Samson kills more Philistines at his death than when he is alive. How could he do this? See pp. 244-246 for the story.

• • • • • • • • • • • • • • • • • • •

God always punishes sin . . . but He is ready at any moment to forgive when you tell Him truthfully that you are sorry for any wrong that you've done.

• • • • • • • • • • • • • • • • • • •

Attacked by a Lion

THE PHILISTINE RAIDERS STRIKE TIME AND AGAIN AT THE ISRAELITE VILLAGES, CARRYING OFF GRAIN, CATTLE—EVEN CHILDREN TO WORK AS SLAVES. BUT ONE ISRAELITE MOTHER AND FATHER WAIT EAGERLY FOR A STRANGE AND WONDERFUL PROMISE TO COME TRUE. ONE DAY THEY TELL THEIR YOUNG SON, SAMSON, ABOUT IT.

BEFORE YOU WERE BORN, AN ANGEL OF GOD TOLD US THAT SOME DAY YOU WOULD BE THE LEADER OF OUR PEOPLE AND SAVE US FROM THE WICKED PHILISTINES.

I WOULD SAVE OUR PEOPLE? HOW?

WE DON'T KNOW HOW, SON, BUT IF YOU TRUST IN GOD, HE WILL SHOW YOU THE WAY. BUT YOU MUST KEEP A PROMISE YOUR MOTHER MADE TO GOD.

A PROMISE? WHAT IS IT?

TO SET YOU APART AS ONE DEDICATED TO GOD, YOU WILL NEVER CUT YOUR HAIR—OR TOUCH STRONG DRINK.

227

SAMSON KEEPS HIS MOTHER'S PROMISE TO GOD. AND AS THE YEARS PASS AND THE PHILISTINES CONTINUE TO ROB AND PLUNDER THE ISRAELITES, HE DREAMS OF THE DAY WHEN HE CAN SAVE HIS PEOPLE. ONE DAY AFTER A RAID, HE STORMS ANGRILY INTO A MEETING OF THE ELDERS.

THEY KILLED MY COUSIN WITH THIS SPEAR! IT HAS AN IRON HEAD...

YES, THE PHILISTINES KNOW HOW TO MAKE IRON SPEARS, BUT WE DON'T. HOW CAN WE FIGHT THEM WITH WOODEN SPEARS?

SOME DAY I'LL FIGHT THEM, AND WHEN I DO...

HE SNAPPED THAT SPEAR AS IF IT WERE A TWIG.

IF HE IS THAT STRONG NOW, WHAT WILL HE BE LIKE WHEN HE IS A MAN?

AS SAMSON GROWS, HIS STRENGTH GROWS UNTIL AT LAST HE IS THE STRONGEST MAN IN ALL THE TRIBE OF DAN. SOME OF THE PEOPLE WATCH ANXIOUSLY AS HE SETS OUT ONE DAY SEEKING ADVENTURE IN A PHILISTINE VILLAGE.

I HOPE HE DOESN'T GET INTO ANY TROUBLE.

NO MAN IN HIS RIGHT MIND WOULD RISK A FIGHT WITH SAMSON.

NO—NOT ONE MAN, BUT A WHOLE VILLAGE MIGHT. AND THAT COULD MEAN TROUBLE FOR US, TOO.

228

229

ON THE DAY SAMSON SETS OUT FOR HIS WEDDING, HE STOPS TO EXAMINE THE BODY OF THE LION HE HAD KILLED--AND FINDS THAT BEES HAVE MADE HONEY IN THE CARCASS.

FOOD FROM A LION-- HONEY FROM THE STRONG. GIVES ME AN IDEA FOR A RIDDLE TO TRY ON THE WEDDING GUESTS.

IN TIMNATH HE IS GREETED BY A GROUP OF YOUNG MEN.

I AM YOUR BEST MAN, AND I HAVE BROUGHT 29 OF MY FRIENDS TO BE YOUR GUESTS.

GOOD! NOW WILL YOU TRY TO GUESS MY RIDDLE. IF YOU DO, I'LL GIVE EACH OF YOU A SHIRT AND A ROBE. IF YOU CAN'T, EACH OF YOU WILL GIVE ME A SHIRT AND ROBE.

WE'LL TAKE YOU UP ON THAT-- WHAT'S THE RIDDLE?

OUT OF THE EATER CAME FOOD; OUT OF THE STRONG CAME SWEETNESS. YOU HAVE A WEEK TO GUESS THE ANSWER.

BUT AS THE WEEK GOES BY, NEITHER THE BEST MAN NOR ANY OF HIS FRIENDS CAN GUESS SAMSON'S RIDDLE.

WHAT WILL WE DO? I CAN'T AFFORD TO GIVE HIM A SHIRT AND ROBE.

NEITHER CAN I. WE'LL HAVE TO GET THE ANSWER FROM HIS WIFE. AFTER ALL, SHE IS A PHILISTINE.

GET THE ANSWER FROM SAMSON, OR WE'LL SET FIRE TO YOUR FATHER'S HOUSE WITH YOU IN IT!

NO! NO! GIVE ME TIME.

231

Fire!

From Judges 14:19—15:12

SAMSON IS FURIOUS! HE HAS LOST THE WAGER OF THIRTY ROBES TO THE PHILISTINES WHO FORCED HIS WIFE TO TELL THEM THE ANSWER TO HIS RIDDLE. HE LEAVES HIS WEDDING FEAST AND ENTERS ANOTHER CITY...

AH! ENOUGH PHILISTINES TO PAY MY DEBT--AND ALL OF THEM HANDSOMELY DRESSED, TOO.

WHO HIT ME?

WHAT'S HAPPENING?

PHILISTINES TRICKED ME, SO PHILISTINES WILL PAY THE DEBT.

STILL IN A RAGE, SAMSON RETURNS TO THE WEDDING FEAST...

HERE-- THE DEBT IS PAID! AND BY THE LIVES OF YOUR OWN COUNTRYMEN!

BACK HOME AS SAMSON'S ANGER COOLS, HE THINKS OF HIS WIFE WAITING FOR HIM.

IN THE PHILISTINE CITY HE GOES STRAIGHT TO THE HOME OF HIS WIFE'S FATHER.

IT WASN'T HER FAULT. THEY FORCED HER TO TELL THE ANSWER. I'LL GO TO HER AND TELL HER I'M SORRY.

I'VE COME TO SEE MY WIFE.

YOUR WIFE? WE THOUGHT YOU HATED HER. SHE IS NOW MARRIED TO YOUR BEST MAN.

HERE IS HER YOUNGER SISTER--SHE'S EVEN MORE BEAUTIFUL. DO YOU WANT TO MARRY HER?

NO! I SHOULD HAVE KNOWN BETTER THAN TO TRUST A PHILISTINE. WHATEVER I DO NOW YOU WILL HAVE COMING TO YOU.

ON THE WAY HOME, HE GOES THROUGH FIELDS RICH WITH RIPENED GRAIN.

FIELDS AND VINEYARDS STOLEN FROM MY PEOPLE! I KNOW HOW I CAN MAKE THE PHILISTINES SORRY FOR WHAT THEY DID TO ME.

QUICKLY SAMSON SETS FOXES RACING THROUGH THE FIELDS AND VINEYARDS WITH FLAMING TORCHES. IN A MATTER OF MINUTES THE WHOLE COUNTRYSIDE IS ABLAZE.

IN THE CITY THE PHILISTINES WATCH WITH TERROR AS THE SKY GROWS RED.

SAMSON DID THIS! HE'S GETTING EVEN WITH HIS WIFE'S FATHER FOR MARRYING HER TO ANOTHER.

HER FATHER SHOULD HAVE KNOWN BETTER THAN TO TRICK SAMSON. COME ON, LET'S GIVE OUR COUNTRYMAN A TASTE OF HIS OWN MEDICINE.

THE ANGRY PHILISTINES SET FIRE TO THE HOME OF SAMSON'S FATHER-IN-LAW...BUT THEY DO NOT COUNT ON SAMSON'S RETURN.

THAT'S MY WIFE'S HOUSE-- WHERE IS SHE?

IN THERE!

DEAD! YOU KILLED HER WHILE SHE SLEPT! IF YOU'RE SO BRAVE, SHOW IT NOW.

The Gaza Trap

FROM JUDGES 15:13—16:2

WHEN THE PHILISTINE ARMY DEMANDS THAT THE TRIBE OF JUDAH TURN SAMSON OVER TO THEM, THE TRIBAL LEADERS AGREE. "IT'S YOU," THEY TELL SAMSON, "OR EVERY MAN, WOMAN AND CHILD IN JUDAH." SO SAMSON SURRENDERS...

THAT OUGHT TO DO IT. THE ROPES ARE NEW, AND THE KNOTS ARE TIGHT. HE'S HELPLESS-- LET'S GO.

O GOD, BE WITH ME WHEN I FACE MY ENEMY.

IT'S A GREAT MOMENT FOR THE PHILISTINES WHEN SAMSON IS BOUND AND DELIVERED INTO THEIR HANDS.

WONDER HOW THE STRONG MAN FEELS NOW?

I'D LIKE TO BE THE FIRST ONE TO GET EVEN WITH HIM.

NOT I-- I DON'T TRUST ROPES TO HOLD SAMSON.

WAIT TILL WE SHOW THE MIGHTY MAN OF JUDAH TO THE PEOPLE BACK HOME.

THAT JAWBONE-- IT'S JUST WHAT I NEED!

235

SUDDENLY, SAMSON BURSTS THE ROPES...
AND SEIZES THE JAWBONE OF AN ASS.

NOW WHAT ARE YOU GOING TO SHOW THE PEOPLE BACK HOME?

WITH DEADLY AIM SAMSON STRIKES DOWN ONE PHILISTINE SOLDIER AFTER ANOTHER. THOSE WHO CAN, RUN FOR THEIR LIVES. IN A SHORT WHILE THE ONE-MAN ATTACK IS OVER...

THEN, WEARY AND THIRSTY, SAMSON PRAYS TO GOD.

LORD, YOU GAVE ME THE VICTORY. DON'T LET ME NOW DIE OF THIRST.

WHEN HE FINISHES PRAYING, HE TURNS... AND THERE BEFORE HIM IS A BUBBLING SPRING.

WATER! O GOD, I THANK THEE!

SAMSON RETURNS TO HIS OWN TRIBE IN THE HILLS... AND FOR TWENTY YEARS HE SERVES AS JUDGE OF HIS PEOPLE.

THEN ONE EVENING HE VISITS THE PHILISTINE CITY OF GAZA.

WHAT IS YOUR BUSINESS IN GAZA?

I HAVE COME TO SEE A FRIEND.

I JUST SAW SAMSON ENTERING A HOUSE DOWN THE STREET. HOW DID HE GET IN?

SAMSON? HE DIDN'T LOOK DIFFERENT FROM ANY OTHER TRAVELER.

NEVER MIND--CLOSE THE GATE AND WE'LL TRAP HIM IN THE CITY. CALL OUT ALL THE GUARDS-- SAMSON WILL NEVER LEAVE GAZA ALIVE.

The Big Bribe

From Judges 16:3–5

WHO CAN STOP A MAN WITH STRENGTH ENOUGH TO CARRY OFF THE CITY GATES? I TELL YOU, SUCH STRENGTH IS NOT HUMAN.

NEWS OF SAMSON'S ESCAPE FROM GAZA SPREADS THROUGH THE COUNTRY. RULERS OF PHILISTINE CITIES ARE WORRIED AND CALL A MEETING.

SAMSON **MUST** BE CAPTURED. LET'S PUT ALL OF OUR ARMIES TOGETHER AND...

I'M NOT RISKING **MY** ARMY ON SAMSON. WE'VE GOT TO FIND ANOTHER WAY.

AND I KNOW THE WAY!

WE KNOW SAMSON HAS STRENGTH NOT GIVEN TO OTHER MEN. IF WE CAN LEARN THE SOURCE OF THAT STRENGTH...

Blind Captive

FROM JUDGES 16:6–21

FOR 5500 PIECES OF SILVER DELILAH HAS PROMISED TO FIND OUT THE SOURCE OF SAMSON'S STRENGTH AND REPORT IT TO HIS PHILISTINE ENEMIES. SO SHE PRETENDS SHE LOVES HIM...

YOU'RE SO STRONG, SAMSON... ARE THERE NO BONDS THAT CAN HOLD YOU?

IF I WERE TIED WITH SEVEN NEW BOWSTRINGS, I'D BE NO STRONGER THAN ANY OTHER MAN.

ON SAMSON'S NEXT VISIT, HE FALLS ASLEEP AND DELILAH TIES HIM WITH SEVEN NEW BOWSTRINGS.

THIS WILL HOLD HIM! SOON THE REWARD WILL BE MINE!

WAKE UP, SAMSON! THE PHILISTINES ARE HERE!

WATCH OUT--HE'S FREE! RUN FOR YOUR LIVES!

SAMSON TRICKED ME!

DELILAH KEEPS TRYING TO LEARN THE SECRET OF SAMSON'S STRENGTH. SHE BINDS HIM IN DIFFERENT WAYS, BUT EACH TIME HE BREAKS FREE. AT LAST...

YOU DON'T LOVE ME, SAMSON! IF YOU DID, YOU'D TELL ME THE TRUTH.

I DO LOVE YOU, AND TO PROVE IT, I'LL TELL YOU MY SECRET. WHEN I WAS DEDICATED TO GOD A PROMISE WAS MADE NEVER TO CUT MY HAIR. IF I BREAK THAT PROMISE, GOD WILL TAKE AWAY MY STRENGTH. I'LL BE AS WEAK AS ANY MAN.

AT LAST DELILAH HAS THE REAL SECRET. SHE CALLS THE PHILISTINES AND PLANS TO TRAP SAMSON THAT NIGHT.

HAVE YOUR CHAINS READY-- AND TELL YOUR MASTERS TO BRING THE MONEY THEY PROMISED ME.

THAT EVENING SAMSON CALLS ON DELILAH. WHEN HE FALLS ASLEEP...

NOW'S YOUR CHANCE.

I'VE NEVER SEEN SUCH LONG HAIR-- BUT I STILL DON'T SEE HOW THIS WILL TAKE HIS STRENGTH AWAY.

SAMSON! WAKE UP-- THE PHILISTINES ARE HERE.

MY HAIR! GONE! I HAVE BROKEN MY VOW AND NOW GOD HAS TAKEN AWAY MY STRENGTH.

YOU CAN BREAK BOWSTRINGS-- LET'S SEE IF YOU CAN BREAK OUR CHAINS!

SAMSON'S STRENGTH IS GONE! CHAINED--AND UNDER HEAVY GUARD--HE IS TAKEN AWAY...

WHAT WILL THEY DO TO HIM?

PUT OUT HIS EYES AND THEN THROW HIM INTO PRISON. OUR TROUBLES WITH SAMSON ARE OVER!

HERE'S YOUR MONEY, DELILAH--YOU HAVE EARNED IT.

5500 PIECES OF SILVER-- ALL MINE!

WHILE DELILAH COUNTS HER MONEY, SAMSON IS LED THROUGH THE STREETS OF GAZA--A CAPTIVE IN CHAINS.

HA! HA! THE MIGHTY JUDGE OF ISRAEL IS A WEAKLING NOW!

243

Samson's Victory

FROM JUDGES 16:21-30

SO SAMSON IS BROUGHT OUT OF PRISON AND LED UP THE TEMPLE STEPS...

BRING HIM UP HERE SO EVERYONE CAN SEE WHAT THE MIGHTY JUDGE OF ISRAEL LOOKS LIKE NOW!

SHOW US HOW YOU CARRIED OFF THE GATES OF GAZA!

LET'S SEE YOU TEAR A LION APART WITH YOUR HANDS.

AS SAMSON'S HAIR HAS GROWN— SO HAS HIS STRENGTH...

WHERE ARE THE PILLARS? I WANT TO LEAN AGAINST THEM.

HERE— I'LL PUT YOUR HANDS ON THEM.

RUN, BOY—AND DON'T STOP UNTIL YOU'RE OUTSIDE THE TEMPLE.

USING ALL HIS MIGHTY STRENGTH, SAMSON PUSHES AGAINST THE PILLARS—AND THE GIANT TEMPLE TO THE HEATHEN GOD, DAGON, CRASHES TO THE GROUND. CRUSHED BENEATH IT ARE THE PHILISTINES WHO HAD MADE SLAVES OF SAMSON'S PEOPLE...

BUT THE FIGHT IS NOT YET OVER...AND IN THE MIDST OF THESE TROUBLESOME TIMES THERE COMES A WOMAN FROM A FOREIGN LAND WHO GIVES ISRAEL A VICTORIOUS KING.

Naomi's Strategy

FROM RUTH 2:6—3:18

THE GLEANERS WATCH EAGERLY AS BOAZ, THE OWNER OF THE FIELDS, QUESTIONS HIS FOREMAN ABOUT THE YOUNG WOMAN GATHERING GRAIN IN HIS FIELDS.

HER NAME IS RUTH—SHE IS THE MOABITE WOMAN WHO TAKES CARE OF HER MOTHER-IN-LAW, NAOMI.

HOW BEAUTIFUL SHE IS!

I HAVE HEARD HOW KIND YOU ARE TO YOUR MOTHER-IN-LAW. GLEAN IN MY FIELDS AS MUCH AS YOU LIKE —AND MAY GOD REWARD AND PROTECT YOU.

THANK YOU. YOU ARE VERY KIND.

AT LUNCH TIME BOAZ INVITES RUTH TO EAT WITH HIM AND HIS REAPERS...

AND WHEN THE MEAL IS OVER AND
RUTH HAS GONE BACK TO WORK—

DROP SOME GRAIN
ON PURPOSE FOR HER
TO PICK UP. AND
SEE THAT NO
HARM COMES
TO HER!

HAVE NO
FEAR, BOAZ.
SHE WILL
BE SAFE—AND
SHE WILL FIND
ALL THE GRAIN
SHE NEEDS.

THAT
EVENING—

LOOK AT
ALL THE GRAIN
I FOUND! OH,
NAOMI, YOUR
GOD IS GOOD
TO US.

I THOUGHT WHEN
MY HUSBAND
AND SONS DIED
THAT GOD HAD
FORGOTTEN ME.
NOW I KNOW HOW
MUCH HE LOVES ME,
FOR HE HAS GIVEN ME
A DAUGHTER-IN-LAW
WHO CARES FOR ME AS
A DAUGHTER. BUT—NOW
—TELL ME ABOUT THE
DAY. IN WHOSE
FIELD DID YOU
GLEAN?

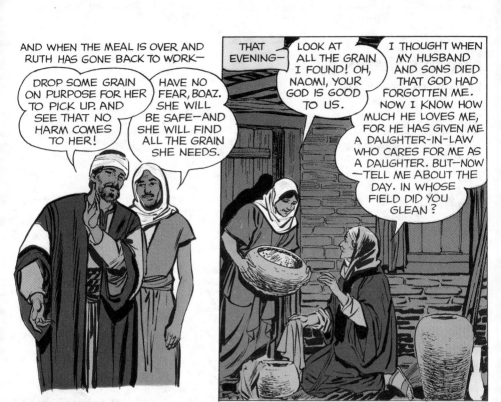

HIS NAME WAS
BOAZ—HE WAS
VERY KIND.

AND VERY
HANDSOME,
TOO.

BOAZ? HE IS
A RELATIVE OF
MY HUSBAND'S
FAMILY. GOD BLESS
HIM FOR BEING
KIND TO YOU.

ALL THROUGH THE HARVEST SEASON RUTH
GLEANS IN BOAZ' FIELD AND TAKES CARE
OF NAOMI. ONE EVENING...

I BELIEVE BOAZ LOVES YOU,
BUT HE DOESN'T KNOW HOW
YOU FEEL. WE ISRAELITES HAVE
A CUSTOM ABOUT THE RIGHTS OF
RELATIVES IN MARRIAGE. TONIGHT
BOAZ WILL STAY AT THE
THRESHING FLOOR TO
GUARD HIS GRAIN. IF YOU
DO AS I SAY—

I LOVE
BOAZ, AND
I'LL DO WHAT
YOU TELL
ME.

RUTH GOES TO THE THRESHING FLOOR AS NAOMI TOLD HER TO DO.

I ASK YOUR HELP AND PROTECTION, BOAZ, BECAUSE YOU ARE A RELATIVE OF MY HUSBAND'S FAMILY.

I LOVE YOU, RUTH, AND I AM GLAD YOU HAVE ASKED ME TO TAKE CARE OF YOU. BUT THERE IS A CLOSER RELATIVE THAN I, AND, ACCORDING TO OUR CUSTOM, HE HAS THE FIRST RIGHT TO TAKE YOUR DEAD HUSBAND'S PLACE.

THE NEXT MORNING...

BOAZ DOES LOVE ME; BUT OH, NAOMI, HE SAYS THERE IS A CLOSER RELATIVE WHO HAS MORE RIGHT THAN HE.

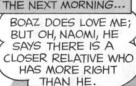

DON'T WORRY— BOAZ WILL NOT REST UNTIL HE HAS HANDLED THIS ACCORDING TO OUR CUSTOM.

A Joyful Wedding
FROM RUTH 4

NEXT MORNING BOAZ WATCHES FOR THE RELATIVE WHO HAS FIRST RIGHT TO BUY THE LAND THAT BELONGED TO NAOMI'S DEAD HUSBAND—AND TO MARRY RUTH.

GOOD MORNING! WILL YOU STOP AND DISCUSS A MATTER THAT IS IMPORTANT TO BOTH OF US?

GOOD MORNING TO YOU, BOAZ. WHAT IS THE PROBLEM?

WHEN THE MAN IS SEATED BOAZ INVITES THE ELDERS OF THE CITY TO JOIN THEM...

THE LAND THAT BELONGED TO NAOMI'S HUSBAND IS FOR SALE. ONE OF US MUST BUY IT TO KEEP IT IN THE FAMILY. YOU ARE THE CLOSEST RELATIVE... WILL YOU BUY THE LAND?

YES, I WILL BUY IT!

"ACCORDING TO OUR CUSTOM, THE DAY YOU BUY THE LAND YOU MUST ALSO MARRY NAOMI'S DAUGHTER-IN-LAW, RUTH."

"I AM MARRIED SO I WILL FORFEIT MY RIGHTS."

AND TO SHOW THAT HE IS GIVING UP HIS RIGHTS, THE MAN TAKES OFF HIS SHOE AND GIVES IT TO BOAZ. THE DEAL IS CLOSED.

"YOU ARE WITNESSES THAT I NOW HAVE THE RIGHT TO BUY THE LAND AND MARRY RUTH?"

"WE ARE WITNESSES. GOD BLESS YOU, BOAZ, AND MAY RUTH BECOME THE MOTHER OF A FAMOUS FAMILY IN ISRAEL."

BOAZ HURRIES TO NAOMI'S HOUSE WITH THE NEWS...

"THIS IS INDEED A HAPPY DAY FOR ME. I HAVE ARRANGED TO BUY THE LAND, AND NOW I HAVE COME TO CLAIM RUTH IN MARRIAGE."

"GOD BLESS YOU, BOAZ. SHE WILL BE A GOOD WIFE."

THE NEWS OF RUTH AND BOAZ' COMING MARRIAGE SPREADS RAPIDLY THROUGHOUT ALL BETHLEHEM, FOR BOAZ IS A WELL-TO-DO LANDOWNER. AT THE WEDDING THERE IS FEASTING, MUSIC AND LAUGHTER...

ARE YOU HAPPY, MY DEAR?

HAPPIER THAN I EVER DREAMED I COULD BE. GOD HAS BEEN GOOD TO ME.

AFTER HER MARRIAGE, RUTH MOVES INTO THE BIG HOUSE OF BOAZ. LATER, WHEN A SON IS BORN TO RUTH, NAOMI PROUDLY CARES FOR THE CHILD. HE IS NAMED OBED, WHICH MEANS "SERVANT."

OH, RUTH, I THANK GOD FOR THE DAY YOU LEFT MOAB TO COME WITH ME TO BETHLEHEM. FOR NOW I HAVE A GRANDSON TO SERVE ME IN MY OLD AGE.

I THANK HIM, TOO, NAOMI— FOR TRULY YOUR PEOPLE HAVE BECOME MY PEOPLE—AND YOUR GOD MY GOD...

AND MY PRAYER IS THAT OBED WILL SERVE GOD AND HIS PEOPLE.

RUTH'S PRAYER COMES TRUE— FOR HER SON BECOMES THE GRANDFATHER OF DAVID, ISRAEL'S GREATEST KING, WHO FREES HIS PEOPLE FROM THEIR ENEMIES...

Call in the Night

FROM 1 SAMUEL 1:1—3:17

HUNDREDS OF YEARS HAVE PASSED SINCE THE ISRAELITES SETTLED IN THE PROMISED LAND OF CANAAN. DURING THAT TIME THEY OFTEN TURNED FROM GOD TO WORSHIP HEATHEN IDOLS. AS A RESULT THEY HAVE BECOME WEAK— ALMOST SLAVES OF THEIR ENEMIES, THE PHILISTINES. TO SOME IT SEEMS THAT GOD HAS FORGOTTEN HIS PROMISE TO MAKE ISRAEL STRONG.

THE BOOK OF **1 SAMUEL** BEGINS...

AT THE TABERNACLE AT SHILOH, ELI, THE HIGH PRIEST, WATCHES THE FAITHFUL COME TO WORSHIP. HE NOTICES A WOMAN AND SUDDENLY HE BECOMES ANGRY...

SHE ACTS AS IF SHE'S DRUNK! HOW DARE SHE INSULT GOD!

ANGRILY HE ACCUSES HER...

NO! NO! I AM NOT DRUNK, I AM UNHAPPY; AND IN MY SORROW I HAVE POURED OUT MY HEART TO GOD, ASKING HIM TO HELP ME.

GO IN PEACE, HANNAH, AND MAY GOD GRANT THEE THY PRAYER.

HANNAH IS SO HAPPY THAT SHE RUSHES OUT OF THE TABERNACLE TO FIND HER HUSBAND.

OH, ELKANAH, I PRAYED TO GOD FOR A SON— AND ELI BLESSED ME AND ASKED GOD TO GIVE ME WHAT I PRAYED FOR.

A SON? I, TOO, PRAY THAT GOD WILL GRANT YOUR PRAYER.

GOD ANSWERS HANNAH'S PRAYER—AND WHEN THE BOY IS OLD ENOUGH TO LEAVE HIS MOTHER, SHE BRINGS HIM TO ELI.

WHEN I ASKED GOD FOR A SON, I PROMISED THAT HE WOULD SERVE THE LORD ALL HIS LIFE. SO I HAVE BROUGHT HIM HERE TO BE TRAINED IN GOD'S HOUSE. HIS NAME IS SAMUEL.

GOD BLESS YOU, HANNAH. LEAVE THE BOY WITH ME AND I WILL TEACH HIM TO BE A SERVANT OF THE LORD.

SAMUEL STAYS WITH ELI AND EAGERLY LEARNS WHAT GOD EXPECTS OF THOSE WHO SERVE HIM. EACH YEAR WHEN HANNAH AND HER HUSBAND COME TO WORSHIP, SHE BRINGS SAMUEL A NEW COAT.

IT'S JUST LIKE A PRIEST'S ROBE. THANK YOU, MOTHER.

OLD ELI IS PROUD OF SAMUEL—BUT HE IS BROKENHEARTED WHEN HE THINKS OF HIS OWN TWO SONS. AS PRIESTS, THEY HAVE SINNED AGAINST GOD AND CHEATED THE PEOPLE. ELI KNOWS THAT HE, TOO, IS GUILTY BECAUSE HE HAS DONE NOTHING TO STOP THEM.

In a Heathen Temple

FROM 1 SAMUEL 3:18—5:2

ELI, THE HIGH PRIEST OF ISRAEL, KNOWS THAT GOD HAS SPOKEN TO HIS YOUNG HELPER, SAMUEL. SAMUEL DOESN'T WANT TO REPEAT THE MESSAGE, BUT ELI INSISTS...

GOD SAID, "ELI'S SONS ARE WICKED AND ELI HAS NOT TRIED TO STOP THEM. THEY WILL BE PUNISHED FOR THE EVIL THEY HAVE DONE."

THE LORD WILL DO WHAT IS JUST.

WORD SPREADS THAT GOD HAS SPOKEN TO SAMUEL. AND AS SAMUEL GROWS UP ALL ISRAEL KNOWS THAT HE IS A TRUE PROPHET OF GOD.

IF ONLY OUR PRIESTS WERE MEN OF GOD LIKE SAMUEL. HOW LONG MUST WE SUFFER UNDER THE LYING AND CHEATING OF ELI'S SONS?

MARK MY WORDS, THEY WILL BRING ABOUT THEIR OWN DESTRUCTION.

SUDDENLY WAR BREAKS OUT WITH THE PHILISTINES. A FIERCE BATTLE RAGES, AND THE ISRAELITES ARE BADLY DEFEATED.

WE'VE LOST FOUR THOUSAND MEN.

WHAT CAN WE DO?

I HAVE IT—IF WE BRING THE SACRED ARK HERE, MAYBE IT WILL SAVE US.

YES! YES! SEND FOR THE ARK RIGHT AWAY.

ELI'S TWO SONS GO WITH THE OTHERS TO GET THE SACRED ARK FROM THE TABERNACLE. WHEN THEY BRING IT TO CAMP, THE ISRAELITES SHOUT WITH SO MUCH JOY...

...THAT THEY ARE HEARD IN THE PHILISTINE CAMP.

THE WAY THE ISRAELITES ARE SHOUTING, YOU'D THINK THEY HAD WON THE BATTLE!

SEND SOMEONE TO FIND OUT WHAT'S GOING ON.

THE MESSENGER RETURNS WITH STARTLING NEWS...

THEY'VE BROUGHT THE ARK OF THEIR GOD INTO CAMP.

YOU MEAN—THE SAME GOD WHO SENT SO MANY PLAGUES ON THE EGYPTIANS THAT THEY HAD TO FREE THE ISRAELITES? HOW CAN WE FIGHT THAT KIND OF POWER?

IF WE DON'T, WE'LL BE SLAVES TO THE ISRAELITES WHO HAVE BEEN _OUR_ SLAVES ...COME ON, LET'S TAKE THE ADVANTAGE AND STRIKE FIRST!

THE PHILISTINES ATTACK! BUT THE ISRAELITES, BELIEVING IN THE POWER OF THE ARK, COUNTER ATTACK WITH SUDDEN FURY.

CAPTURE THE ARK—AND THEY'LL GIVE UP.

THE ARK IS CAPTURED, AND THE ISRAELITES FLEE IN TERROR. A MESSENGER TAKES THE NEWS TO ELI...

THE BATTLE IS LOST—YOUR SONS ARE DEAD—AND THE PHILISTINES HAVE CAPTURED THE ARK.

THE ARK! CAPTURED?

AT THE NEWS, ELI FALLS AND BREAKS HIS NECK. MEANWHILE THE PHILISTINES TRIUMPHANTLY CARRY THE ARK HOME AND PLACE IT IN THE TEMPLE OF THEIR GOD, DAGON.

BUT IN THE MORNING...

257

The Turning Point
FROM 1 SAMUEL 5:3—7:10

WITH SHOUTS OF TRIUMPH THE PHILISTINES PLACE THE SACRED ARK OF GOD IN THEIR HEATHEN TEMPLE. TO THEM IT IS A SIGN THAT THE PHILISTINE GOD, DAGON, HAS CONQUERED THE GOD OF ISRAEL. BUT THE NEXT MORNING THE IDOL LIES ON ITS FACE BEFORE THE ARK. PRIESTS REPLACE THE IDOL, AND ON THE FOLLOWING MORNING...

LOOK! OUR GREAT GOD, DAGON, LIES BROKEN BEFORE THE ARK OF THE ISRAELITES!

SO THE ARK IS TAKEN FROM ONE PHILISTINE CITY TO ANOTHER...AND IN EACH CITY A PLAGUE BREAKS OUT...

NOT A FAMILY HAS ESCAPED THIS STRANGE ILLNESS.

OUR FIELDS ARE OVER RUN WITH MICE. I TELL YOU—A CURSE HAS BEEN PUT UPON THIS CITY.

THE PHILISTINES SOON REALIZE THAT THEIR TROUBLES BEGAN WHEN THEY CAPTURED THE HOLY ARK OF ISRAEL. FINALLY THEY RETURN THE ARK TO ISRAEL, BUT ISRAEL IS WORSHIPING IDOLS. THE ARK IS PLACED IN A HOUSE AND ALMOST FORGOTTEN.

BUT AFTER YEARS OF STRUGGLE UNDER THE PHILISTINES, THE ISRAELITES ARE READY TO LISTEN WHEN SAMUEL SPEAKS...

RETURN TO THE LORD! WORSHIP HIM WITH ALL YOUR HEARTS, AND GOD WILL DELIVER YOU FROM THE PHILISTINES.

SAMUEL IS RIGHT! LET US THROW AWAY OUR IDOLS AND WORSHIP GOD.

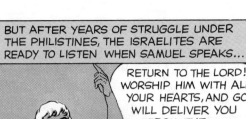

LET US ALL GO TO THE CITY OF MIZPEH AND PRAY TOGETHER!

EAGERLY THE PEOPLE FOLLOW THIS MAN WHO SPEAKS BOLDLY FOR GOD. BY THE THOUSANDS THEY SET OUT...

BUT THE GREAT MARCH TO MIZPEH IS DISCOVERED BY THE PHILISTINES.

IF THOUSANDS OF ISRAELITES ARE MASSING AT MIZPEH IT CAN MEAN ONLY ONE THING —THEY PLAN TO ATTACK US.

LET'S STRIKE BEFORE THEY DO, AND **THIS** TIME WE'LL CRUSH THEM SO BADLY THEY'LL NEVER FIGHT AGAIN!

260

Samuel Prays for a King

FROM 1 SAMUEL 7:10—9:20

GOD HAS ANSWERED OUR PRAYER.

LET'S GO AFTER THEM.

THE PHILISTINE DEFEAT IS A TURNING POINT IN ISRAEL'S HISTORY—NEVER AGAIN DO THE PHILISTINES INVADE ISRAEL WHILE SAMUEL IS ITS LEADER. TO REMIND HIS PEOPLE THAT IT WAS GOD WHO HELPED THEM WIN THEIR VICTORY, SAMUEL ERECTS A STONE WHICH HE CALLS EBENEZER (STONE OF HELP).

FOR YEARS SAMUEL JUDGES THE PEOPLE OF ISRAEL, AND THERE IS PEACE. BUT AS HE GROWS OLD THE TRIBAL LEADERS BECOME WORRIED...

SAMUEL, YOU ARE GROWING OLD, AND YOUR SONS ARE NOT WORTHY TO TAKE YOUR PLACE AS JUDGE OF ISRAEL. GIVE US A KING LIKE OTHER NATIONS HAVE.

I WILL PRAY TO GOD ABOUT YOUR REQUEST.

LATER—

THE LORD HAS TOLD ME TO WARN YOU WHAT A KING WILL DO—HE WILL SEND YOUR SONS TO BATTLE, YOUR DAUGHTERS WILL BECOME HIS SERVANTS, AND YOUR BEST CROPS WILL BE USED TO FEED HIS COURT.

MAYBE SO, BUT WE STILL WANT A KING!

262

AGAIN SAMUEL PRAYS TO GOD, THEN—

GOD WANTS ME TO DO AS YOU HAVE ASKED. GO HOME, AND I WILL SEND WORD WHEN I HAVE FOUND A KING FOR YOU.

A FEW DAYS LATER SAMUEL SETS OUT EAGERLY FOR THE GATE OF THE CITY—

YESTERDAY GOD TOLD ME THAT TODAY I WOULD MEET A MAN, HERE, WHO IS THE ONE TO BE THE KING OF ISRAEL.

AT THE GATE, A YOUNG FARMER WHO IS LOOKING FOR HIS LOST DONKEYS STOPS SAMUEL.

I NEED HELP. CAN YOU TELL ME WHERE I MIGHT FIND THE PROPHET, SAMUEL?

I AM THE PROPHET. DON'T WORRY ABOUT YOUR DONKEYS—THEY HAVE BEEN FOUND. COME WITH ME TO WORSHIP THE LORD, AND TOMORROW I WILL TELL YOU WHAT GREAT THINGS ARE IN STORE FOR YOU.

GREAT THINGS—FOR ME? WHAT DOES HE MEAN?

Test for a King

FROM 1 SAMUEL 9:20—11:7

THE YOUNG FARMER, SAUL, IS STUNNED WHEN SAMUEL TELLS HIM THAT GREAT THINGS ARE IN STORE FOR HIM. THEY WORSHIP GOD TOGETHER, THEN SAMUEL INVITES SAUL TO A SPECIAL FEAST.

WHY SHOULD THIS YOUNG MAN BE SO HIGHLY HONORED?

SAMUEL MAKES NO EXPLANATION TO HIS GUESTS, BUT EARLY THE NEXT MORNING HE ACCOMPANIES SAUL AND HIS SERVANT AS THEY LEAVE THE CITY.

SEND YOUR SERVANT ON AHEAD, SAUL. I HAVE A MESSAGE FOR YOU FROM GOD.

THE LORD HAS ANOINTED YOU TO RULE OVER HIS PEOPLE. CALL ON THE LORD, AND HE WILL BE WITH YOU.

SURPRISED—AND A LITTLE FRIGHTENED—AT ALL THAT HAS HAPPENED TO HIM, SAUL STARTS HOME. BUT ON THE WAY THE SPIRIT OF GOD COMES TO HIM. HOWEVER, WHEN HE REACHES HOME, HE DOES NOT TELL ANYONE THAT HE HAS BEEN ANOINTED KING!

WHEN SAMUEL CALLS THE PEOPLE TO MIZPEH, SAUL GOES, TOO. BEFORE ALL ISRAEL SAMUEL MAKES A SURPRISING ANNOUNCEMENT.

GOD HAS CHOSEN SAUL TO RULE OVER YOU.

WHERE IS HE?

A SEARCH IS QUICKLY MADE, AND SAUL—WHO IS AWED BY THE THOUGHT OF BEING KING—IS FOUND HIDING.

WHEN HE IS BROUGHT FORTH, THE PEOPLE SHOUT: LONG LIVE THE KING!

AT MIZPEH THE PEOPLE SHOUTED THEIR PRAISES TO SAUL—BUT AFTER HE RETURNS HOME, SOME COMPLAIN.

FINE THING—THERE GOES OUR KING—BACK TO THE FARM.

HE'LL BE NO HELP TO US.

SAUL'S TEST AS A LEADER COMES WHEN HE RETURNS HOME FROM HIS FIELDS ONE DAY AND FINDS THE WHOLE VILLAGE WEEPING.

WHAT'S THE MATTER?

HAVEN'T YOU HEARD? THE AMMONITES HAVE SURROUNDED JABESH. THEY THREATEN TO PUT OUT AN EYE OF EVERY MAN IN THE CITY.

WE'LL SHOW THE AMMONITES THEY CAN'T THREATEN ISRAEL!

IT'S NO USE. YOU'LL NEVER GET ENOUGH PEOPLE TO HELP YOU FIGHT THE AMMONITES.

I'M KING—AND I'LL **MAKE** THEM FIGHT!

BIG TALK—BUT WAIT UNTIL HE TRIES TO BACK IT UP.

Prophet, Priest, and Judge

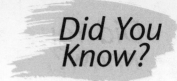

▶ Read about Samuel on pp. 253-296.

Samuel is one of greatest leaders of Israel. Called as a small boy, Samuel dedicates his life to serving God. Here are some of the things he does:

▶ Samuel grows up in the Tabernacle, learning how to be a priest (p. 254).

▶ Samuel is a man who prays (Psalm 99:6).

▶ He may have written some books of the Bible, such as Judges and Ruth.

▶ He prays for Israel's deliverance from the Philistines and erects a stone to remind the people of God's help (p. 261).

▶ He anoints Saul to be the first king (p. 264).

▶ He is a true prophet of God (p. 255).

▶ He is the last major judge in Israel, traveling from town to town (1 Samuel 7:15-17).

THE LORD BLESS YOU, FOR YOU WILL BE THE NEXT KING OF ISRAEL,

He anoints David to be king (p. 278).

267

Israel's First King— Saul

From the beginning, Saul looks like a good candidate for king. But as time goes by, things change and his life seems in a downward spin.

Looking for lost donkeys when he is chosen king (p. 263).

Saul is a humble Benjamite farmer, a head taller than other men (p. 264).

Found hiding in the baggage at his coronation (p. 265).

His army is crushed; his sons are killed (p. 305).

Wins the people's confidence (p. 269).

Falls on his own sword and dies (p. 305).

Big Mistake #3
He visits a witch (p. 300).

Big mistake #1
Offers sacrifices as a priest, then makes excuses for doing so (p. 272).

Jealous of David and tries to kill him (p. 289).

Big mistake #2
Disobeys God, lies to Samuel, and is rejected as king (p. 274).

By Order of the King

FROM 1 SAMUEL 11—13:9

WHEN WORD COMES THAT THE AMMONITES HAVE SURROUNDED AN ISRAELITE CITY, SAUL FACES HIS FIRST TEST AS KING. TO HIS AMAZEMENT—AND ANGER—HE DISCOVERS THAT SOME OF HIS PEOPLE ARE AFRAID TO FIGHT! HE ACTS AT ONCE...

BY ORDER OF THE KING WE ARE TO KILL THE OXEN OF ANY MAN WHO REFUSES TO DEFEND HIS COUNTRY!

ER—I'LL JOIN THE ARMY RIGHT NOW!

AN ARMY IS QUICKLY FORMED, AND SAUL ATTACKS AT DAWN. CAUGHT BY SURPRISE, THE AMMONITES ARE DEFEATED.

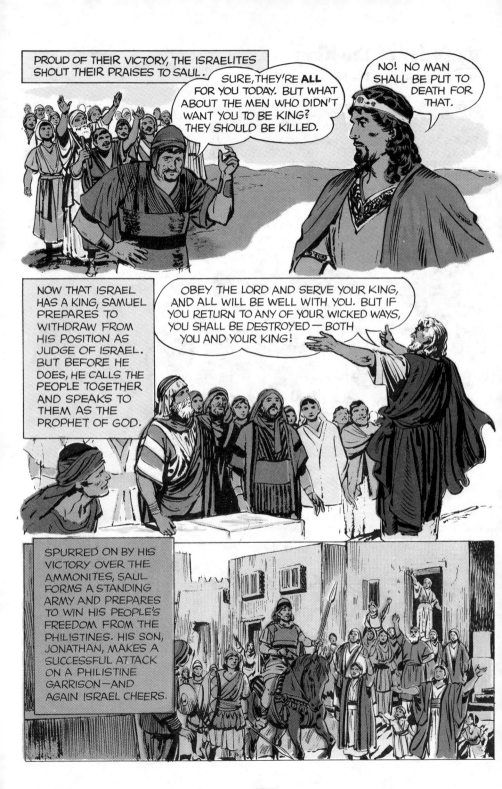

PROUD OF THEIR VICTORY, THE ISRAELITES SHOUT THEIR PRAISES TO SAUL.

SURE, THEY'RE **ALL** FOR YOU TODAY. BUT WHAT ABOUT THE MEN WHO DIDN'T WANT YOU TO BE KING? THEY SHOULD BE KILLED.

NO! NO MAN SHALL BE PUT TO DEATH FOR THAT.

NOW THAT ISRAEL HAS A KING, SAMUEL PREPARES TO WITHDRAW FROM HIS POSITION AS JUDGE OF ISRAEL. BUT BEFORE HE DOES, HE CALLS THE PEOPLE TOGETHER AND SPEAKS TO THEM AS THE PROPHET OF GOD.

OBEY THE LORD AND SERVE YOUR KING, AND ALL WILL BE WELL WITH YOU. BUT IF YOU RETURN TO ANY OF YOUR WICKED WAYS, YOU SHALL BE DESTROYED — BOTH YOU AND YOUR KING!

SPURRED ON BY HIS VICTORY OVER THE AMMONITES, SAUL FORMS A STANDING ARMY AND PREPARES TO WIN HIS PEOPLE'S FREEDOM FROM THE PHILISTINES. HIS SON, JONATHAN, MAKES A SUCCESSFUL ATTACK ON A PHILISTINE GARRISON—AND AGAIN ISRAEL CHEERS.

TAKE THIRTY THOUSAND CHARIOTS, SIX THOUSAND HORSEMEN AND ALL OUR INFANTRY—SET UP A CAMP AT MICHMASH. FROM THERE WE CAN SEND OUT RAIDING PARTIES THAT WILL DRAW SAUL FROM HIS STRONGHOLD AT GILGAL.

IN SPITE OF FORMER VICTORIES MANY OF THE ISRAELITES LOSE COURAGE WHEN THEY SEE THE SIZE OF THE ENEMY FORCES.

THE PHILISTINES OUTNUMBER US BY THOUSANDS. I'M HIDING OUT UNTIL THIS IS OVER.

THERE'S A PIT DOWN THE VALLEY— I'LL HIDE THERE.

EVEN IN THE CAMP OF KING SAUL, THE SOLDIERS ARE AFRAID.

A RAID ON A PHILISTINE GARRISON IS ONE THING—FIGHTING THE WHOLE PHILISTINE ARMY IS ANOTHER.

THE MEN ARE LOSING THEIR NERVE. WE CAN'T WAIT MUCH LONGER FOR SAMUEL TO COME AND OFFER THE SACRIFICE TO GOD.

YOU'RE RIGHT. WE'LL WAIT NO LONGER. **I'LL** MAKE THE OFFERING!

The King Disobeys

FROM 1 SAMUEL 13:10—15:14

THE ISRAELITES WATCH WITH GROWING TERROR AS THE PHILISTINE ARMY SETS UP CAMP AT MICHMASH. SAUL, AFRAID THAT HIS PEOPLE WILL PANIC, LOSES FAITH IN GOD'S GUIDANCE. INSTEAD OF WAITING FOR SAMUEL TO OFFER THE SACRIFICE, HE MAKES THE OFFERING HIMSELF. HE NO SOONER FINISHES THAN HE SEES SAMUEL COMING...

I WAS AFRAID MY PEOPLE WOULD FLEE BEFORE YOU GOT HERE, SO I OFFERED THE SACRIFICE.

YOU HAVE DISOBEYED GOD. YOU CANNOT DO THAT AND HOLD YOUR KINGDOM!

MEANTIME—INSTEAD OF MAKING AN OPEN ATTACK, THE PHILISTINES SEND OUT RAIDING PARTIES TO DRAW SAUL FROM CAMP—BUT SAUL WILL NOT COME OUT. HIS SON, PRINCE JONATHAN, DECIDES TO TAKE ACTION...

LET'S ATTACK THE PHILISTINE GARRISON BY OURSELVES.

I'M WITH YOU!

SECRETLY JONATHAN AND HIS ARMOR-BEARER LEAVE CAMP. WHEN THEY REACH THE FOOT OF THE CLIFF THAT LEADS TO THE PHILISTINE GARRISON, THE ENEMY DARES THEM TO COME UP AND FIGHT. BOLDLY, JONATHAN AND HIS FRIEND SCALE THE CLIFF...

FOLLOW ME, FOR WITH THE LORD THERE IS NO NEED FOR LARGE NUMBERS.

AT THE TOP THEY ATTACK WITH SUCH DARING THAT THE PHILISTINES FLEE IN PANIC. IN THEIR CONFUSION, THE PHILISTINES EVEN ATTACK ONE ANOTHER.

WHEN SAUL LEARNS THE PHILISTINES ARE RETREATING, AND DISCOVERS THAT IT IS JONATHAN WHO HAS ATTACKED THEM, HE LEADS HIS ARMY AGAINST THE ENEMY AND DRIVES THEM BACK TO THEIR OWN COUNTRY.

AFTER THIS VICTORY, SAUL ATTACKS THE OTHER ENEMIES OF ISRAEL AND DRIVES THEM AWAY. BUT THE RAIDS OF THE DESERT TRIBE OF THE AMALEKITES CONTINUE —

FINALLY SAMUEL CALLS SAUL TO HIM...

THE LORD WANTS YOU TO DESTROY THE AMALEKITES WHO HAVE BEEN ENEMIES OF ISRAEL EVER SINCE OUR PEOPLE LEFT EGYPT. BRING NOTHING AWAY WITH YOU, FOR THIS IS NOT A WAR TO GAIN WEALTH.

SAUL ATTACKS THE AMALEKITES AND DRIVES THEM BACK TOWARD EGYPT, BUT HE BRINGS THE BEST OF THE SHEEP AND OXEN HOME WITH HIM.

AT GILGAL, HE COMES FACE TO FACE WITH SAMUEL...

I HAVE OBEYED THE COMMANDMENT OF GOD AND DESTROYED THE AMALEKITES.

IF YOU HAVE OBEYED GOD, THEN WHAT IS THE MEANING OF THIS NOISE OF SHEEP AND CATTLE THAT I HEAR?

AT GOD'S COMMAND, SAMUEL GOES TO BETHLEHEM WHERE HE IS GREETED BY JESSE, THE GRANDSON OF RUTH AND BOAZ.

HAVE WE DONE ANYTHING WRONG THAT YOU HAVE COME TO JUDGE US?

NO, I HAVE COME TO GIVE AN OFFERING TO GOD.

JESSE, GOD WANTS ME TO CHOOSE ONE OF YOUR SONS FOR A SPECIAL SERVICE. WILL YOU BRING THEM TO ME?

OF COURSE.

THIS IS MY OLDEST SON, ELIAB.

HOW TALL AND STRONG HE IS — SURELY THIS IS GOD'S CHOSEN ONE.

BUT SAMUEL HEARS GOD'S VOICE: "MAN LOOKS ON THE OUTWARD APPEARANCE, BUT THE LORD LOOKS ON THE HEART. THIS IS NOT THE ONE."

I'M SORRY, ELIAB IS NOT THE ONE. CALL ANOTHER.

ABINADAB!

The Chosen One
FROM 1 SAMUEL 16:12–19

WHEN SAMUEL, THE PROPHET OF GOD, ASKS TO SEE ALL OF JESSE'S SONS, JESSE HAS TO SEND FOR HIS YOUNGEST, DAVID, WHO IS AWAY TENDING SHEEP. THE MESSENGERS REACH THE FIELDS IN TIME TO SEE A LION ABOUT TO SPRING ON THE YOUNG SHEPHERD. DAVID'S KEEN EARS HEAR A SWISH IN THE TALL GRASS. HE WHIRLS...

A LION!

DAVID! THE LION—YOU KILLED IT!

I KILLED A BEAR A FEW DAYS AGO. NOTHING'S GOING TO HURT MY FATHER'S SHEEP IF I CAN HELP IT.

YOU'RE A BRAVE SHEPHERD, DAVID. BUT HURRY HOME—SAMUEL WANTS TO SEE YOU. I'VE BROUGHT A MAN TO STAY WITH THE SHEEP.

ME? BUT WHY?

ON THE HIKE BACK TO THE CITY, DAVID CONTINUES TO WONDER. BUT WHEN SAMUEL SEES THE YOUNG SHEPHERD BOY, HE KNOWS HIS SEARCH HAS ENDED, FOR HE HEARS GOD SAY: *"THIS IS MY CHOSEN ONE."*

BEFORE JESSE AND HIS SONS, SAMUEL BLESSES DAVID AND ANOINTS HIS HEAD WITH OIL.

THE LORD BLESS YOU, FOR YOU WILL BE THE NEXT KING OF ISRAEL.

DAVID DOES NOT KNOW WHEN HE WILL BE MADE KING. BUT AS HE GOES BACK TO HIS SHEEP HE HAS A SPECIAL FEELING OF GOD'S PRESENCE WITH HIM.

THE LORD IS MY STRENGTH. WHAT HAVE I TO FEAR?

279

BACK AT THE PALACE THE MEN GO TO SEE KING SAUL—BUT THEY FIND HIM STARING WILDLY INTO SPACE.

A Giant's Challenge

1 Samuel 16:23—17:26

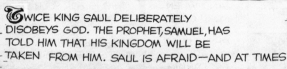

TWICE KING SAUL DELIBERATELY DISOBEYS GOD. THE PROPHET, SAMUEL, HAS TOLD HIM THAT HIS KINGDOM WILL BE TAKEN FROM HIM. SAUL IS AFRAID—AND AT TIMES HIS MIND BECOMES UNBALANCED. WHEN HIS ADVISORS TELL HIM ABOUT DAVID, A YOUNG SHEPHERD, WHO SINGS AND PLAYS A HARP, SAUL SENDS FOR HIM. DAVID ARRIVES AT THE PALACE...

THE KING IS VERY ILL TODAY—SO HE MAY BE DANGEROUS. NEVER TAKE YOUR EYES OFF HIM.

QUIETLY DAVID ENTERS THE KING'S ROOM AND BEGINS TO PLAY...SAUL STARES AT HIM WILDLY... BUT DAVID CONTINUES TO PLAY AND SING OF HIS FAITH IN GOD.

AT LAST KING SAUL RELAXES AND FALLS QUIETLY ASLEEP. AFTER THAT DAVID IS OFTEN CALLED TO THE PALACE. HIS MUSIC QUIETS SAUL'S TORTURED MIND—AND IN TIME THE KING SEEMS WELL AGAIN.

AND WHEN WORD COMES THAT THE PHILISTINES ARE PREPARING FOR AN ATTACK, SAUL LEADS HIS ARMY AGAINST THEM. DAVID'S THREE OLDEST BROTHERS JOIN THE KING'S FORCES.

ONE EVENING DAVID COMES IN FROM THE FIELDS TO FIND HIS FATHER BUSY PACKING FOOD.

THIS IS FOR YOUR BROTHERS. I WANT YOU TO TAKE IT TO THEM.

I'LL LEAVE RIGHT AWAY. WHAT'S THE LATEST NEWS FROM THE FRONT?

NOT GOOD, AND I'M WORRIED.

WHEN DAVID REACHES THE ISRAELITE CAMP, HE FINDS THE SOLDIERS STRANGELY QUIET.

WHAT'S THE MATTER?

THE MATTER? LISTEN TO THAT GIANT!

SEND OUT A MAN WHO DARES TO FIGHT ME. IF HE KILLS ME, THE PHILISTINES WILL BE YOUR SERVANTS, BUT IF I KILL HIM, YOU WILL BE OUR SERVANTS.

WHO IS THAT PHILISTINE THAT HE CAN DEFY THE ARMY OF GOD?

THAT'S THE GIANT, GOLIATH— THE BIGGEST, STRONGEST, MOST FEARED OF ALL THE PHILISTINE SOLDIERS. NO MAN DARES TO TAKE UP HIS CHALLENGE.

NO MAN? IS EVERY ISRAELITE SOLDIER A COWARD?

THOSE ARE STRONG WORDS, BOY. BUT—LOOK —HERE COMES YOUR BIG BROTHER. YOU'D BETTER GET OUT OF HERE BEFORE HE HEARS WHAT YOU'VE SAID.

The Challenge Is Met

FROM 1 SAMUEL 17:28–48

WHEN DAVID REACHES THE ISRAELITE CAMP, HE FINDS THAT NO ISRAELITE SOLDIER IS BRAVE ENOUGH TO ACCEPT THE PHILISTINE GIANT'S CHALLENGE TO FIGHT. DAVID IS ANGRY—BUT SO IS ELIAB, HIS BIG BROTHER...

WHAT ARE **YOU** DOING HERE? WHY AREN'T YOU HOME WHERE YOU BELONG—TAKING CARE OF THE SHEEP?

FATHER SENT ME HERE WITH FOOD FOR YOU—NOW **YOU** TELL ME WHY NO ONE HAS ACCEPTED GOLIATH'S CHALLENGE TO FIGHT?

EVER SINCE THE PROPHET SAMUEL CHOSE DAVID INSTEAD OF HIM, ELIAB HAS BEEN FILLED WITH JEALOUSY...NOW IT BURSTS INTO THE OPEN.

YOU'RE JUST A SHOW-OFF.

I'M NOT AFRAID. I'LL FIGHT THE GIANT.

MEANWHILE IN KING SAUL'S TENT...

EVERY DAY THAT GIANT DEFIES US. I HAVE OFFERED A HANDSOME REWARD—EVEN MY DAUGHTER IN MARRIAGE—BUT NOT ONE SOLDIER IN MY WHOLE ARMY WILL ACCEPT THE CHALLENGE.

O KING—THERE IS ONE OUTSIDE WHO ACCEPTS, BUT—

BRING HIM HERE AT ONCE!

DAVID ENTERS—BUT SAUL DOES NOT REMEMBER THE SHEPHERD WHO PLAYED FOR HIM.

A SHEPHERD BOY! YOU CAN'T FIGHT A GIANT!

THE LORD WHO HELPED ME KILL A LION AND A BEAR WILL HELP ME NOW.

MAYBE YOU'RE RIGHT—AT LEAST YOU HAVE COURAGE, GO, AND THE LORD BE WITH THEE. YOU CAN WEAR MY OWN ARMOR.

I CAN'T WEAR THIS—I'M NOT USED TO FIGHTING IN ARMOR. BESIDES, MY PLAN IS NOT TO DEFEND MYSELF, BUT TO ATTACK!

286

The Jealous King

FROM 1 SAMUEL 17:48—18:9

FOR FORTY DAYS THE PHILISTINE GIANT, GOLIATH, CHALLENGES THE ISRAELITES TO FIGHT. BUT NOT ONE SOLDIER IN ALL OF KING SAUL'S ARMY IS BRAVE ENOUGH TO ACCEPT THE CHALLENGE, UNTIL DAVID, THE YOUNG SHEPHERD, OFFERS TO MEET THE GIANT WITH ONLY A STAFF, A SLING—AND HIS FAITH IN GOD! EVEN WHILE DAVID WHIRLS HIS SLING, THE GIANT LAUGHS, BUT THE STONE HITS ITS MARK...AND THE GIANT FALLS!

GOLIATH'S DEAD!

IN TERROR, THE PHILISTINES FLEE FOR THEIR LIVES. SPURRED ON BY THIS SUDDEN TURN OF EVENTS, THE EXCITED ISRAELITES CHASE THE PHILISTINES BACK TO THEIR OWN LAND.

WHEN THE ARMY RETURNS, SAUL'S GENERAL, ABNER, TAKES DAVID TO SEE THE KING.

YOU SAVED ISRAEL, DAVID. FROM NOW ON YOU WILL LIVE IN THE PALACE. PRINCE JONATHAN WILL TAKE YOU BACK WITH HIM.

DAVID AND JONATHAN BECOME TRUE FRIENDS— AND MAKE A PACT OF FRIENDSHIP.

DAVID, I'M PROUD TO BE THE FRIEND OF THE BRAVEST MAN IN ISRAEL. I WANT TO GIVE YOU MY ROBE AND ARMOR AS A SIGN THAT I WILL BE LOYAL TO YOU—FOREVER!

THANK YOU, JONATHAN. GOD IS MY WITNESS THAT I WILL BE YOUR FRIEND UNTIL DEATH.

TRIUMPHANTLY, KING SAUL AND HIS VICTORIOUS SOLDIERS RETURN HOME...THE WOMEN RUSH OUT OF THE CITIES TO GREET THEM AND SING THEIR PRAISES.

SAUL HAS SLAIN HIS THOUSANDS—AND DAVID HIS TEN THOUSANDS!

WHEN SAUL HEARS THESE WORDS, HE THINKS OF WHAT THE PROPHET SAMUEL TOLD HIM: "BECAUSE YOU HAVE DISOBEYED GOD, YOUR KINGDOM WILL BE GIVEN TO ANOTHER."

THE PEOPLE KNOW DAVID IS A GREATER WARRIOR THAN I. MAYBE *HE'S* THE ONE WHO WILL TAKE MY KINGDOM FROM ME!

THAT NIGHT SAUL CANNOT SLEEP.

DAVID! HE'S THE HERO NOW! BUT HE CAN'T TAKE MY KINGDOM FROM ME—IF HE'S DEAD!

Jonathan Defends David

From 1 Samuel 19:22—20:33

I'LL KILL HIM MYSELF! DAVID MAY BE A HERO TO THE PEOPLE, BUT HE WON'T LIVE TO TAKE _MY_ KINGDOM FROM ME!

THREE TIMES SAUL SENDS MEN TO RAMAH TO CAPTURE DAVID. BUT EACH TIME THE MEN FAIL. IN A FIT OF RAGE, SAUL SETS OUT...

—BUT ON THE WAY A STRANGE THING HAPPENS...

GOD TAKES CONTROL OF SAUL. AND WHEN SAUL REACHES RAMAH HE FALLS TO THE GROUND AND LIES THERE FOR A DAY AND A NIGHT.

WHILE SAUL IS IN RAMAH, DAVID HURRIES BACK TO THE PALACE TO SEE HIS FRIEND, PRINCE JONATHAN

INSIDE THE PALACE DAVID SEEKS OUT HIS FRIEND.

DAVID! WHAT BRINGS YOU BACK HERE?

I MUST KNOW WHY YOUR FATHER WANTS TO KILL ME. COME—LET'S GO WHERE WE CAN TALK WITHOUT BEING HEARD.

MY FATHER MEANS YOU NO HARM, DAVID. HE WOULD TELL ME IF HE DID.

NO, JONATHAN. HE WOULD NOT TELL YOU BECAUSE YOU ARE MY FRIEND.

TOMORROW STARTS THE KING'S FEAST OF THE NEW MOON—BUT I WON'T ATTEND. IF YOUR FATHER ASKS ABOUT ME, TELL HIM I HAVE GONE TO BETHLEHEM TO SEE MY FAMILY. IF HE IS NOT ANGRY, THEN ALL IS WELL. BUT IF HE IS—REMEMBER THE AGREEMENT WE MADE BEFORE GOD TO BE FRIENDS, ALWAYS.

I'LL FIND OUT THE TRUTH. NOW, LET'S GO OUT IN THE FIELD WHERE WE CAN SET UP A SECRET PLAN FOR ME TO LET YOU KNOW HOW MY FATHER FEELS.

JONATHAN AND DAVID MAKE
THEIR PLANS, THEN—

WHATEVER HAPPENS, DAVID, THE LORD IS A WITNESS TO OUR AGREEMENT THAT WE WILL BE LOYAL TO EACH OTHER—AND TO EACH OTHER'S CHILDREN.

YES, NOTHING WILL EVER BREAK UP OUR FRIENDSHIP. GOOD-BY.

ON THE SECOND DAY OF THE KING'S FEAST—

WHERE'S DAVID?

HE ASKED TO VISIT HIS FAMILY IN BETHLEHEM —I LET HIM GO.

DON'T YOU KNOW THAT AS LONG AS DAVID LIVES YOU WILL NEVER BE KING? BRING HIM HERE, FOR HE MUST DIE!

WHY SHOULD HE BE KILLED? WHAT HAS HE DONE BUT SERVE YOU WELL IN BATTLE?

EVEN MY OWN SON IS FOR DAVID.

Trapped in a Cave

FROM 1 SAMUEL 21:13—24:5

FORCED TO FLEE FOR HIS LIFE FROM KING SAUL, DAVID TRIES TO FIND SAFETY IN ENEMY COUNTRY. BUT SOME OF THE PHILISTINES REMEMBER DAVID AND WARN THEIR KING AGAINST HIM. TO FOOL THEM, DAVID PRETENDS HE IS CRAZY.

THIS IS DAVID, THE ISRAELITE WHO KILLED GOLIATH.

HE'S MAD! TAKE THAT CRAZY MAN OUT OF MY SIGHT!

DAVID RETURNS TO ISRAEL...AND THE NEWS OF HIS WHEREABOUTS SPREADS QUICKLY AMONG HIS FRIENDS.

KING SAUL HAS ORDERED US TO FIGHT **AGAINST** YOU— BUT WE WANT TO FIGHT **FOR** YOU.

GOOD. THAT MAKES FOUR HUNDRED MEN ON OUR SIDE.

BUT NEWS ABOUT DAVID ALSO REACHES SAUL.

THE PRIESTS AT NOB ARE HELPING DAVID. ONE OF THEM GAVE HIM GOLIATH'S SWORD. I SAW THE WHOLE THING WITH MY OWN EYES.

BRING THE PRIESTS TO ME—I'LL MAKE AN EXAMPLE OF TRAITORS WHO HELP DAVID.

THE PRIESTS OF NOB PLEAD INNOCENT TO THE CHARGE OF PLOTTING AGAINST SAUL—BUT HE WILL NOT LISTEN!

YOU HELPED MY ENEMY—AND FOR THIS YOU WILL DIE!

IN HIS INSANE DESIRE FOR REVENGE, SAUL ORDERS THE DEATH OF NOT ONLY THE PRIESTS OF NOB, BUT OF EVERY MAN, WOMAN AND CHILD IN THEIR CITY. ONLY ONE MAN ESCAPES, ABIATHAR...

...WHO CARRIES THE TRAGIC NEWS TO DAVID.

GOD FORGIVE ME. I AM PARTLY TO BLAME. I ASKED FOR HELP, AND YOUR FATHER GAVE IT. STAY WITH ME—FOR NOW SAUL SEEKS YOUR LIFE AS WELL AS MINE.

REPORTS OF DAVID'S MOVEMENTS ARE AGAIN BROUGHT TO SAUL—AND THIS TIME THE JEALOUS KING SETS OUT WITH THREE THOUSAND MEN.

Saul Is Spared

FROM 1 SAMUEL 24:5—25:13

WHY DOESN'T DAVID KILL HIM?

HE JUST STANDS THERE!

AFRAID THAT DAVID WILL TAKE HIS KINGDOM FROM HIM, KING SAUL SETS OUT WITH HIS ARMY TO CAPTURE DAVID. ON THE WAY HE STOPS TO REST IN A CAVE— UNAWARE THAT DAVID AND HIS MEN ARE HIDING IN THE BACK OF IT.

DAVID LOOKS DOWN AT THE KING—AND THINKS OF ALL THE TIMES SAUL HAS TRIED TO KILL HIM. NOW THE JEALOUS KING IS AT HIS MERCY—BUT DAVID ONLY BENDS DOWN AND CAREFULLY CUTS OFF A PIECE OF THE ROYAL ROBE.

HE'S YOUR WIFE'S FATHER— SO IF YOU DON'T WANT TO KILL HIM, I'LL DO IT FOR YOU.

NO—HE WAS CHOSEN BY GOD TO BE OUR KING. IT IS NOT FOR US TO DECIDE WHEN HE WILL DIE.

AFTER A TIME SAUL LEAVES THE CAVE—AND DAVID CALLS AFTER HIM.

MY LORD THE KING.

DAVID!

WHY DO YOU KEEP HUNTING ME? I MEAN YOU NO HARM. SEE THIS PIECE OF CLOTH? I CUT IT FROM YOUR ROBE. I COULD HAVE KILLED YOU, BUT I DIDN'T.

I AM ASHAMED. YOU ARE A BETTER MAN THAN I AM, DAVID. I WILL GO NOW AND LEAVE YOU ALONE.

SAUL LEADS HIS ARMY AWAY ...BUT A SHORT TIME LATER DAVID LEARNS THAT SAUL HAS FORCED MICHAL, DAVID'S WIFE, TO MARRY ANOTHER MAN. DAVID KNOWS NOW THAT SAUL IS STILL ANGRY AND THAT HE WILL NEVER BE SAFE AS LONG AS SAUL LIVES. WORD COMES, TOO, THAT HIS OLD FRIEND, SAMUEL, THE PROPHET, IS DEAD.

David's Dilemma

FROM 1 SAMUEL 26:6—28:2

KING SAUL AND HIS ARMY ARE CAMPED IN THE VALLEY—PREPARING TO ATTACK DAVID. BUT DAVID IS WARNED, AND IN THE DARK OF NIGHT HE AND HIS YOUNG NEPHEW, ABISHAI, STEAL PAST THE SLEEPING GUARDS IN SEARCH OF THE KING. ONE FALSE MOVE AND THE WHOLE CAMP WILL BE AROUSED...

STEALTHILY THEY CREEP UP BESIDE THE SLEEPING KING.

GOD HAS PUT YOUR ENEMY IN OUR HANDS. I'LL PIN HIM TO THE GROUND WITH ONE BLOW.

NO! THE LORD ANOINTED SAUL KING OF ISRAEL, AND THE LORD WILL DECIDE WHEN AND HOW SAUL IS TO DIE.

HAND ME HIS SPEAR AND WATER JUG. THEN WE'LL LEAVE THE SAME WAY WE CAME INTO CAMP.

THE NEXT MORNING DAVID CALLS DOWN TO SAUL'S CAMP.

KING SAUL! LOOK! I HAVE YOUR SPEAR AND WATER JUG!

YOU TOOK THEM WHILE I SLEPT! AGAIN YOU COULD HAVE KILLED ME— AND YOU DIDN'T. I HAVE BEEN A FOOL! I'LL NEVER TRY TO HARM YOU AGAIN.

ASHAMED, KING SAUL ORDERS HIS MEN TO BREAK CAMP AND RETURN HOME.

LOOK! THEY'RE LEAVING—YOU'RE SAFE!

NO—SAUL PROMISED THAT BEFORE. I'LL NEVER BE SAFE AS LONG AS THE KING LIVES.

AND I'M TIRED OF BEING HUNTED LIKE AN OUTLAW. I'M GOING BACK TO THE LAND OF THE PHILISTINES.

PHILISTINES! BUT, UNCLE DAVID, THEY'RE ENEMIES OF ISRAEL. THEY'LL KILL YOU ON SIGHT.

SO—FOR THE FIRST TIME SINCE THEY JOINED DAVID—HIS FOLLOWERS HAVE A SETTLED PLACE IN WHICH TO LIVE.

DAVID REASONS THAT THE PHILISTINES KNOW OF HIS TROUBLE WITH SAUL AND THAT THIS TIME THEY WILL ACCEPT HIM. AND HE IS RIGHT. KING ACHISH OF THE PHILISTINES IS GLAD TO HAVE DAVID'S SIX HUNDRED WARRIORS ON HIS SIDE. HE EVEN GIVES THEM THE CITY OF ZIKLAG TO LIVE IN.

IT'S GOOD, ABIGAIL, TO SEE MY MEN RAISING THEIR FAMILIES IN PEACE.

AND I'M SO GLAD YOUR LIFE IS NO LONGER IN DANGER.

ONE DAY DAVID SEES KING ACHISH RIDING INTO THE CITY.

I WONDER WHAT BRINGS HIM HERE?

I PRAY HIS VISIT IS A FRIENDLY ONE.

DAVID GOES OUT TO WELCOME THE KING.

GREETINGS, DAVID. WE ARE PLANNING AN ATTACK ON YOUR OLD ENEMY, KING SAUL, AND WE EXPECT YOU TO HELP US.

HOW CAN I FIGHT MY OWN PEOPLE? KING SAUL AND PRINCE JONATHAN WILL BE LEADING THE ISRAELITES!

At the Witch's House

FROM 1 SAMUEL 28:5–11; 29

DAVID IS ON THE SPOT! KING ACHISH HAS ORDERED HIM TO JOIN THE ATTACK ON KING SAUL AND HIS OWN PEOPLE. IF HE REFUSES, THE PHILISTINES WILL TURN ON HIM. SO—AGAINST HIS WILL—HE JOINS THE MARCH AGAINST ISRAEL.

O GOD—HELP ME SO THAT I WILL NOT HAVE TO FIGHT SAUL AND JONATHAN.

UNKNOWN TO DAVID, SOME OF THE PHILISTINE LEADERS ARE HOPING TO KEEP HIM OUT OF THE FIGHT—FOR ANOTHER REASON. THAT NIGHT THEY GO TO KING ACHISH'S TENT.

I DON'T LIKE HAVING DAVID AND HIS MEN BRINGING UP THE REAR. REMEMBER, DAVID IS AN ISRAELITE.

AND HE COULD CUT US TO PIECES WHILE WE'RE BUSY AT THE FRONT.

I THINK DAVID IS LOYAL TO ME. BUT, IF YOU WISH, I'LL SEND HIM HOME.

ACHISH CALLS FOR DAVID.

I FIND NO FAULT IN YOU, DAVID, BUT THE OTHERS DON'T TRUST YOU. YOU'D BETTER RETURN HOME AS SOON AS IT IS LIGHT.

DAVID'S PRAYER HAS BEEN ANSWERED. AT DAWN HE LEADS HIS SOLDIERS OUT OF THE CAMP AND BACK TOWARD THEIR CITY OF ZIKLAG. THE PHILISTINES MARCH ON...

WHEN SAUL SEES THE POWERFUL PHILISTINE ARMY, HE IS AFRAID. FRANTICALLY HE CALLS UPON GOD FOR HELP—BUT GOD DOES NOT ANSWER. TERRIFIED, HE CALLS FOR A SERVANT.

WHERE CAN I FIND A WOMAN WHO SPEAKS WITH THE SPIRITS OF THE DEAD? I NEED SOME ADVICE.

THERE'S A WITCH AT ENDOR. IT'S NEAR THE PHILISTINE CAMP, SO WE'LL HAVE TO GO BY NIGHT.

THAT NIGHT SAUL AND TWO SERVANTS STEAL ACROSS THE HILL TO THE VILLAGE OF ENDOR...

AND KNOCK ON A DOOR.

I'LL PAY YOU WELL TO CALL UP THE SPIRIT OF THE ONE I NAME.

IS THIS A TRAP? YOU KNOW KING SAUL HAS ORDERED ALL WITCHES PUT TO DEATH.

HAVE NO FEAR, NOTHING WILL HAPPEN TO YOU FOR WHAT I ASK.

WHOSE SPIRIT DO YOU WANT CALLED UP?

A Voice from the Dead

FROM 1 SAMUEL 28:11–25; 31:1–6; 30:1–3

SAUL IS TERRIFIED BY THE SIGHT OF THE APPROACHING PHILISTINE ARMY. IN DESPERATION, HE DISGUISES HIMSELF AND STEALS THROUGH THE NIGHT TO SEEK THE ADVICE OF A WITCH.

CALL UP THE SPIRIT OF THE PROPHET SAMUEL.

FOR A MOMENT ALL IS STILL...THE WOMAN CALLS FOR THE SPIRIT OF SAMUEL. SUDDENLY SHE CRIES OUT IN TERROR...

THEN SAUL HEARS THE VOICE OF SAMUEL: BECAUSE YOU DISOBEYED GOD, THE LORD WILL DELIVER ISRAEL INTO THE HANDS OF THE PHILISTINES. TOMORROW YOU AND YOUR SONS WILL BE DEAD.

THE NEXT MORNING THE PHILISTINES ATTACK. ISRAEL, UNDER A WEAK AND FRIGHTENED KING, RETREATS IN PANIC.

THE ENEMY IS EVERYWHERE! WE CAN'T STOP THEM!

MY SONS— WHERE ARE THEY?

DEAD, SIR.

DEAD! AND I AM BADLY WOUNDED.

DRAW YOUR SWORD AND KILL ME. I WOULD RATHER DIE BY YOUR HAND THAN BE CAPTURED BY THE PHILISTINES.

KILL MY KING? I CAN'T— I CAN'T!

SO SAUL DRAWS HIS OWN SWORD— AND FALLS UPON IT.

WHEN THE PEOPLE OF ISRAEL LEARN THAT THEIR KING IS DEAD AND THE ARMY HAS FLED, THEY DESERT THEIR CITIES, LEAVING THEM TO THE CONQUERING PHILISTINES. SO— SAMUEL'S PROPHECY COMES TRUE!

MEANTIME, DAVID AND HIS MEN RIDE TOWARD ZIKLAG...

LOOK! WHAT'S THAT RED GLOW AGAINST THE SKY?

305

On the Robber's Trail

FROM 1 SAMUEL 30:1–11

DAVID AND HIS MEN RETURN TO FIND THEIR CITY OF ZIKLAG IN SMOLDERING RUINS.

IN VAIN THEY SEARCH THROUGH THE RUBBLE AND ASHES FOR THEIR FAMILIES.

Front-line News

FROM 1 SAMUEL 30; 2 SAMUEL 1:1–3

307

SO IT WAS THE AMALEKITES WHO RAIDED ZIKLAG? DO YOU KNOW WHERE THEY ARE NOW?

I'LL TAKE YOU TO THEIR CAMP— IF YOU PROMISE NOT TO TURN ME OVER TO MY MASTER. HE'D KILL ME.

DAVID PROMISES. AND, TRUE TO HIS WORD, THE SLAVE GUIDES DAVID TO THE AMALEKITE CAMP— WHERE THE SOLDIERS ARE CELEBRATING THEIR VICTORY.

WE'LL SOON END **THAT** PARTY!

DAVID MAKES A LIGHTNING ATTACK—THE AMALEKITES RALLY THEIR FORCES, BUT THEY ARE NO MATCH FOR COURAGEOUS MEN FIGHTING FOR THEIR WIVES AND CHILDREN.

WHEN THE BATTLE IS OVER...

OH, DAVID, I KNEW **YOU** WOULD COME!

THANK GOD, ABIGAIL, YOU ARE SAFE!

THE AMALEKITE WHO LEFT HIS SLAVE TO DIE PAID DEARLY FOR HIS CRUELTY, FOR BY THIS ACT HE AND MOST OF HIS COUNTRYMEN LOST THEIR LIVES. BUT DAVID, WHO OBEYED GOD, RESCUES ALL OF THE ISRAELITE WOMEN AND CHILDREN. AND WHEN HE DIVIDES THE SPOIL OF BATTLE HE SHARES IT NOT ONLY WITH HIS MEN, BUT WITH LEADERS OF THE TOWNS OF JUDAH.

TRIUMPHANTLY DAVID AND HIS MEN BRING THEIR FAMILIES AND POSSESSIONS BACK TO THE BURNED CITY. THEY TALK EAGERLY OF HOW THEY WILL REBUILD THEIR HOMES AND ONCE AGAIN LIVE IN PEACE. BUT DAVID'S THOUGHTS ARE FAR AWAY...

YOU LOOK WORRIED, DAVID.

YES, I KEEP WONDERING HOW THE BATTLE BETWEEN THE PHILISTINES AND KING SAUL CAME OUT.

TWO DAYS LATER...

WHO ARE YOU — AND WHAT DO YOU WANT?

I WAS WITH SAUL IN THE BATTLE WITH THE PHILISTINES — AND I HAVE GOOD NEWS FOR DAVID.

Rival Kings

From 2 Samuel 1:2—2:9

THE BOOKS OF 2 SAMUEL AND 1 CHRONICLES RECORD THE SAME PERIOD OF HISTORY—THE REIGN OF DAVID, ISRAEL'S GREATEST KING. 2 SAMUEL PRESENTS IT THROUGH THE EYES OF THE PROPHETS, WHILE 1 CHRONICLES RELATES IT FROM THE VIEWPOINT OF THE PRIESTS.

SOON AFTER DAVID AND HIS MEN RETURN TO ZIKLAG, A MESSENGER COMES WITH NEWS FOR DAVID.

WHO ARE YOU—AND WHAT BRINGS YOU HERE?

I COME FROM THE BATTLE BETWEEN THE PHILISTINES AND ISRAEL. YOUR OLD ENEMY, KING SAUL, IS DEAD—SO IS CROWN PRINCE JONATHAN!

HOW DO YOU KNOW THIS?

I DO NOT KNOW HOW JONATHAN DIED, BUT I FOUND THE KING ON THE BATTLEFIELD. HE WAS INJURED, AND HE ASKED ME TO KILL HIM. I DID—AND HERE ARE HIS CROWN AND BRACELETS TO PROVE IT!

DAVID DOES NOT KNOW THAT THE MAN IS TELLING A LIE, WITH THE HOPE OF RECEIVING A REWARD. FOR A MOMENT HE IS LOST IN GRIEF—THEN HE TURNS IN ANGER UPON THE MAN WHO BROUGHT THE NEWS.

EVEN IF THE KING ASKED YOU TO KILL HIM, YOU HAD NO RIGHT TO TAKE THE LIFE OF THE MAN CHOSEN BY GOD TO BE KING OF ISRAEL. FOR THIS CRIME YOU WILL PAY—WITH YOUR LIFE!

SO THE MAN WHO LIED TO WIN FAVOR WITH DAVID LOSES NOT ONLY THE FAVOR—BUT HIS LIFE!

THEN, BEFORE ALL OF HIS FAITHFUL FOLLOWERS, DAVID SINGS A MEMORIAL SONG FOR JONATHAN AND THE KING.

Song of the Bow

...HOW ARE THE MIGHTY FALLEN! ...
THE BOW OF JONATHAN TURNED NOT BACK,
AND THE SWORD OF SAUL RETURNED NOT EMPTY....
IN THEIR DEATH THEY WERE NOT DIVIDED:
THEY WERE SWIFTER THAN EAGLES,
THEY WERE STRONGER THAN LIONS....
I AM DISTRESSED FOR YOU, MY BROTHER JONATHAN:
VERY PLEASANT HAVE YOU BEEN TO ME:
YOUR LOVE TO ME WAS WONDERFUL,
PASSING THE LOVE OF WOMEN.
HOW ARE THE MIGHTY FALLEN,
AND THE WEAPONS OF WAR PERISHED!

NOW THAT SAUL IS DEAD, DAVID KNOWS THAT HE CAN RETURN TO HIS HOMELAND. BUT BEFORE HE MAKES ANY PLANS, HE PRAYS TO GOD.

LORD, SHALL I RETURN NOW TO MY OWN PEOPLE IN JUDAH?

GOD TELLS DAVID TO RETURN—AND WHEN HE DOES, THE PEOPLE OF JUDAH WELCOME THEIR HERO, AND MAKE HIM KING OF THEIR TRIBE.

GOD BLESS KING DAVID!

LONG LIVE THE KING!

BUT DAVID'S TROUBLES ARE NOT OVER...FOR ACROSS THE JORDAN RIVER SAUL'S YOUNGEST SON, ISHBOSHETH, HAS BEEN CROWNED KING OF THE OTHER TRIBES OF ISRAEL...

312

The Road to Becoming a King

As a boy, David never dreams that one day he will be king over Israel. But God has plans for this talented shepherd boy. . . .

▶ David grows up in Bethlehem. He is the youngest of Jesse's eight sons. As he watches his father's sheep, he writes songs, practices playing the harp, and learns to use a sling.

▶ When the Philistine giant Goliath challenges Saul's army, David meets the challenge and defeats the giant, using only a sling and his faith in God. He becomes a national hero.

▶ The king's jealousy causes David to flee and he becomes leader of a group of fugitives. He has two occasions to kill Saul, but out of honor and respect, he does not harm the king.

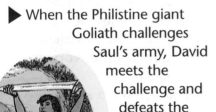

After Saul's death, David becomes king of Judah and for two years civil war wages as David tries to unite Israel and Judah. After seven years, the northern kingdom accepts David as their king. David was king for over 40 years.

David, A Man After God's Heart

▶ **Read about David on pp. 276-367.**

In 1 Samuel 13:14, Samuel tells Saul that God wants a person after His own heart to be the next king. God wants a person of good character who will do what God asks him to do. He finds the qualities He is looking for in David.

As Warrior
- Is resourceful and courageous
- Demonstrates faith in God
- Shows respect for Saul by not killing him when he has the chance.

As King
- Unites the kingdom
- Makes Jerusalem—the City of David—the capital.

As Shepherd
- Responsible keeper of his father's sheep
- Shows courage by killing a lion and a bear

As Religious Leader
- Moves the ark of the covenant to Jerusalem
- Organizes the worship of God
- Plans to build a temple

As Musician/Writer:
- Writes at least 73 Psalms
- Plays harp skillfully
- Organizes priestly singers for worship of God (1 Chr. 6:31)

When David sins, he:
- Repents
- Asks God for forgiveness
- Follows God's leadership

David and Jesus were related. See Matthew 1 and Luke 3.

Warring Kingdoms of Israel

FROM 2 SAMUEL 2:12—3:25

WHEN JOAB LEARNS OF ASAHEL'S DEATH, HE IS TORN WITH GRIEF — AND ANGER.

I'LL GET REVENGE!

THE WAR CONTINUES BETWEEN THE TWO KINGDOMS. BUT WITH EACH BATTLE DAVID GROWS STRONGER, AND IN ISH-BOSHETH'S PALACE FEAR AND TENSION MOUNT UNTIL ONE DAY ABNER TURNS ON THE KING...

HOW DARE YOU QUESTION ME? FOR THAT, I WILL TRANSFER MY ALLEGIANCE TO DAVID—AND YOUR KINGDOM WITH IT.

ABNER CARRIES OUT HIS THREAT AND OFFERS TO HELP DAVID ADD THE REST OF ISRAEL TO HIS KINGDOM. DAVID REPLIES WITH AN INVITATION TO A FEAST.

THANK YOU FOR YOUR KINDNESS. I'LL JOIN FORCES WITH YOU...YOU, MY LORD, WILL SOON REIGN OVER ALL ISRAEL!

ABNER JUST LEFT—DAVID HAD A BIG FEAST FOR HIM.

ABNER _HERE_? AND DAVID LET HIM GO?

ANGRILY JOAB RUSHES IN TO SEE DAVID...

DON'T YOU KNOW THAT ABNER CAME HERE AS A SPY—TO FIND OUT YOUR STRENGTH?

DAVID REFUSES TO LISTEN—AND IN A RAGE JOAB STORMS OUT.

I'LL HANDLE THIS _MY_ WAY!

JOAB IS FURIOUS! THIS COULD MEAN TROUBLE!

HE WOULDN'T DARE DEFY THE KING!

Plot against the King!

FROM 2 SAMUEL 3:26—4:5

JOAB IS ANGRY BECAUSE KING DAVID HAS HONORED ABNER, THE GENERAL OF AN ENEMY KING. SECRETLY, JOAB INVITES ABNER TO SEE HIM...

HERE COMES ABNER—THE MAN WHO KILLED MY BROTHER! HE MUST BE WILLING TO BETRAY HIS OWN KING TO WIN FAVOR AND POWER WITH DAVID—MORE POWER THAN I WOULD HAVE!

WHEN ABNER ENTERS THE CITY...

WELCOME, ABNER. I HAVE AN IMPORTANT MATTER TO TAKE UP WITH YOU—WILL YOU STEP OVER HERE WHERE WE CAN TAKE IT UP QUIETLY?

GREETINGS, JOAB. OF COURSE.

JOAB LEADS ABNER TO A QUIET CORNER OF THE BUSY GATE. AND THERE, BEFORE ABNER CAN SUSPECT WHAT IS GOING ON— JOAB STABS HIM.

DAVID IS ANGRY WHEN HE LEARNS OF ABNER'S MURDER. HE CALLS THE PEOPLE TOGETHER AND ACCUSES JOAB.

THE PUNISHMENT OF JOAB IS IN THE HANDS OF GOD!

TO FURTHER SHOW HIS DISAPPROVAL FOR WHAT JOAB HAS DONE, DAVID LEADS THE MOURNERS IN ABNER'S FUNERAL PROCESSION. BUT EVEN AS KING, DAVID IS NOT SECURE ENOUGH IN HIS NEW KINGDOM TO PUNISH JOAB, FOR JOAB IS THE LEADER OF DAVID'S ARMY.

DAVID MOURNS THE DEATH OF ABNER, BUT ABNER'S MASTER, KING ISH-BOSHETH, IS SHAKEN WITH FRIGHT.

WHAT BAD NEWS! WITHOUT ABNER, I'M LOST.

KING ISH-BOSHETH'S FEARS ARE WELL GROUNDED. FOR EVEN AS HE RECEIVES THE NEWS OF ABNER'S DEATH, TWO OF HIS OWN ARMY OFFICERS ARE PLOTTING...

WITHOUT ABNER, KING ISH-BOSHETH IS A WEAKLING. IF DAVID ATTACKS US, WE'LL BE WIPED OUT.

I HAVE AN IDEA THAT COULD GIVE US POWER —AND A REWARD! LISTEN—JUST THE TWO OF US...

WONDERFUL! LET'S DO IT NOW WHILE IT'S DARK.

NO—IT WILL BE EASIER IF WE JUST WALK INTO THE PALACE IN BROAD DAYLIGHT— AS IF WE WERE GETTING GRAIN. THEN NO ONE WOULD SUSPECT.

AT NOON THE NEXT DAY, WHILE THE KING IS TAKING HIS NAP...

THE REWARD WILL SOON BE OURS!

Hail to the King!

FROM 2 SAMUEL 4:6—5:4

THE WAR AGAINST KING DAVID LEAVES KING ISH-BOSHETH WITH FEW LOYAL FOLLOWERS. IN BROAD DAYLIGHT TWO OF HIS OWN OFFICERS ENTER THE KING'S PALACE...

THE KING'S ROOM IS DOWN THIS HALL.

HE IS ASLEEP.

GOOD—BUT WE MUST ACT SWIFTLY!

BOLDLY THE MEN ENTER THE KING'S BEDROOM AND—WHILE THE PALACE IS RESTING DURING THE HEAT OF THE DAY—THEY KILL HIM. THEN...

321

QUIETLY, SO THAT NO ONE WILL SUSPECT THEIR ERRAND...THEY WALK OUT OF THE PALACE AND INTO THE STREET. NIGHT FINDS THEM TRAVELING DOWN THE PLAIN TOWARD DAVID'S CAPITAL IN HEBRON.

BEFORE DAVID THEY PROUDLY TELL THEIR STORY.

WE BRING GOOD NEWS, O KING. **WE** HAVE KILLED YOUR ENEMY, KING ISH-BOSHETH!

WE THOUGHT SOME REWARD...

REWARD! DO YOU THINK I WILL REWARD YOU FOR KILLING AN INNOCENT MAN? THERE'S NO ROOM IN MY KINGDOM FOR TRAITORS WHO BETRAY THEIR KING! GUARDS! TAKE THEM AWAY—EXECUTE THEM.

Underground Attack

FROM 2 SAMUEL 5:5–9; 1 CHRONICLES 11:6

325

God's Promise to David

FROM 2 SAMUEL 6—8; 9:5;
1 CHRONICLES 13, 15, 16

JERUSALEM, THE CAPITAL OF ISRAEL, IS NOW A WELL-FORTIFIED CITY. BUT KING DAVID KNOWS THAT HIS NATION LACKS ONE THING TO MAKE IT SPIRITUALLY STRONG— A WAY FOR ISRAEL TO WORSHIP THE LORD. HE CALLS ON THE PEOPLE TO GO WITH HIM TO BRING GOD'S HOLY ARK TO JERUSALEM.

FATHER, WHAT'S IN THE GOLDEN CHEST?

TWO STONE TABLETS ON WHICH GOD'S TEN COMMANDMENTS ARE WRITTEN.

WHERE HAS IT BEEN?

THE PHILISTINES CAPTURED IT—BUT WHEN TROUBLE CAME TO THEM, THEY WERE AFRAID AND SENT IT BACK. IT HAS BEEN STORED AWAY FOR MANY YEARS.

328

BUT ONE DAY DAVID LOOKS AT THE TENT AND CALLS NATHAN, THE PROPHET OF GOD, TO HIM.

IT ISN'T RIGHT FOR GOD'S HOUSE TO BE A TENT WHILE I LIVE IN A PALACE. I'D LIKE TO BUILD A TEMPLE TO GOD.

I'M SURE GOD WOULD BE PLEASED.

THAT NIGHT GOD SPEAKS TO NATHAN — AND THE NEXT DAY NATHAN TELLS DAVID THAT GOD DOES NOT WANT HIM TO BUILD THE TEMPLE. DAVID IS A MAN OF WAR, AND THE TEMPLE IS TO BE BUILT BY A MAN OF PEACE. GOD PROMISES TO GIVE DAVID A SON WHO WILL BUILD A HOUSE FOR GOD.

THEN DAVID REMEMBERS A PROMISE HE HIMSELF MADE YEARS BEFORE TO HIS BEST FRIEND, JONATHAN. EACH HAD VOWED TO BE KIND TO THE OTHER'S CHILDREN. DAVID INQUIRES ABOUT JONATHAN'S FAMILY.

SEND FOR HIM.

REMEMBER, HE IS ALSO KING SAUL'S GRANDSON. BUT FOR YOU HE MIGHT BE SITTING ON THE THRONE OF ISRAEL. HE MAY HATE YOU...

YES, PRINCE JONATHAN HAD A SON, MEPHIBOSHETH.

329

A King Is Tempted

FROM 2 SAMUEL 9:6—11:14

DAVID ORDERS JONATHAN'S SON BROUGHT TO HIM. BUT HE IS SHOCKED WHEN MEPHIBOSHETH APPEARS -- A CRIPPLE.

HAVE MERCY ON YOUR SERVANT AND HIS CHILD, O KING.

MERCY? WHY DO YOU ASK FOR MERCY?

I AM THE GRANDSON OF YOUR ENEMY, KING SAUL. DID YOU NOT SEND FOR ME TO PUT ME TO DEATH?

NO, MEPHIBOSHETH -- NO! I SENT FOR YOU BECAUSE I LOVED YOUR FATHER, JONATHAN. I DID NOT KNOW YOU WERE LAME.

"I WAS ONLY FIVE WHEN THE NEWS OF MY FATHER'S DEATH CAME. AS MY NURSE RAN IN FRIGHT, SHE DROPPED ME. I HAVE BEEN CRIPPLED EVER SINCE."

"I AM SORRY--AND I REGRET THAT YOUR GRANDFATHER'S LAND WAS NOT RESTORED TO YOU BEFORE. IT IS NOW YOURS--AND I INVITE YOU TO EAT EVERY DAY AT MY TABLE."

"I AM GRATEFUL FOR YOUR KINDNESS."

"AND I THANK GOD I AM ABLE TO KEEP MY PROMISE TO YOUR FATHER."

UNDER DAVID'S LEADERSHIP, ISRAEL GROWS STRONGER EVERY DAY. BUT RULERS OF THE COUNTRIES AROUND GROW WORRIED.

"WORD HAS COME THAT THE SYRIANS AND AMMONITES ARE JOINING FORCES AGAINST US."

"I CAN'T LEAVE JERUSALEM NOW, JOAB. CALL UP THE ARMY AND GO OUT TO MEET THEM."

JOAB TAKES CHARGE OF THE WAR. ABOUT A YEAR LATER, AS DAVID STROLLS ON THE ROOF OF HIS PALACE...

"WHO IS THAT BEAUTIFUL WOMAN?"

"BATH-SHEBA, THE WIFE OF URIAH, A SOLDIER IN YOUR ARMY."

DAVID SENDS A MESSENGER TO BRING BATH-SHEBA TO HIS COURT.

YOU SENT FOR ME, O KING?

SHE IS EVEN MORE BEAUTIFUL THAN I THOUGHT!

IF ONLY I COULD MARRY HER! THE PROBLEM IS... URIAH IS HER HUSBAND.

BUT SOLDIERS SOMETIMES DIE IN BATTLE. THAT'S IT!

THINKING ONLY OF HIS LOVE FOR BATH-SHEBA DAVID SENDS FOR URIAH ON THE EXCUSE OF ASKING ABOUT THE WAR.

THE ENEMY IS STRONG. BUT JOAB THINKS WE CAN FORCE THEIR SURRENDER SOON.

I AM SURE OF IT. PREPARE TO RETURN TO THE FRONT--AND TAKE THIS MESSAGE TO JOAB.

King David's Sin

FROM 2 SAMUEL 11:14–27

URIAH, THE HUSBAND OF BATH-SHEBA, RETURNS TO THE BATTLEFRONT WITH A MESSAGE FROM KING DAVID TO JOAB, GENERAL OF THE ISRAELITE FORCES.

WELCOME BACK, URIAH. DID YOU SEE THE KING?
YES, HE ASKED ABOUT THE CAMPAIGN. I TOLD HIM OF YOUR PLANS TO FORCE THE CITY INTO SURRENDER. HERE IS A MESSAGE FROM HIM.
JOAB BREAKS THE KING'S SEAL AND READS...
"SET URIAH IN THE THICK OF THE FIGHT SO THAT HE WILL BE KILLED."

JOAB IS STUNNED.
ER--WE ARE TO ATTACK THE CITY AT ONCE. TOMORROW YOU WILL LEAD AN ASSAULT AGAINST THE MAIN GATE. THAT IS ALL...
THE MAIN GATE? IT'S HELD BY THE BEST TROOPS OF THE CITY... VERY WELL, I WILL OBEY.
URIAH OBEYS AND BOLDLY ATTACKS THE GATE, BUT HE IS KILLED BY ARCHERS PROTECTING THE WALL. THE ISRAELITE ATTACK FAILS. JOAB CALLS BACK HIS TROOPS...

WE FOUGHT BRAVELY--BUT THE ARCHERS ON THE CITY WALLS HAD THE ADVANTAGE. URIAH, THE LEADER OF THE ATTACK, WAS KILLED.

TELL JOAB NOT TO FEEL BADLY-- WAR ALWAYS TAKES SOME OF OUR BEST MEN. STEP UP THE ATTACK AND TAKE THE CITY.

ACROSS THE CITY, BATH-SHEBA MOURNS FOR HER HUSBAND-- BUT IN HER HEART SHE KNOWS THAT NOW SHE IS FREE TO MARRY THE KING.

WHEN BATH-SHEBA'S TIME OF MOURNING IS OVER, DAVID CALLS HER TO THE PALACE, AND THEY ARE MARRIED.

LONG LIVE THE KING! LONG LIVE THE QUEEN!

LATER, WHEN A SON IS BORN TO BATH-SHEBA, THE KING AND ALL ISRAEL REJOICE... BUT GOD IS NOT PLEASED! EVEN WHILE THE PEOPLE SHOUT THEIR PRAISES, A MAN OF GOD IS ON HIS WAY TO THE PALACE...

The King's Punishment

From 2 Samuel 12:1–14

DAVID HAS MARRIED THE BEAUTIFUL BATH-SHEBA. WHEN THEIR SON IS BORN, DAVID IS PROUD AND HAPPY UNTIL ONE DAY... NATHAN, THE PROPHET OF GOD, COMES TO SEE HIM.

WELCOME, NATHAN. WHAT CAN I DO FOR YOU?

I HAVE COME TO TELL YOU ABOUT A GREAT INJUSTICE THAT HAS BEEN DONE IN YOUR KINGDOM.

337

YOU, O KING, ARE THAT MAN! GOD MADE YOU RICH AND POWERFUL. BUT YOU WANTED BATH-SHEBA, THE WIFE OF ONE OF YOUR MOST LOYAL SOLDIERS. YOU HAD HIM KILLED SO THAT YOU MIGHT MARRY HER--JUST AS THE RICH MAN TOOK THE POOR MAN'S LAMB!

I HAVE SINNED! I HAVE SINNED AGAINST THE LORD!

AND YOUR SIN WILL BRING TROUBLE TO YOU AND YOUR FAMILY. THE CHILD WHICH HAS BEEN BORN TO YOU AND BATH-SHEBA WILL DIE!

NO, NATHAN! NOT MY CHILD!

HE'S GONE!

338

Flight of the Brothers

FROM 2 SAMUEL 12:15—13:29

BOLDLY THE PROPHET NATHAN CHARGES KING DAVID WITH SINNING AGAINST THE LORD, AND FORETELLS THE DEATH OF DAVID'S YOUNGEST SON. WHEN NATHAN LEAVES, DAVID IS ALONE IN HIS SHAME. HE IS TRULY SORRY FOR THE CRIME HE HAS COMMITTED, AND TURNS TO GOD IN PRAYER...

CREATE IN ME A CLEAN HEART, O GOD; AND RENEW A RIGHT SPIRIT WITHIN ME.

THE SAME DAY WORD COMES THAT THE KING'S INFANT SON IS ILL...AND DAVID RUSHES TO THE SICKROOM.

HOW IS HE?

THERE IS LITTLE HOPE.

DAVID IS SICK WITH SORROW. HE FASTS AND PRAYS... BUT ON THE SEVENTH DAY HIS CHILD DIES.

MEANWHILE JOAB, DAVID'S GENERAL, CONTINUES THE SIEGE AGAINST THE CITY OF RABBAH. TO HONOR DAVID, HE SENDS WORD FOR THE KING TO COME AND MAKE THE FINAL ATTACK. DAVID LEADS THE CHARGE-- AND THE CITY SURRENDERS.

RETURNING VICTORIOUS INTO JERUSALEM, DAVID IS GREETED WITH SHOUTS OF PRAISE. HE IS PLEASED AND PROUD-- ISRAEL IS STRONG, AND NO NATION WOULD DARE ATTACK IT, BUT...

DAVID DOES NOT REALIZE THAT TROUBLE BUILDING UP WITHIN HIS OWN PALACE WALLS WILL ENDANGER HIS THRONE.

SOON AFTER DAVID'S TRIUMPHAL RETURN, PRINCE ABSALOM MAKES A SPECIAL VISIT TO HIS FATHER.

IT'S SHEEPSHEARING TIME, AND I'M HAVING A BIG FEAST IN THE COUNTRY. WILL YOU HONOR MY GUESTS WITH YOUR PRESENCE?

THANK YOU, ABSALOM, BUT IF YOU ARE HAVING A BIG FEAST, I DON'T WANT TO ADD TO YOUR EXPENSES.

THEN MAY MY BROTHERS COME? PRINCE AMNON CAN REPRESENT YOU.

AMNON? I THOUGHT ABSALOM HATED HIM.

YES, I'M PLEASED THAT YOU WANT TO HONOR YOUR BROTHERS THIS WAY.

ABSALOM DOES HATE HIS OLDER HALF-BROTHER, AMNON, WHO HAS FIRST RIGHT TO DAVID'S THRONE. WHEN AMNON ACCEPTS THE INVITATION, ABSALOM CALLS IN HIS SERVANTS.

AMNON IS COMING TO THE FEAST. WHEN I GIVE THE WORD -- KILL HIM!

AT THE HEIGHT OF THE FEAST, AMNON IS KILLED... AFRAID FOR THEIR LIVES, THE REST OF THE BROTHERS FLEE INTO THE NIGHT...

341

A Prince's Command
FROM 2 SAMUEL 13:30—14:30

MESSENGERS BRING WORD TO THE PALACE IN JERUSALEM THAT KING DAVID'S SON, ABSALOM, HAS KILLED ALL OF HIS BROTHERS. STUNNED BY SHOCK AND GRIEF, DAVID FALLS TO THE GROUND--WEEPING. BUT HIGH ON THE CITY WALLS THE MAN IN THE TOWER KEEPS WATCH...

LOOK! A BAND OF MEN RIDING THIS WAY!

THE MEN ARE DAVID'S SONS AND THEIR SERVANTS.

AT FULL SPEED THEY RIDE INTO THE CITY AND RUSH TO THEIR FATHER.

MY SONS! THEY TOLD ME YOU WERE ALL KILLED! WHAT HAPPENED?

ABSALOM MURDERED AMNON -- THE REST OF US ESCAPED!

THANK GOD, YOU ARE SAFE -- BUT AMNON, MY FIRST-BORN IS DEAD! KILLED BY HIS OWN BROTHER! WHERE IS ABSALOM NOW?

HE FLED -- WE THINK HE WENT TO GESHUR.

FOR THREE YEARS DAVID GRIEVES FOR THE SON WHO RAN AWAY. FINALLY HE SENDS HIS GENERAL, JOAB, TO ABSALOM.

YOUR FATHER MISSES YOU, ABSALOM. HE HAS SENT ME TO BRING YOU BACK TO JERUSALEM.

I'M GLAD HE'S FORGIVEN ME.

343

FOR TWO YEARS ABSALOM LIVES IN JERUSALEM WITHOUT SEEING HIS FATHER. HE RESENTS THIS TREATMENT AND HIS ANGER GROWS UNTIL AT LAST HE CAN STAND IT NO LONGER. HE SENDS FOR JOAB. JOAB REFUSES TO COME. ABSALOM SENDS A SECOND TIME.

Treason?

FROM 2 SAMUEL 14:31—15:4

WHEN DAVID'S GENERAL, JOAB, REFUSES TO OBEY PRINCE ABSALOM'S REQUEST TO COME TO HIM, ABSALOM ORDERS JOAB'S GRAINFIELD SET ON FIRE. AT THE SIGHT OF THE BURNING FIELD JOAB SETS OUT AT ONCE FOR ABSALOM'S HOUSE...

HE MAY BE A PRINCE--BUT SOME DAY I'LL GET EVEN WITH HIM FOR THIS.

YOUR SERVANTS SET FIRE TO MY GRAIN. WHY?

I SENT FOR YOU--AND YOU REFUSED TO COME. I THOUGHT **THIS** WOULD BRING YOU.

I'M A PRINCE, AND I SHOULD BE TREATED LIKE MY BROTHERS. GO TO MY FATHER AND ASK HIM IF HE WILL SEE ME.

BUT... HE ASKED ME TO COME BACK TO JERUSALEM. IF HE WANTS TO PUNISH ME FOR WHAT I DID, LET HIM DO IT. IF NOT, THEN LET HIM TREAT ME LIKE A SON AGAIN.

JOAB CARRIES ABSALOM'S MESSAGE TO KING DAVID.

YOUR SON MISSES YOU — HE WISHES TO BE FORGIVEN AND WELCOMED BACK INTO THE FAMILY.

HE MISSES ME? NO MORE THAN I MISS HIM. TELL HIM TO COME TO ME.

ABSALOM PRETENDS TO BE HUMBLE AS HE BOWS BEFORE HIS FATHER--ASKING FORGIVE-NESS. BUT IN HIS HEART HE HAS AN EVIL PLAN.

RISE UP, ABSALOM. YOU ARE FORGIVEN. FROM NOW ON YOU WILL BE WELCOME AT THE PALACE AS A PRINCE OF ISRAEL.

349

MEANWHILE MORE AND MORE PEOPLE RUSH TO HEBRON.

WHAT'S THE EXCITEMENT?

ABSALOM HAS LED A REVOLT AGAINST DAVID. WE'RE GIVING OUR ALLEGIANCE TO ABSALOM.

ABSALOM IS FOR THE PEOPLE. THESE ARE GREAT DAYS FOR ISRAEL. COME ON -- JOIN US.

MY SHEEP -- I MUST TAKE CARE OF THEM FIRST.

INSTEAD OF JOINING THE CROWDS ON THE WAY TO HEBRON, THE FAITHFUL SHEPHERD RUNS NORTH -- UNTIL HE REACHES THE GATES OF DAVID'S CAPITAL, JERUSALEM.

OPEN UP -- THE KING'S LIFE IS IN DANGER!

THE PEOPLE HAVE REVOLTED... THEY ARE PROCLAIMING ABSALOM KING IN HEBRON!

MY SON -- HAS DONE **THIS** TO ME?

350

Council of War

FROM 2 SAMUEL 15:13—17:13

THE NEWS THAT HIS OWN SON, ABSALOM, HAS LED A REVOLT AGAINST HIM LEAVES DAVID IN A STATE OF SHOCK.

ABSALOM! HOW CAN I FIGHT MY OWN SON--MY OWN PEOPLE? WHOM CAN I COUNT ON TO STAND WITH ME?

YOUR FRIENDS WILL MAKE THEMSELVES KNOWN.

WE MUST ESCAPE BEFORE ABSALOM ATTACKS THE CITY! TELL MY FAMILY-- MY SERVANTS -- ALL WHO ARE LOYAL--TO GET READY TO LEAVE JERUSALEM!

AT DAWN DAVID LEADS HIS PEOPLE OUT OF THE CITY--AT THE LAST HOUSE HE STOPS TO WATCH HIS FOLLOWERS PASS BY.

IN THE PROCESSION ARE THE PRIESTS CARRYING GOD'S HOLY ARK.

STOP--TAKE IT BACK TO THE CITY. IF GOD WILLS IT, I WILL RETURN TO THE CITY AND WORSHIP AGAIN BEFORE HIS ARK.

THE NUMBER WHO CHOOSE TO JOIN DAVID GROWS WITH EACH PASSING HOUR. BUT DAVID SENDS ONE OF THEM BACK...

HUSHAI, YOU CAN SERVE ME BETTER IF YOU OFFER TO HELP ABSALOM. MAYBE YOU CAN KEEP HIM FROM FOLLOWING THE ADVICE OF THOSE WHO HAVE BETRAYED ME.

YOU ARE MY KING, AND I WILL SERVE IN ANY WAY YOU ASK.

HUSHAI RETURNS -- IN TIME TO SEE ABSALOM RIDE INTO THE CITY. IN THE CROWDS THERE ARE SHOUTS OF JOY AND PRAISE -- BUT THERE IS ALSO FEAR...

THIS MEANS WAR!

LIKE THE MAN IN THE CROWD, HUSHAI KNOWS THAT WAR WILL SOON BE UPON THEM. HE OFFERS HIS SERVICES TO ABSALOM -- AND ALONG WITH AHITHOPHEL IS CALLED TO THE FIRST COUNCIL OF WAR. AHITHOPHEL SPEAKS FIRST.

WE MUST ATTACK WHILE DAVID IS WEAK AND ON THE RUN.

NO, AHITHOPHEL'S ADVICE IS NOT GOOD. DAVID AND HIS MEN ARE ISRAEL'S BEST FIGHTERS. AND RIGHT NOW THEY ARE ANGRY AS BEARS ROBBED OF THEIR YOUNG. IF YOU ATTACK AND SUFFER ANY DEFEAT, THE PEOPLE WILL TURN AGAINST YOU. WAIT UNTIL YOU CAN CALL UP THOUSANDS OF MEN... THEN IF YOU, O KING, LEAD THEM...

Hide—out in a Well

FROM 2 SAMUEL 17:14–23

AHITHOPHEL HAS ADVISED ABSALOM TO ATTACK KING DAVID WHILE HE IS FLEEING FOR HIS LIFE. BUT HUSHAI -- SECRETLY WORKING FOR DAVID -- TELLS ABSALOM TO WAIT UNTIL HIS OWN FORCES ARE BETTER PREPARED.

NO! NO! HUSHAI'S ADVICE WILL HELP YOUR FATHER MORE THAN YOU. GIVE DAVID TIME TO GET HIS FORCES PREPARED, AND THE BATTLE IS HIS. REMEMBER -- DEFEAT MEANS DEATH TO ALL OF US!

BUT ABSALOM WILL NOT LISTEN. AHITHOPHEL IS SO SURE THE REBELLION WILL FAIL -- AND HE WILL DIE A TRAITOR'S DEATH -- THAT HE GOES HOME AND COMMITS SUICIDE.

MEANWHILE, BACK IN JERUSALEM, HUSHAI'S WELL-ORGANIZED PLAN IS BEING CARRIED OUT.

TWO OF OUR MEN ARE WAITING AT THE KIDRON FOUNTAIN. TELL THEM WHAT WE HAVE TOLD YOU. BE CAREFUL -- KING DAVID'S LIFE IS IN YOUR HANDS!

WITH A WATER JUG ON HER HEAD, THE GIRL WALKS BOLDLY OUT OF THE CITY GATE...

354

AND AT THE APPOINTED PLACE MEETS THE TWO MEN.

TELL KING DAVID NOT TO STOP UNTIL HE HAS REACHED THE OTHER SIDE OF THE JORDAN RIVER.

THE MEN LEAVE, BUT ON THE WAY...

DON'T LOOK NOW, BUT I THINK WE HAVE BEEN SEEN. LET'S PLAY IT SAFE AND HIDE OUT IN BAHURIM.

SPIES!

THE BOY RACES BACK TO THE CITY AND REPORTS WHAT HE HAS SEEN TO PRINCE ABSALOM.

FIND THOSE SPIES AND BRING THEM TO ME!

ABSALOM'S SOLDIERS FOLLOW THE TRAIL UNTIL THEY REACH A HOUSE IN BAHURIM...

WE'RE SEARCHING FOR SPIES...HAS ANYONE BEEN HERE?

YES, TWO MEN. BUT THEY LEFT-- IN THE DIRECTION OF THE RIVER.

THE SOLDIERS SEARCH THE HOUSE, BUT WHEN THEY FIND NOTHING, THEY MOVE ON.

COME UP-- THE SOLDIERS HAVE GONE.

EVEN ABSALOM'S MEN WOULDN'T KNOW THERE WAS A WELL HERE. I'M GLAD IT WAS A DRY ONE.

I'M PROUD TO HELP MY KING, BUT--GO-- THE SOLDIERS MIGHT RETURN.

THE MESSENGERS HURRY ON... AND THAT NIGHT DAVID AND HIS FOLLOWERS CROSS OVER THE JORDAN.

Father against Son

FROM 2 SAMUEL 17:24—18:9

ABSALOM'S SOLDIERS SEARCH FOR THE MESSENGERS WHO HAVE BEEN SENT TO WARN DAVID. WHEN THEY CANNOT FIND THEM, THEY RETURN TO JERUSALEM. MEANWHILE, DAVID AND HIS FOLLOWERS REACH THE CITY OF MAHANAIM.

HERE'S SOME FOOD AND BEDDING MY MASTER HAS SENT FOR KING DAVID AND HIS FRIENDS.

GOD BLESS YOU. TELL YOUR MASTER I WILL NOT FORGET HIS KINDNESS.

DAVID QUICKLY ORGANIZES HIS ARMY AND WAITS FOR THE MESSAGE HE EXPECTS — BUT DREADS.

PRINCE ABSALOM AND HIS FORCES HAVE CROSSED THE JORDAN RIVER!

THE ARMIES MEET HEAD-ON IN THE WOODS OF EPHRAIM. DAVID'S MEN ATTACK WITH SUCH FURY THAT ABSALOM'S ARMY IS THROWN INTO PANIC ...AND RETREATS.

THE BATTLE IS LOST. ABSALOM IS AFRAID THAT IF HE IS CAUGHT HE WILL SUFFER A TRAITOR'S DEATH. HE TRIES TO ESCAPE...

AND IS CAUGHT IN THE LOW-HANGING BRANCH OF AN OAK!

The King Returns

PRINCE ABSALOM'S REVOLT AGAINST HIS FATHER, KING DAVID, LEADS TO A TERRIBLE BATTLE IN THE WOODS OF EPHRAIM. WHEN ABSALOM SEES THAT THE FIGHT IS GOING AGAINST HIM, HE TRIES TO ESCAPE, BUT...

GENERAL JOAB! ABSALOM IS CAUGHT-- BACK THERE-- IN A TREE!

ABSALOM? WHY DIDN'T YOU KILL HIM ON THE SPOT!

KILL THE KING'S SON? NEVER! I HEARD DAVID TELL YOU AND THE OTHER LEADERS TO BE CAREFUL OF ABSALOM.

WE'RE WASTING TIME-- I'LL DO IT MYSELF!

MESSENGERS CARRY NEWS OF THE BATTLE TO DAVID.

MY SON, ABSALOM. IS HE ALL RIGHT?

MAY ALL THE KING'S ENEMIES BE AS THAT YOUNG MAN!

JOAB AND HIS ARMOR-BEARERS RUSH BACK TO THE TREE AND KILL ABSALOM. THE TRUMPET OF VICTORY IS SOUNDED-- THE BATTLE IS OVER!

BROKENHEARTED, DAVID CLIMBS TO THE LOOKOUT ABOVE THE GATE. ALONE, HE MOURNS FOR HIS SON.

O MY SON ABSALOM. WOULD I HAD DIED INSTEAD OF YOU. MY SON! MY SON!

IN HIS GRIEF DAVID TURNS HIS BACK ON THE MEN WHO WON THE VICTORY FOR HIM. FINALLY JOAB GOES TO SEE THE KING.

YOU ACT AS IF YOU WISH ABSALOM HAD WON THE VICTORY! HAVE YOU FORGOTTEN THE MEN WHO FOUGHT TO SAVE YOU-- YOUR FAMILY--AND YOUR KINGDOM? IF THIS KEEPS UP, ALL YOUR FRIENDS WILL TURN AGAINST YOU!

DAVID SEES THE TRUTH OF JOAB'S WORDS. HE MAKES PEACE WITH THE TRIBES THAT HAD SIDED WITH ABSALOM... AND GOES BACK TO JERUSALEM.

SOON AFTER THE ROYAL FAMILY IS SETTLED AGAIN IN THE PALACE, QUEEN BATH-SHEBA SPEAKS TO DAVID.

WHEN OUR SON, SOLOMON, WAS BORN, YOU PROMISED THAT HE WOULD BE KING AFTER YOU. BUT I FEAR HIS HALF-BROTHERS WILL CAUSE TROUBLE.

HAVE NO FEAR. SOLOMON WILL RULE ISRAEL.

YEARS PASS -- AND DAVID GROWS OLD. FINALLY WORD SPREADS THROUGHOUT JERUSALEM THAT THE KING'S HEALTH IS FAILING FAST. THE PEOPLE KNOW THAT DAVID HAS CHOSEN SOLOMON TO BE KING AND TO BUILD THE TEMPLE OF GOD. BUT THERE ARE RUMORS...

AND IN THE PALACE, ONE OF DAVID'S SONS, ADONIJAH, MEETS WITH THE HIGH PRIEST, ABIATHAR, AND GENERAL JOAB.

MY FATHER IS GROWING WEAKER -- AND THE TIME HAS COME FOR ME TO CARRY OUT OUR PLAN. BRING ALL THE KING'S SONS -- EXCEPT MY HALF-BROTHER, SOLOMON — AND MEET ME AT THE SERPENT'S STONE.

The Plot that Failed

FROM 1 KINGS 1:9–49

THE BOOKS, 1 AND 2 KINGS AND 2 CHRONICLES, RECORD THE HISTORY OF THE HEBREW EMPIRE THROUGH THE YEARS OF SOLOMON'S REIGN, THE DIVISION OF THE KINGDOM INTO TWO SEPARATE NATIONS, JUDAH AND ISRAEL-- AND THE FALL OF BOTH.

KING DAVID IS GROWING WEAKER... HIS OLDEST SON, ADONIJAH, KNOWS THAT IF HE IS TO ACCOMPLISH HIS PURPOSE, HE MUST ACT SWIFTLY. SECRETLY HE INVITES SOME OF HIS FRIENDS TO A FEAST OUTSIDE THE CITY... AND PROCLAIMS HIMSELF KING.

EAT AND BE MERRY — BEFORE THIS DAY IS OVER I WILL SIT ON THE THRONE OF ISRAEL. AND YOU, MY FRIENDS, WILL BE REWARDED FOR YOUR LOYALTY.

BUT WHILE ADONIJAH IS FEASTING, NATHAN, THE PROPHET OF GOD, IS TALKING WITH QUEEN BATH-SHEBA.

HAVE YOU HEARD--ADONIJAH HAS PROCLAIMED HIMSELF KING! IF YOU WOULD SAVE YOURSELF AND YOUR SON, SOLOMON, DO AS I SAY.

TELL ME-- AND I'LL DO IT.

FOLLOWING NATHAN'S ADVICE, SHE GOES AT ONCE TO DAVID.

MY LORD, YOU PROMISED THAT MY SON SOLOMON WOULD RULE AFTER YOU—BUT EVEN NOW HIS HALF-BROTHER, ADONIJAH, HAS DECLARED HIMSELF KING.

SEND FOR NATHAN AND ZADOK, THE PRIEST.

TAKE SOLOMON TO THE SACRED SPRING OF GIHON AND DECLARE HIM KING.

ZADOK AND NATHAN ACT AT ONCE... SOLOMON RIDES HIS FATHER'S MULE TO THE SPRING OF GIHON...

AND THERE HE IS MADE KING OF ISRAEL. THE TRUMPET SOUNDS...

GOD SAVE KING SOLOMON!

AS SOLOMON RETURNS TO THE CITY, THE PEOPLE GREET THEIR NEW KING WITH SHOUTS OF JOY.

SO GREAT IS THE NOISE OF THE CELEBRATION THAT IT REACHES ADONIJAH'S FEAST.

WHAT'S GOING ON IN THE CITY?

AT THAT MOMENT A MESSENGER ENTERS...

WHAT GOOD NEWS DO YOU HAVE FOR US?

THE NOISE YOU HEAR IS THE SHOUTING OF ALL JERUSALEM! DAVID HAS MADE SOLOMON KING.

KNOWING THAT THEY MAY BE BRANDED AS TRAITORS, ADONIJAH'S GUESTS FLEE IN TERROR.

THERE'S ONLY ONE CHANCE TO SAVE MY LIFE.

Death of a King

FROM 1 KINGS 1—5; 2 CHRONICLES 2:16

WHEN PRINCE ADONIJAH LEARNS THAT HIS FATHER, KING DAVID, HAS MADE SOLOMON KING OF ALL ISRAEL, ADONIJAH KNOWS THAT HIS OWN PLOT TO STEAL THE THRONE HAS FAILED. IN FEAR FOR HIS LIFE, HE RUNS TO THE TABERNACLE AND GRABS HOLD OF THE HORNS ON THE ALTAR OF SACRIFICE.

I WILL NOT LET GO UNTIL SOLOMON PROMISES NOT TO KILL ME.

SOLOMON AGREES TO SPARE ADONIJAH'S LIFE **IF** HE PROVES HIMSELF WORTHY OF THE KING'S TRUST. ADONIJAH PROMISES AND IS BROUGHT BEFORE HIS YOUNG HALF-BROTHER.

MY LORD AND KING!

SOLOMON LATER BELIEVES BOTH ADONIJAH AND GENERAL JOAB TO BE DISLOYAL, AND THEY ARE EXECUTED.

ONE DAY DAVID CALLS SOLOMON TO HIM.

MY SON, I AM DYING. THIS IS MY LAST COUNSEL TO YOU: BE STRONG AND SHOW YOURSELF A MAN. KEEP GOD'S COMMANDMENTS AND WALK IN HIS WAYS...

AND IS BURIED IN A TOMB WITHIN THE WALLS OF JERUSALEM, THE CAPITAL OF HIS KINGDOM.

THEN DAVID, WHO RULED ISRAEL FOR FORTY YEARS, DIES...

ALL ISRAEL MOURNS THE DEATH OF THE SHEPHERD BOY WHO BUILT ISRAEL INTO A MIGHTY EMPIRE AND WHOSE FAITH IN GOD IS REVEALED IN ONE OF HIS PSALMS.

Psalm 23

THE LORD IS MY SHEPHERD;
  SO I SHALL LACK NOTHING.
HE MAKES ME LIE DOWN IN
  GREEN PASTURES;
HE LEADS ME BESIDE
  STILL WATERS.
HE RESTORES MY VERY SELF.
HE GUIDES ME IN CORRECT
  PATHS FOR HIS NAME'S SAKE.
YES, THOUGH I WALK THROUGH
  THE VALLEY OF THE
  SHADOW OF DEATH,
I WILL NOT FEAR HARM,
FOR YOU ARE WITH ME.
YOUR ROD AND STAFF
  ARE A COMFORT TO ME.

YOU LAY OUT A TABLE BEFORE
  ME IN THE PRESENCE OF
  MY ENEMIES.
YOU'VE ANOINTED MY HEAD
  WITH OIL;
MY CUP RUNS OVER.
SURELY GOODNESS AND
  FAITHFULNESS WILL FOLLOW
  ME ALL THE DAYS OF
  MY LIFE,
AND I WILL LIVE IN THE
  HOUSE OF THE LORD
  FOREVER.

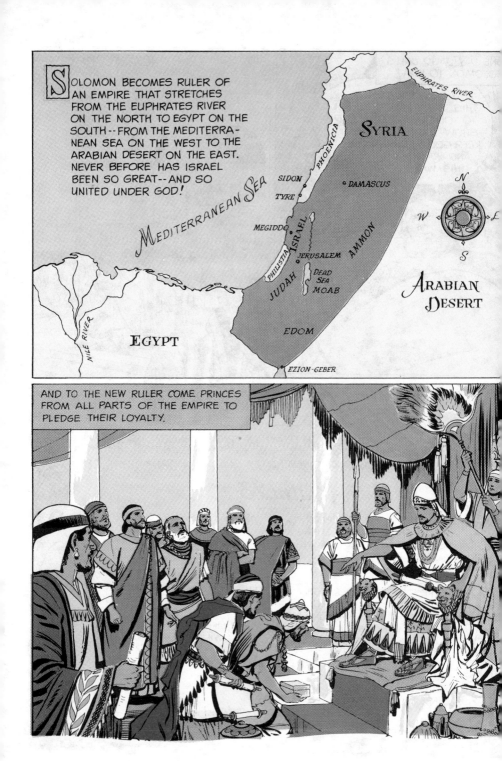

SOLOMON BECOMES RULER OF AN EMPIRE THAT STRETCHES FROM THE EUPHRATES RIVER ON THE NORTH TO EGYPT ON THE SOUTH--FROM THE MEDITERRANEAN SEA ON THE WEST TO THE ARABIAN DESERT ON THE EAST. NEVER BEFORE HAS ISRAEL BEEN SO GREAT--AND SO UNITED UNDER GOD!

AND TO THE NEW RULER COME PRINCES FROM ALL PARTS OF THE EMPIRE TO PLEDGE THEIR LOYALTY.

THE PEOPLE ARE HAPPY. ISRAEL IS AT PEACE. SOLOMON ESTABLISHES GOOD RELATIONS WITH MANY OF THE NEIGHBORING COUNTRIES BY MARRYING PRINCESSES OF THOSE NATIONS. RULERS OF THE COUNTRIES CONQUERED BY DAVID PAY TRIBUTE MONEY TO SOLOMON'S TREASURY. SO BEGINS THE GOLDEN AGE OF ISRAEL.

TO LAUNCH HIS FIRST GREAT BUILDING PROJECT, SOLOMON SENDS A MESSENGER TO HIS FATHER'S OLD FRIEND, KING HIRAM OF TYRE.

KING SOLOMON SENDS HIS GREETINGS--AND ASKS IF YOU WILL SEND HIM CEDAR AND CYPRESS LOGS AND SKILLED WORKERS TO HELP HIM BUILD A TEMPLE TO GOD IN JERUSALEM.

BLESSED BE THE LORD FOR GIVING MY FRIEND DAVID SUCH A WISE SON. TELL YOUR KING I WILL GIVE HIM WHAT HE ASKS IN EXCHANGE FOR WHEAT AND OIL, WHICH ARE SCARCE IN OUR COUNTRY.

THE DEAL IS MADE--AND SOON MEN BY THE THOUSANDS ARE ORDERED TO WORK IN THE FORESTS OF LEBANON, CUTTING CEDAR TREES FOR SOLOMON'S TEMPLE.

ON THE SEACOAST WEST OF THE LEBANON FORESTS THE LOGS ARE TIED TOGETHER TO FORM GIANT RAFTS. THESE ARE FLOATED DOWN TO ISRAEL.

AT THE SEAPORT OF JOPPA THE LOG RAFTS ARE BROKEN UP, AND THE TIMBERS ARE DRAGGED MORE THAN THIRTY MILES ACROSS RUGGED COUNTRY TO JERUSALEM.

NEAR JERUSALEM, THOUSANDS OF MEN TOIL IN THE GREAT QUARRIES.

CHISEL A BIT FROM THIS SIDE. EVERY STONE MUST BE MADE TO FIT PERFECTLY.

MEANWHILE, WOOD CARVERS AND GOLDBEATERS ARE AT WORK IN JERUSALEM.

THESE DOORS WOULD BE BEAUTIFUL JUST AS THEY ARE.

COVERED WITH GOLD, THEY'LL BE THE FINEST IN THE WORLD.

SLOWLY, CAREFULLY, FOR SEVEN LONG YEARS THE WORK GOES ON, UNTIL AT LAST, THE MOST BEAUTIFUL BUILDING IN ALL ISRAEL IS FINISHED...

The Temple of God

FROM 1 KINGS 8:1—10:1

AFTER SEVEN LONG YEARS OF HARD WORK, THE MAGNIFICENT TEMPLE OF GOD IS COMPLETED. MEN, WOMEN, AND CHILDREN FROM ALL CORNERS OF ISRAEL CROWD INTO JERUSALEM TO WATCH THE PRIESTS CARRY THE SACRED ARK INTO THE TEMPLE. INSIDE, IN THE HOLY OF HOLIES-- A DARK, WINDOWLESS, HEAVILY CURTAINED ROOM-- THE ARK IS CAREFULLY PLACED BENEATH THE PROTECTING WINGS OF TWO FIFTEEN-FOOT GOLDEN CHERUBIM.

THEN, BEFORE ALL THE PEOPLE OF ISRAEL, SOLOMON KNEELS IN PRAYER.

O LORD, THERE IS NO GOD LIKE YOU! FORGIVE AND GUIDE YOUR PEOPLE AS YOU GUIDED MOSES WHO BROUGHT US OUT OF SLAVERY IN EGYPT.

BUT SOLOMON'S BUILDING PROGRAM DOES NOT END WITH THE TEMPLE. SOON A LARGE PALACE IS UNDER CONSTRUCTION.

O SOLOMON, IT WILL BE BEAUTIFUL. CEDAR-- BRONZE AND GOLD!

I MEAN TO MAKE JERUSALEM THE MOST BEAUTIFUL CITY IN THE WORLD.

AND RICHES KEEP POURING IN FROM MANY COUNTRIES. SHIPS FROM ARABIA AND AFRICA BRING RARE AND PRECIOUS GIFTS.

PEACOCKS --IVORY--OF WHAT USE ARE THEY?

WHEN YOU'RE AS RICH AS SOLOMON, THINGS DON'T HAVE TO BE USEFUL.

BUT NOT EVERYONE IN ISRAEL IS RICH. OUTSIDE THE CITY OF JERUSALEM PEOPLE ARE BEGINNING TO COMPLAIN...

THERE! THAT'S MY SHARE OF GRAIN FOR KING SOLOMON'S HORSES.

HORSES! BETWEEN FEEDING HIS FOREIGN WIVES, HIS SERVANTS, AND HIS HORSES, THERE'S LITTLE LEFT FOR THE POOR-- LIKE US!

STILL THE BUILDING PLANS GO ON...

OUR CARAVANS TRAVEL NORTH, SOUTH, EAST, AND WEST-- BUT WE HAVE MISSED ONE VITAL TRADE ROUTE.

WHERE?

THE SEA! I HAVE DECIDED TO BUILD MERCHANT SHIPS TO SAIL BEYOND THE RED SEA!

THE FLEET IS BUILT. ITS SHIPS BRING TREASURES INTO JERUSALEM AND CARRY AWAY WITH THEM STORIES OF THE CITY'S BEAUTY AND THE RULER'S WISDOM. THE STORIES REACH FAR AND WIDE — EVEN TO THE KINGDOM OF SHEBA IN THE ARABIAN PENINSULA.

SOLOMON! SOLOMON! ALL I HEAR ARE TALES OF HIS WEALTH AND WISDOM. I'M GOING TO JERUSALEM AND FIND OUT FOR MYSELF WHETHER THEY ARE TRUE!

A Queen's Visit

FROM 1 KINGS 10:2—11:8

THE FAME OF SOLOMON'S WEALTH AND WISDOM SPREADS FAR AND WIDE. IN THE ARABIAN PENINSULA, THE QUEEN OF SHEBA IS SO CURIOUS THAT SHE SETS OUT ON A TRIP TO JERUSALEM TO SEE FOR HERSELF WHETHER THE STORIES ARE TRUE.

WHAT A BEAUTIFUL CITY! IT SITS ON THE HILL LIKE A GLISTENING CROWN.

INSIDE THE CITY, SHE IS EVEN MORE IMPRESSED WITH THE THRONE OF ISRAEL'S KING.

I HAVE HEARD SO MUCH OF YOUR WEALTH AND WISDOM THAT I HAD TO SEE YOU.

WELCOME, GRACIOUS QUEEN. ONCE I PRAYED TO GOD TO MAKE ME WISE. I HOPE YOU FIND THAT HE HAS.

SOLOMON ANSWERS ALL OF THE QUEEN'S QUESTIONS -- THEN HE TAKES HER FOR A TOUR OF THE CITY TO SEE THE BEAUTIFUL TEMPLE OF GOD-THE GIANT MARBLE PALACES- STABLES HOLDING THOUSANDS OF FINE HORSES.

JERUSALEM HAS OUTGROWN ITS OLD WALLS OF DEFENSE, SO WE ARE BUILDING NEW ONES.

THAT FOREMAN SEEMS TO KNOW WHAT HE IS DOING.

HOW OBSERVING YOU ARE! THAT IS JEROBOAM, MY CHIEF LABOR FOREMAN.

WHEN HER CURIOSITY IS SATISFIED, THE QUEEN OF SHEBA PRESENTS SOLOMON WITH GIFTS OF GOLD, RARE SPICES, PRECIOUS STONES — AND DEPARTS FOR HER HOME.

SOLOMON CONTINUES TO BUILD -- BUT NOW THE PEOPLE ARE WORRIED AND SHOCKED BY WHAT THEY SEE.

ANOTHER TEMPLE TO THE IDOL OF ONE OF THE KING'S FOREIGN WIVES. AND OUR TAXES USED TO BUILD IT!

THOSE HEATHEN TEMPLES MAKE IT CLEAR THAT SOLOMON IS NO LONGER ASKING GOD FOR GUIDANCE. THERE'S TROUBLE AHEAD FOR ISRAEL...

AHIJAH TEARS THE ROBE INTO TWELVE STRIPS.

HERE, TAKE THESE TEN PIECES. THEY REPRESENT THE TEN TRIBES OF ISRAEL OVER WHICH YOU WILL RULE WHEN SOLOMON DIES. THE OTHER TWO TRIBES WILL BE GIVEN TO SOLOMON'S SON.

SOLOMON FLIES INTO A RAGE WHEN HE LEARNS OF AHIJAH'S PROPHECY.

I MADE JEROBOAM A LEADER-- NOW HE IS USING HIS POSITION TO TURN PEOPLE AGAINST ME! FIND HIM AND KILL HIM!

BUT FRIENDS WARN JEROBOAM-- AND HE ESCAPES INTO EGYPT.

I'LL STAY HERE UNTIL SOLOMON DIES. THEN WE'LL SEE IF AHIJAH SPOKE THE TRUTH ABOUT MY RULING THE NORTHERN TRIBES OF ISRAEL.

REPORTS OF YOUR PEOPLE'S COMPLAINTS HAVE BEEN REACHING US FOR SOME TIME.

BUT SOLOMON CONTINUES TO LIVE IN LUXURY -- AND SO FAR REMOVED FROM HIS PEOPLE THAT THEIR COMPLAINTS DO NOT REACH HIM. HE EVEN IGNORES AHIJAH'S PROPHECY AND GOD'S WARNING THAT THE KINGDOM WILL BE DIVIDED BECAUSE HE WORSHIPS FALSE GODS.

AT LAST HE EVEN JOINS HIS FOREIGN WIVES IN THEIR WORSHIP OF HEATHEN IDOLS.

JUST TO PLEASE ME, PRAY TO MY GOD, SOLOMON.

IT CAN DO NO HARM--I STILL PRAY EVERY DAY TO THE GOD OF ISRAEL.

FIRST THE KING--AND NOW THE PEOPLE. WORSHIP HEATHEN IDOLS. NO COUNTRY THAT TURNS AWAY FROM GOD CAN REMAIN STRONG AND FREE. ISRAEL IS DOOMED.

THEN SOLOMON DIES! WITH GOD'S HELP HE HAD BUILT ISRAEL INTO A STRONG NATION. BUT IN HIS GREED FOR MORE WEALTH AND POWER HE HAD TURNED AWAY FROM GOD--AND HIS MIGHTY KINGDOM BEGINS TO CRUMBLE...

WHILE ISRAEL MOURNS THE DEATH OF ITS KING, A MESSENGER CARRIES THE NEWS OF HIS DEATH TO EGYPT.

JEROBOAM, I BRING NEWS! KING SOLOMON IS DEAD. HIS SON, REHOBOAM, HAS TAKEN HIS PLACE. THE PEOPLE WANT YOU TO COME HOME AND PRESENT THEIR CASE TO THE NEW KING.

I'LL GO AT ONCE!

The Kingdom Is Divided

FROM 1 KINGS 12:4–27

THIS IS A MESSAGE FROM GOD! YOU MEN OF JUDAH SHALL NOT FIGHT YOUR BROTHERS OF ISRAEL. RETURN EVERY MAN TO HIS OWN HOUSE.

WHO IS THIS MAN WHO GIVES **US** ORDERS?

SHEMAIAH, A PROPHET OF GOD. I, FOR ONE, WILL NOT DISOBEY ORDERS FROM GOD.

REHOBOAM IS AFRAID TO DEFY THE PROPHET, SO THE ARMY BREAKS UP AND GOES HOME. BUT IN THE NORTH KING JEROBOAM KNOWS THAT REHOBOAM WILL STOP AT NOTHING TO GET HIS KINGDOM BACK.

KING JEROBOAM, DO YOU KNOW THAT PEOPLE ARE GOING TO JERUSALEM TO WORSHIP IN THE TEMPLE?

YES, AND REHOBOAM WILL DO HIS BEST TO TURN THEM AGAINST ME.

THEY'RE GOING TO JERUSALEM, BECAUSE THERE IS NO TEMPLE HERE.

I KNOW-- I MUST KEEP THEM AWAY FROM JERUSALEM AND REHOBOAM-- AND I THINK I KNOW HOW TO DO IT!

Two Kingdoms

When Saul is anointed Israel's first king, all twelve tribes are considered one nation. After Solomon's reign, the kingdom is divided and each kingdom has its own kings.

Saul
↓
David
↓
Solomon

↙ ↘

Israel	**Judah**
Northern Kingdom	Southern Kingdom
10 tribes	2 tribes (Judah and Benjamin)
Has 19 kings	20 kings
No godly kings	Has 8 kings that please God:

Asa
Jehoshaphat
Joash (p. 440)
Amaziah
Azariah (Uzziah)
Jotham
Hezekiah (p. 449)
Josiah (p. 458)

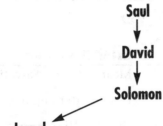

DO YOU PROMISE TO OBEY GOD'S LAW AND RULE YOUR PEOPLE ACCORDING TO HIS WORD?

I PROMISE!

▶ Josiah is 8 years old when he becomes king.

▶ Jehoshaphat tries to abolish idol worship and teach the people God's laws.

As a baby, Joash is hidden in the temple. He becomes king at age 7, and rules with the help of the High Priest, Jehoiada.

▶ Hezekiah reopens the temple and destroys many idols.

Did You Know?

Two Prophets—The Same but Different

In 1 and 2 Kings, we read about two men who are called by God to be prophets in Northern Israel. Their names are Elijah and Elisha. Sometimes it's easy to mix them up, but even though they basically have the same job, God uses them in different ways.

Elijah (See p. 389-412)	**Elisha** (See p. 402-435)
Means "The Lord is my God"	Means "God is Salvation"
Lives 800 years before Jesus	Comes after Elijah
Wears hairy clothes (2 King 1:8)	Wears Elijah's mantle (p. 402)
A loner and an outsider	Welcomed by everyone
Performs many miracles	Performs many miracles
Lives in caves (1 Kings 17:3; 19:9)	Lives in a house (2 King 6:32)
Confronts kings	Advises kings
Brings judgement	Brings compassion
Carried away in whirlwind (2 Kings 2:1-11)	Dies a natural death

Elisha's bones bring a dead man back to life (2 Kings 13:21)

ONLY GOD CAN GRANT YOUR WISH. YOU'LL HAVE TO WAIT AND SEE WHAT HAPPENS...

Idol Worship in Israel

FROM 1 KINGS 12:28—16:34

KING JEROBOAM RULES THE NORTHERN TRIBES, KNOWN AS ISRAEL, AND KING REHOBOAM RULES THE SOUTHERN KINGDOM OF JUDAH.

Mediterranean Sea

ISRAEL

JUDAH MOAB

EGYPT EDOM

KING JEROBOAM IS AFRAID THAT IF HIS PEOPLE GO TO JERUSALEM TO WORSHIP IN THE TEMPLE, KING REHOBOAM WILL WIN THEM BACK TO HIS KINGDOM. TO PREVENT THIS, JEROBOAM MAKES TWO GOLDEN CALVES...

YEARS AGO WHEN OUR PEOPLE ESCAPED FROM EGYPT, THEY WORSHIPED THIS GOD. WORSHIP IT NOW AND YOU WILL NOT NEED TO MAKE THE LONG, HARD TRIP TO JERUSALEM.

HAVING GIVEN THE PEOPLE IDOLS TO WORSHIP, JEROBOAM FEELS THAT ALL IS WELL IN HIS KINGDOM, UNTIL ONE DAY...

OUR SON IS VERY ILL, JEROBOAM. I'M WORRIED.

SO AM I. IF ONLY I KNEW -- BUT I KNOW SOMEONE WHO DOES--

AHIJAH, THE PROPHET! HE TOLD ME I WOULD BE KING. HE KNOWS WHAT WILL HAPPEN. DISGUISE YOURSELF SO THAT HE WILL NOT KNOW YOU AND GO TO HIM.

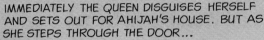

IMMEDIATELY THE QUEEN DISGUISES HERSELF AND SETS OUT FOR AHIJAH'S HOUSE. BUT AS SHE STEPS THROUGH THE DOOR...

I AM BLIND--BUT I KNOW WHO YOU ARE AND WHY YOU HAVE COME! TELL YOUR HUSBAND, JEROBOAM, THAT HE HAS DONE EVIL--AND EVIL WILL COME TO HIM. HIS CHILD WILL DIE--AND ONE DAY THE PEOPLE OF ISRAEL WILL BE SCATTERED IN OTHER LANDS BECAUSE THEY HAVE WORSHIPED IDOLS.

THE FIRST PART OF AHIJAH'S PROPHECY COMES TRUE AT ONCE-- WHEN THE QUEEN RETURNS HOME SHE FINDS HER SON DEAD! BUT JEROBOAM IS NOT WISE ENOUGH TO HEED THIS WARNING. HE CONTINUES TO LEAD HIS PEOPLE IN IDOL WORSHIP, AND EVERY KING OF ISRAEL AFTER HIM FOLLOWS HIS EVIL PRACTICE. AT LAST KING AHAB COMES TO THE THRONE, AND...

ONE DAY A CARAVAN ENTERS SAMARIA, THE CAPITAL OF NORTHERN ISRAEL, WHERE KING AHAB HAS HIS PALACE.

THAT'S A RICH CARAVAN-- WONDER WHERE IT'S FROM AND WHO CAN AFFORD TO TRAVEL IN SUCH STYLE?

IT'S AHAB'S NEW WIFE-- JEZEBEL -- THE DAUGHTER OF THE HEATHEN KING OF TYRE.

387

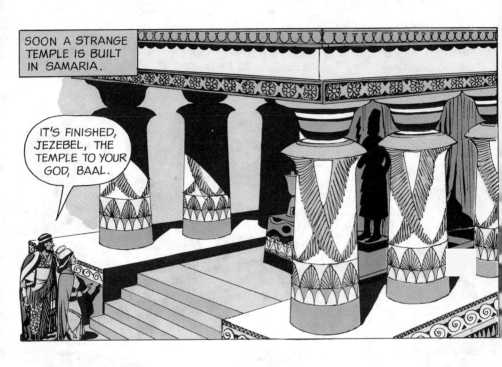

SOON A STRANGE TEMPLE IS BUILT IN SAMARIA.

IT'S FINISHED, JEZEBEL, THE TEMPLE TO YOUR GOD, BAAL.

MY GOD? YOUR GOD, AHAB, AND EVERYBODY'S GOD. ONLY BAAL SHALL BE WORSHIPED WHERE I AM QUEEN.

THAT WON'T BE EASY --THERE ARE STILL PEOPLE IN ISRAEL WHO WORSHIP ISRAEL'S GOD.

THEY'LL WORSHIP ISRAEL'S GOD NO LONGER-- I HAVE ORDERED THEM PUT TO DEATH!

A Prophet Speaks

FROM 1 KINGS 17:1–7

Challenge on Mt. Carmel

FROM 1 KINGS 18:17–37

MONTHS GO BY AND STILL THERE IS NO RAIN IN ISRAEL. AT LAST KING AHAB HIMSELF IS FORCED TO SEARCH THE COUNTRY TO FIND PASTURES FOR HIS ANIMALS. MEANTIME GOD SENDS THE PROPHET, ELIJAH, TO SEE THE KING. THE TWO MEET.

ELIJAH! IS IT YOU -- THE ONE WHO HAS CAUSED US SO MUCH TROUBLE?

IT IS NOT **I** WHO BROUGHT DROUGHT TO ISRAEL, BUT YOU, O KING. IT IS **YOU** WHO HAVE BROKEN GOD'S COMMANDMENTS AND WORSHIPED BAAL.

SEND FOR THE PROPHETS OF BAAL -- ALL 450 OF THEM -- AND THE LEADERS OF ISRAEL. THEN MEET ME ON MOUNT CARMEL.

AHAB IS SO AWED BY THE AUTHORITY WITH WHICH ELIJAH SPEAKS THAT HE DOES AS THE PROPHET COMMANDS. SOON A GREAT CROWD GATHERS ON TOP OF THE MOUNTAIN BY THE SEA.

PEOPLE OF ISRAEL! HOW LONG WILL YOU WANDER BACK AND FORTH BETWEEN THE LORD AND BAAL? IF BAAL IS GOD, WORSHIP HIM. IF THE LORD IS GOD, WORSHIP HIM AND HIM ONLY. BUT TODAY, YOU MUST CHOOSE.

LET ALL OF BAAL'S PROPHETS MAKE AN OFFERING AND PRAY TO HIM. I, ALONE, WILL PRAY TO THE LORD. THE GOD WHO ANSWERS WITH FIRE IS THE REAL GOD.

THAT'S A REAL TEST.

FAIR ENOUGH -- BUT IF ELIJAH FAILS, HE'LL LOSE HIS LIFE. AHAB WILL SEE TO THAT.

THE PROPHETS OF BAAL ARE FORCED TO ACCEPT THE CHALLENGE. WITH GREAT CEREMONY THEY PREPARE THE SACRIFICE... AND BEGIN TO CHANT AND CALL UPON THEIR GOD.

AS THE HOURS PASS THEY SING LOUDER AND LOUDER.

CALL A LITTLE LOUDER-- PERHAPS BAAL IS TALKING --OR OFF ON A JOURNEY-- OR ASLEEP.

BY MIDAFTERNOON THE PROPHETS ARE STILL CALLING UPON BAAL TO SEND DOWN FIRE-- BUT THERE IS NO ANSWER. AT LAST THEY GIVE UP.

THEN ELIJAH BUILDS AN ALTAR TO GOD.

WHEN IT IS FINISHED, AND THE SACRIFICE PREPARED, ELIJAH ORDERS MEN TO POUR WATER OVER IT.

POUR ON MORE WATER. FILL THE TRENCH WITH IT.

THEN--BEFORE THE WATER-SOAKED ALTAR--ELIJAH PRAYS.

HEAR ME, O LORD, HEAR ME, THAT THE PEOPLE OF ISRAEL MAY KNOW THAT YOU ARE THE LORD GOD.

THEN ELIJAH CLIMBS TO A PEAK ON THE MOUNTAIN TO PRAY. HE SENDS HIS SERVANT TO WATCH THE HORIZON.

GO UP A LITTLE HIGHER AND LOOK TOWARD THE SEA. TELL ME WHAT YOU SEE.

SIX TIMES THE SERVANT LOOKS OUT TOWARD THE SEA, AND REPORTS THAT HE SEES NOTHING. BUT WHEN ELIJAH SENDS HIM BACK THE SEVENTH TIME...

I SAW A CLOUD --NO LARGER THAN A MAN'S HAND.

RUN. TELL KING AHAB TO GET INTO HIS CHARIOT AND HURRY TO THE CITY BEFORE THE RAIN STOPS HIM.

ELIJAH IS SO EXCITED ABOUT HIS VICTORY OVER BAAL AND THE COMING RAIN THAT HE STARTS RUNNING FOR THE CITY. GOD GIVES HIM STRENGTH TO OUTRUN EVEN THE KING'S CHARIOT.

IN THE HOMES OF ISRAEL, THERE IS JOY-- THANKSGIVING -- AND REPENTANCE.

RAIN AT LAST! THE LORD BE PRAISED!

YES, IT WAS THE LORD WHO ANSWERED WITH FIRE! WE SHOULD NEVER HAVE WORSHIPED BAAL.

BUT IN THE PALACE QUEEN JEZEBEL IS FURIOUS...

WHEN THE PEOPLE SAW THE FIRE FROM GOD, THEY TURNED ON THE PROPHETS OF BAAL AND KILLED THEM. ELIJAH---

ELIJAH! ELIJAH! THAT'S ALL I HEAR! WELL, I'LL HEAR HIS NAME NO MORE!

SHE CALLS FOR A MESSENGER.

GO TO ELIJAH AND TELL HIM THAT BY THIS TIME TOMORROW HE WILL BE AS THOSE PROPHETS HE HAD PUT TO DEATH ON MOUNT CARMEL...

A Voice in the Mountain
FROM 1 KINGS 19:3–18

THEN, HUNGRY AND TIRED, ELIJAH FALLS ASLEEP. WHILE HE IS SLEEPING AN ANGEL APPEARS WITH BREAD AND WATER.

WAKE UP, ELIJAH, AND EAT.

ELIJAH IS ENCOURAGED BY THE FACT THAT GOD IS TAKING CARE OF HIM. AFTER HE EATS AND RESTS, HE CONTINUES HIS JOURNEY...

AND FORTY DAYS LATER HE REACHES MOUNT SINAI WHERE GOD TALKED TO MOSES.

I PRAY THAT I, TOO, MAY RECEIVE A MESSAGE FROM GOD ON THIS MOUNTAIN.

SUDDENLY A GREAT STORM STRIKES. THE WIND HURLS ROCKS DOWN THE MOUNTAIN-- AN EARTHQUAKE SHAKES THE GROUND ON WHICH ELIJAH STANDS -- AND LIGHTNING SPLITS THE SKY! THE POWER OF GOD IS REVEALED IN THE STORM--BUT THERE IS NO MESSAGE.

THEN, IN THE QUIETNESS AFTER THE STORM, ELIJAH HEARS THE STILL, SMALL VOICE OF GOD.

ELIJAH, WHAT ARE YOU DOING HERE?

O LORD, THE PEOPLE OF ISRAEL DO NOT SERVE THEE. THEY WORSHIP IDOLS. THEY HAVE KILLED ALL OF YOUR OTHER PROPHETS--AND NOW THEY WANT TO KILL ME.

BUT GOD TELLS ELIJAH THERE IS WORK FOR HIM TO DO IN ISRAEL. SO--HIS COURAGE RENEWED-- ELIJAH STARTS BACK.

O GOD, I AM READY NOW TO FACE ANY DANGER.

Forged Letters

FROM 1 KINGS 19:19–21; 21:1–8

ELIJAH RETURNS TO ISRAEL TO SERVE AS GOD'S PROPHET. PASSING BY A FIELD HE STOPS AND THROWS HIS CLOAK OVER A YOUNG FARMER'S SHOULDERS.

ELIJAH! YOUR CLOAK! DOES THIS MEAN THAT YOU ARE CALLING **ME** TO BE A PROPHET?

YES, ELISHA, YOU HAVE BEEN APPOINTED BY GOD TO BE HIS SPOKESMAN IN ISRAEL.

WAIT--LET ME GO HOME AND SAY GOOD-BYE TO MY MOTHER AND FATHER; THEN I'LL GO WITH YOU.

OF COURSE--BUT JOIN ME SOON, FOR THERE IS WORK TO BE DONE FOR GOD.

SO ELISHA RETURNS HOME AND GIVES A FAREWELL FEAST FOR HIS FAMILY AND FRIENDS.

YOU'RE GIVING UP A SAFE LIFE FOR A DANGEROUS ONE, ELISHA.

I KNOW, BUT GOD HAS CALLED ME, AND I MUST OBEY.

I'M PROUD OF YOU, SON.

ELISHA GOES TO WORK WITH ELIJAH, AND WHILE THEY ARE TRAINING OTHER PROPHETS, KING AHAB MAKES A SURPRISE VISIT TO ONE OF HIS SUBJECTS.

NABOTH, I WANT TO BUY THIS VINEYARD. OR, IF YOU LIKE, I'LL GIVE YOU ANOTHER FOR IT.

I'M SORRY, O KING, BUT OUR FAMILY HAS OWNED THIS VINEYARD FOR MANY YEARS. IT WOULD NOT BE RIGHT TO SELL IT TO SOMEONE OUTSIDE THE FAMILY.

YOU MAY ALSO FIND THAT IT IS NOT RIGHT TO DISPLEASE YOUR KING!

LIKE A SPOILED CHILD WHO CANNOT HAVE HIS OWN WAY, AHAB RETURNS TO THE PALACE.

WHAT IS THE MATTER? ARE YOU ILL?

NO--I WANT NABOTH'S VINEYARD, BUT HE WON'T SELL IT TO ME.

WON'T? ARE YOU KING OF ISRAEL, OR AREN'T YOU?

BUT DON'T WORRY, I'LL GET THE VINEYARD FOR YOU.

QUICKLY JEZEBEL WRITES SOME LETTERS AND SIGNS THE KING'S NAME TO THEM.

DELIVER THESE TO THE ELDERS AND NOBLES OF THE CITY.

The Price of a Vineyard

FROM 1 KINGS 21:9—22:29

QUEEN JEZEBEL SIGNED KING AHAB'S NAME TO LETTERS SHE SENT TO THE ELDERS AND NOBLES OF THE CITY. WHEN THE MEN RECEIVE THE MESSAGES...

THIS SAYS WE ARE TO ACCUSE NABOTH OF CURSING GOD AND THE KING--AND TO HAVE HIM STONED TO DEATH.

NABOTH? HE'S A GOOD MAN. THIS LOOKS LIKE THE WORK OF JEZEBEL.

RIGHT--THE MESSENGER SAID THE LETTER CAME FROM THE QUEEN HERSELF.

DO WE DARE DISOBEY THESE ORDERS? THEY CAME FROM THE QUEEN!

NOT IF WE VALUE OUR LIVES. NO MAN CAN SAVE NABOTH IF JEZEBEL WANTS HIS LIFE.

405

406

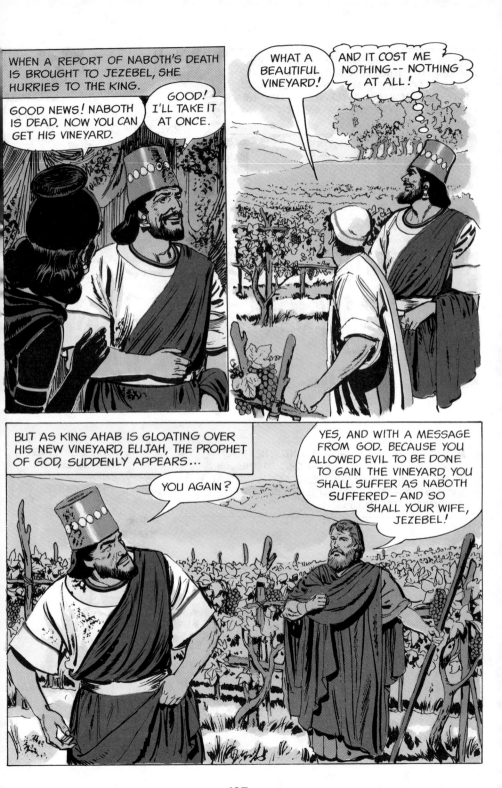

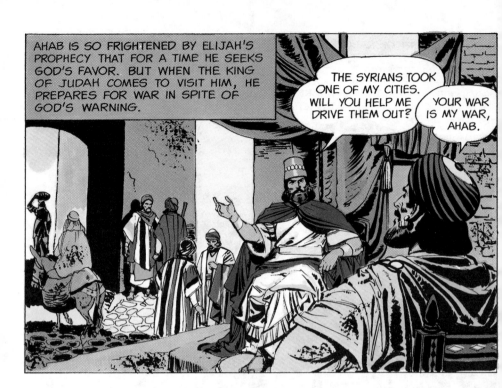

AHAB IS SO FRIGHTENED BY ELIJAH'S PROPHECY THAT FOR A TIME HE SEEKS GOD'S FAVOR. BUT WHEN THE KING OF JUDAH COMES TO VISIT HIM, HE PREPARES FOR WAR IN SPITE OF GOD'S WARNING.

THE SYRIANS TOOK ONE OF MY CITIES. WILL YOU HELP ME DRIVE THEM OUT?

YOUR WAR IS MY WAR, AHAB.

THE ARMIES ARE FORMED, AND THE TWO KINGS LEAD THEIR FORCES ACROSS THE JORDAN RIVER TOWARD THE CONQUERED CITY. BUT AT THE THOUGHT OF THE COMING BATTLE, AHAB BECOMES FRIGHTENED.

I'LL DISGUISE MYSELF SO THE ENEMY WON'T RECOGNIZE ME!

The Last Journey

FROM 1 KINGS 22:30—2 KINGS 2:10

As KING AHAB OF ISRAEL PREPARES FOR BATTLE AGAINST THE SYRIAN INVADERS, HE BECOMES SO FRIGHTENED THAT HE DISGUISES HIMSELF.

THE ENEMY WILL NEVER RECOGNIZE ME IN THIS ARMOR.

AHAB IS RIGHT— THE ENEMY DOESN'T RECOGNIZE HIM. BUT IN THE HEAT OF BATTLE A STRAY ARROW STRIKES AHAB. ALTHOUGH BADLY WOUNDED, HE STAYS WITH HIS ARMY UNTIL EVENING.

THE BATTLE TURNS AGAINST THE ISRAELITES. SUDDENLY...

LOOK! THE KING IS DEAD!

WITHOUT THEIR KING, THE ISRAELITES RETREAT, AND THE CAMPAIGN FAILS. KING AHAB'S BODY IS BROUGHT BACK TO HIS CAPITAL FOR BURIAL, AND HIS CHARIOT TAKEN OUTSIDE THE CITY TO BE WASHED.

REMEMBER--ELIJAH SAID THAT AHAB'S FAMILY WOULD PAY FOR NABOTH'S MURDER.

YES, AND HE SAID THAT AHAB'S FAMILY WOULD BE DESTROYED. I WONDER IF THAT WILL COME TRUE, TOO.

AHAB'S KINGDOM PASSES ON TO HIS SONS, BUT QUEEN JEZEBEL REMAINS THE POWER BEHIND THE THRONE. IT IS DURING THE REIGN OF HER SECOND SON, JEHORAM, THAT ELIJAH RECEIVES A MESSAGE FROM GOD.

THE LORD HAS TOLD ME TO GO TO JORDAN. YOU DON'T NEED TO GO ALONG, ELISHA.

I WANT TO GO WITH YOU, ELIJAH.

410

SO THEY SET OUT TOGETHER. GOD HAS REVEALED TO BOTH OF THEM THAT THIS IS ELIJAH'S LAST JOURNEY, BUT THEY SAY NOTHING. WHEN THEY REACH THE JORDAN RIVER, ELIJAH STRIKES IT WITH HIS CLOAK-- THE WATERS PART, AND THEY WALK ACROSS ON DRY LAND.

ON THE OTHER SIDE, ELIJAH STOPS--AS IF HE HAS REACHED THE END OF HIS JOURNEY.

IS THERE ANY REQUEST YOU WANT TO MAKE BEFORE GOD TAKES ME AWAY?

YES, GIVE ME THE SPIRITUAL POWER TO CARRY ON THE WORK YOU HAVE BEEN DOING FOR GOD.

ONLY GOD CAN GRANT YOUR WISH. YOU'LL HAVE TO WAIT AND SEE WHAT HAPPENS...

Chariot of Fire!

FROM 2 KINGS 2:11–18; 4:1

ELISHA ASKS FOR THE SPIRITUAL POWER TO CARRY ON ELIJAH'S WORK. AND ELIJAH PROMISES: "IF YOU SEE ME WHEN I AM TAKEN FROM YOU, IT WILL BE A SIGN THAT GOD HAS GRANTED YOUR WISH." SUDDENLY A CHARIOT OF FIRE SWEEPS DOWN AND SEPARATES ELIJAH FROM ELISHA, AND ELIJAH IS TAKEN UP IN A WHIRLWIND...

ELIJAH! ELIJAH! I SEE NOW--THE POWER THAT PROTECTED AND GUIDED YOU IS GREATER THAN ALL THE ARMIES OF EARTH!

FOR A LONG TIME ELISHA STANDS LOOKING UP INTO THE SKY. THEN, PICKING UP THE PROPHET'S CLOAK, HE TURNS BACK. AT THE JORDAN HE STRIKES THE WATER WITH HIS CLOAK--AND THE WATERS PART.

O GOD, I THANK THEE FOR THE GIFT OF THY POWER.

ON THE OTHER SIDE OF THE RIVER ELISHA IS MET BY A GROUP OF YOUNG PROPHETS WHO HAD BEEN TRAINED BY ELIJAH.

WE KNOW GOD HAS TAKEN ELIJAH'S SPIRIT, BUT LET US SEARCH FOR HIS BODY THAT WE MAY BURY IT.

NO, ELIJAH WAS TAKEN UP INTO HEAVEN BY A WHIRLWIND.

BUT THE PROPHETS CANNOT BELIEVE WHAT ELISHA TELLS THEM. THEY PLEAD UNTIL ELISHA TELLS THEM TO CARRY OUT THEIR SEARCH. FOR THREE DAYS THE MEN LOOK-- THEN THEY RETURN, CONVINCED THAT THE BODY OF ELIJAH IS NOT TO BE FOUND.

NEWS THAT ELIJAH IS GONE SPREADS QUICKLY. IN THE PALACE OF SAMARIA, QUEEN JEZEBEL GLADLY PASSES THE NEWS ON TO HER SON.

WITH ELIJAH OUT OF THE WAY, WE CAN RULE ISRAEL AS WE PLEASE.

414

A Miracle of Oil

FROM 2 KINGS 4:2–7

ELISHA PROMISES A SURPRISE FOR THE MONEYLENDER WHO DEMANDS THAT A WIDOW GIVE HER SONS IN PAYMENT FOR A DEBT SHE CANNOT PAY.

415

THERE, THAT'S THE LAST JAR WE HAVE-- AND MINE IS STILL FULL. IT'S A MIRACLE.

SHE HURRIES WITH HER NEWS TO ELISHA...

EVERY JAR IS FILLED-- AND WITH THE VERY BEST OIL, TOO. HOW CAN I THANK YOU?

THANK GOD--FOR IT WAS HE WHO HELPED YOU. NOW, SELL THE OIL, PAY THE MONEYLENDER, AND LIVE ON THE REST OF THE MONEY.

WITH A GRATEFUL HEART, THE WOMAN THANKS GOD FOR SAVING HER SONS. THEN SHE SELLS THE OIL, AND WAITS FOR THE MONEYLENDER. THE NEXT MORNING, EARLY...

WHERE ARE MY SLAVES? I TOLD YOU TO BE READY FOR ME.

I **AM** READY FOR YOU. COME OUT, BOYS.

HERE IS THE MONEY I OWE YOU. NOW LET GO OF MY SON.

MONEY? I DON'T UNDERSTAND. I'LL --I'LL TAKE IT, BUT--

GOD SAVED US FROM SLAVERY, DIDN'T HE, MOTHER?

YES, THROUGH HIS PROPHET, ELISHA, WHO IS NEVER TOO BUSY TO HELP THOSE OF US WHO NEED HIM.

ELISHA HELPS MANY PEOPLE BY KEEPING THEIR FAITH IN GOD STRONG. STORIES OF HIS GOOD DEEDS SPREAD THROUGHOUT ALL OF ISRAEL.

EVEN TO A SMALL GIRL WHO WANDERS AWAY FROM HER FATHER'S FLOCK...

SHE'D MAKE A GOOD SLAVE FOR GENERAL NAAMAN'S WIFE.

YES--I'LL TAKE HER. THE REST OF YOU TAKE THE SHEEP.

A Prophet's Prescription

FROM 2 KINGS 5:1–14A

AN ISRAELITE GIRL, KIDNAPPED BY SYRIAN RAIDERS, BECOMES A SERVANT TO THE WIFE OF SYRIA'S GENERAL, NAAMAN.

THANK YOU, DEAR, I'M NOT HUNGRY.

ARE YOU ILL?

NO, BUT MY HUSBAND IS. HE HAS LEPROSY AND NO ONE CAN CURE HIM.

I KNOW A PROPHET OF GOD IN ISRAEL WHO CAN.

NAAMAN'S WIFE BELIEVES THE GIRL AND RUNS TO TELL HER HUSBAND. NAAMAN QUICKLY TAKES THE NEWS TO THE KING.

I CAN'T BELIEVE IT, NAAMAN, BUT I'LL GIVE YOU A LETTER TO TAKE TO THE KING OF ISRAEL.

IN SAMARIA, THE CAPITAL OF ISRAEL, NAAMAN HAS THE LETTER DELIVERED TO KING JEHORAM. THE LETTER DOES NOT MENTION ELISHA, SO THE KING MISINTERPRETS IT.

WHAT'S THIS — THE KING OF SYRIA ASKS **ME** TO CURE HIS GENERAL?

AM I A GOD THAT I CAN CURE AN INCURABLE DISEASE? IS THE KING OF SAMARIA TRYING TO PICK A QUARREL WITH ME?

REPORTS OF KING JEHORAM'S PROBLEM SPREAD THROUGHOUT THE CITY. WHEN ELISHA HEARS THEM HE SENDS HIS SERVANT TO THE KING.

ELISHA SAYS IF YOU SEND NAAMAN TO HIM, THE GENERAL WILL LEARN THE POWER OF GOD'S PROPHET.

I'LL SEND WORD TO NAAMAN AT ONCE.

NAAMAN LOSES NO TIME IN GOING TO ELISHA'S HOUSE WHERE HE IS MET BY A SERVANT.

GREETINGS, NAAMAN. ELISHA SAYS THAT IF YOU WILL WASH SEVEN TIMES IN THE JORDAN RIVER YOU WILL BE CURED.

WASH IN THE JORDAN? THAT'S SILLY! I THOUGHT ELISHA WOULD CALL ON HIS GOD TO CURE ME.

NAAMAN THINKS HE HAS BEEN MADE A FOOL OF -- AND IN A RAGE HE DRIVES AWAY.

THINK AGAIN, NAAMAN. IF ELISHA HAD ASKED YOU TO DO SOMETHING HARD, YOU WOULD HAVE DONE IT. WHY NOT DO THIS EASY THING HE ASKS?

THE GENERAL TAKES HIS SERVANT'S ADVICE AND GOES TO THE JORDAN RIVER.

I DON'T SEE HOW THIS MUDDY WATER WILL CURE LEPROSY.

Surrounded

FROM 2 KINGS 5:14–16; 6:8–16

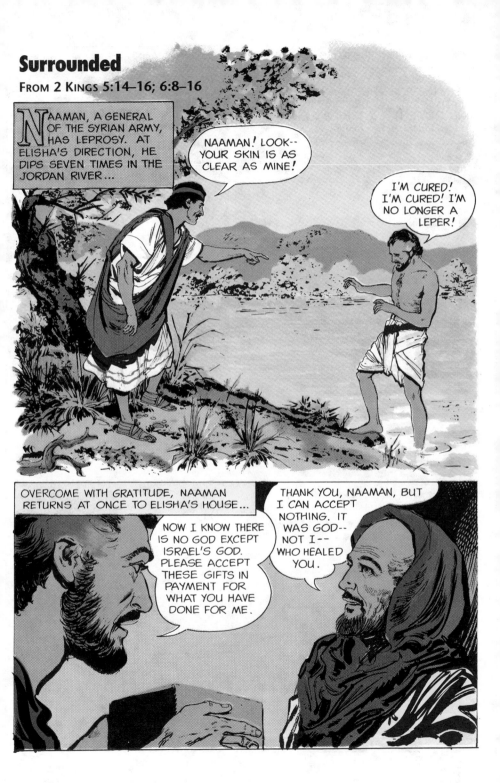

NAAMAN, A GENERAL OF THE SYRIAN ARMY, HAS LEPROSY. AT ELISHA'S DIRECTION, HE DIPS SEVEN TIMES IN THE JORDAN RIVER...

NAAMAN! LOOK-- YOUR SKIN IS AS CLEAR AS MINE!

I'M CURED! I'M CURED! I'M NO LONGER A LEPER!

OVERCOME WITH GRATITUDE, NAAMAN RETURNS AT ONCE TO ELISHA'S HOUSE...

NOW I KNOW THERE IS NO GOD EXCEPT ISRAEL'S GOD. PLEASE ACCEPT THESE GIFTS IN PAYMENT FOR WHAT YOU HAVE DONE FOR ME.

THANK YOU, NAAMAN, BUT I CAN ACCEPT NOTHING. IT WAS GOD-- NOT I-- WHO HEALED YOU.

THEN NAAMAN RETURNS TO HIS HOME IN SYRIA.

I THANK GOD EVERY DAY FOR HEALING ME, AND I OWE IT ALL TO ELISHA...

AND TO THE LITTLE GIRL WHO ALSO BELIEVES IN ELISHA'S GOD.

BUT THE HEALING OF NAAMAN DOES NOT KEEP THE KING OF SYRIA FROM PLOTTING AGAINST ISRAEL.

MY SPIES TELL ME THAT THE KING OF ISRAEL WILL SOON BE RETURNING TO SAMARIA. SET UP AN AMBUSH AND CAPTURE HIM.

A FEW DAYS LATER ON THE ROAD TO SAMARIA...

STOP! ELISHA SENDS WORD FOR YOU TO TAKE ANOTHER ROAD. THE SYRIANS ARE WAITING ON THIS ROAD TO CAPTURE YOU.

FOR DAYS THE SYRIAN SOLDIERS WAIT FOR THE ISRAELITE KING -- BUT HE DOESN'T COME. AGAIN THE SYRIAN KING SETS A TRAP AND AGAIN ELISHA WARNS HIS KING TO ESCAPE. FINALLY THE SYRIAN KING BECOMES SO ANGRY THAT HE ACCUSES HIS OWN MEN OF TREASON.

WE'RE NOT GUILTY, O KING. IT'S ELISHA, THE PROPHET IN ISRAEL, WHO IS TELLING YOUR PLANS.

ELISHA, IS IT? HAVE OUR SPIES FIND OUT WHERE HE IS AND I'LL SEND AN ARMY TO GET HIM.

A FEW DAYS LATER...

I HAVE GOOD NEWS FOR YOU -- ELISHA IS AT DOTHAN.

SEND AN ARMY AT ONCE TO SURROUND THE CITY.

THE SYRIANS MARCH -- AND SET UP THEIR CAMP BY NIGHT. THE NEXT MORNING -- ELISHA'S SERVANT RISES EARLY AND SEES THE SYRIAN ARMY.

ELISHA! WE'RE SURROUNDED -- BY THE WHOLE SYRIAN ARMY!

FEAR NOT -- THERE'S MORE POWER ON OUR SIDE THAN ON THEIRS.

One against an Army

FROM 2 KINGS 6:17–24

ELISHA'S SERVANT IS FRIGHTENED WHEN HE SEES THE SYRIAN ARMY. BUT AS ELISHA PRAYS, THE SERVANT LOOKS UP TO SEE CHARIOTS OF FIRE SURROUNDING THE PROPHET.

THE ARMY OF HEAVEN IS WITH ELISHA!

TO SAVE THE CITY FROM ATTACK, ELISHA AND HIS SERVANT GO OUT TO MEET THE ENEMY. AT ONCE THE SYRIAN SOLDIERS CLOSE IN ON THEM. BUT ELISHA PRAYS, AND SUDDENLY...

I CAN'T SEE--WHAT'S HAPPENED?

I'M BLIND-- I--

COME WITH ME. I KNOW THE ONE YOU SEEK, AND I'LL TAKE YOU TO HIM.

424

ELISHA LEADS THE ENEMY SOLDIERS TEN MILES SOUTH AND INTO THE CAPITAL CITY OF ISRAEL.

O LORD, OPEN THEIR EYES, THAT THEY MAY SEE.

INSTANTLY, SIGHT RETURNS TO THE SYRIANS.

WE'RE IN SAMARIA--

WE'RE TRAPPED-- THEY'LL KILL US!

SHALL WE KILL THEM, ELISHA?

NO. FEED THEM AND SEND THEM HOME.

425

TO THE AMAZEMENT OF THE SYRIANS, THEY ARE GIVEN FOOD AND TOLD TO RETURN HOME.

I CAN'T BELIEVE IT! WE TRIED TO KILL BOTH THE KING AND ELISHA-- AND NOW THEY TREAT US LIKE FRIENDS!

BACK HOME, THE SYRIANS TELL ABOUT THE KINDNESS OF THE ISRAELITES, AND FOR A TIME THERE IS PEACE BETWEEN THE TWO NATIONS. BUT AFTER A WHILE...

WE'LL CUT OFF ALL FOOD SUPPLIES TO SAMARIA, SURROUND IT, AND STARVE THE PEOPLE INTO SURRENDER.

EXCELLENT! AND THE LONGER THEY HOLD OUT, THE EASIER THEY WILL BE TO TAKE.

SO THE SYRIAN ARMY PITCHES ITS TENTS AROUND THE WALLS OF SAMARIA AND WAITS...

I WONDER HOW LONG THEY CAN HOLD OUT.

426

A Starving City

FROM 2 KINGS 6:25—7:5

SAMARIA, THE CAPITAL OF ISRAEL, IS SURROUNDED BY THE SYRIAN ARMY. THE CITY MAKES A BRAVE STAND TO HOLD OUT, BUT AS MONTHS PASS, AND NO FOOD IS ALLOWED INTO THE GATES, THE PEOPLE PLEAD FOR ACTION FROM THE KING.

OUR CHILDREN ARE DYING. WE MUST HAVE FOOD.

I'D RATHER TAKE MY CHANCES FIGHTING THE ENEMY THAN STARVING TO DEATH!

WHO HAS STRENGTH ENOUGH TO FIGHT NOW?

THIS IS THE MOMENT THE QUEEN MOTHER, JEZEBEL, HAS BEEN WAITING FOR.

YOUR PEOPLE ARE STARVING-- AND WHAT IS ELISHA'S GOD DOING ABOUT IT? NOTHING! GET RID OF ELISHA AND CALL ON MY GOD, BAAL!

YOU'RE RIGHT, MOTHER. I'LL ORDER HIM PUT TO DEATH AT ONCE.

AS KING JEHORAM'S SOLDIER SETS OUT ON HIS ERRAND OF DEATH, ELISHA IS VISITING WITH FRIENDS.

BAR THE DOOR, PLEASE. THE KING IS SENDING A SOLDIER TO KILL ME.

HOW COULD ELISHA KNOW THAT?

BUT THE KING SUDDENLY BECOMES WORRIED ABOUT KILLING THE PROPHET. HE RUSHES AFTER HIS SOLDIER, AND REACHES ELISHA JUST IN TIME.

IF GOD ISN'T GOING TO HELP US, WE MIGHT AS WELL SURRENDER NOW. OUR PEOPLE ARE STARVING.

NO! THE LORD SAYS THERE WILL BE FOOD ENOUGH FOR EVERYONE TOMORROW.

THE ANXIOUS KING IS WILLING TO WAIT UNTIL THE NEXT DAY, BUT OUTSIDE THE CITY FOUR LEPERS HAVE NOT HEARD ELISHA'S PROPHECY...

I'M STARVING. I'M GOING TO TRY TO BREAK INTO THE CITY AND GET SOME FOOD.

WHY DO THAT? THERE'S NO FOOD IN THERE.

THEN LET'S GO OVER TO THE SYRIAN CAMP. MAYBE THEY'LL GIVE US SOMETHING TO EAT. MAYBE THEY'LL KILL US. EITHER WAY, THERE'S NOTHING TO LOSE-- WE'LL STARVE IF WE STAY HERE.

IN DESPERATION THE FOUR HUNGRY LEPERS APPROACH THE SYRIAN CAMP.

SOMETHING STRANGE IS GOING ON. THERE'S NOT A GUARD IN SIGHT. MAYBE IT'S A TRAP--

MAYBE IT IS-- BUT I'D RATHER DIE QUICKLY THAN STARVE TO DEATH. COME ON--

THERE'S NOBODY HERE!

The Missing Enemy

FROM 2 KINGS 7:8–16

THEIR HUNGER SATISFIED, THE LEPERS QUICKLY SEARCH THE SYRIAN TENTS.

LOOK! WON'T PEOPLE BE SURPRISED TO SEE ME IN THIS?

MORE GOLD-- WE'RE RICH!

SURPRISED? THEY'LL SAY YOU STOLE IT. THEN YOU'LL REALLY BE IN TROUBLE.

HE'S RIGHT-- LET'S HIDE EVERYTHING.

IT ISN'T RIGHT FOR US TO KEEP ALL OF THIS FOOD FROM THE STARVING PEOPLE IN THE CITY.

IF WE DON'T TELL THE GOOD NEWS, SOME PUNISHMENT MAY COME UPON US.

THE MEN GO BACK TO THE CITY AND POUND ON THE GATES UNTIL A GUARD ANSWERS.

THE SYRIANS ARE GONE!

GONE? WHERE? HOW DO YOU KNOW?

431

WE DON'T KNOW WHERE OR WHY--BUT WE WERE IN THEIR CAMP. THEY LEFT THEIR FOOD, TENTS, HORSES --EVERYTHING!

I'LL GET WORD TO THE KING RIGHT AWAY.

ROUSED FROM HIS BED, KING JEHORAM RECEIVES THE NEWS AND CALLS HIS ADVISERS.

IT'S A TRAP-- THE SYRIANS ARE WAITING IN AMBUSH TO CAPTURE US IF WE LEAVE THE CITY.

MAYBE -- BUT LET'S SEND OUT A FEW MEN TO SEE WHAT'S GOING ON.

THE KING'S MEN QUICKLY PICK UP THE SYRIAN TRAIL BY FOLLOWING THE CLOTHING, WEAPONS, AND VESSELS DROPPED ALONG THE WAY.

WHAT COULD HAVE HAPPENED TO MAKE TRAINED SOLDIERS THROW AWAY THEIR WEAPONS AND RUN FOR THEIR LIVES?

LOOK-- MORE SHIELDS. THE SYRIANS ARE LETTING NOTHING SLOW THEM DOWN IN THEIR FLIGHT.

The Sound of Marching Men

FROM 2 KINGS 7:5-7, 14—9:12

THE ISRAELITE SCOUTS FOLLOW THE FLEEING SYRIAN ARMY TO THE JORDAN RIVER. ALONG THE WAY THEY OVERTAKE ONE OF THE ENEMY SOLDIERS.

PULL UP--HERE'S ONE WHO DROPPED BEHIND. MAYBE HE CAN TELL US WHAT HAPPENED.

WHY DID YOU SYRIANS DESERT CAMP IN THE MIDDLE OF THE NIGHT?

WE WERE GOING TO BE ATTACKED! WE THOUGHT THE HITTITES WERE COMING FROM THE NORTH -- AND THE EGYPTIANS FROM THE SOUTH -- TO TRAP US.

433

WE RODE AROUND YOUR CAMP. THERE WAS NO SIGN OF EVEN A SCOUTING PARTY-- LET ALONE **TWO** ARMIES. DID YOU REALLY **SEE** THEM?

NO--BUT WE HEARD THEM! THOUSANDS OF SOLDIERS, HORSES AND CHARIOTS --WE WOULDN'T HAVE HAD A CHANCE AGAINST SUCH MIGHT.

THE **SOUND** OF ARMIES-- REAL ENOUGH TO FRIGHTEN THE WHOLE SYRIAN CAMP. WHAT DO YOU MAKE OF IT?

IT WAS A MIRACLE--USED BY ELISHA'S GOD TO FRIGHTEN THE SYRIANS AWAY.

ELISHA'S GOD--YES. THAT FITS IN WITH THE PROMISE THAT BY TODAY THERE WOULD BE FOOD FOR EVERYONE!

BACK IN SAMARIA THE STARVING ISRAELITES RUSH OUT TO THE SYRIAN CAMP, EAT THEIR FILL, AND HAUL THE REST OF THE FOOD BACK TO THE CITY.

YOU SAID THERE WOULD BE FOOD, ELISHA, BUT I DIDN'T BELIEVE YOU.

IT WAS THE LORD WHO PROMISED THE FOOD--AND YOU CAN ALWAYS COUNT ON THE PROMISES OF GOD!

IN SPITE OF THE FACT THAT GOD HAS SAVED ISRAEL, KING JEHORAM AND HIS MOTHER KEEP ON WORSHIPPING BAAL. WHEN ONE OF HIS BORDER CITIES IS ATTACKED BY THE KING OF SYRIA, JEHORAM GOES TO ITS DEFENSE. WOUNDED IN THE BATTLE, HE LEAVES CAPTAIN JEHU IN CHARGE AND RETURNS HOME.

WHILE THE KING IS AWAY FROM THE ARMY, ELISHA CALLS FOR A YOUNG PROPHET TO MAKE A QUICK JOURNEY FOR HIM.

TAKE THIS OIL--GO OUT TO WHERE OUR ARMY IS CAMPED, AND DO WHAT I TELL YOU.

AT THE CAMP THE YOUNG PROPHET SEARCHES UNTIL HE FINDS A GROUP OF OFFICERS.

CAPTAIN JEHU! PLEASE COME WITH ME--I MUST SPEAK TO YOU ALONE.

THUS SAYS THE LORD; "I HAVE ANOINTED YOU TO BE KING OVER ISRAEL, TO FIGHT FOR THOSE WHO WORSHIP ME, AND AGAINST THOSE WHO WORSHIP BAAL."

WHAT DID THAT FELLOW WANT?

HE WAS A MESSENGER FROM GOD--AND HE ANOINTED ME KING-- KING OF ISRAEL!

WHAT'S GOING TO HAPPEN WHEN KING JEHORAM LEARNS OF THIS?

435

The Revenge of Israel

FROM 2 KINGS 9:13–32

JEHU, A CAPTAIN IN THE ARMY, HAS JUST BEEN ANOINTED KING OF ISRAEL. HIS MEN GO WILD WITH JOY! THEY BLOW THEIR TRUMPETS AND THROW DOWN THEIR GARMENTS TO MAKE A THRONE...

JEHU IS KING!

LONG LIVE THE KING!

MY FIRST JOB IS TO GET RID OF JEZEBEL'S SON, KING JEHORAM. ARE YOU WITH ME?

WE'RE WITH YOU -- TO A MAN.

JEHORAM IS IN JEZREEL. WE'LL HAVE TO GET TO HIM BEFORE HE LEARNS WHAT'S HAPPENED.

JEHU AND A COMPANY OF MEN SET OUT AT ONCE--AND AS THEY APPROACH JEZREEL...

CHARIOTS! A WHOLE LINE OF THEM. THE LEADER MUST BE JEHU. HE'S DRIVING SO FAST.

WHEN THE NEWS REACHES KING JEHORAM, HE BELIEVES JEHU IS BRINGING NEWS OF THE WAR. SO, WITH HIS VISITOR, KING AHAZIAH OF JUDAH, HE RIDES OUT TO MEET JEHU.

DO YOU BRING NEWS OF PEACE?

HOW CAN THERE BE PEACE IN ISRAEL WHILE YOUR MOTHER, JEZEBEL, WORSHIPS BAAL?

TOO LATE, JEHORAM SEES THAT JEHU HAS COME TO OVERTHROW THE KINGDOM. HE TRIES TO ESCAPE, BUT JEHU'S ARROW STRIKES HIM DOWN.

THAT'S THE FIRST BLOW STRUCK FOR ISRAEL.

BUT NOT THE LAST! NOW JEZEBEL MUST PAY FOR HER SINS!

IN SPITE OF JEHU'S SURPRISE ATTACK, THE NEWS REACHES THE PALACE BEFORE HE DOES...

QUEEN JEZEBEL! JEHU HAS KILLED YOUR SON-- HIS MEN ARE AFTER THE KING OF JUDAH. JEHU--

JEHU! HE'LL BE HERE NEXT.

QUICKLY SHE PUTS ON HER CROWN-- AND GOES TO THE WINDOW IN TIME TO SEE JEHU RIDE THROUGH THE GATE.

THERE SHE IS-- JEZEBEL, THE MOST EVIL WOMAN IN ALL ISRAEL!

WHO IS ON MY SIDE?

438

A Queen's Plot

FROM 2 KINGS 9:32—11:3

WHEN THE PALACE SERVANTS DISCOVER THAT JEHU IS NOW KING OF ISRAEL, THEY SHOW THEIR ALLEGIANCE TO HIM BY PUSHING QUEEN JEZEBEL FROM THE WINDOW TO HER DEATH IN THE STREET BELOW. SO JEZEBEL PAYS WITH HER LIFE FOR THE EVIL SHE HAS DONE--AND ELIJAH'S PROPHECY IS FULFILLED. JEHU WIPES OUT THE WORSHIP OF BAAL IN ISRAEL.

DESTROY THE IDOL OF BAAL!

BREAK DOWN THE HEATHEN TEMPLE! FROM THIS DAY ON IT SHALL BE A PLACE TO DUMP REFUSE.

TO THE SOUTH, IN THE KINGDOM OF JUDAH, JEZEBEL'S DAUGHTER, ATHALIAH, RECEIVES THE NEWS...

I BRING BAD NEWS. YOUR MOTHER, QUEEN JEZEBEL, AND YOUR SON, KING AHAZIAH, HAVE BEEN KILLED BY ISRAEL'S NEW KING -- JEHU.

POOR LITTLE JOASH! YOUR FATHER IS DEAD, AND YOUR GRANDMOTHER HATES YOU.

STOP WHISPERING! TAKE MY GRANDSON AWAY AND LEAVE ME ALONE IN MY TERRIBLE GRIEF.

BUT ATHALIAH'S GRIEF IS ONLY A COVER FOR HER PLAN.

MY SON IS DEAD. NOW IF **HIS** SONS WERE DEAD, **I** COULD RULE OVER JUDAH. THEN WE WOULD BE FREE TO WORSHIP BAAL.

SHE ACTS AT ONCE TO CARRY OUT HER BOLD PLOT.

ORDER YOUR SOLDIERS TO KILL ALL OF THE KING'S MALE RELATIVES. DON'T LET ONE OF THEM ESCAPE -- NOT ONE!

441

The Temple Secret

UNDER COVER OF DARKNESS THE TWO WOMEN HURRY TO THE TEMPLE OF GOD. THE HIGH PRIEST, JEHOIADA, ANSWERS THEIR FRANTIC KNOCK.

WE HAVE BABY JOASH. HELP US SAVE HIM FROM THE QUEEN.

COME IN-- HURRY!

ONLY THE PRIESTS USE THIS ROOM. JOASH WILL BE SAFE HERE AS LONG AS IT IS NECESSARY TO HIDE HIM.

442

A FEW HOURS LATER THE QUEEN'S OFFICER GIVES HIS REPORT.

THE KING'S RELATIVES HAVE BEEN PUT TO DEATH --AS YOU COMMANDED.

GOOD! NOW THERE IS NO ONE TO SAY I CAN-- NOT RULE JUDAH.

FOR SIX YEARS ATHALIAH RULES JUDAH WITH A CRUEL HAND UNTIL AT LAST THE PEOPLE BEGIN TO COMPLAIN. UNKNOWN TO THEM --IN A SECRET ROOM OF THE TEMPLE--YOUNG PRINCE JOASH IS BEING TRAINED BY THE HIGH PRIEST.

WHAT'S THIS?

THE IDOL BAAL--THE CAUSE OF ALL THE TROUBLE IN JUDAH. YOUR GRANDMOTHER WORSHIPS IT. WHEN YOU ARE KING, YOU MUST DESTROY IT AND LEAD YOUR PEOPLE BACK TO GOD.

NOW, TELL ME THE WORD OF GOD YOU HAVE LEARNED TODAY.

YOU MUST LOVE THE LORD YOUR GOD WITH ALL YOUR HEART, AND WITH ALL YOUR SOUL, AND WITH ALL YOUR MIGHT!

ONE DAY A PRIEST OF THE TEMPLE COMES TO JEHOIADA.

I PRAY THAT GOD WILL DELIVER JUDAH FROM THIS IDOL WORSHIP.

AND GOD HAS ANSWERED YOUR PRAYER. I HAVE SENT FOR ALL THE CAPTAINS OF THE GUARD TO MEET SECRETLY IN THE TEMPLE. COME--

IN THE TEMPLE...

MEN-- THIS IS PRINCE JOASH, YOUR RIGHTFUL RULER. I AM GOING TO CROWN HIM KING OF JUDAH ON THIS COMING SABBATH. BE THERE WITH ALL YOUR MEN TO PROTECT HIM.

THE NEXT SABBATH IN THE PALACE...

THE SOUND OF CHEERING --IT COMES FROM THE TEMPLE. I WONDER WHAT IT MEANS!

444

Boy King of Judah

FROM 2 KINGS 11:13–21; 2 CHRONICLES 24:1–23

WHO IS HE?

YOUR GRANDSON, JOASH, NOW KING OF JUDAH.

THAT'S A LIE-- JOASH IS DEAD. GET RID OF THIS BOY!

STOP! TAKE HER OUT OF THE TEMPLE!

QUEEN ATHALIAH IS FORCED FROM THE TEMPLE, AND PUT TO DEATH.

IN THE TEMPLE THE CORONATION OF KING JOASH CONTINUES...

DO YOU PROMISE TO OBEY GOD'S LAW AND RULE YOUR PEOPLE ACCORDING TO HIS WORD?

I PROMISE!

UNDER THE GUIDANCE OF JEHOIADA, THE HIGH PRIEST, JOASH DESTROYS THE TEMPLE OF BAAL AND LEADS HIS PEOPLE BACK TO THE WORSHIP OF GOD. THE HOUSE OF GOD IS REPAIRED, AND FOR YEARS JUDAH PROSPERS. BUT WHEN JEHOIADA DIES, JOASH IS TOO WEAK TO STAND UP UNDER THE PRESSURE OF THOSE WHO WOULD TURN HIM AWAY FROM GOD. FINALLY, JEHOIADA'S SON, ZECHARIAH, GOES TO THE KING...

KING JOASH, I SPEAK TO YOU AS MY FATHER WOULD SPEAK. YOUR PEOPLE ARE RETURNING TO BAAL AND FORSAKING GOD. JUDAH WILL BE DESTROYED UNLESS YOU STOP THEM!

AS SOON AS ZECHARIAH LEAVES, THE WORSHIPERS OF BAAL GIVE **THEIR** ADVICE.

ZECHARIAH IS A TROUBLE-MAKER.

HE SHOULD BE PUT TO DEATH BEFORE HE TURNS ALL JUDAH AGAINST YOU.

YOU'RE RIGHT. STIR UP THE PEOPLE SO THAT THEY WILL GET RID OF HIM.

AND SO JOASH, WHO WAS ONCE A GOOD KING, LISTENS TO EVIL ADVICE. ZECHARIAH IS STONED TO DEATH BY A MOB--AND SOON HIS PROPHECY OF DISASTER COMES TRUE...

447

Dagger in the Night

FROM 2 KINGS 12—18:10; 2 CHRONICLES 24:20–27

WHEN KING JOASH TURNED AWAY FROM GOD, ZECHARIAH PREDICTED DISASTER. IT COMES SOON-- IN AN ATTACK BY THE KING OF SYRIA WHO IS ON A CAMPAIGN OF CONQUEST. DURING THE ATTACK THE MEN WHO HAD ADVISED JOASH AGAINST ZECHARIAH ARE KILLED. IN AN ATTEMPT TO SAVE JERUSALEM, JOASH TRIES TO BUY OFF THE ENEMY.

GIFTS FROM MY LORD, KING JOASH OF JUDAH. HE ASKS THAT YOU ACCEPT THEM AND LEAVE JERUSALEM IN PEACE.

TELL YOUR KING I ACCEPT HIS OFFER.

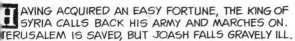

HAVING ACQUIRED AN EASY FORTUNE, THE KING OF SYRIA CALLS BACK HIS ARMY AND MARCHES ON. JERUSALEM IS SAVED, BUT JOASH FALLS GRAVELY ILL.

HOW IS THE KING TODAY?

NO BETTER-- NO WORSE. TOO BAD THE SYRIANS DIDN'T KILL THE KING ALONG WITH THE MEN WHO ADVISED HIM TO MURDER ZECHARIAH. WITH THEM GONE WE COULD SAVE JUDAH --IF IT WEREN'T FOR...

IF YOU'RE THINKING WHAT I AM--

SH! THIS ISN'T THE TIME.

BUT THAT NIGHT-- WHEN ALL THE PALACE IS ASLEEP...

REMEMBER-- WE'RE DOING THIS TO SAVE OUR COUNTRY.

SO KING JOASH IS MURDERED-- BY HIS OWN MEN. FOR ALMOST A HUNDRED YEARS JUDAH IS RULED BY KINGS WHO WAVER BETWEEN WORSHIPING GOD AND HEATHEN IDOLS. THEN HEZEKIAH COMES TO THE THRONE...

449

OUR FATHERS DISOBEYED GOD, AND JUDAH HAS BECOME WEAK. WE WILL SERVE THE LORD, AND WITH HIS HELP MAKE OUR NATION STRONG AGAIN.

AT HEZEKIAH'S ORDERS, THE TEMPLE IS REPAIRED, AND THE KING LEADS HIS PEOPLE BACK TO THE WORSHIP OF GOD.

BUT ONE DAY THE STREETS OF JERUSALEM ARE FILLED WITH ALARM.

HAVE YOU HEARD-- THE KING OF ASSYRIA HAS DESTROYED THE CITY OF SAMARIA AND TAKEN THE PEOPLE OF ISRAEL AWAY AS CAPTIVES.

AND SAMARIA IS ONLY FORTY MILES AWAY!

WITH THE FALL OF SAMARIA, THE NORTHERN KINGDOM OF ISRAEL COMES TO AN END. GREAT MASSES OF THE PEOPLE ARE CARRIED AWAY, NEVER TO RETURN. THOSE LEFT IN THE LAND MIX WITH THE RACES BROUGHT IN BY THE CONQUERORS.

450

THEN HEZEKIAH CALLS THE PEOPLE TOGETHER...

DO NOT BE AFRAID. THERE IS MORE POWER ON OUR SIDE THAN ON THE SIDE OF THE ENEMY. THE LORD GOD IS WITH US.

BUT INSTEAD OF MAKING AN ARMED ATTACK ON THE CITY, THE ASSYRIAN KING SENDS A TASK FORCE TO TRY TO FRIGHTEN THE PEOPLE OF JERUSALEM INTO SURRENDERING.

WE HAVE CONQUERED OTHER CITIES AND COUNTRIES. WHAT MAKES YOU THINK YOUR GOD CAN SAVE YOU?

AFTER A WHILE THIS KIND OF ATTACK BEGINS TO HAVE ITS EFFECT.

HOW DO WE KNOW GOD WILL SAVE US?

OTHER CITIES HAVE FALLEN. AND, REMEMBER, IT WAS THE ASSYRIANS WHO TOOK ISRAEL.

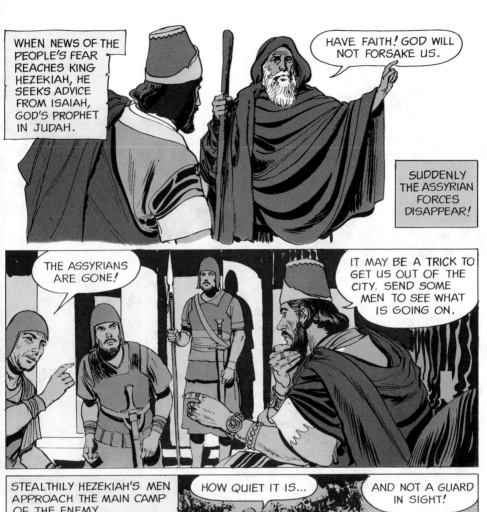

WHEN NEWS OF THE PEOPLE'S FEAR REACHES KING HEZEKIAH, HE SEEKS ADVICE FROM ISAIAH, GOD'S PROPHET IN JUDAH.

HAVE FAITH! GOD WILL NOT FORSAKE US.

SUDDENLY THE ASSYRIAN FORCES DISAPPEAR!

THE ASSYRIANS ARE GONE!

IT MAY BE A TRICK TO GET US OUT OF THE CITY. SEND SOME MEN TO SEE WHAT IS GOING ON.

STEALTHILY HEZEKIAH'S MEN APPROACH THE MAIN CAMP OF THE ENEMY...

HOW QUIET IT IS...

AND NOT A GUARD IN SIGHT!

A Foolish King

FROM 2 CHRONICLES 32:21—33:12

WHEN THE ASSYRIANS SUDDENLY STOP THREATENING THE PEOPLE OF JERUSALEM, KING HEZEKIAH SENDS MEN TO SCOUT THE ENEMY CAMP. THEY FIND IT STRANGELY QUIET.

WHY-- THEY'RE ASLEEP, OR--

A PLAGUE MUST HAVE STRUCK DOWN THE MAIN FORCE OF THE ENEMY.

AT THE NEWS, ALL JERUSALEM GOES WILD WITH JOY...

HEZEKIAH SAID GOD WAS ON OUR SIDE.

AND GOD DOESN'T FORSAKE THOSE WHO BELIEVE AND TRUST HIM ...

NO SOONER IS MANASSEH ON THE THRONE THAN THE FOLLOWERS OF BAAL BEGIN THEIR CAMPAIGN TO LEAD HIM AWAY FROM GOD.

TO BECOME RICH AND POWERFUL AS THE ASSYRIANS, WE SHOULD WORSHIP IDOLS, AS THEY DO.

NEVER AGAIN WHILE HEZEKIAH LIVES DO THE ASSYRIANS TRY TO TAKE JERUSALEM. HEZEKIAH CONTINUES TO LEAD HIS PEOPLE IN THEIR WORSHIP OF GOD, AND THEY ARE HAPPY. AT HIS DEATH, HIS YOUNG SON, MANASSEH, IS CROWNED KING.

MANASSEH LISTENS TO THEIR ADVICE, AND RESTORES IDOL WORSHIP IN ISRAEL. HE EVEN DARES TO PLACE AN IDOL IN THE TEMPLE OF GOD.

BUT WORSHIPING THE IDOLS OF THE SURROUNDING NATIONS DOES NOT SAVE MANASSEH. THE ASSYRIAN KING SUSPECTS MANASSEH IS PLOTTING AGAINST HIM AND SENDS TROOPS TO JERUSALEM. IN A SURPRISE MOVE THE ASSYRIANS OVERCOME MANASSEH'S FORCES AND TAKE THE KING PRISONER.

BOUND BY CHAINS, MANASSEH IS PARADED THROUGH THE STREETS OF JERUSALEM...

WHERE ARE HIS ADVISORS NOW?

AND IN BABYLON, WHICH IS CONTROLLED BY ASSYRIA, HE IS CAST INTO PRISON.

ALONE -- AND IN THE DARKNESS OF HIS CELL -- MANASSEH REVIEWS THE PAST. HE REMEMBERS THAT WHEN HIS FATHER RULED JUDAH, THE ASSYRIANS TRIED TO TAKE JERUSALEM, AND GOD HAD DESTROYED THEM WITH A PLAGUE. ASSYRIA HAD NOT DARED TO STRIKE AGAIN WHILE HIS FATHER LIVED. BUT HIS FATHER HAD OBEYED GOD -- AND HE, MANASSEH...

O GOD, I HAVE SINNED AGAINST THEE. I REPENT AND PRAY THAT YOU WILL FORGIVE ME.

The Lost Book
FROM 2 CHRONICLES 33:13—34:18;
2 KINGS 22:1–10

IN AN ASSYRIAN DUNGEON, KING MANASSEH OF JUDAH REPENTS FOR DISOBEYING GOD, AND ASKS FORGIVENESS. ONE DAY HE IS SUDDENLY BROUGHT BEFORE THE KING OF ASSYRIA.

REMOVE HIS CHAINS. TAKE HIM HOME AND LET HIM RULE JUDAH AGAIN-- UNDER MY COMMAND.

NO ONE KNOWS WHAT PROMPTED THE ASSYRIAN KING TO FREE MANASSEH--BUT WHEN HE RETURNS TO JERUSALEM HIS PEOPLE WELCOME HIM...

THE KING HAS RETURNED!

LONG LIVE THE KING OF JUDAH!

BUT THE PEOPLE ARE AMAZED AT HIS FIRST SPEECH...

I WAS WRONG TO TURN AWAY FROM GOD. DESTROY THE IDOLS, AND JOIN ME IN WORSHIPING GOD.

MANASSEH TRIES TO SAVE HIS NATION, BUT IT IS TOO LATE. MOST OF THE PEOPLE CONTINUE TO WORSHIP IDOLS. MANASSEH DIES, AND AFTER TWO YEARS, HIS EIGHT-YEAR-OLD GRANDSON, JOSIAH, COMES TO THE THRONE.

AS THE KING GROWS UP, THE IDOL WORSHIPERS TRY TO INFLUENCE JOSIAH, BUT THE YOUNG KING REMAINS TRUE TO GOD. HE RULES JUDAH WITH A FIRM BUT JUST HAND. ONE DAY HE CALLS FOR THREE OF HIS OFFICIALS.

THE WALLS OF THE TEMPLE ARE CRUMBLING-- I WANT THEM REPAIRED IMMEDIATELY.

WORKMEN BEGIN AT ONCE. AFTER A WHILE THE HIGH PRIEST COMES TO CHECK THEIR PROGRESS...

STOP! WHAT'S THAT OBJECT BEHIND THOSE STONES?

HE TAKES HIS DISCOVERY TO THE KING'S SCRIBE.

LOOK WHAT I HAVE FOUND! THE BOOK OF THE LAW!

IT HAS BEEN LOST FOR YEARS! LET ME READ IT!

SLOWLY, CAREFULLY, THE SCRIBE READS THE ANCIENT SCROLL.

WHAT DOES IT SAY?

IT GIVES GOD'S LAWS--BUT IT ALSO TELLS WHAT WILL HAPPEN IF THE LAWS ARE NOT OBEYED. I MUST READ THIS TO THE KING.

BUT I'M AFRAID THERE'S NOTHING HE--OR ANYBODY ELSE--CAN DO TO SAVE JUDAH!

459

A Prophetess Speaks

FROM 2 KINGS 22:11—24:20; 2 CHRONICLES 34:19—36:16

THE SCRIBE READS TO KING JOSIAH FROM THE LOST BOOK THAT HAS BEEN FOUND IN THE TEMPLE WALLS.

GOD'S LAWS ARE CLEARLY STATED --AND SO IS THE PUNISHMENT FOR ANYONE WHO DISOBEYS THEM.

THEN JUDAH IS DOOMED! FOR IT HAS BROKEN GOD'S LAW MANY TIMES.

JOSIAH IS SO UPSET THAT HE QUICKLY SENDS SEVERAL HIGH-RANKING OFFICIALS TO THE PROPHETESS HULDAH.

THE KING HAS SENT US TO ASK FOR A MESSAGE FROM GOD ABOUT THE BOOK WE HAVE JUST READ.

THUS SAITH THE LORD: BECAUSE JUDAH HAS DISOBEYED ME, JUDAH SHALL BE DESTROYED... BUT THE DESTRUCTION WILL NOT COME IN THE DAYS OF JOSIAH.

HOPING HE MAY YET WIN GOD'S FORGIVENESS FOR HIS NATION, JOSIAH CALLS A MEETING OF THE PEOPLE.

AT JOSIAH'S COMMAND PAGAN WORSHIP IS WIPED OUT IN ALL THE LAND. OBJECTS USED IN IDOL WORSHIP ARE REMOVED FROM GOD'S TEMPLE IN JERUSALEM, TAKEN OUTSIDE THE CITY, AND BURNED.

I HAVE READ GOD'S LAWS TO YOU. LET US NOW PROMISE TO OBEY THEM FROM THIS DAY ON. AND MAY GOD HAVE MERCY ON US.

461

While Josiah lives, Judah obeys the laws of God. But after his death, one king after another turns back to the worship of idols. Lacking God's help, Judah comes under the control of a new world power, Babylonia.

JUDAH IS ALLOWED TO REMAIN UNDER ITS OWN RULERS, BUT AFTER KING ZEDEKIAH COMES TO THE THRONE HE FOOLISHLY TRIES TO REGAIN HIS COUNTRY'S INDEPENDENCE. IN REPLY THE GREAT BABYLONIAN ARMY SETS OUT...

The Fall of Jerusalem

FROM 2 CHRONICLES 36:17–20; 2 KINGS 25:1–11

FOR 2 YEARS AND A HALF, FORCES FROM THE GREAT BABYLONIAN ARMY BESIEGE THE CITY OF JERUSALEM. AT LAST THEY BREAK THROUGH THE WALL...

THAT NIGHT KING ZEDEKIAH AND HIS ARMY TRY TO ESCAPE.

IF WE CAN MAKE IT TO THE HILL REGION EAST OF THE JORDAN, THEY'LL NEVER FIND US.

IT'S OUR ONLY CHANCE --IF THEY CAPTURE US...

BUT THE BABYLONIANS PURSUE THEM, AND ZEDEKIAH IS CAPTURED BEFORE HE CAN REACH THE RIVER. HE IS BLINDED AND TAKEN TO BABYLON.

HUNGRY, WEARY, AND AFRAID, THE PEOPLE OF JERUSALEM ARE FORCED TO BEGIN THE LONG MARCH OF 900 MILES FROM JERUSALEM TO BABYLON--AS CAPTIVES.

GOD HAS FORSAKEN US.

NO. GOD WARNED US, BUT WE WOULD NOT LISTEN. IT IS WE WHO HAVE FORSAKEN GOD!

SILVER, GOLD, AND ALL OBJECTS OF VALUE ARE STRIPPED FROM THE TEMPLE AND PALACE BUILDINGS.

SET FIRE TO EVERY CORNER OF THE CITY-- LET NOTHING REMAIN THAT WILL GIVE ANYONE IDEAS ABOUT REBUILDING IT.

FOR DAYS THE FIRES RAGE -- UNTIL ALL THAT IS LEFT OF THE BEAUTIFUL CITY OF JERUSALEM IS A HEAP OF ASHES AND BLACKENED STONES...

BUT ON THE WAY TO BABYLON A FEW BRAVE CAPTIVES DREAM OF A DAY WHEN THEY MAY RETURN...

Return of the Captives

FROM EZRA 1—2; DANIEL 5; ISAIAH 45:1–2,13

FROM THE MOMENT THEY ARE CARRIED AWAY AS CAPTIVES TO BABYLON, THE JEWS DREAM OF RETURNING TO THEIR HOMELAND, JUDAH. THE BOOK OF **EZRA** TELLS WHAT HAPPENS TO THAT DREAM.

FOR MANY YEARS THE JEWS LIVE AS CAPTIVES OF THE GREAT BABYLONIAN EMPIRE. THEY WATCH ANXIOUSLY AS PERSIA, A STRONG COUNTRY TO THE EAST, RISES UP TO CHALLENGE BABYLON.

WHEN THE PERSIAN ARMY APPEARS OUTSIDE THE CITY WALLS, KING BELSHAZZAR IS SO SURE OF BABYLON'S STRENGTH THAT HE SPENDS THE NIGHT IN A DRUNKEN FEAST WITH HIS COURT. PERSIAN TROOPS STEAL INTO THE CITY-- INVADE THE PALACE--AND SLAY BELSHAZZAR. WITHIN HOURS THE BABYLONIAN EMPIRE FALLS TO PERSIA.

TWO WEEKS LATER KING CYRUS OF PERSIA RIDES TRIUMPHANTLY INTO THE CITY.

SO THAT'S OUR NEW RULER. I WONDER--DOES THIS MEAN GOOD OR EVIL FOR US JEWS?

I'VE HEARD THAT CYRUS IS A JUST MAN. WE'LL HAVE TO WAIT AND SEE.

SOON AFTER CYRUS TAKES OVER THE BABYLONIAN EMPIRE, AN OFFICIAL ANNOUNCEMENT IS READ.

THESE ARE THE WORDS OF KING CYRUS: THE GOD OF ISRAEL COMMANDS THAT A HOUSE BE BUILT FOR HIM IN JERUSALEM. ANY OF HIS PEOPLE WHO WANT TO DO SO MAY RETURN. THOSE WHO DO NOT GO BACK SHOULD GIVE OF THEIR POSSESSIONS TO HELP THOSE WHO RETURN TO JUDAH.

GIFTS OF MONEY, HORSES, MULES, CAMELS, GOLD AND SILVER, FOOD AND CLOTHING POUR IN. AT LAST THE DAY COMES WHEN THE GREAT CARAVAN IS READY TO LEAVE.

THANK GOD, I'LL SEE MY HOMELAND AGAIN.

ON THE LONG ROAD HOME, THEY FOLLOW MUCH THE SAME ROUTE THAT ABRAHAM, THE FATHER OF THE JEWISH NATION, TRAVELED 1,500 YEARS BEFORE WHEN HE OBEYED GOD'S COMMAND TO LEAVE UR AND MAKE A NEW NATION IN PALESTINE.

BUT NO MATTER HOW MUCH THEY PREPARE THEMSELVES FOR THE RUINED CITY, THEY ARE BROKENHEARTED WHEN THEY WALK THROUGH THE RUBBLE OF JERUSALEM.

WHEN WE LEFT JERUSALEM IT WAS IN FLAMES -- I WONDER WHAT IT LOOKS LIKE NOW.

SOLOMON'S BEAUTIFUL TEMPLE STOOD OVER THERE.

OUR HOME-- LET'S TRY TO FIND IT.

HOW PROUD WE WERE WHEN WE BUILT IT-- WITH OUR OWN HANDS, TOO. NOW LOOK AT IT--A HOME FOR WILD DOGS.

MAYBE WE SHOULD NOT HAVE COME BACK. MAYBE...

OUR FOREFATHERS BUILT MUCH OF THIS CITY. WE'LL REBUILD IT -- JERUSALEM WILL RISE AGAIN. YOU'LL SEE...

468

Jerusalem Rises Again

FROM EZRA 3—10

ALTHOUGH THE CITY OF JERUSALEM IS IN RUINS, THE JEWS WHO HAVE RETURNED FROM CAPTIVITY IN BABYLON SET TO WORK TO REBUILD IT. WHEN THE FOUNDATION OF THE TEMPLE IS IN PLACE, THE HIGH PRIEST LEADS THE PEOPLE IN A SERVICE OF WORSHIP AND REJOICING.

O GIVE THANKS UNTO THE LORD, FOR HE IS GOOD. HIS MERCY ENDURETH FOR EVER.

BUT THE SOUND OF REJOICING BRINGS TROUBLE. THE SAMARITANS WHO LIVE NEAR JERUSALEM COME WITH A REQUEST TO HELP BUILD THE TEMPLE.

WE'RE SORRY-- BUT YOU DO NOT WORSHIP AS WE DO, SO WE CANNOT LET YOU HELP US BUILD OUR TEMPLE TO GOD.

SO THEY "CAN'T" LET US HELP THEM BUILD THE TEMPLE! WELL, WE'LL MAKE THEM SORRY THEY EVER CAME BACK TO JERUSALEM TO BUILD ANYTHING.

WHAT DO YOU MEAN?

THE JEWS SOON LEARN WHAT THE SAMARITAN MEANT. ONE DAY WHILE THEY ARE AT WORK AN OFFICER OF KING CYRUS RIDES UP.

BY ORDER OF THE KING, THIS WORK IS TO STOP!

STOP? WHY? IT WAS KING CYRUS HIMSELF WHO TOLD US WE SHOULD RETURN TO JERUSALEM TO REBUILD THE TEMPLE!

UNHAPPILY, THE WORKMEN LAY DOWN THEIR TOOLS AND GO HOME.

FATHER, WHAT COULD HAVE HAPPENED? KING CYRUS SAID...

YES, BUT THE SAMARITANS WROTE HIM THAT WE WERE TRYING TO DESTROY HIS POWER HERE. THE KING IS INVESTIGATING THE CHARGES AND HAS ORDERED WORK ON THE TEMPLE STOPPED.

FORCED TO OBEY, THE JEWS TURN TO WORK ON THEIR HOMES AND GARDENS. SEVERAL YEARS PASS -- CYRUS DIES AND NEW KINGS COME TO THE THRONE IN PERSIA, BUT STILL THE TEMPLE IN JERUSALEM IS NOT COMPLETED. THEN, ONE DAY, THE JEWS ARE APPROACHED BY TWO PROPHETS OF GOD.

HAGGAI, ZECHARIAH! WHAT BRINGS YOU HERE?

WE HAVE NEWS.

A NEW KING, DARIUS, HAS COME TO THE THRONE. LET'S START WORK AGAIN ON THE TEMPLE -- MAYBE HE WON'T STOP US.

KING DARIUS NOT ONLY LETS THE JEWS COMPLETE THE TEMPLE -- HE EVEN ORDERS HIS OFFICERS TO GIVE THEM THE MATERIAL THEY NEED.

SO -- AT LAST -- THE NEW TEMPLE OF GOD IS FINISHED. WITH THANKFUL HEARTS THE PEOPLE OFFER THEIR SACRIFICES AND PRAYERS TO GOD.

SOME YEARS LATER, EZRA, A PRIEST, GAINS PERMISSION FROM THE PERSIAN KING TO GO TO JERUSALEM TO TEACH THE PEOPLE THE LAWS OF GOD. HE TAKES A GROUP OF JEWS WITH HIM. UNDER EZRA JERUSALEM GROWS IN SIZE AND SPIRITUAL STRENGTH, BUT IS STILL WITHOUT WALLS AND SURROUNDED BY HOSTILE NEIGHBORS.

ONE NIGHT, WHILE THE CITY SLEEPS, A STRANGER AND HIS GUARDS RIDE TOWARD JERUSALEM ...

Two Lines of Defense

FROM NEHEMIAH

THE BOOK OF **NEHEMIAH** CONTINUES THE STORY OF THE JEWS' STRUGGLE TO REBUILD JERUSALEM.

AT NIGHT, SO THAT NO ONE WILL SEE HIM, A STRANGER TO JERUSALEM RIDES AROUND THE CITY AND EXAMINES THE WALLS.

THIS CITY COULD BE WIPED OUT IN ONE QUICK ATTACK.

YOU'RE RIGHT, NEHEMIAH. BUT IT MUST HAVE BEEN A GREAT FORTRESS AT ONE TIME. THESE WALLS ARE AS THICK AS ANY WE HAVE IN PERSIA.

THE NEXT DAY NEHEMIAH CALLS ON THE PRIESTS AND RULERS OF THE CITY.

I HAVE EXAMINED THE WALLS OF JERUSALEM. THEY ARE JUST HEAPS OF BROKEN STONE. THE CITY IS DEFENSELESS.

YOU ARE RIGHT, BUT WHY--

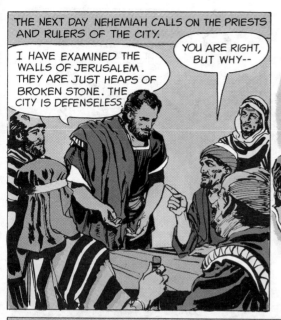

WHY HAVE I COME? BECAUSE I, TOO, AM A JEW. AND WHILE I WAS SERVING THE KING OF PERSIA AS HIS CUPBEARER, I LEARNED THAT JERUSALEM WAS WITHOUT ANY DEFENSE. I PRAYED TO GOD-- AND THE KING GAVE ME HIS PERMISSION TO COME HERE AND BUILD UP THE WALLS. ARE YOU WITH ME?

WE ARE-- AND WE'LL START AT ONCE.

THE WORK BEGINS. EVERY ABLE-BODIED MAN AND BOY DOES HIS PART. THE WOMEN HELP... AND SLOWLY THE WALLS BEGIN TO RISE.

BUT SOME OF THE NEIGHBORING COUNTRIES DO NOT WANT TO SEE JERUSALEM PROTECTED.

IF THOSE WALLS ARE FINISHED, THE CITY WILL BE TOO STRONG TO ATTACK. WE MUST STOP IT **NOW**.

DOWN WITH THE WALLS!

BUT WHILE THE ENEMIES OF JERUSALEM PLAN TO TAKE THE CITY, NEHEMIAH PREPARES TO DEFEND IT.

PASS THESE OUT TO EVERY WORKER. LET NO MAN WORK WITHOUT A WEAPON IN HIS HAND -- READY TO FIGHT!

THE ENEMY APPROACHES -- BUT TO THEIR SURPRISE ARMED WORKERS RISE UP -- THEIR SPEARS RAISED AND THEIR BOWS PULLED.

THEY'RE ARMED!

RETREAT!

THE WORKERS GO BACK TO THEIR JOBS, AND SOON STRONG WALLS AND HEAVY GATES AGAIN PROTECT THE CITY OF JERUSALEM. BUT INSIDE THERE IS AN EVEN STRONGER LINE OF DEFENSE -- A NATION LED BY EZRA AND NEHEMIAH TO LOVE AND OBEY GOD!

The Search for a Queen

FROM ESTHER 1:1—2:11

THE BOOK OF ESTHER IS THE STORY OF A YOUNG JEWISH WOMAN WHO RISKS HER LIFE TO SAVE HER PEOPLE.

WHEN THE BABYLONIANS CAPTURE JERUSALEM, THEY TAKE THOUSANDS OF JEWS BACK HOME AS CAPTIVES. LATER, WHEN THE PERSIAN KING CONQUERS BABYLON, HE FREES THE JEWS. MANY RETURN TO JERUSALEM, BUT OTHERS REMAIN IN BABYLON AND PERSIA.

AT THIS TIME THE PERSIAN EMPIRE IS THE MOST POWERFUL IN ALL THE WORLD--REACHING FROM INDIA TO ETHIOPIA. ON THE THRONE AT SHUSHAN SITS KING AHASUERUS.

FOR MONTHS THE KING HAS BEEN ENTERTAINING HIGH-RANKING OFFICIALS OF HIS REALM. HOW MUCH LONGER WILL THIS FEASTING GO ON?

UNTIL HE HAS IMPRESSED ALL OF HIS SUBJECTS WITH HIS WEALTH AND POWER.

A Plot against the King

FROM ESTHER 2:11—3:6

476

477

HAMAN IS VERY PROUD AND ENJOYS HAVING PEOPLE BOW BEFORE HIM. BUT MORDECAI REFUSES TO RISE FROM HIS PLACE BY THE GATE.

WHO IS THAT MAN WHO DOES NOT SHOW PROPER RESPECT FOR ME?

THAT'S MORDECAI — A JEW. AND JEWS BOW ONLY TO THEIR GOD.

MORDECAI WILL PAY FOR THIS -- AND SO WILL EVERY JEW IN PERSIA!

A New Law

FROM ESTHER 3:8—4:16

479

THE ORDERS ARE WRITTEN AND DELIVERED. THROUGHOUT THE KINGDOM JEWISH FAMILIES ARE TERRIFIED...

WHY? WHY? WE HAVE DONE NO WRONG!

AND WHEREVER WE GO THERE'S A PRICE ON OUR HEADS!

WHEN MORDECAI HEARS THE ORDERS HE DRESSES IN CLOTHES OF MOURNING AND POURS ASHES OVER HIS HEAD TO SHOW HIS GRIEF...

FROM HER PALACE WINDOW ESTHER SEES THAT SOMETHING IS WRONG.

FIND OUT WHAT IS TROUBLING MORDECAI.

THE QUEEN ASKS WHY I MOURN? DOESN'T SHE KNOW THAT HAMAN'S ORDER MEANS DEATH TO EVERY JEW IN PERSIA? SHOW THIS TO HER-- TELL HER SHE MUST GO TO THE KING AND ASK HIM TO SPARE THE JEWS.

481

A Queen Risks Her Life

FROM ESTHER 5:1—6:10

QUEEN ESTHER BREAKS A LAW BY APPEARING UNINVITED BEFORE THE KING--AN ACT PUNISHABLE BY DEATH. BUT THE LIVES OF HER PEOPLE, THE JEWS, ARE IN DANGER, AND SHE IS THE ONLY ONE WHO MAY BE ABLE TO SAVE THEM.

ESTHER! WHAT DOES SHE WANT THAT SHE WOULD RISK HER LIFE TO GET?

SURPRISED AS HE IS BY HER SUDDEN APPEARANCE, THE KING IS PLEASED AT THE SIGHT OF HIS BEAUTIFUL QUEEN. HE HOLDS OUT HIS SCEPTOR TO SHOW THAT SHE IS FORGIVEN, AND ASKS WHAT SHE WANTS.

I ASK THAT YOU AND HAMAN COME TO A DINNER THAT I SHALL PREPARE FOR YOU.

THE KING ACCEPTS. SO DOES HAMAN -- WHO IS OVERJOYED UNTIL HE LEAVES THE PALACE.

THAT STUBBORN JEW -- HE STILL WON'T BOW BEFORE ME! WELL, HE'LL SOON BE DEAD WITH ALL THE OTHER JEWS.

AT HOME HAMAN COMPLAINS THAT MORDECAI HAS INSULTED HIM.

DON'T STAND FOR IT, HAMAN. BUILD A GALLOWS AND TELL THE KING YOU WANT MORDECAI HANGED. THEN YOU CAN ENJOY YOUR DINNER WITH THE QUEEN.

I'LL DO IT! I'LL HAVE THE GALLOWS MADE AND GO TO SEE THE KING EARLY IN THE MORNING.

483

BUT THAT NIGHT THE KING CANNOT SLEEP. HE CALLS FOR A SCRIBE TO READ TO HIM FROM THE RECORDS OF THE KINGDOM. WHEN THE READING REACHES THE STORY OF MORDECAI, THE KING INTERRUPTS.

AT THAT MOMENT HAMAN ENTERS THE COURT AND IS BROUGHT BEFORE THE KING.

STOP! WHAT REWARD DID HE RECEIVE FOR SAVING MY LIFE?

NONE, MY LORD.

HAMAN, YOU'RE JUST THE MAN I WANTED TO SEE. WHAT SHALL I DO TO HONOR A MAN WHO HAS PLEASED ME?

I KNEW THE KING WOULD RECOGNIZE MY SERVICES.

LET HIM WEAR ONE OF YOUR ROBES -- AND RIDE YOUR HORSE. THEN HAVE ONE OF YOUR NOBLES LEAD HIM THROUGH THE CITY TELLING EVERYONE THAT THIS IS THE WAY THE KING HONORS THOSE WHO PLEASE HIM.

GOOD! GET THE ROBE AND THE HORSE AND DO EXACTLY AS YOU HAVE SUGGESTED -- FOR MORDECAI.

MORDECAI! BUT I -- YES -- SIR!

The Unchangeable Law

FROM ESTHER 6:11—10

NGRY AND HUMILIATED, HAMAN IS FORCED TO PERFORM FOR HIS ENEMY, MORDECAI, THE CEREMONY THAT HE HAD PLANNED FOR HIMSELF...

THE CEREMONY OVER, HAMAN COVERS HIS HEAD IN SHAME AND HURRIES HOME TO TELL HIS FAMILY.

THIS LOOKS BAD FOR YOU, HAMAN.

ALL IS NOT LOST! THE KING HAS SIGNED AN ORDER TO KILL THE JEWS, AND NOT EVEN HE CAN CHANGE IT! NOW I MUST DRESS TO GO TO QUEEN ESTHER'S DINNER. AT LEAST SHE RECOGNIZES ME!

LATER AT THE PALACE.

QUEEN ESTHER, WHEN YOU DARED TO COME TO THE THRONE ROOM I THINK YOU WANTED A GREATER FAVOR THAN TO ASK ME TO DINNER. DIDN'T YOU?

YES, MY LORD, I DID.

WHAT IS IT? I'LL GRANT WHATEVER YOU ASK.

I ASK FOR THE LIFE OF MYSELF AND MY PEOPLE. BY THE CRUEL PLAN OF A CERTAIN MAN WE ARE TO BE PUT TO DEATH.

PUT **YOU** TO DEATH? WHO WOULD DARE DO SUCH A THING?

HAMAN!

N OW, FOR THE FIRST TIME THE KING KNOWS THAT HIS WIFE IS JEWISH, AND THAT HAMAN TRICKED HIM INTO SIGNING HER DEATH WARRANT. IN ANGER THE KING LEAVES THE ROOM.

QUEEN ESTHER! I'LL DO ANYTHING YOU SAY-- ONLY SPARE ME! SPARE ME!

THE KING'S SERVANT KNOWS THAT HAMAN IS DOOMED TO DIE AND HE COVERS THE MAN'S HEAD WITH A CLOTH.

487

BUT--I CAN SEND A NEW ORDER!

THE ORDER IS WRITTEN AND RUSHED TO GOVERNORS THROUGHOUT THE EMPIRE.

LISTEN--THE KING SAYS THE JEWS MAY ARM TO PROTECT THEMSELVES, AND THAT MORDECAI, A JEW, HAS BEEN MADE PRIME MINISTER.

AH! THE KING IS ON THE SIDE OF THE JEWS! WE'D BETTER BE, TOO.

AND AT THE PALACE...

I'VE WRITTEN AN ORDER THAT EVERY YEAR ALL JEWS MUST CELEBRATE THE DAYS WHEN WE WERE SAVED FROM OUR ENEMY. THEY SHOULD BE DAYS OF JOY AND GIVING OF GIFTS, AND SHALL BE CALLED THE FEAST OF PURIM.

ON THE THIRTEENTH DAY OF THE 12TH MONTH THE JEWS THROUGHOUT THE PERSIAN EMPIRE GATHER TOGETHER TO DEFEND THEMSELVES. WITH THE HELP OF THE KING'S GOVERNORS, THEY ARE SUCCESSFUL.

THE FEAST OF PURIM IS STILL CELEBRATED BY JEWISH PEOPLE THROUGHOUT THE WORLD.

Women Who Change Their World...

Deborah is a judge and a prophetess who becomes a military advisor. See pp. 214-217 (Judges 4–5).

Delilah is bribed by the enemy to get information from her boyfriend. She betrays him and he is taken prisoner. See pp. 240–243 (Judges 16).

Esther is an orphan who wins a beauty contest and later risks her life to save her people. See pp. 476–488 (the Book of Esther).

Eve is created, not born as a baby, but becomes known as the mother of all human beings. She disobeys God in a big way when she and her husband eat fruit that God tells them not to eat. See pp. 19–26 (Genesis 2–4).

Hannah is falsely accused by a priest of being drunk when she prays earnestly for a child. God grants her request and a son is born. When he is young, she takes her son to be raised in God's house. See pp. 253–254 (1 Samuel 1–2).

Did You Know?

Women Who Change Their World . . .

Jezebel is a wicked queen who worships idols. She tries to kill all the prophets of God, and in the end is thrown over a wall and run over by horses. See pp. 386-439 (1 Kings 16,18–21; 2 Kings 9).

Mary is a young woman who becomes mother to the Son of God. See pp. 550-566 (Matthew 1–2 and Luke 1–2).

Miriam helps her mother save her little brother by putting him in a basket riverboat. See pp. 125–128 (Exodus 2).

Rahab hides two spies in her house and later she and her whole family are saved because she hangs a red cord out of her window. See pp. 193–202 (Joshua 2 and 6).

Rebekah agrees to move away from home and marry a man she has never met. Later she becomes the mother of twin boys. See pp. 68-81 (Genesis 24–28).

Ruth is from an enemy country, but she risks her future to help her mother-in-law. It pays off and she becomes King David's grandmother. See pp. 247–252 (the Book of Ruth).

A Man with a Message

FROM ISAIAH

AT THIS POINT IN OUR BIBLE STORY, WE NOW RETURN TO PICK UP MATERIAL NOT COVERED AT OTHER PLACES IN THE BIBLE.

THINGS SEEMED TO BE GOING WELL IN THE LAND OF JUDAH, BUT TROUBLE WAS ON THE WAY. IN THEIR HEARTS THE PEOPLE WERE TURNING AWAY FROM GOD. THE RICH WERE CHEATING THE POOR. AND ALTHOUGH THE WALLS OF JERUSALEM WERE STRONG, THERE WAS ALWAYS THE DANGER OF INVASION BY AN ENEMY. IN THIS TIME OF NEED, GOD SENT A YOUNG MAN WITH A MESSAGE. HE WAS ISAIAH, ONE OF THE GREATEST OF THE HEBREW PROPHETS.

HOLY, HOLY, HOLY, IS THE LORD GOD OF HOSTS.

THE CALL TO BE-COME A PROPHET OF GOD COMES TO ISAIAH WHEN HE IS WORSHIPING IN THE TEMPLE. AS HE PRAYS, HE SEES A GLORIOUS VISION.

O GOD, I AM NOT WORTHY TO BE IN THY PRESENCE. I AM A SINFUL MAN IN A SINFUL NATION.

AN ANGEL TOUCHES ISAIAH'S LIPS WITH A COAL OF FIRE AND SAYS, "YOUR SIN IS TAKEN AWAY." THEN ISAIAH HEARS GOD ASK: "WHOM SHALL I SEND TO SPEAK TO THIS SINFUL NATION?"

HERE I AM; SEND ME.

FOR MORE THAN FIFTY YEARS ISAIAH PLEADS WITH HIS PEOPLE TO DESTROY THEIR IDOLS AND WORSHIP GOD. BUT ONLY A FEW LISTEN. HE WARNS THE KINGS OF WHAT WILL HAPPEN IF THEY DISOBEY GOD, BUT THE KINGS IGNORE THE WARNINGS. AT LAST ISAIAH PROPHESIES DESTRUCTION...

BECAUSE JUDAH HAS TURNED AWAY FROM GOD, IT WILL BE DESTROYED AND ITS PEOPLE CARRIED AWAY AS CAPTIVES.

IS THERE NO HOPE FOR GOD'S PEOPLE?

YES, GOD WILL SEND A DELIVERER TO SAVE ALL WHO BELIEVE IN HIM. AND HIS NAME SHALL BE CALLED WONDERFUL, COUNSELLOR, THE MIGHTY GOD... THE PRINCE OF PEACE.

A Call from God

FROM JEREMIAH 1:11;
2 KINGS 22:1—23:29

"JUDAH WILL BE DESTROYED FOR DISOBEYING GOD!" THE PROPHET ISAIAH WARNED. BUT THE PEOPLE OF JUDAH IGNORED THE WARNING AND CONTINUED THEIR MAD RUSH TOWARDS RUIN. THEN GOD CALLED ANOTHER PROPHET NAMED JEREMIAH TO SOUND THE ALARM AGAIN.

IT'S AN EXCITING DAY FOR JEREMIAH WHEN HE GOES TO JERUSALEM WITH HIS FATHER TO SEE JUDAH'S NEW KING.

WHY! HE'S JUST ABOUT MY AGE! I WONDER WHAT IT WOULD BE LIKE TO HAVE SUCH AN IMPORTANT JOB.

LONG LIVE KING JOSIAH!

A FEW YEARS LATER JEREMIAH FINDS OUT, FOR GOD CALLS HIM TO AN EVEN GREATER TASK-- TO BECOME SPOKESMAN FOR HIM.

O GOD--I DON'T KNOW HOW TO SPEAK SO THAT PEOPLE WILL LISTEN. I'M TOO YOUNG FOR SUCH A BIG JOB.

BUT GOD PROMISES THAT HE WILL GIVE JEREMIAH THE WORDS TO SPEAK AND THE COURAGE TO SAY THEM. THAT EVENING...

A WONDERFUL THING HAPPENED TO ME TODAY --GOD CALLED ME TO BE A PROPHET.

A PROPHET! KING JOSIAH WORSHIPS GOD--BUT MANY OF THE COURT LEADERS SECRETLY WORSHIP IDOLS. THEY WILL MAKE IT HARD FOR YOU--AND YOU'RE SO SHY...

THE PEOPLE OF JUDAH ARE DOOMED UNLESS THEY TURN BACK TO GOD. GOD HAS CALLED ME TO WARN THEM.

THE MESSAGE JEREMIAH IS TO GIVE HIS PEOPLE COMES TO HIM WHILE HE IS WATCHING A BOILING KETTLE.

INVADERS COMING DOWN FROM THE NORTH TO DESTROY JUDAH! BUT WILL ANYONE BELIEVE ME?

HE SOON FINDS OUT-- WHEN HE TELLS THE PRIESTS IN HIS OWN TOWN THAT JUDAH WILL BE DESTROYED BECAUSE THE PEOPLE HAVE TURNED FROM GOD TO WORSHIP IDOLS.

WHO IS THIS YOUNG UPSTART TO TELL US HOW TO LIVE?

LET'S GET RID OF HIM BEFORE HE STARTS TROUBLE.

SO, TO SAVE HIS LIFE, JEREMIAH IS FORCED TO LEAVE HIS HOME TOWN AND GO TO JERUSALEM.

KING JOSIAH LOVES AND WORSHIPS GOD; HE WILL HELP ME TRY TO SAVE JUDAH.

FOR SEVERAL YEARS JEREMIAH AND THE KING WORK TOGETHER TO DESTROY IDOL WORSHIP. THEN, ONE DAY, JEREMIAH HEARS SOME FRIGHTENING NEWS.

THE ASSYRIAN EMPIRE IS CRACKING UP. EGYPT IS MARCHING NORTH TO GRAB WHAT'S LEFT. KING JOSIAH DECLARES HE WILL STOP THE EGYPTIAN ARMY FROM MARCHING THROUGH JUDAH.

STOP EGYPT? WHY, IT'S ONE OF THE STRONGEST COUNTRIES IN THE WORLD! THE KING IS MAKING A BIG MISTAKE.

BUT KING JOSIAH LEADS HIS SOLDIERS OUT OF THE GATES OF JERUSALEM — AND INTO THE PATH OF THE ONCOMING EGYPTIAN ARMY.

The Broken Vase

FROM JEREMIAH 18—20:2;
2 KINGS 23:29-37

KING JOSIAH IS KILLED AS HE ATTEMPTS TO DEFEAT THE EGYPTIANS. NOW HIS SON, JEHOIAKIM, SITS ON THE THRONE OF JUDAH AS A PUPPET RULER FOR EGYPT. AT ONCE THE IDOL WORSHIPERS BEGIN THEIR CAMPAIGN AGAINST GOD AND HIS PROPHET, JEREMIAH.

O KING, YOUR FATHER ORDERED US NOT TO WORSHIP ANY GOD BUT JEHOVAH. AND WHAT HAPPENED? JUDAH IS NO LONGER A FREE COUNTRY. JOIN US IN WORSHIPING OUR GODS SO THAT JUDAH WILL BECOME STRONG-- LIKE OUR NEIGHBORS.

JEHOIAKIM AGREES--AND IN SPITE OF JEREMIAH'S WARNINGS, MANY OF THE PEOPLE FOLLOW THE KING'S LEAD.

GO AWAY, JEREMIAH. NOBODY WANTS TO LISTEN TO YOUR FAR-FETCHED STORIES ABOUT JUDAH BEING DESTROYED!

Surextender

From Jeremiah 20—36

BECAUSE JEREMIAH HAS DARED TELL THE PEOPLE THAT JUDAH WILL BE DESTROYED FOR ITS WICKEDNESS, THE PRIESTS HAVE HIM BEATEN AND PLACED IN STOCKS. WHEN HE IS RELEASED, A YOUNG SCRIBE, BARUCH, OFFERS TO HELP HIM.

COME WITH ME AND GET SOME REST.

REST? THERE'S TOO MUCH TO DO, AND TOO LITTLE TIME.

JEREMIAH IS RIGHT-- THERE IS LITTLE TIME. NEWS OF A GREAT BATTLE IS ALREADY SPREADING THROUGHOUT JERUSALEM...

THE BABYLONIANS HAVE DEFEATED EGYPT!

WE'VE BEEN UNDER EGYPT'S CONTROL-- WHAT'S GOING TO HAPPEN TO US NOW?

JUDAH DOESN'T HAVE LONG TO WAIT FOR ITS ANSWER. BABYLON ATTACKS JERUSALEM, AND KING JEHOIAKIM IS FORCED TO SURRENDER.

YOU MAY REMAIN ON THE THRONE, JEHOIAKIM, BUT NOW YOU MUST PAY TRIBUTE MONEY TO ME. AND TO SEE THAT YOU DO, I'LL TAKE YOUR BEST PRINCES AS HOSTAGES.

WITHIN DAYS ALL JERUSALEM SADLY WATCHES ITS FINEST YOUNG MEN BEING MARCHED AWAY.

KNOWING THAT THE DOWNFALL OF JUDAH IS NOT FAR OFF, JEREMIAH DICTATES ALL OF THE MESSAGES HE HAS RECEIVED FROM GOD.

THE PEOPLE MUST BE TOLD THAT GOD IS ALLOWING JUDAH TO BE PUNISHED FOR ITS SINS.

THEN-- BECAUSE HE IS NOT ALLOWED IN THE TEMPLE --JEREMIAH ASKS BARUCH TO READ GOD'S WORD TO THE PEOPLE.

WE MUST SEE THAT THE KING LEARNS ABOUT THIS.

498

AS THE SCROLL IS READ TO THE KING, HE BE-COMES SO ANGRY THAT HE CUTS IT UP PIECE BY PIECE AND THROWS IT INTO THE FIRE.

ARREST JEREMIAH AND BARUCH. THROW THEM INTO PRISON. THAT WILL KEEP THEM QUIET.

BUT JEREMIAH AND BARUCH ARE PREPARED FOR THE KING'S ANGER-- ALREADY THEY ARE IN HIDING.

THE KING BURNED THE SCROLL--BUT WE WILL WRITE ANOTHER.

WHILE JEREMIAH AND BARUCH ARE BUSY RE-PLACING THE BURNED SCROLL, TROUBLE IS BREWING IN THE PALACE.

WHY SHOULD WE PAY TRIBUTE TO BABYLON? I SAY LET'S STOP IT AND USE THE MONEY TO BUILD UP OUR OWN ARMY. THEN WE'LL BE READY IF BABYLON ATTACKS US AGAIN.

YOU'RE RIGHT-- THOSE HOSTAGES IN BABYLON ARE NOT AS IMPORTANT AS ALL OF US HERE IN JUDAH.

IN TIME, WORD LEAKS OUT THAT KING JEHOIAKIM IS BREAKING HIS AGREEMENT WITH BABYLON. JEREMIAH IS ALARMED.

THE KING'S DECISION IS AGAINST THE WILL OF GOD. AND NO MAN CAN DEFY GOD!

Babylon Strikes!

FROM 2 KINGS 24—25:4
JEREMIAH 27; 28:1–12
37:1–10

WITH FULL FORCE THE ARMY OF BABYLON STORMS THE WALLS OF JERUSALEM.

YOUNG KING JEHOIACHIN, WHO HAS RULED THREE MONTHS, IS FORCED TO SURRENDER TO KING NEBUCHADNEZZAR.

THIS TIME I WILL TAKE YOUR TREASURES, YOUR NOBLES, YOUR SKILLED WORKERS **AND** YOUR KING. LET THIS BE A LESSON TO YOU WHO ARE LEFT!

SO JEREMIAH'S PROPHECY COMES TRUE! THE TEMPLE TREASURES ARE LOOTED, THE KING AND 10,000 OF JUDAH'S ABLEST MEN ARE LED AWAY. PRINCE ZEDEKIAH IS MADE KING-- **AFTER** HE PROMISES LOYALTY TO BABYLON.

FOR A FEW YEARS KING ZEDEKIAH PAYS TRIBUTE TO BABYLON. THEN, IN SPITE OF JEREMIAH'S WARNINGS, HE BEGINS TO LISTEN TO SOME HOT-HEADED YOUNG ADVISERS IN HIS COURT.

WHAT DO **WE** GET FROM THE MONEY PAID TO BABYLON?

WELL-- WE GET PEACE.

PEACE--BUT NOT FREEDOM! MAYBE THE EGYPTIANS WILL HELP US--THEY HATE BABYLON, TOO.

LET ME THINK ABOUT IT.

WHEN JEREMIAH LEARNS THAT THERE IS TALK OF ANOTHER REVOLT, HE PUTS AN OX YOKE ON HIS SHOULDERS AND WALKS THROUGH THE STREETS.

WHAT'S THE MEANING OF THIS?

BABYLON HAS STRUCK TWICE, AND IT WILL STRIKE AGAIN. THE NEXT TIME IT WILL DESTROY JERUSALEM. JUDAH'S ONLY HOPE OF SURVIVAL IS TO WEAR THE YOKE OF BABYLON AS I AM WEARING THIS ONE.

I'LL SHOW YOU WHAT TO DO WITH THE YOKE OF BABYLON. BREAK IT!

DURING ALL OF THIS TIME, EGYPT KEEPS AN ANXIOUS EYE ON THE GROWING TENSIONS IN JUDAH. AT THE RIGHT MOMENT IT SENDS AN AMBASSADOR TO KING ZEDEKIAH.

BABYLON IS YOUR ENEMY AS WELL AS OURS. ALONE, NEITHER ONE OF US CAN DEFEAT THEM, BUT--

TOGETHER WE CAN! AND WE WILL!

Accused

FROM JEREMIAH 37—38:6

BACKED BY EGYPT'S PROMISE TO HELP, KING ZEDEKIAH OF JUDAH REVOLTS AGAINST THE CONTROL OF BABYLON. JEREMIAH ARGUES AGAINST THE DECISION.

BABYLON HAS SPARED JERUSALEM TWICE BEFORE. BUT IF YOU GO THROUGH WITH THIS REVOLT, BABYLON WILL NOT SPARE THE CITY AGAIN.

BUT THIS TIME WE'LL WIN. JUDAH WILL BE FREE!

AS JEREMIAH PROPHESIED, BABYLON ANSWERS THE REVOLT WITH A SWIFT ATTACK. FOR WEEKS THE SOLDIERS OF JUDAH FIGHT TO DEFEND JERUSALEM'S WALLS.

THE EGYPTIANS! WHY DON'T THEY COME AS THEY PROMISED?

THEN -- SUDDENLY -- THE ATTACK CEASES...

THE BABYLONIANS ARE BREAKING CAMP-- THEY'VE GIVEN UP THE SIEGE!

WE'VE WON! JUDAH IS FREE!

LONG LIVE KING ZEDEKIAH!

NO! THE BABYLONIANS HAVE NOT QUIT. THEY'VE GONE TO STOP THE EGYPTIANS WHO WERE COMING TO HELP US. THEY'LL BE BACK.

HOW DOES HE KNOW SO MUCH ABOUT WHAT THE BABYLONIANS ARE DOING?

A FEW DAYS LATER JEREMIAH STARTS ON A TRIP TO HIS HOME TOWN -- A FEW MILES FROM JERUSALEM. BUT BEFORE HE GETS OUT OF THE GATE, HE IS STOPPED.

HALT! YOU'RE UNDER ARREST!

WHY? I HAVE DONE NOTHING WRONG.

IN SPITE OF HIS INNOCENCE, JEREMIAH IS THROWN INTO PRISON. WITHIN A FEW WEEKS THE BABYLONIANS, AFTER DEFEATING THE EGYPTIANS, RETURN TO THE GATES OF JERUSALEM. JEREMIAH'S ENEMIES BRING HIM BEFORE THE KING AND ACCUSE HIM OF BEING A TRAITOR.

I REPEAT THE WARNING GOD HAS GIVEN ME. INVADERS FROM THE NORTH WILL CONQUER JUDAH. GOD HAS CHOSEN THE BABYLONIANS TO DESTROY OUR NATION BECAUSE OF THE SINS OF ITS PEOPLE.

IT'S THIS KIND OF TALK THAT MAKES OUR SOLDIERS LOSE COURAGE. PUT THIS TRAITOR TO DEATH--OR THE CITY **WILL** FALL.

HE IS IN YOUR HANDS--DO WHAT YOU WANT WITH HIM.

QUICKLY-- BEFORE THE KING CAN CHANGE HIS MIND-- JEREMIAH IS PUT INTO AN OLD CISTERN BENEATH THE PRISON FLOOR.

LET HIM STARVE TO DEATH!

A Prophecy Comes True

FROM JEREMIAH 38:7—43:7

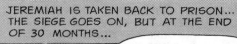

JEREMIAH IS TAKEN BACK TO PRISON... THE SIEGE GOES ON, BUT AT THE END OF 30 MONTHS...

THE BABYLONIANS HAVE BROKEN THROUGH THE WALL!

JERUSALEM WILL BE DESTROYED! BUT IT WILL RISE AGAIN... AND SOMEDAY GOD'S COMMANDMENTS WILL BE WRITTEN IN THE HEARTS OF MEN WHO CHOOSE TO OBEY GOD. THEY WILL LIVE TOGETHER IN PEACE.

KING ZEDEKIAH TRIES TO ESCAPE, BUT IS CAPTURED AND BLINDED. THE KING, JEREMIAH, AND MOST OF THE ABLE-BODIED PEOPLE ARE CAPTURED TO BE TAKEN TO BABYLON.

BUT IN THE CAPTIVE CAMP AT RAMAH...

THE KING OF BABYLON HAS LEARNED THAT YOU TRIED TO KEEP YOUR COUNTRY FROM REBELLING AGAINST HIM, SO HE HAS SENT ORDERS TO SET YOU FREE.

THANK GOD! NOW I CAN HELP THE PEOPLE WHO HAVE BEEN LEFT IN ISRAEL WITHOUT A LEADER.

ABOUT A MONTH AFTER JERUSALEM IS TAKEN, A BABYLONIAN OFFICER RETURNS, TAKES MORE CAPTIVES, AND THEN SETS FIRE TO THE CITY.

THE FIRE RAGES FOR DAYS -- UNTIL THE ONCE-PROUD CAPITAL OF JUDAH BECOMES A HEAP OF SMOULDERING RUINS.

THE BABYLONIANS SET UP HEADQUARTERS AT MIZPAH AND APPOINT AN ISRAELITE TO ACT AS GOVERNOR. JEREMIAH JOINS HIM -- AND BECOMES HIS ADVISER.

TOGETHER WE'LL ENCOURAGE THE PEOPLE TO BUILD UP THEIR HOMES AND REPLANT THEIR VINEYARDS AND FIELDS.

SOMEDAY THE CAPTIVES WILL RETURN-- AND JUDAH WILL BECOME A NATION AGAIN.

BUT BEFORE THE GOVERNOR'S DREAM CAN COME TRUE HE IS MURDERED BY SOME ISRAELITES WHO ARE JEALOUS OF HIS POWER IN THE COUNTRY. FEARFUL THAT BABYLON WILL BLAME ALL ISRAEL FOR THE MURDER, A GROUP OF PEOPLE GO TO JEREMIAH...

WE WANT TO GO TO EGYPT-- WHERE THERE IS PEACE AND PLENTY TO EAT.

YOU WILL FIND NEITHER PEACE NOR PLENTY IN EGYPT. STAY HERE -- THE BABYLONIANS WILL NOT HURT YOU.

BUT THE PEOPLE DO NOT BELIEVE JEREMIAH. THEY FLEE TO EGYPT, FORCING HIM TO GO WITH THEM. AND THERE, UNTIL HE DIES, JEREMIAH TRIES TO LEAD HIS PEOPLE BACK TO GOD.

HE GRIEF OF THE JEWS OVER THE DESTRUCTION OF JERUSALEM IS EXPRESSED IN A GROUP OF POEMS FOUND IN THE

BOOK OF LAMENTATIONS

Ten Thousand Captives

FROM EZEKIEL 1; JEREMIAH 29:1–14

FRIGHTENED AND WEARY FROM THE 900 MILE MARCH, THE 10,000 CAPTIVES FROM JUDAH REACH THE GATES OF BABYLON, THE GIANT CITY OF THEIR CONQUERORS.

TO UNDERSTAND THE **BOOK OF EZEKIEL**, YOU MUST TURN BACK THE PAGES OF TIME-- TO BABYLON'S SECOND SIEGE OF JERUSALEM. JERUSALEM SURRENDERED AND WAS FORCED TO WATCH 10,000 OF ITS PEOPLE MARCHED AWAY AS CAPTIVES. BUT GOD DID NOT FORSAKE THESE CAPTIVES-- HE CALLED ONE OF THEM, A YOUNG PRIEST NAMED EZEKIEL, TO SERVE AS HIS PROPHET AMONG THE EXILES IN BABYLON.

ONLY GOD KNOWS WHAT WILL HAPPEN TO US NOW.

EZEKIEL, A YOUNG PRIEST, AND HIS WIFE ARE AMONG THE CAPTIVES WONDERING WHERE THEY WILL LIVE.

WHERE ARE WE GOING?

TO TEL-ABIB, ON THE CHEBAR CANAL. YOU CAN BUILD YOUR HOMES THERE AND WORK THE FIELDS.

IN THE MONTHS THAT FOLLOW, EZEKIEL WORKS HARD TO MAKE A LIVING IN THE NEW LAND.

IT IS NOT AS BAD AS I FEARED. WE ARE WELL TREATED--AND WE ARE TOGETHER.

YES. WE MAY HAVE TO STAY HERE THE REST OF OUR LIVES, BUT GOD IS WITH US WHEREVER WE ARE.

BUT NOT ALL OF THE CAPTIVES FEEL THE SAME WAY.

WHAT DO YOU THINK OF EZEKIEL PLANTING TREES AND PLANNING TO BUILD A HOUSE? LOOKS AS IF HE INTENDS TO STAY IN BABYLONIA.

HE'S WASTING HIS TIME. WE'LL BE ON OUR WAY HOME IN A COUPLE OF YEARS.

WHEN THIS NEWS REACHES GOD'S PROPHET, JEREMIAH, IN JUDAH, HE WRITES A LETTER TO THE CAPTIVES.

JEREMIAH SAYS IT IS GOD'S WILL THAT WE STAY HERE. WE SHOULD BUILD HOMES AND WORK FOR THE GOOD OF OUR NEW COUNTRY. WE WILL BE HERE FOR SEVENTY YEARS.

DID YOU HEAR THAT, EZEKIEL? SEVENTY YEARS -- I DON'T BELIEVE IT!

JEREMIAH SPEAKS THE WILL OF GOD.

EZEKIEL SHOWS HIS FAITH BY BUILDING A HOUSE.

WE'LL MAKE A LARGE COURTYARD -- BIG ENOUGH TO INVITE PEOPLE HERE TO WORSHIP GOD. I USED TO THINK THAT WE COULD WORSHIP GOD ONLY IN THE TEMPLE IN JERUSALEM, BUT NOW I KNOW WE CAN WORSHIP HIM ANYWHERE.

511

A Message of Hope

FROM EZEKIEL 1—48

512

EZEKIEL KEEPS WARNING THE PEOPLE THAT JERUSALEM WILL BE DESTROYED, BUT THEY REFUSE TO BELIEVE HIM. THEN--SUDDENLY-- EZEKIEL'S WIFE DIES. BUT THE PROPHET SHOWS NO OUTWARD SIGN OF GRIEF.

WE MOURN FOR YOUR WIFE, EZEKIEL. WHY DO YOU NOT MOURN FOR THE ONE YOU LOVED?

YES, I LOVED HER VERY MUCH. BUT GOD HAS COMMANDED ME NOT TO SHOW MY GRIEF, AS A SIGN THAT YOU ARE NOT TO SHOW YOUR GRIEF WHEN JERUSALEM FALLS.

BUT THE PEOPLE WILL NOT GIVE UP BELIEVING THAT JERUSALEM WILL BE STANDING--STRONG AND BEAUTIFUL-- WAITING FOR THEIR RETURN. ONE DAY A MAN STAGGERS WEARILY INTO THEIR MIDST...

WHAT BRINGS YOU HERE?

I'M FROM WHAT **WAS** JERUSALEM.

514

Captives in Babylon

FROM DANIEL 1—2:13

THE STORY OF WHAT HAPPENED TO A ROYAL CAPTIVE FROM JUDAH BEGINS WHEN DANIEL AND HIS THREE FRIENDS—SHADRACH, MESHACH, AND ABEDNEGO—ENTER THE CITY OF BABYLON AT THE END OF THEIR 900 MILE MARCH FROM JERUSALEM.

WHAT DO YOU THINK THEY'LL DO TO US, DANIEL?

I DON'T KNOW, SHADRACH. BUT I AM SURE OF THIS, GOD IS WITH US.

SOON AFTER THE PRISONERS REACH THE CITY, DANIEL AND SEVERAL OTHERS ARE BROUGHT BEFORE AN OFFICER OF KING NEBUCHADNEZZAR.

AS NOBLES FROM JERUSALEM, YOU WILL BE GIVEN A CHANCE TO TRY OUT FOR POSITIONS IN THE KING'S COURT. BUT I WARN YOU--ONLY THE SMARTEST AND STRONGEST CAN PASS OUR TESTS.

FOR DAYS THE YOUNG MEN ARE GIVEN EXAMINATIONS TO TEST THEIR PHYSICAL STRENGTH AND MENTAL ALERTNESS.

THIS IS THE LAST TEST. BY TOMORROW YOU WILL KNOW HOW MANY PASSED.

WHAT IF WE FAIL?

WE'VE DONE OUR BEST-- THAT'S ALL WE CAN DO.

THE NEXT DAY,...

YOU HAVE ALL PASSED -- NOW YOU'LL BE GIVEN THREE YEARS TO STUDY UNDER OUR WISE MEN. AFTER THAT THE KING HIMSELF WILL CHOOSE THOSE BEST QUALIFIED TO BE HIS ADVISERS.

O GOD, THANK YOU. HELP US TO PASS THESE NEW TESTS SO THAT WE MAY ADVISE THE KING IN A WAY THAT WILL PLEASE YOU.

THE YOUNG MEN ARE TAKEN AT ONCE TO THE PALACE TO BEGIN THEIR STUDIES. THEY ARE GIVEN THE BEST OF EVERYTHING -- EVEN FOOD FROM THE KING'S TABLE.

THANK YOU, BUT WE CANNOT EAT THIS MEAT AND DRINK THIS WINE. OUR HEBREW LAWS FORBID IT. GIVE US PLAIN FOOD AND WATER, PLEASE.

BUT IT'S THE KING'S ORDER -- WE DARE NOT DISOBEY. I LIKE YOU, DANIEL, BUT I DON'T WANT TO GET INTO TROUBLE.

GIVE US A TEN-DAY TRIAL. LET US EAT OUR FOOD AND THEN SEE IF WE ARE NOT STRONGER THAN THE OTHERS.

THE TEST IS MADE, AND AT THE END OF TEN DAYS, THERE'S NO DOUBT--DANIEL AND HIS FRIENDS NOT ONLY **LOOK** STRONGER, THEY **ARE** STRONGER.

AT THE END OF THREE YEARS, THE YOUNG MEN ARE BROUGHT BEFORE THE KING. HE TALKS WITH EACH ONE, THEN MAKES HIS DECISION.

I HAVE CHOSEN THESE FOUR--DANIEL, SHADRACH, MESHACH, AND ABEDNEGO -- TO SERVE AS MY ADVISERS.

THERE IS NONE TO EQUAL THEM, SIR.

DANIEL AND HIS FRIENDS BECOME POPULAR MEMBERS OF THE KING'S COURT. BUT ONE DAY THE KING HAS AN UNUSUALLY DIFFICULT PROBLEM AND HE CALLS FOR ONLY HIS OLDER, MORE EXPERIENCED ADVISERS.

I HAD A STRANGE DREAM, BUT I HAVE FORGOTTEN IT. TELL ME WHAT IT WAS AND WHAT IT MEANS.

WE CAN TELL YOU WHAT A DREAM MEANS, SIR, BUT NO MAN CAN TELL YOU WHAT YOU DREAMED.

WHAT GOOD ARE ADVISERS IF THEY CAN'T TELL ME WHAT I WANT TO KNOW? PUT THESE MEN TO DEATH -- AND EVERY WISE MAN IN MY KINGDOM!

THE CAPTAIN OF THE KING'S GUARD IS FORCED TO CARRY OUT HIS UGLY TASK.

DANIEL, YOU AND YOUR FRIENDS ARE UNDER ARREST --THE KING HAS ORDERED ALL OF HIS WISE MEN PUT TO DEATH.

TO DEATH? WHY? WHAT HAVE WE DONE?

The Statue

FROM DANIEL 2:16—3:6

KING NEBUCHADNEZZAR IS FURIOUS! HIS WISE MEN CANNOT TELL HIM WHAT HE HAS DREAMED. SO HE ORDERS ALL OF THEM PUT TO DEATH-- INCLUDING DANIEL AND HIS THREE FRIENDS, SHADRACH, MESHACH, AND ABEDNEGO. DANIEL ASKS FOR PERMISSION TO SPEAK TO THE KING.

O KING, GIVE ME TIME AND I WILL TELL YOU WHAT YOU DREAMED.

YOU HAVE UNTIL TOMORROW AT THIS HOUR-- BUT NOT ONE MINUTE MORE.

DANIEL RUSHES BACK TO HIS FRIENDS WITH THE GOOD NEWS.

BUT, DANIEL, NO MAN ON EARTH CAN DO WHAT YOU HAVE PROMISED TO DO.

YOU ARE RIGHT-- NO MAN CAN DO IT, BUT GOD CAN. AND WE WILL ASK HIM TO GIVE US THE ANSWER.

518

AS THE FOUR YOUNG HEBREWS PRAY, A VISION COMES TO DANIEL.

O GOD, THANK YOU FOR MAKING THE DREAM KNOWN TO ME.

THE NEXT DAY--

HAVE YOU COME TO ASK FOR MORE TIME -- OR CAN YOU TELL ME MY DREAM?

GOD IN HEAVEN HAS REVEALED YOUR DREAM TO ME.

YOU SAW A MIGHTY STATUE -- ITS HEAD WAS MADE OF GOLD AND ITS FEET OF CLAY. THEN YOU SAW A LARGE STONE STRIKE AT THE FEET OF THE STATUE AND BREAK IT INTO MANY PIECES.

YES! YES! THAT'S RIGHT. BUT WHAT DOES IT MEAN?

THE HEAD OF GOLD STANDS FOR YOU AND YOUR GREAT KINGDOM, O KING. OTHER LESSER KINGDOMS WILL FOLLOW. BUT AFTER THEY FALL, GOD WILL SET UP A KINGDOM WHICH SHALL NEVER BE DESTROYED.

YOUR GOD IS A GOD ABOVE ALL GODS. AND YOU SHALL BE RULER OF THE PROVINCE OF BABYLON-- OVER ALL THE WISE MEN WHOSE LIVES YOU SAVED THIS DAY.

DANIEL RELAYS THE GOOD NEWS TO HIS HEBREW FRIENDS.

THE KING HAS MADE ME RULER OVER BABYLON AND EACH OF YOU HAS AN IMPORTANT OFFICE IN THE KINGDOM.

THAT'S WONDERFUL!

BUT THE NEWS DOES NOT PLEASE THE KING'S OTHER ADVISERS.

SO THE KING HAS PUT THIS YOUNG HEBREW OVER **US**! WE MUST GET RID OF HIM.

NOT NOW-- HE'S TOO POWERFUL! BUT IF WE CAN TURN THE KING AGAINST DANIEL'S FRIENDS, WE MIGHT BE ABLE TO CAUSE DANIEL TROUBLE.

THEIR OPPORTUNITY COMES WHEN THE KING BUILDS A STATUE AND ORDERS HIS OFFICIALS TO WORSHIP IT--OR BE THROWN INTO A FIERY FURNACE.

THE KING IS PLAYING RIGHT INTO OUR HANDS --HE DOESN'T KNOW THAT HEBREWS WILL WORSHIP ONLY THEIR GOD.

DANIEL HOLDS TOO HIGH A POSITION FOR ANY ONE OF US TO REPORT ON HIM--BUT NOT HIS FRIENDS...

RIGHT--AND TOMORROW WHEN THE TRUMPET SOUNDS FOR ALL MEN TO BOW BEFORE THE STATUE, WE'LL KEEP OUR EYES ON SHADRACH, MESHACH, AND ABEDNEGO.

Trial by Fire

FROM DANIEL 3:1–25

521

EAGERLY, THE JEALOUS ADVISERS REPORT TO THE KING.

O KING, THREE OF YOUR HEBREW OFFICIALS HAVE DEFIED YOU. THEY REFUSE TO WORSHIP YOUR STATUE.

WHAT? HAVE THEM BROUGHT TO ME AT ONCE!

WORSHIP THE STATUE -- OR BE THROWN INTO THE FIERY FURNACE. AND TELL ME -- WHAT GOD CAN SAVE YOU FROM THAT?

IF WE ARE CAST INTO THE FIRE, THE GOD WHOM WE SERVE WILL BE ABLE TO DELIVER US! BUT EVEN IF WE MUST DIE, WE WILL NOT WORSHIP AN IDOL.

HEAT THE FURNACE -- SEVEN TIMES HOTTER THAN EVER BEFORE -- AND THROW THEM IN IT!

THE THREE HEBREWS ARE QUICKLY BOUND AND THROWN INTO THE RAGING FIRE.

A King's Boast

FROM 3:26—5:6

WHEN KING NEBUCHADNEZZAR SEES THAT DANIEL'S FRIENDS ARE NOT BURNED IN THE FIERY FURNACE, HE IS AFRAID AND ORDERS THEM OUT.

BLESSED BE THE GOD OF SHADRACH, MESHACH AND ABEDNEGO, WHO SENT HIS ANGEL TO SAVE THEM. AND IF ANY MAN DARES TO SAY A WORD AGAINST THEIR GOD, HE WILL DIE!

IT WOULDN'T BE SMART FOR US TO MAKE ANY MORE ATTACKS ON THE HEBREWS.

WHEN THE KING HAS ANOTHER DREAM, HE AGAIN CALLS FOR DANIEL.

NONE OF MY OTHER ADVISERS CAN TELL ME WHAT IT MEANS. CAN YOU?

YES--BUT YOU WILL NOT LIKE IT.

THE TREE YOU DREAMED ABOUT IS YOU, O KING-- TALL, STRONG, AND PROUD. YOU SAW THE TREE CUT DOWN. THIS MEANS THAT YOUR POWER AS KING WILL BE TAKEN FROM YOU IF YOU DO NOT HONOR GOD ABOVE YOURSELF.

THE KING IS UPSET BY WHAT DANIEL SAYS, BUT IN TIME HE FORGETS... ONE DAY AS HE WALKS IN HIS PALACE ROOF GARDEN...

LOOK AT THE GREAT CITY I HAVE BUILT! LONG AFTER I AM GONE IT WILL BE A TRIBUTE TO MY POWER AND MIGHT!

AS THE BOASTFUL WORDS ARE SPOKEN, DANIEL'S WARNING COMES TRUE. THE KING LOSES HIS MIND-- AND FOR SEVEN YEARS HE LIVES LIKE A BEAST OF THE FIELD. THEN ONE DAY THE KING REALIZES HE IS BEING PUNISHED FOR FAILING TO HONOR GOD.

O GOD OF DANIEL AND THE HEBREWS, I HONOR AND PRAISE THEE, WHOSE KINGDOM IS GREAT AND EVERLASTING-- WHOSE WORK IS TRUTH AND JUSTICE.

INSTANTLY KING NEBUCHADNEZZAR'S MIND IS RESTORED. HE RETURNS TO THE THRONE AND RULES WISELY WITH DANIEL AS HIS ADVISER.

BUT AFTER HIS DEATH THE RULERS WHO FOLLOW HIM TURN AWAY FROM DANIEL. ONE OF THEM, BELSHAZZAR, IS SO SURE OF HIS OWN WISDOM THAT...

HE LAUGHS AT TWO GREAT THREATS TO HIS KINGDOM: ANGRY PRIESTS WHO ARE TURNING AGAINST HIM, AND THE APPROACH OF THE MIGHTY PERSIAN ARMY. INSTEAD, HE PREPARES A GREAT FEAST TO WHICH HE INVITES A THOUSAND GUESTS...

THE PARTY IS AT ITS MERRIEST WHEN SUDDENLY BELSHAZZAR STARES AT A PLACE HIGH ON THE BANQUET WALL. HE TURNS PALE-- HIS HANDS TREMBLE...

LOOK! ON THE WALL! WHAT IS IT? WHAT DOES IT MEAN?

Handwriting on the Wall

FROM DANIEL 5:7—6:15

It is midnight! Outside the walls of Babylon the Persian army waits for traitors within to open the city gates. But inside-- in the banquet hall of the palace-- King Belshazzar eats and drinks merrily with his guests. Suddenly he sees a hand write four words on the wall.

MENE MENE TEKEL UPHARSIN

TERRIFIED, BELSHAZZAR CALLS FOR HIS ADVISERS TO EXPLAIN THE WORDS, BUT THEY CANNOT. WHEN THE KING'S MOTHER HEARS THE EXCITEMENT IN THE BANQUET HALL SHE RUSHES TO HER SON.

MY SON, THERE'S A MAN IN YOUR KINGDOM NAMED DANIEL WHO CAN INTERPRET DREAMS. CALL HIM.

DANIEL! YES! YES! BRING HIM HERE AT ONCE!

NOT A SOUND IS HEARD IN THE GREAT BANQUET HALL UNTIL DANIEL APPEARS BEFORE THE KING.

TELL ME WHAT THOSE WORDS MEAN AND YOU SHALL BE SECOND ONLY TO ME IN ALL BABYLON.

O KING, THEY ARE A WARNING FROM GOD. YOU HAVE BEEN MEASURED AND FOUND LACKING IN THE QUALITIES OF A RULER. YOUR KINGDOM WILL BE GIVEN TO THE PERSIANS.

I DON'T BELIEVE YOUR MESSAGE, BUT I'LL KEEP MY PROMISE. HERE, THIS CHAIN MAKES YOU NEXT TO ME IN ALL THE KINGDOM. NOW, ON WITH THE FEAST!

AS BELSHAZZAR SPEAKS, PERSIAN SOLDIERS SUDDENLY FILL THE HALL--AND TAKE HIM PRISONER.

SOLDIERS? WHERE DID THEY COME FROM? MY GUARDS! WHERE ARE MY GUARDS?

528

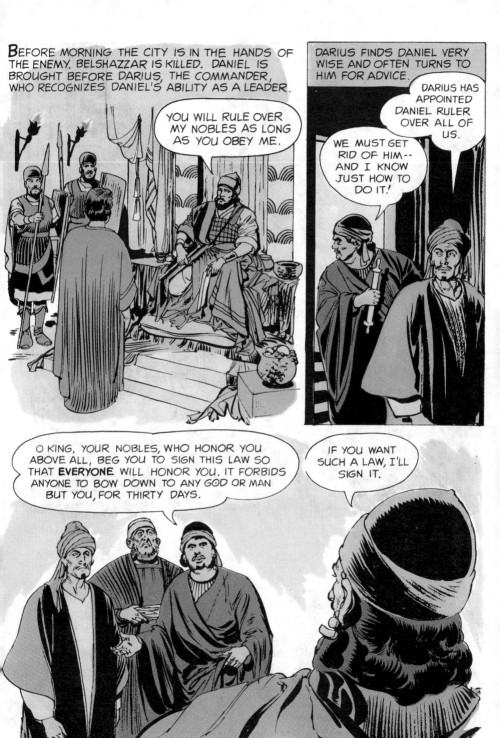

529

The Lions' Den

FROM DANIEL 6:16–28

SEAL THE DEN WITH A STONE SO THAT EVERYONE WILL KNOW I AM ENFORCING THE LAW.

IF ONLY I COULD CHANGE THIS ONE LAW TO SAVE MY FRIEND.

THAT NIGHT THE KING CAN NEITHER EAT NOR SLEEP. HE PACES UP AND DOWN HIS ROOM -- THINKING OF DANIEL.

AT DAYBREAK HE RUSHES TO THE LIONS' DEN.

ROLL AWAY THAT STONE!

DANIEL! DANIEL! DID YOUR GOD PROTECT YOU?

Twelve Men of God

FROM THE MINOR PROPHETS

THE LAST TWELVE BOOKS OF THE OLD TESTAMENT ARE CALLED THE MINOR PROPHETS. EACH IS NAMED FOR A MAN WHOM GOD CALLED TO SPEAK FOR HIM AT A CRUCIAL TIME IN THE HISTORY OF ISRAEL AND JUDAH.

HOSEA -- the Prophet of Love

HOSEA LOVES HIS WIFE, GOMER, VERY MUCH. BUT ONE DAY SHE RUNS AWAY. HOSEA IS BROKENHEARTED. THEN SUDDENLY HE SEES THAT THE PEOPLE OF ISRAEL HAVE TREATED GOD THE WAY GOMER HAS TREATED HIM. GOD LOVE. HIS PEOPLE, BUT THEY HAVE RUN AWAY TO WORSHIP IDOLS.

CAN GOD FORGIVE THEM? "YES," HOSEA SAYS, "FOR I CAN FORGIVE GOMER, AND GOD'S LOVE IS GREATER THAN MINE."

"GOD LOVES YOU. HE WILL FORGIVE YOUR SINS IF YOU CONFESS THEM AND WORSHIP HIM." THIS IS HOSEA'S MESSAGE TO THE PEOPLE OF ISRAEL.

AMOS -- and the Crooked Wall

JOEL -- and the Plague of Locusts

LIKE A MIGHTY ARMY DESTROYING EVERYTHING IN ITS PATH, MILLIONS OF LOCUSTS SWARM OVER THE LAND OF JUDAH. THEY DEVOUR THE CROPS -- LEAVING ONLY BARREN FIELDS BEHIND.

"WHAT WILL WE DO?" THE PEOPLE CRY.

THE PROPHET JOEL ANSWERS: "REPENT OF YOUR SINS. SEEK GOD'S HELP, AND HE WILL RESTORE THE LAND."

THEN HE ADDS THIS PROMISE: "ONE DAY GOD WILL SEND HIS HOLY SPIRIT INTO THE HEARTS OF HIS PEOPLE."

AMOS, A SHEPHERD OF JUDAH, IS WATCHING HIS SHEEP WHEN GOD CALLS HIM TO A DANGEROUS JOB. "GO," GOD SAYS, "TO THE NEIGHBORING COUNTRY OF ISRAEL AND TELL THE PEOPLE THAT THEY ARE GOING TO BE PUNISHED FOR THEIR SINS."

WITHOUT PROTESTING, AMOS ACCEPTS THE JOB AND GOES TO THE CITY OF BETHEL IN ISRAEL.

"PREPARE TO MEET THY GOD," HE TELLS THE PEOPLE OF ISRAEL, "FOR YOU ARE LIKE A CROOKED WALL THAT MUST BE DESTROYED BEFORE A NEW ONE CAN BE BUILT."

OBADIAH -- the Angry Prophet

OBADIAH IS ANGRY AT JUDAH'S NEIGHBOR, THE NATION OF EDOM. "YOU CHEERED," HE CRIES TO EDOM, "WHEN BABYLON DESTROYED JERUSALEM. YOU HELPED TO ROB THE CITY OF ITS TREASURES. YOU CAPTURED THE PEOPLE AS THEY TRIED TO ESCAPE AND TURNED THEM OVER TO THE ENEMY."

THEN HE PREDICTS EDOM'S PUNISHMENT: "BECAUSE YOUR CAPITAL CITY IS PROTECTED BY ROCKY CLIFFS, YOU THINK IT CANNOT BE DESTROYED. BUT IT CAN! AND IT WILL-- AS WILL EVERY NATION THAT DISOBEYS GOD."

JONAH -- the Man Who Ran Away

NINEVEH IS ONE OF THE MOST WICKED CITIES IN THE WORLD. SO, WHEN GOD TELLS JONAH TO GO TO NINEVEH WITH A MESSAGE TO SAVE THE CITY FROM ITS ENEMIES, JONAH RUNS THE OTHER WAY.

BUT AFTER A LESSON FROM GOD, JONAH OBEYS. HE TELLS NINEVEH TO REPENT OF ITS SINS-- AND HE PREACHES HIS MESSAGE SO SUCCESSFULLY THAT THE CITY DOES REPENT AND IS SAVED FROM DESTRUCTION.

THE MESSAGE OF THE BOOK OF JONAH IS THIS: GOD LOVES ALL PEOPLE. THOSE WHO KNOW GOD MUST TELL OTHERS ABOUT HIM.

MICAH -- Champion of the Poor

MICAH, A SMALL-TOWN PROPHET, IS A CHAMPION OF THE POOR. HE DARES TO CON- DEMN THE WEALTHY LEADERS OF JUDAH AND ISRAEL.

"YOU HATE JUSTICE," HE SHOUTS, "AND YOU OPPRESS THE POOR. BECAUSE YOU DO, JUDAH AND ISRAEL HAVE BECOME SO WEAK AND CORRUPT THAT THEY WILL BE DESTROYED."

WHEN THE PEOPLE ASK WHAT GOD EXPECTS THEM TO DO, MICAH ANSWERS: "DO JUSTLY, LOVE MERCY, AND WALK HUMBLY WITH THY GOD."

AND TO THOSE WHO WILL LISTEN HE MAKES A WONDERFUL PROMISE: "IN THE LITTLE TOWN OF BETHLEHEM A SAVIOR WILL BE BORN--A SAVIOR WHOSE KINGDOM OF PEACE WILL LAST FOREVER."

NAHUM Condemns a City

WHEN THE PROPHET JONAH WARNED NINEVEH OF ITS WICKEDNESS, THE CITY REPENTED-- AND WAS SPARED.

NOW, ONE HUNDRED AND FIFTY YEARS LATER, ANOTHER PROPHET, NAHUM, IS CALLED TO CONDEMN NINEVEH FOR RETURN- ING TO A LIFE OF SIN.

"THE LORD IS SLOW TO ANGER," NAHUM TELLS THE CITY, "BUT HE IS NOT BLIND. HE WILL NOT LET THE WICKED GO UNPUNISHED."

THIS TIME THE CITY IS NOT SPARED-- THE ARMIES OF BABYLON SO COMPLETELY DESTROY NINEVEH THAT IT IS NEVER REBUILT.

HABAKKUK--
The Man Who Asks Questions

Habakkuk is a man who asks questions -- of God.

HABAKKUK: The people of Judah are getting more wicked every day. How long will they go unpunished?

GOD: Not for long. The Babylonians are coming. I am using them to teach Judah that evil must be destroyed.

HABAKKUK: The Babylonians? Aren't they more wicked than Judah?

GOD: Yes, but have faith. In time you will understand my plans.

In the midst of all the evil around him, Habakkuk is comforted in knowing that God is in charge of the world. "God is in his holy temple," Habakkuk says, "and no matter what happens, I am not afraid, for the Lord is my strength."

ZECHARIAH and the Triumphal Entry

Zechariah is a friend of Haggai and works with him to rebuild the temple in Jerusalem.

ZEPHANIAH: Repent or Die

"The day of the Lord is at hand," Zephaniah warned Judah. "God will punish all nations of the earth that have disobeyed him. Neither gold nor silver will be able to deliver those who have turned from God."

Zephaniah pleads with his people to repent and seek God's forgiveness. "Those who do," he promises, "will live in peace under the rule of God."

HAGGAI -- A Temple Builder

When the Hebrews first return to Jerusalem -- after years of captivity in Babylon -- their first thought is to rebuild the temple. They start -- but they soon get discouraged and quit. For fifteen years nothing is done.

God speaks to Haggai and he takes the message to the people.

"Build God's temple," he preaches. And in four years it is built!

MALACHI -- The Final Warning

The people of Judah have returned to Jerusalem from captivity in Babylon -- the temple has been rebuilt. But still they are unhappy. And Malachi tells them why --

"You do not show respect to God. You would not dare bring cheap gifts to the governor. Yet you bring cheap and faulty offerings to God."

"God knows those who are faithful to him. He will reward them. But the unfaithful will perish as stubble in the burning fields after the harvest."

The Final Message FROM MALACHI

THE VOICE OF THE PROPHET MALACHI IS THE LAST TO BE HEARD IN THE STORY OF THE OLD TESTAMENT. BUT BEFORE WE HEAR HIS FINAL MESSAGE--WHICH IS FOUND IN THE BOOK THAT BEARS HIS NAME -- LET US BRIEFLY REVIEW THE HISTORY OF THE PEOPLE TO WHOM HE SPOKE.

IN OUR STORY OF THE BIBLE WE HAVE BEEN TRACING THE LIVES OF THE PEOPLE WHO DESCENDED FROM ABRAHAM. GOD CALLED HIM TO BE THE FATHER OF A NATION THAT WOULD TEACH THE WORLD ABOUT THE ONE TRUE GOD. ABRAHAM OBEYED GOD AND WENT TO CANAAN WHERE HIS FAMILY LIVED AND GREW. HIS GRANDSON, JACOB (OR ISRAEL), BECAME THE FATHER OF 12 SONS. THEIR FAMILIES WERE CALLED THE 12 TRIBES OF ISRAEL.

WHEN A FAMINE STRUCK CANAAN THE TRIBES WENT DOWN TO EGYPT WHERE THEY LIVED FOR MANY YEARS. BUT AFTER A TIME THE EGYPTIANS TURNED AGAINST THE ISRAELITES AND FORCED THEM TO WORK AS SLAVES. THE PEOPLE CRIED TO GOD FOR HELP...

GOD HEARD THE CRIES OF HIS PEOPLE AND SENT MOSES TO LEAD THEM OUT OF EGYPT -- ACROSS THE RED SEA -- AND BACK TO THE PROMISED LAND OF CANAAN. WITH GOD'S HELP THEY CONQUERED THE LAND AND MADE IT THEIR HOME. FOR MANY YEARS JUDGES RULED OVER THE TRIBES OF ISRAEL, BUT THE PEOPLE LONGED FOR A KING.

GOD HEARD THEIR PLEA AND GAVE THEM A KING, SAUL. HE WAS FOLLOWED BY DAVID, WHO BUILT ISRAEL INTO A POWERFUL NATION. BUT IN THE YEARS THAT FOLLOWED, THE PEOPLE TURNED FROM GOD TO WORSHIP IDOLS. THEY QUARRELED AMONG THEMSELVES, AND THE NATION WAS SPLIT INTO TWO KINGDOMS -- ISRAEL IN THE NORTH AND JUDAH IN THE SOUTH. WEAK AND CORRUPT, THEY WERE OPEN TO THE ATTACKS OF STRONGER NATIONS AROUND THEM.

IN TIME BOTH KINGDOMS WERE CONQUERED. MANY OF THE PEOPLE WERE TAKEN AWAY TO FOREIGN LANDS. AFTER 70 YEARS OF CAPTIVITY, THE JEWS WERE ALLOWED TO RETURN TO JUDAH AND REBUILD JERUSALEM.

BUT STILL THE PEOPLE WERE UNHAPPY, AND THE PROPHET MALACHI TELLS THEM WHY...

DO YOU CALL THAT GOD'S SHARE OF YOUR GRAIN? HOW CAN YOU BE HAPPY WHEN YOU ROB GOD? BRING YOUR RIGHTFUL GIFTS AND OFFERINGS TO GOD, AND YOU WILL PROSPER.

BUT PEOPLE WHO CHEAT AND BRING NONE OF THEIR GRAIN TO THE TEMPLE PROSPER MORE THAN WE DO.

GOD KNOWS WHO LOVES AND OBEYS HIM. HE WILL REWARD THE RIGHTEOUS AND PUNISH THE WICKED.

WHEN WILL HE DO THIS?

FIRST, GOD WILL SEND A PROPHET AS HIS MESSENGER TO GET THE PEOPLE READY. THEN THE LORD HIMSELF WILL COME AND DELIVER HIS OWN PEOPLE FROM EVIL. BUT HE WILL DESTROY THE WICKED WHO DISOBEY.

SO, WITH A WARNING -- AND A PROMISE -- THE OLD TESTAMENT ENDS. BUT TO THE JEWS THE QUESTION REMAINS: WHEN WILL THE GREAT DELIVERER COME?

The Years of Waiting

BETWEEN THE OLD TESTAMENT AND THE NEW TESTAMENT

THE LAND OF JUDAH IS STILL UNDER THE RULE OF THE
PERSIANS WHEN ALEXANDER, THE YOUNG KING OF MACEDONIA,
SETS OUT TO CONQUER THE WORLD.
RIDING HIS FAMOUS HORSE, BUCEPHALUS,
HE LEADS HIS ARMY AGAINST THE COUNTRIES
OF THE MIGHTY PERSIAN EMPIRE. ONE
AFTER ANOTHER THEY FALL, AND IN 332 B.C....

THE CITY WAITS IN TERROR! BUT WHEN ALEXANDER'S ARMY COMES IN SIGHT, THE HIGH PRIEST OPENS THE GATES AND LEADS A PROCESSION OUT TO GREET THE CONQUEROR. ALEXANDER RECOGNIZES THE PRIEST AS A MAN OF GOD AND BOWS BEFORE HIM. THEN HE ENTERS THE CITY AND WORSHIPS IN THE TEMPLE. UNDER THE RULE OF THIS DARING YOUNG WARRIOR THE JEWS ARE ALLOWED TO KEEP THEIR OWN RELIGIOUS CUSTOMS -- AND THEY ARE HAPPY.

BUT--SUDDENLY--ALEXANDER DIES... AND THE GIANT EMPIRE IS DIVIDED AMONG HIS GENERALS. WHEN THE RULER OVER JUDAH COMMANDS THE PEOPLE TO WORSHIP AN IDOL, A PRIEST SLAYS THE KING'S MESSENGER. THIS BOLD ACT STIRS ALL JUDAH TO REVOLT...

UNDER THE LEADERSHIP OF THE PRIEST'S BRAVE FAMILY (KNOWN AS THE MACCABEES), THE JEWS DRIVE THE ENEMY FROM THEIR LAND. ONE OF THE FIRST THINGS THEY DO IS TO REDEDICATE THE TEMPLE, WHICH THE ENEMY HAD USED TO WORSHIP IDOLS. FOR A HUNDRED GLORIOUS YEARS JUDAH IS FREE!

BUT ONCE AGAIN A CONQUEROR COMES FROM ACROSS THE MEDITERRANEAN SEA. ROMAN SHIPS AND ROMAN SOLDIERS CONQUER EVERYTHING IN THEIR PATH. AND IN 63 B.C. THE MIGHTY ROMAN ARMY TAKES JERUSALEM. AGAIN JUDAH IS DOWN-- AND THIS TIME IT IS TOO WEAK TO RISE.

AFTER A TIME THE ROMANS APPOINT A MAN NAMED HEROD TO RULE THE JEWS. A CRAFTY, CRUEL MAN, HE TRIES TO WIN THEIR FAVOR BY BUILDING THEM A NEW AND MORE BEAUTIFUL TEMPLE, BUT THEY DESPISE HIM. BITTERLY THE JEWS CRY OUT: "WHEN WILL GOD SEND THE DELIVERER PROMISED TO US BY THE PROPHETS OF OLD?"

Next week: THE WORLD INTO WHICH JESUS CAME

STORIES FROM THE

New Testament

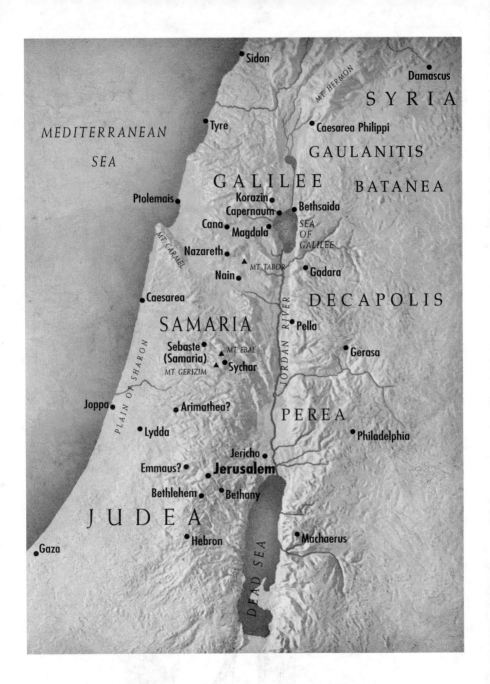

New Testament
Palestine

The Life of Jesus

FROM MATTHEW, MARK, LUKE, AND JOHN

THE FIRST FOUR BOOKS OF THE NEW TESTAMENT ARE CALLED THE GOSPELS, WHICH MEANS "GOOD NEWS"--ABOUT JESUS: HIS LIFE, TEACHINGS, DEATH, AND RESURRECTION. BECAUSE THE BOOKS ARE ALIKE IN MANY WAYS, THE FACTS HAVE BEEN COMBINED HERE TO TELL ONE STORY.

TO EVERYONE, JESUS SAYS-- I AM THE WAY... NO ONE CAN COME TO GOD BUT BY ME.

HERE, OLD MAN, CARRY THIS FOR ME.

FOR ALMOST SIXTY YEARS PALESTINE, THE HOME OF THE JEWS, HAS BEEN RULED BY THE MIGHTY ROMAN EMPIRE. TO MAINTAIN THEIR CONTROL, THE ROMANS APPOINTED HEROD, A CLEVER BUT CRUEL MAN, TO RULE THE LAND. THE JEWS HATE HIM -- AND THE ROMAN OFFICIALS WHO COME TO HIS COURT. THE TIME IS NOW 6 B.C....

THAT CHEST IS TOO HEAVY FOR SUCH AN OLD MAN.

THE ROMANS DON'T CARE.

HOURS LATER THE OLD MAN REACHES HOME...

GRANDFATHER! WHAT'S THE MATTER?

A ROMAN SOLDIER MADE HIM CARRY A HEAVY CHEST TO HEROD'S PALACE.

THAT AFTERNOON -- AS THE JEWS IN JERUSALEM GATHER IN THE TEMPLE FOR PRAYER -- AN OLD PRIEST, ZACHARIAS, ENTERS THE HOLY PLACE TO PRAY AND OFFER INCENSE.

THIS IS THE GREATEST DAY IN MY LIFE. AFTER ALL THESE YEARS IT IS FINALLY MY TURN TO OFFER INCENSE ON GOD'S HOLY ALTAR.

HE STAYS SO LONG IN THE SECRET ROOM THAT THE PEOPLE BEGIN TO WONDER.

ZACHARIAS' PRAYER IS LONGER THAN THAT OF MOST PRIESTS.

HE IS A GOOD MAN. IT'S TOO BAD HE HAS NO SON TO TAKE HIS PLACE.

AT LAST ZACHARIAS COMES OUT AND FACES THE PEOPLE -- BUT HE CANNOT SPEAK!

WHAT HAPPENED IN THE HOLY PLACE OF GOD?

A Secret from God

From Luke 1:23–55

Zacharias, the aged priest, has not spoken a word since he entered the holy place of the temple to offer incense. Most of the people in Jerusalem believe he saw a vision, but Zacharias makes no explanation. He completes his time of service in the temple, and returns to his home in the hills of Judah. His wife, Elisabeth, meets him at the door...

ZACHARIAS! WHAT IS WRONG? WHY DON'T YOU SPEAK TO ME?

Quickly Zacharias writes his answer and hands it to Elisabeth to read.

WHILE I WAS PRAYING IN THE HOLY PLACE, AN ANGEL SPOKE TO ME. HE TOLD ME THAT WE WOULD HAVE A SON. HIS NAME WILL BE JOHN, AND HE WILL PREPARE OUR PEOPLE FOR THE DELIVERER FROM GOD.

A SON! AND HE WILL PREPARE THE WAY FOR GOD'S CHOSEN ONE!

BUT, ZACHARIAS, WHY DO YOU WRITE THIS INSTEAD OF TELLING ME?

ZACHARIAS WRITES A SECOND MESSAGE AND GIVES IT TO HIS WIFE.

GOD FORGIVE ME. I DOUBTED THE ANGEL'S MESSAGE, AND HE TOLD ME I WOULD NOT BE ABLE TO SPEAK UNTIL THE MESSAGE CAME TRUE.

Overjoyed--and awed by the great trust God has placed in them--Zacharias and Elisabeth prepare for the birth of their son. In the months that pass they often read together the parts of scripture that tell about God's promises to his people.

As the aged priest and his wife wait for the coming of their son, the angel Gabriel appears to Elisabeth's cousin Mary, who is engaged to Joseph, a carpenter, in Nazareth.

DO NOT BE AFRAID, MARY. GOD HAS CHOSEN YOU TO BE THE MOTHER OF HIS SON. HIS NAME WILL BE "JESUS." HE WILL BE A KING WHOSE REIGN WILL NEVER END.

I AM THE LORD'S SERVANT AND I WILL DO WHATEVER HE SAYS.

MARY TELLS NO ONE OF THE ANGEL'S MESSAGE, BUT IN A FEW DAYS SHE GOES TO THE CARPENTER SHOP TO SEE JOSEPH.

I HAVE DECIDED TO GO AND VISIT MY COUSIN, ELISABETH.

IN JUDAH? I HATE TO HAVE YOU GO ALONE, MARY. IF ONLY THE PERIOD OF OUR ENGAGEMENT WERE OVER AND WE WERE MARRIED. THEN I COULD TAKE YOU THERE.

BUT, MARY LEAVES NAZARETH ALONE.

THE ANGEL SAID THAT ELISABETH IS GOING TO HAVE A SON, TOO. IT WILL BE GOOD TO TALK WITH HER.

AND WHEN SHE REACHES HER COUSIN...

MARY, HOW WONDERFULLY GOD HAS BLESSED YOU! BUT, TELL ME, WHY HAS THE MOTHER OF MY LORD COME TO VISIT ME?

FROM THIS GREETING MARY KNOWS THAT ELISABETH SHARES HER WONDERFUL SECRET. JOYFULLY SHE SINGS ALOUD HER PRAISE TO GOD.

MY SOUL MAGNIFIES THE LORD... FOR GOD WHO IS MIGHTY HAS DONE GREAT THINGS FOR ME; AND HOLY IS HIS NAME.

551

A Father's Prophecy

FROM LUKE 1:57–80; 2:1–5

THE DAYS PASS SWIFTLY IN THE HOME OF THE OLD PRIEST, ZACHARIAS. HIS WIFE, ELISABETH, AND HER YOUNG COUSIN, MARY, SPEND MANY HOURS TALKING ABOUT THE SONS GOD HAS PROMISED THEM. WHEN ELISABETH AND ZACHARIAS' CHILD IS BORN, NEIGHBORS AND RELATIVES COME TO SEE HIM.

HOW PROUD ZACHARIAS MUST BE TO HAVE A SON TO BEAR HIS NAME.

HE IS PROUD TO HAVE A SON, BUT, THE CHILD'S NAME IS JOHN.

JOHN? THEN YOU AREN'T NAMING HIM FOR ANYONE IN YOUR FAMILY?

ZACHARIAS-- WHO HAS NOT BEEN ABLE TO SPEAK A WORD SINCE HE DOUBTED THE ANGEL'S MESSAGE ABOUT THE BIRTH OF HIS SON-- MOTIONS FOR A TABLET. QUICKLY HE WRITES HIS ANSWER, AND HANDS IT TO THE WOMAN TO READ.

HIS NAME IS JOHN.

SO THE BABY IS NAMED ACCORDING TO THE INSTRUCTIONS OF THE ANGEL-- AND AT THAT MOMENT ZACHARIAS IS ABLE TO SPEAK.

BLESSED BE THE LORD GOD OF ISRAEL; FOR HE HAS VISITED AND REDEEMED HIS PEOPLE... AND YOU, CHILD, SHALL BE CALLED THE PROPHET OF THE HIGHEST: FOR YOU WILL GO BEFORE THE FACE OF THE LORD TO PREPARE HIS WAYS.

ON THEIR WAY HOME THE PEOPLE TALK ABOUT THE STRANGE EVENTS CONNECTED WITH THE BIRTH OF ZACHARIAS' SON.

THE NAME JOHN --WHAT DOES IT MEAN?

IT MEANS, "GOD HAS BEEN GRACIOUS." GOD MUST HAVE A SPECIAL PURPOSE FOR THAT CHILD.

HOME AGAIN IN NAZARETH, MARY THINKS ABOUT THE PURPOSE GOD HAS FOR HER CHILD. BUT JOSEPH, THE CARPENTER TO WHOM SHE IS ENGAGED, DOES NOT UNDERSTAND WHAT THE ANGEL HAS TOLD MARY ABOUT THE SON THAT IS TO BE BORN. ONE NIGHT AN ANGEL COMES TO HIM.

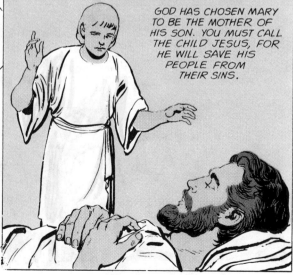

GOD HAS CHOSEN MARY TO BE THE MOTHER OF HIS SON. YOU MUST CALL THE CHILD JESUS, FOR HE WILL SAVE HIS PEOPLE FROM THEIR SINS.

EARLY THE NEXT MORNING, JOSEPH HURRIES TO SEE MARY.

O MARY, IN A DREAM LAST NIGHT AN ANGEL TOLD ME THAT YOU ARE TO BE THE MOTHER OF THE LORD. I SEE NOW THAT GOD HAS CHOSEN ME TO TAKE CARE OF YOU AND YOUR SON.

SO MARY AND JOSEPH ARE MARRIED, AND MOVE INTO JOSEPH'S HOUSE BESIDE THE CARPENTER SHOP. IN THE EVENINGS WHEN THE DAY'S WORK IS DONE, THEY REST ON THE ROOF TOP--WATCHING THE STARS AND TALKING ABOUT GOD'S PROMISE TO MARY.

BUT ONE DAY JOSEPH COMES HOME FROM THE MARKET PLACE WITH BAD NEWS: CAESAR AUGUSTUS HAS ORDERED EVERYONE TO REGISTER HIS NAME AND PROPERTY. SINCE JOSEPH AND MARY ARE DESCENDANTS OF KING DAVID, JOSEPH MUST GO TO BETHLEHEM, THE CITY OF DAVID.

BUT I CAN'T GO NOW--AND LEAVE YOU...

YOU MUST GO, JOSEPH, AND I'LL GO WITH YOU. DON'T WORRY--GOD WILL BE WITH US.

EAGER TO HAVE THE REGISTRATION OVER, THEY SET OUT. SOON OTHERS JOIN THEM ON THE WAY. BUT THE JOURNEY TAKES SEVERAL DAYS, AND AFTER A WHILE JOSEPH AND MARY FALL BEHIND-- UNTIL THEY ARE AMONG THE LAST TO REACH BETHLEHEM.

WE HAVE TRAVELED A LONG WAY AND MY WIFE IS VERY TIRED. I NEED A ROOM.

I'M SORRY, BUT BETHLEHEM IS CROWDED THESE DAYS. THERE'S NO ROOM HERE.

The Night the Angels Sang

FROM LUKE 2:1–15

555

THAT SAME NIGHT SOME SHEPHERDS ARE WATCHING THEIR SHEEP ON THE HILLS OUTSIDE THE CITY. THEY TALK OF THE CROWDS THAT HAVE COME TO BETHLEHEM.

I'VE HEARD THAT CAESAR AUGUSTUS ORDERED THIS REGISTRATION SO THAT HE CAN COLLECT MORE TAXES. WILL WE NEVER BE FREE FROM THESE FOREIGN TYRANTS?

GOD HAS PROMISED US A DELIVERER. AND ALL MY LIFE I HAVE PRAYED THAT I WOULD LIVE TO SEE HIM.

SUDDENLY-- A GREAT LIGHT SHINES AROUND THE SHEPHERDS.

WHAT IS IT?

O GOD, PROTECT US.

FEAR NOT; FOR I BRING YOU GOOD NEWS OF GREAT JOY FOR ALL THE PEOPLE. FOR TO YOU IS BORN IN THE CITY OF DAVID A SAVIOR, WHO IS CHRIST THE LORD. YOU WILL FIND THE BABY LYING IN A MANGER.

THEN THE SKY IS FILLED WITH A GREAT CHOIR OF ANGELS -- SINGING THEIR PRAISE TO GOD.

Glory to God in the highest, and on earth peace, good will toward men.

THE ANGELS LEAVE -- THE BEAUTIFUL LIGHT DISAPPEARS. ONCE AGAIN IT IS DARK AND STILL ON THE BETHLEHEM HILLS.

I CAN SCARCELY BELIEVE WHAT I HAVE SEEN AND HEARD. GOD HAS SENT OUR DELIVERER, OUR SAVIOR--**TONIGHT!**

AND TO THINK HE SENT HIS ANGEL TO TELL POOR SHEPHERDS LIKE US!

THE ANGEL SAID WE WOULD FIND THE SAVIOR IN A MANGER. LET'S GO TO BETHLEHEM AND SEE HIM.

EAGERLY -- AND WITH AWE AND WONDER -- THE SHEPHERDS HURRY TO BETHLEHEM. INSIDE THE GATE THEY TURN TOWARD THE INN...

LOOK -- THERE'S A LIGHT IN THE STABLE!

OUR SAVIOR IS HERE! AND I'M GOING TO SEE HIM!

A King Is Born

FROM LUKE 2:7, 16–20;
MATTHEW 2:1–8

IT IS A STRANGE AND HOLY NIGHT. WHILE THE CROWDED CITY OF BETHLEHEM SLEEPS, THE SON OF GOD IS BORN. LOVINGLY, MARY WRAPS HER BABY IN SWADDLING CLOTHES AND LAYS HIM IN A MANGER... AND THERE THE SHEPHERDS FIND HIM.

AN ANGEL TOLD US THAT THE SAVIOR HAS BEEN BORN. MAY WE SEE HIM?

MARY NODS, AND JOSEPH TURNS THE LAMP A LITTLE SO THAT ITS LIGHT FALLS ON THE MANGER. REVERENTLY THE SHEPHERDS LOOK AT THE BABY JESUS.

O GOD, WE THANK YOU FOR SENDING OUR SAVIOR, AND FOR LETTING US SEE HIM.

QUIETLY, THE SHEPHERDS TURN AWAY...

...AND GO BACK TO THEIR FLOCKS, STILL PRAISING GOD FOR WHAT HAS HAPPENED THAT NIGHT. AT THE SAME TIME IN A LAND FAR TO THE EAST, WISE MEN TALK ABOUT A STRANGE THING THEY HAVE JUST SEEN.

THAT NEW STAR-- IT'S BRIGHTER THAN ALL THE REST. IT MUST HAVE A SPECIAL MEANING.

IT IS A SIGN FROM GOD THAT THE GREAT KING OF THE JEWS HAS BEEN BORN.

LET US GO TO JERUSALEM AND FIND THE KING.

AFTER MONTHS OF TRAVEL, THE WISE MEN REACH JERUSALEM.

WE HAVE COME TO WORSHIP THE ONE BORN TO BE KING OF THE JEWS. PLEASE TELL US WHERE WE CAN FIND HIM.

YOU MUST BE MISTAKEN. NO KING HAS BEEN BORN HERE RECENTLY.

560

Flight in the Night

FROM MATTHEW 2:9–14

OLLOWING HEROD'S INSTRUCTIONS, THE WISE MEN SET OUT FOR BETHLEHEM. AS THEY LEAVE JERUSALEM, THEY AGAIN SEE THE STAR THEY HAD SEEN IN THE EAST. IT LEADS THEM TO BETHLEHEM, AND THERE...

LOOK! THE STAR HAS STOPPED ABOVE THAT HOUSE!

OUR JOURNEY IS FINISHED! SOON WE'LL SEE THE CHILD WHO IS TO BE KING OF THE JEWS!

PEOPLE IN BETHLEHEM ARE SURPRISED TO SEE THE IMPORTANT-LOOKING STRANGERS STOP BEFORE THE HOUSE WHERE JOSEPH AND MARY NOW LIVE. WHEN THE WISE MEN TELL THEIR REASON FOR COMING, THEY ARE INVITED INSIDE. THERE THEY KNEEL BEFORE THE BABY JESUS.

WE HAVE COME A LONG WAY TO WORSHIP THE ROYAL CHILD.

AND TO BRING HIM GIFTS OF GOLD, FRANKINCENSE, AND MYRRH.

THAT NIGHT AT THE INN THE WISE MEN MAKE PLANS FOR THEIR RETURN HOME.

I'M GLAD THAT WE CAN GO BACK TO JERUSALEM AND TELL KING HEROD WHERE HE CAN FIND THE BABY.

THE NEXT MORNING...

I HAD A DREAM—

SO DID I! IN MY DREAM GOD WARNED US NOT TO RETURN TO JERUSALEM BECAUSE HEROD IS JEALOUS AND WANTS TO KILL THE CHILD.

I HAD THE SAME DREAM! HEROD WILL FIND OUT NOTHING FROM US. WE'LL GO HOME BY ANOTHER ROUTE.

BUT THE WISE MEN ARE NOT THE ONLY ONES WHO ARE WARNED OF HEROD'S ANGER. AN ANGEL OF GOD APPEARS TO JOSEPH, TOO...

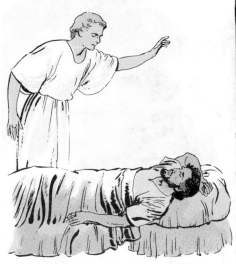

MARY! AN ANGEL HAS TOLD ME WE MUST ESCAPE AT ONCE -- TO EGYPT. HEROD WANTS TO KILL JESUS.

KILL JESUS! OH, NO!

IN THE MIDDLE OF THE NIGHT, JOSEPH AND MARY WITH THE BABY JESUS STEAL QUIETLY OUT OF THE CITY.

IN JERUSALEM, HEROD WAITS FOR THE RETURN OF THE WISE MEN. WHEN THEY DO NOT COME, HE SUSPECTS THEY ARE TRYING TO PROTECT THE CHILD -- FROM HIM.

THAT CHILD WILL NEVER LIVE TO TAKE **MY** THRONE. I'LL KILL EVERY BABY IN BETHLEHEM BEFORE I LET HIM ESCAPE.

Boy in the Temple

FROM MATTHEW 2:16–23; LUKE 2:40–52

FEARING THAT THE BABY JESUS WILL TAKE HIS THRONE, HEROD ORDERS ALL BOY BABIES IN BETHLEHEM KILLED. BUT JOSEPH AND MARY ESCAPE WITH JESUS TO EGYPT. AFTER A FEW MONTHS, AN ANGEL TELLS JOSEPH THAT HEROD IS DEAD AND THAT IT IS NOW SAFE TO TAKE JESUS HOME. IN NAZARETH...

MARY! AND JOSEPH! HOW GOOD TO HAVE YOU BACK. WHAT IS THE BABY'S NAME?

HIS NAME IS JESUS.

JESUS. THE NAME MEANS "GOD SAVES." WE NEED SOMEONE TO SAVE US FROM THE TYRANTS WHO RULE PALESTINE.

JOSEPH SETS UP HIS CARPENTER SHOP--AND AS THE YEARS PASS, JESUS LEARNS TO HELP HIM. WHEN THE DAY'S WORK IS OVER JESUS LISTENS TO THE ELDERS OF THE TOWN...

IN THE DAYS OF KING DAVID, **WE** WERE THE RULERS.

YES, BUT IN THOSE DAYS PEOPLE OBEYED GOD. TODAY, TOO MANY IGNORE HIS LAWS.

BUT JOSEPH AND MARY OBEY GOD'S COMMANDMENTS, AND TEACH JESUS TO OBEY THEM, TOO. EACH SPRING THEY ATTEND THE PASSOVER FEAST IN JERUSALEM TO THANK GOD FOR DELIVERING THEIR ANCESTORS FROM SLAVERY IN EGYPT. IN THE CARAVAN THAT MAKES THE ANNUAL JOURNEY FROM NAZARETH, THERE IS NO ONE MORE EXCITED THAN JESUS.

THIS YEAR, AS HE WORSHIPS IN THE TEMPLE, JESUS THINKS OF MANY QUESTIONS HE WOULD LIKE TO ASK THE TEACHERS OF THE JEWS.

AFTER THE FEAST IS OVER, THE PEOPLE SET OUT FOR THEIR HOMES. THAT NIGHT WHEN THEY MAKE CAMP...

JOSEPH, WHERE IS JESUS?

HE'S WITH HIS FRIENDS. I'LL FIND HIM.

BUT NO ONE HAS SEEN JESUS. FRANTICALLY, JOSEPH AND MARY TURN BACK TO JERUSALEM. THEY SEARCH THE INNS, THE CROWDED STREETS, AND FINALLY THE TEMPLE.

JESUS! WE HAVE BEEN LOOKING FOR YOU EVERYWHERE.

BUT, MOTHER, DIDN'T YOU KNOW THAT I WOULD BE IN MY FATHER'S HOUSE?

WE ARE SURPRISED AT YOUR SON'S KNOWLEDGE OF THE SCRIPTURES. HIS QUESTIONS SHOW THAT HE HAS THOUGHT A GREAT DEAL ABOUT GOD AND HIS LAWS FOR MAN.

JESUS IS NOT LIKE ANYONE ELSE. EVEN I, HIS MOTHER, DO NOT UNDERSTAND EVERYTHING ABOUT HIM.

JESUS RETURNS WITH JOSEPH AND MARY TO NAZARETH, WHERE HE LIVES UNTIL HE IS 30 YEARS OLD. HE GROWS TALL AND STRONG, AND IS WELL LIKED BY THE PEOPLE OF NAZARETH. GOD IS ALSO PLEASED WITH HIM. SEVENTY MILES AWAY, IN THE WILDERNESS NEAR THE DEAD SEA, A MAN OF THE SAME AGE PREPARES FOR AN ASSIGNMENT THAT WAS PLANNED FOR HIM -- EVEN BEFORE HE WAS BORN.

Tempted!

FROM LUKE 3:1—4:4

*A*S SOON AS JOHN, THE COUSIN OF JESUS, IS OLD ENOUGH TO UNDERSTAND, HIS FATHER TELLS HIM: "BEFORE YOU WERE BORN, GOD PLANNED FOR YOU TO SERVE HIM IN A SPECIAL WAY." JOHN GROWS UP PREPARING TO SERVE GOD. AND AFTER THE DEATH OF HIS PARENTS HE GOES INTO THE WILDERNESS TO PRAY AND STUDY. THERE GOD CALLS HIM TO BEGIN HIS WORK.

O GOD, I'M READY TO PREPARE THE WAY FOR THE COMING OF THE SAVIOR.

JOHN PUTS HIS WORDS INTO ACTION AND BEGINS PREACHING ALONG THE JORDAN RIVER.

REPENT OF YOUR SINS AND BE BAPTIZED, FOR GOD'S KINGDOM IS CLOSE AT HAND.

NEWS SPREADS FAR AND WIDE ABOUT THE MAN WHO LOOKS AND SPEAKS LIKE A PROPHET OF OLD. CROWDS COME OUT FROM JERUSALEM TO HEAR THE MAN CALLED JOHN THE BAPTIST. SOME ARE ONLY CURIOUS, BUT JOHN KNOWS THEIR THOUGHTS.

DO YOU THINK THAT JUST BECAUSE YOU ARE JEWS YOU WILL BE ALLOWED IN GOD'S KINGDOM? NO, YOU MUST REPENT--

THE SCOFFERS TURN AWAY, BUT MANY PEOPLE LISTEN EAGERLY. ONE DAY A CROWD GATHERS AT THE JORDAN RIVER.

ARE YOU THE SAVIOR GOD HAS PROMISED US?

NO. I BAPTIZE WITH WATER, BUT HE WILL BAPTIZE WITH THE HOLY SPIRIT OF GOD. PREPARE YOURSELVES; THE SAVIOR IS COMING!

UNKNOWN TO JOHN, THE VERY ONE HE IS TALKING ABOUT IS IN THE CROWD. JESUS HAS COME DOWN FROM NAZARETH TO HEAR HIM. HE ASKS TO BE BAPTIZED.

WHY DO YOU COME TO ME FOR BAPTISM? IT IS I WHO NEED TO BE BAPTIZED BY YOU.

JOHN, THIS IS WHAT GOD WOULD WANT US TO DO.

SO JOHN BAPTIZES JESUS. AND WHEN JESUS COMES UP OUT OF THE WATER, THE SPIRIT OF GOD DESCENDS LIKE A DOVE UPON HIM. THEN A VOICE FROM HEAVEN SPEAKS:

THIS IS MY BELOVED SON IN WHOM I AM WELL PLEASED.

THE CROWDS DO NOT UNDERSTAND WHAT HAS HAPPENED--THEY GO HOME, NOT REALIZING THAT THEY HAVE SEEN THEIR SAVIOR. JOHN CONTINUES PREACHING -- REPENT OF YOUR SINS, FOR THE KINGDOM OF GOD IS COMING SOON.

TO JESUS, THE WORDS OF HIS FATHER ARE A SIGN OF APPROVAL, AND THE GIFT OF THE HOLY SPIRIT IS AN ASSURANCE OF HELP FOR THE WORK GOD HAS SENT HIM TO DO. HE GOES INTO THE WILDERNESS -- ALONE -- TO THINK ABOUT HIS PLAN FOR ESTABLISHING GOD'S KINGDOM.

AT THE END OF FORTY DAYS, JESUS IS HUNGRY. AS HE THINKS OF FOOD, HE HEARS THE VOICE OF THE DEVIL TEMPTING HIM TO USE HIS DIVINE POWER FOR HIS OWN BENEFIT. "IF YOU ARE REALLY THE SON OF GOD," THE DEVIL SAYS, "TURN THIS STONE INTO BREAD. AFTER ALL, GOD WOULD NOT WANT HIS BELOVED SON TO BE HUNGRY."

SCRIPTURE SAYS, "MAN SHALL NOT LIVE BY BREAD ALONE, BUT BY THE WORD OF GOD."

THE DEVIL DOESN'T GIVE UP EASILY. HE TRIES AGAIN-- AND THIS TIME WITH A MORE POWERFUL TEMPTATION ...

Victory in the Wilderness

FROM MATTHEW 4:5–11; JOHN 1:35–46

TO PREVENT JESUS FROM CARRYING OUT GOD'S WORK, THE DEVIL TEMPTS HIM TO SEEK EARTHLY POWERS FOR HIMSELF. BUT JESUS REFUSES. THE DEVIL TRIES AGAIN--THIS TIME HE TEMPTS JESUS TO MAKE HIMSELF POPULAR BY DOING SOMETHING SENSATIONAL.

"LET PEOPLE SEE YOUR DIVINE POWER BY THROWING YOURSELF FROM THE ROOF OF THE TEMPLE," THE DEVIL SAYS. "FOR, IF YOU ARE THE SON OF GOD, HIS ANGELS WILL TAKE CARE OF YOU."

THE SCRIPTURES SAY, "THOU SHALT NOT TEMPT GOD."

HAVING REJECTED EVERY TEMPTATION, JESUS LEAVES THE WILDERNESS AND GOES BACK TO BETHANY BEYOND THE JORDAN.

AS JESUS ENTERS BETHANY, JOHN THE BAPTIST POINTS HIM OUT TO TWO OF HIS OWN DISCIPLES -- ANDREW AND JOHN.

THERE IS THE SAVIOR I HAVE BEEN TELLING YOU ABOUT.

THE TWO MEN TURN AND QUICKLY FOLLOW JESUS.

MASTER-- MAY WE TALK WITH YOU?

YES, COME WITH ME TO MY LODGING PLACE.

LISTENING TO JESUS IS SUCH A WON-DERFUL EXPERIENCE THAT HOURS GO BY BEFORE ANDREW SUDDENLY REMEMBERS...

MY BROTHER! HE CAME DOWN HERE FROM CAPERNAUM WITH ME TO HEAR JOHN THE BAPTIST. I MUST FIND HIM AND BRING HIM TO SEE YOU.

ANDREW RUNS TO THE HOUSE WHERE HE AND HIS BROTHER ARE STAYING.

SIMON! I HAVE FOUND THE SAVIOR!

SIMON EAGERLY FOLLOWS ANDREW BACK THROUGH THE WINDING STREETS OF BETHANY.

THIS IS SIMON, MY BROTHER.

YES, YOU ARE SIMON, BUT FROM NOW ON YOU SHALL BE CALLED PETER, BECAUSE YOU WILL BE LIKE A ROCK.

THE NEXT DAY JESUS GOES NORTH TO GALILEE. HE INVITES ANOTHER YOUNG MAN, PHILIP, TO BE HIS DISCIPLE AND GO WITH HIM.

PHILIP ACCEPTS JESUS' INVITATION. LIKE ANDREW, HE WANTS TO SHARE HIS GOOD NEWS, SO HE HURRIES TO TELL A FRIEND.

NATHANAEL--COME WITH ME! I HAVE FOUND THE SAVIOR! HE IS JESUS OF NAZARETH.

NAZARETH? CAN ANYTHING GOOD COME FROM **THAT** TOWN?

IF WHAT YOU SAY IS TRUE, MEN WOULD GIVE UP EVERYTHING THEY HAVE TO FOLLOW HIM.

COME AND SEE FOR YOURSELF!

NATHANAEL SEES JESUS, BUT HE STILL DOESN'T BELIEVE. THEN JESUS SPEAKS...

Six Jars of Water

FROM JOHN 1:47–51; 2:1–11, 23–25; 3:1–2

PHILIP IS SO EXCITED ABOUT SEEING JESUS THAT HE HURRIES TO TELL A FRIEND. "NATHANAEL, COME WITH ME. I HAVE FOUND THE SAVIOR!" NATHANAEL DOUBTS SUCH NEWS, BUT HE AGREES TO SEE FOR HIMSELF. AS THEY APPROACH JESUS...

BEHOLD, A MAN IN WHOM THERE IS NOTHING DECEITFUL.

HOW DO **YOU** KNOW ANYTHING ABOUT ME?

BEFORE PHILIP CALLED YOU, YOU WERE SITTING UNDER A FIG TREE THINKING ABOUT GOD. I SAW YOU THERE.

YOU **ARE** THE SAVIOR FOR WHOM WE HAVE WAITED SO LONG!

HAVING FOUND HIS SAVIOR, NATHANAEL FORGETS EVERYTHING ELSE AND JOINS JESUS AND HIS FRIENDS AS THEY TRAVEL NORTH TO GALILEE. AT THE CROSSROADS, PETER AND ANDREW TURN OFF TO THEIR HOME NEAR THE SEA OF GALILEE; THE OTHERS GO ON TO CANA.

WHEN THEY REACH THE TOWN THEY ARE GREETED BY A FRIEND OF JESUS.

PLEASE COME TO MY WEDDING FEAST --YOUR MOTHER WILL BE THERE.

THANK YOU-- WE WOULD LIKE TO SHARE YOUR HAPPINESS.

DURING THE FEAST MARY DISCOVERS SOMETHING THAT WILL EMBARRASS THE GROOM--THERE IS NO MORE WINE. SHE TELLS JESUS, THEN SHE GOES TO THE SERVANTS.

DO WHATEVER HE TELLS YOU.

FILL THESE JARS WITH WATER.

WHY WATER? IT'S WINE WE NEED.

BUT THE SERVANTS SENSE A STRANGE AUTHORITY IN JESUS, AND THEY OBEY HIM.

NOW TAKE SOME TO THE HEADWAITER.

WHY--IT IS WINE! IT'S A MIRACLE!

THIS MAN MUST BE A PROPHET OF GOD--NO ORDINARY MAN COULD DO SUCH A THING!

THE HEADWAITER IS SO SURPRISED WHEN HE TASTES THE WINE THAT HE CALLS THE GROOM AWAY FROM THE FEAST.

SIR, THE BEST WINE IS USUALLY SERVED FIRST. BUT YOU HAVE SAVED THE BEST TO THE LAST.

I'M GLAD IF PEOPLE ARE HAPPY.

WHEN JESUS' DISCIPLES HEAR ABOUT THE MIRACLE, THEY TOO ARE EXCITED. THEY TALK ABOUT IT AS THEY GO DOWN TO JERUSALEM WITH JESUS FOR THE PASSOVER FEAST. THE CITY IS CROWDED WITH PEOPLE WHO HAVE HEARD JOHN THE BAPTIST TELL ABOUT THE COMING OF THE MESSIAH. "HOW WILL WE RECOGNIZE HIM?" THEY ASK.

AS JESUS WALKS THROUGH THE BUSY STREETS, HE HEALS THE LAME AND THE SICK.

I CAN WALK! PRAISE BE TO GOD--THIS MAN HEALED ME!

BECAUSE OF THESE MIRACLES, PEOPLE BEGIN TO ASK: "IS JESUS THE MESSIAH?" ONE NIGHT, AFTER THE STREETS ARE EMPTY, A JUDGE OF THE JEWISH SUPREME COURT STEALS THROUGH THE STREETS OF JERU- SALEM ON A SECRET MISSION.

The Judge's Problem

FROM JOHN 3:3—4:6; MARK 6:14–17

NICODEMUS, A JUDGE OF THE JEWISH SUPREME COURT, HAS A PROBLEM HE CAN'T SOLVE. PEOPLE IN JERUSALEM ARE ASKING, "IS JESUS THE SAVIOR WHO WILL OVERTHROW THE ROMANS AND SET UP GOD'S KINGDOM IN PALESTINE?"

NICODEMUS ISN'T SURE, AND HE WONDERS: "WHAT MUST A MAN DO TO ENTER GOD'S KINGDOM?" HE HAS TO FIND OUT. SO SECRETLY-- BY NIGHT-- HE GOES TO THE PLACE WHERE JESUS IS STAYING, AND JESUS ANSWERS HIS QUESTION EVEN BEFORE HE ASKS IT...

A MAN MUST BE BORN OVER AGAIN TO ENTER GOD'S KINGDOM.

BORN AGAIN? HOW CAN I BE BORN AGAIN WHEN I AM OLD?

YOU WERE BORN ONCE OF EARTHLY PARENTS. BUT YOU MUST BE BORN AGAIN OF GOD'S SPIRIT TO LIVE IN GOD'S KINGDOM.

I DON'T UNDERSTAND.

YOU CAN'T SEE THE WIND, BUT YOU CAN SEE WHAT IT DOES. YOU CANNOT SEE THE SPIRIT OF GOD, BUT YOU CAN TELL BY THE WAY A MAN LIVES IF HE HAS BEEN BORN AGAIN AND HAS THE SPIRIT OF GOD IN HIS HEART. GOD LOVES THE WORLD, AND HE HAS SENT ME TO GIVE THIS NEW LIFE TO ALL WHO BELIEVE IN ME.

NICODEMUS GOES AWAY--STILL PUZZLED, BUT WANTING TO LEARN MORE ABOUT JESUS AND HIS TEACHINGS.

JESUS SEES THAT MANY OF THE PEOPLE IN JERUSALEM ARE NOT READY TO RECEIVE HIM AS THEIR SAVIOR, SO HE LEAVES THE CITY. IN JUDEA HE TELLS THE PEOPLE ABOUT GOD'S KINGDOM AND WHAT THEY MUST DO TO ENTER IT. HERE, THE PEOPLE LISTEN EAGERLY.

THIS TEACHER IS GREATER THAN ALL THE PROPHETS.

NEWS OF JESUS' SUCCESSFUL MINISTRY IN JUDEA REACHES JOHN THE BAPTIST.

I'VE HEARD THAT JESUS IS BECOMING MORE POPULAR EVERY DAY.

THANK GOD, I HAVE FULFILLED MY MISSION OF PREPARING THE WAY FOR HIM. JESUS' INFLUENCE MUST INCREASE, AND MINE DECREASE.

SOMETIME LATER JESUS RECEIVES NEWS ABOUT HIS LOYAL FRIEND.

HEROD HAS PUT JOHN THE BAPTIST IN PRISON FOR TRYING TO START A REVOLUTION.

REVOLUTION? NO-- THE REAL REASON IS THAT JOHN CONDEMNED HEROD FOR MARRYING HIS BROTHER'S WIFE.

SOON AFTER THIS, JESUS DECIDES TO EXTEND HIS MINISTRY INTO ANOTHER AREA. HE SETS OUT FOR GALILEE, NORTH OF SAMARIA.

AS THEY APPROACH A TOWN IN SAMARIA, JESUS SENDS HIS DISCIPLES ON AHEAD TO BUY SOME FOOD.

IT MAY BE QUICKER TO GO TO GALILEE BY WAY OF SAMARIA, BUT I WONDER IF IT'S WISE. SAMARITANS HATE US JEWS.

WHILE JESUS IS RESTING BESIDE THE WELL, A WOMAN COMES UP WITH A JAR FOR WATER.

A JEW! DOESN'T HE KNOW JEWS AREN'T WELCOME IN SAMARIA?

In Enemy Territory

FROM JOHN 4:6–44;
LUKE 4:16–28; MARK 1:16–20

THE JEWS AND SAMARITANS HAVE BEEN BITTER ENEMIES FOR OVER 500 YEARS, SO WHEN JESUS ASKS A SAMARITAN WOMAN FOR A DRINK OF WATER SHE IS SURPRISED.

WHAT? YOU, A JEW, ASK ME, A SAMARITAN, FOR A DRINK?

IF YOU KNEW WHO I AM YOU WOULD ASK ME TO GIVE YOU LIVING WATER.

BUT THE WELL IS DEEP AND YOU HAVE NO WAY TO GET WATER.

ANYONE WHO DRINKS FROM THIS WELL WILL THIRST AGAIN, BUT THE PERSON WHO DRINKS OF THE WATER I GIVE WILL NEVER THIRST, FOR IT IS GOD'S GIFT OF ETERNAL LIFE.

WHEN JESUS TELLS HER THAT HE IS THE SAVIOR FROM GOD, SHE BELIEVES HIM AND RUNS BACK TO THE TOWN TO TELL THE WONDERFUL NEWS.

COME! SEE A MAN WHO HAS TOLD ME THINGS ABOUT MY LIFE THAT NO STRANGER COULD KNOW. HE IS THE PROMISED MESSIAH! THE SAVIOR!

WHILE THE WOMAN IS IN THE TOWN, JESUS' DISCIPLES RETURN AND INVITE HIM TO SHARE THE FOOD THEY HAVE BOUGHT.

THANK YOU, BUT NOT NOW-- I HAVE FOOD THAT YOU DON'T KNOW ABOUT.

WHAT DO YOU MEAN?

MY FOOD IS TO DO THE WILL OF HIM WHO SENT ME. LOOK AT THE PEOPLE WHO ARE EAGER TO HEAR WHAT GOD HAS SENT ME TO TELL THEM.

ALTHOUGH THE SAMARITANS HATE JEWS, MANY OF THEM BELIEVE JESUS TO BE THEIR SAVIOR. "STAY," THEY PLEAD, "AND TELL US MORE ABOUT GOD AND HIS KINGDOM." JESUS REMAINS FOR TWO DAYS-- THEN GOES ON TO THE REGION OF GALILEE.

ON THE SABBATH, IN HIS TOWN OF NAZARETH, HE GOES TO THE SYNAGOGUE. THERE HE READS FROM THE BOOK OF ISAIAH WHICH TELLS ABOUT THE COMING OF THE MESSIAH. THEN HE SITS DOWN TO TEACH.

TODAY THIS SCRIPTURE HAS BEEN FULFILLED IN YOUR EARS.

YOU -- THE MESSIAH? WHY, YOU'RE JUST THE SON OF A NAZARETH CARPENTER!

NO PROPHET IS ACCEPTED IN HIS OWN COUNTRY. REMEMBER -- IN THE DAYS OF ELISHA THERE WERE MANY LEPERS IN ISRAEL, BUT THE PROPHET HEALED ONLY ONE -- A FOREIGNER, NAAMAN.

THE THOUGHT THAT GOD WOULD DO MORE FOR FOREIGNERS THAN FOR THEM -- HIS CHOSEN PEOPLE -- TURNS THE WORSHIPERS INTO AN ANGRY MOB.

DRIVE HIM OUT OF THE CITY!

KILL HIM!

BUT--SUDDENLY--JESUS TURNS AND LOOKS INTO THE FACES OF THE MEN AND WOMEN WHO HAVE KNOWN HIM FOR THIRTY YEARS. THEN HE WALKS--SLOWLY--THROUGH THEIR MIDST... AND, STRANGELY, NOT A PERSON DARES TO TOUCH HIM.

FROM NAZARETH JESUS GOES TO CAPERNAUM ON THE SEA OF GALILEE. THERE HE FINDS THE BROTHERS HE MET NEAR THE JORDAN RIVER.

PETER! ANDREW! COME WITH ME, AND I'LL MAKE YOU FISHERS OF MEN.

THEY LEAVE THEIR NETS AND GO AT ONCE WITH JESUS. FARTHER DOWN THE SHORE JESUS SEES TWO MORE FRIENDS--JAMES AND JOHN.

COME WITH ME AND BE MY DISCIPLES.

Through the Roof

FROM MARK 2:1–14

EVERYWHERE JESUS GOES THE CROWDS FOLLOW HIM. ONE DAY IN CAPERNAUM SO MANY PEOPLE CROWD INTO THE HOUSE WHERE HE IS TEACHING THAT NO ONE ELSE CAN ENTER. SOME MEN WHO HAVE BROUGHT A SICK FRIEND TO SEE JESUS CANNOT GET THROUGH THE CROWD, SO THEY CARRY THE MAN TO THE ROOF TOP.

MAKING A HOLE SO YOU CAN GET IN.

WHAT ARE YOU DOING?

AFTER A FEW MINUTES OF HARD WORK, THE SICK MAN IS LET DOWN THROUGH THE ROOF. JESUS IS PLEASED TO HELP, FOR HE KNOWS THE MAN'S REAL NEED.

YOUR SINS ARE FORGIVEN.

THE PEOPLE ARE AMAZED. BUT THE PHARISEES,* WHO HAVE COME OUT OF CURIOSITY TO HEAR JESUS, ARE ANGRY.

WHO IS THIS MAN WHO PRETENDS TO FORGIVE SINS?

HOW DARE HE ACT AS IF HE IS GOD!

*The Pharisees are a group of Jews who believe in obeying not only the laws God gave to Moses but the hundreds of rules *they* have made--such as how far a man can walk on the Sabbath. Because Jesus is more concerned about helping people than obeying their rules, the Pharisees turn against him.

JESUS KNOWS WHAT THE PHARISEES ARE THINKING.

WHICH IS EASIER-- TO SAY TO THE SICK, "YOUR SINS ARE FORGIVEN," OR TO SAY, "ARISE, TAKE UP YOUR BED, AND WALK"?

BUT SO THAT ALL MAY KNOW THAT I HAVE DIVINE POWER TO DO BOTH, I SAY TO YOU, "ARISE, TAKE UP YOUR BED, AND GO TO YOUR HOME."

MY SINS ARE FORGIVEN! I'M HEALED! GLORY BE TO GOD!

I'VE NEVER SEEN ANYTHING LIKE IT.

NEITHER HAVE I. BUT IF HE IS TRYING TO MAKE US THINK HE IS THE MESSIAH, WHY DOESN'T HE DO SOMETHING ABOUT OVERTHROWING THE ROMANS?

JESUS LEAVES THE HOUSE WHERE HE HAS BEEN TEACHING, AND AS HE PASSES BY THE TOLL HOUSE AT THE CITY GATE...

YOU TAX COLLECTORS ARE ALL ROBBERS. I CAN'T PAY THAT MUCH TAX, AND YOU KNOW IT.

YOU'D BETTER PAY IT! REMEMBER — I HAVE THE POWER OF THE WHOLE ROMAN EMPIRE BEHIND ME.

One Man's Answer

FROM MATTHEW 9:9–13; 12:9–14

IN ALL CAPERNAUM THERE IS NO ONE MORE DESPISED THAN MATTHEW, A TAX COLLECTOR FOR ROME. ONE DAY AS HE AND A MERCHANT ARE ARGUING ABOUT TAXES ON A CARAVAN OF GOODS, JESUS PASSES BY. HE LOOKS STRAIGHT INTO THE EYES OF THE HATED TAX COLLECTOR...

MATTHEW, FOLLOW ME.

TO THE AMAZEMENT OF THE CROWD, MATTHEW TURNS FROM HIS WORK AND FOLLOWS JESUS.

I CAN'T BELIEVE IT! MATTHEW IS GIVING UP HIS JOB TO GO WITH A MAN OF GOD!

STRANGE -- NO GOOD JEW EVER WANTED MATTHEW FOR A FRIEND.

MATTHEW IS SO HAPPY TO START A NEW LIFE WITH JESUS THAT HE GIVES A BIG FEAST AND INVITES HIS FRIENDS TO MEET JESUS. SOME PHARISEES WHO ARE PASSING BY LOOK ON -- SURPRISED.

WHY DOES YOUR MASTER EAT WITH ALL THOSE SINNERS?

JESUS ANSWERS FOR HIS DISCIPLE.

ONLY THE SICK NEED A DOCTOR. I HAVE COME NOT TO CALL THE RIGHTEOUS BUT SINNERS TO REPENT.

THE PHARISEES HAVE NO ANSWER TO THIS -- BUT IT MAKES THEM EVEN MORE ANGRY. SO EVERYWHERE JESUS GOES THEY WATCH FOR A CHANCE TO CRITICIZE HIM. ONE SABBATH DAY IN THE SYNAGOGUE...

LOOK -- JESUS IS TALKING TO THAT MAN WITH THE WITHERED HAND. LET'S SEE IF WE CAN CATCH HIM BREAKING A SABBATH LAW. THEN WE'LL HAVE A CASE AGAINST HIM.

Sermon on the Mount

FROM LUKE 6:12–16;
MATTHEW 5; 6; 7; 8:5–13; 13:45–46;
MARK 4:35–37

JESUS KNOWS THAT THE PHARISEES ARE PLOTTING TO TAKE HIS LIFE BUT HE DOES NOT LET THIS KEEP HIM FROM CARRYING ON THE WORK GOD SENT HIM TO DO. HE GOES TO A NEARBY MOUNTAIN-- AND SPENDS THE NIGHT IN PRAYER.

IN THE MORNING HE CALLS HIS DISCIPLES TO HIM -- AND FROM THE GROUP HE NAMES TWELVE TO BE HIS FULL-TIME HELPERS: SIMON PETER, ANDREW, JAMES, JOHN, PHILIP, NATHANAEL BARTHOLOMEW, MATTHEW, THOMAS, JAMES THE SON OF ALPHEUS, THADDEUS, SIMON THE ZEALOT, AND JUDAS ISCARIOT. THESE ARE KNOWN AS THE TWELVE APOSTLES.

AS THEY COME DOWN THE MOUNTAIN, THEY FIND A LARGE CROWD
WAITING FOR JESUS. SO THERE--ON--THE MOUNTAINSIDE JESUS PREACHES
A SERMON IN WHICH HE EXPLAINS WHAT MEMBERS OF
GOD'S KINGDOM ARE LIKE:

BLESSED ARE THE MERCIFUL: FOR THEY SHALL OBTAIN MERCY.
BLESSED ARE THE PURE IN HEART: FOR THEY SHALL SEE GOD.
BLESSED ARE THE PEACEMAKERS: FOR THEY SHALL BE CALLED
THE CHILDREN OF GOD ....
YOU ARE THE LIGHT OF THE WORLD .... LET YOUR LIGHT SO SHINE
BEFORE OTHERS, THAT THEY MAY SEE YOUR GOOD WORKS,
AND GLORIFY YOUR FATHER WHO IS IN HEAVEN ....
LOVE YOUR ENEMIES, BLESS THOSE WHO CURSE YOU, DO
GOOD TO THOSE WHO HATE YOU, AND PRAY FOR
THOSE WHO MISUSE YOU, AND PERSECUTE YOU;
THAT YOU MAY BE THE CHILDREN OF YOUR FATHER WHO IS IN
HEAVEN: FOR HE MAKES HIS SUN TO RISE ON THE EVIL AND
ON THE GOOD, AND SENDS RAIN ON THE JUST AND ON THE
UNJUST .... THEREFORE ALL THINGS YOU WOULD WANT
PEOPLE TO DO TO YOU, DO THOSE THINGS TO OTHERS:
FOR THIS IS THE SUM OF THE LAW AND THE PROPHETS.

(THE FULL SERMON IS
FOUND IN MATTHEW,
CHAPTERS 5, 6, 7.)

591

EVEN THOUGH THE PHARISEES ARE STILL PLOTTING AGAINST HIM, JESUS KEEPS ON TEACHING IN CAPERNAUM. ONE DAY THE CROWDS THAT COME TO HEAR HIM ARE SO GREAT THAT HE HAS TO GET INTO A BOAT AND PUSH OUT FROM SHORE IN ORDER TO TEACH THEM.

A MERCHANT ONCE SAW A RARE AND BEAUTIFUL PEARL. HE WANTED IT MORE THAN ANYTHING ELSE. SO HE SOLD EVERYTHING HE OWNED AND BOUGHT IT. THE KINGDOM OF GOD IS LIKE THAT PEARL -- IT IS WORTH EVERYTHING YOU HAVE TO POSSESS IT.

WHEN EVENING COMES JESUS SUGGESTS TO HIS DISCIPLES THAT THEY CROSS OVER TO THE OTHER SIDE OF THE LAKE.

IT'S THE KIND OF A NIGHT WHEN A SUDDEN STORM COULD HIT.

Mad Man by the Sea

FROM MARK 4:37–41; 5:1–24, 35

AT THE END OF A DAY OF TEACHING, JESUS ASKS HIS DISCIPLES TO TAKE HIM ACROSS THE SEA OF GALILEE. BUT SOON AFTER HE LIES DOWN TO SLEEP A SUDDEN AND VIOLENT STORM STRIKES.

LOWER THE SAIL!

SECONDS LATER GIANT WAVES ARE POURING OVER THE SHIP.

HELP! WE'RE BEING SWAMPED!

IN TERROR THE DISCIPLES RUSH TO THE STERN OF THE BOAT.

MASTER! DON'T YOU CARE IF WE DROWN?

JESUS RISES AND FACES THE STORMY SEA.

PEACE, BE STILL!

INSTANTLY THE WIND DIES AND THE WAVES VANISH.

WHO IS HE, THAT EVEN THE WINDS AND THE SEA OBEY HIM?

IN THE MORNING THE BOAT REACHES SHORE; AND AS JESUS AND HIS DISCIPLES ARE WALKING UP THE BEACH, A MAN POSSESSED BY AN EVIL SPIRIT RUSHES DOWN THE BANK TO MEET JESUS.

BE CAREFUL-- HE'S BROKEN HIS CHAINS.

COME OUT OF THE MAN, THOU UNCLEAN SPIRIT.

LET ME GO WITH YOU.

IT WOULD BE BETTER IF YOU WENT HOME AND TOLD YOUR FRIENDS WHAT GOD HAS DONE FOR YOU.

THE MAN IS CURED -- THE PEOPLE WHO SEE IT ARE AMAZED, AND THEY WONDER, TOO, WHAT POWER JESUS HAS TO MAKE EVIL SPIRITS OBEY HIM.

AFTER A WHILE JESUS AND HIS DISCIPLES RETURN TO CAPERNAUM. ONCE AGAIN A CROWD GATHERS TO HEAR HIM. BUT JUST AS JESUS BEGINS TO TEACH, JAIRUS, THE CHIEF RULER OF THE SYNAGOGUE, PUSHES HIS WAY THROUGH THE CROWD AND FALLS AT JESUS' FEET.

MY LITTLE GIRL -- SHE'S DYING! PLEASE COME!

JESUS GOES WITH JAIRUS -- BUT ON THE WAY THEY ARE MET BY A SERVANT FROM JAIRUS' HOUSEHOLD...

IT'S TOO LATE -- YOUR DAUGHTER IS DEAD!

The Mocking Crowd

FROM MARK 5:38–43;
MATTHEW 9:35–11:1; 14:1–12; JOHN 6:1–10

WHEN JESUS AND HIS DISCIPLES REACH THE HOME OF JAIRUS, THEY FIND A CROWD OF PEOPLE WEEPING BECAUSE JAIRUS' DAUGHTER IS DEAD.

WHY ARE YOU CRYING? THE LITTLE GIRL IS JUST ASLEEP.

ASLEEP? HOW DARE YOU RAISE FALSE HOPE FOR THIS FAMILY? THE CHILD IS DEAD, AND EVERYONE KNOWS IT!

QUIETLY JESUS LEADS THE CHILD'S PARENTS INTO HER ROOM. THERE HE TAKES THE GIRL'S HAND AND SAYS, "ARISE." INSTANTLY SHE GETS UP-- AND LOOKS AT JESUS IN SURPRISE AND WONDER.

GIVE HER SOMETHING TO EAT-- BUT DO NOT TELL ANYONE WHAT HAS HAPPENED IN THIS ROOM.

BUT JAIRUS IS AN IMPORTANT MAN. NEWS ABOUT HIS DAUGHTER SPREADS QUICKLY. AND AS JESUS TRAVELS THROUGH GALILEE, PREACHING AND HEALING, HIS FAME INCREASES. THE PHARISEES WATCH ANGRILY. AS YET THEY HAVE NO REAL CASE AGAINST JESUS AND WITH-OUT ONE THEY DARE NOT STIR UP THE EXCITED CROWDS THAT FOLLOW HIM.

BUT JESUS IS CONCERNED ABOUT THE MANY PEOPLE WHO STILL HAVE NOT HEARD HIS MESSAGE. HE CALLS HIS DISCIPLES ASIDE.

THE PEOPLE ARE LIKE SHEEP WITHOUT A SHEPHERD. I WANT YOU TO GO OUT BY TWOS TO PREACH AND HEAL THE SICK AS I HAVE DONE. DO NOT BE WORRIED ABOUT WHAT TO SAY, FOR THE SPIRIT OF GOD WILL SPEAK THROUGH YOU.

THE DISCIPLES PREACH THROUGHOUT GALILEE. WHEN THEY RETURN JESUS PREPARES TO TAKE THEM TO A QUIET PLACE TO REST AND TALK ABOUT FUTURE PLANS. AS THEY ARE STARTING, A DISCIPLE OF JOHN THE BAPTIST BRINGS THEM TRAGIC NEWS.

JOHN HAS BEEN BEHEADED BY KING HEROD!

HEROD IS A WICKED MAN. BUT THIS IS THE WORST OF HIS SINS.

Jesus—A Miracle Worker ▶ Read more about miracles on pp. 573-634 in your Picture Bible.

▶ Read more about miracles on pp. 573-634 in your Picture Bible.

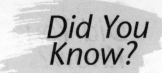

Did You Know?

A miracle is an extraordinary happening—something that couldn't happen without God stepping in to do what no human being could do. It is a way for God to show His power and love for people. Jesus, God's Son, did many miracles while He was on earth. Here are a few:

Blind man gets his sight (p. 614).

▶ Dead man comes to life (p. 626).

▶ 153 large fish caught (p. 670).

▶ Jesus' resurrection is the greatest miracle of all! (p. 665)

▶ 1st miracle
Turns water into wine at a wedding reception (p. 573).

▶ Jairus' daughter healed (p. 595).

▶ Walks on water. Disciples think He is a ghost (p. 601).

Stormy sea is made calm (p. 593).

There are about 35 miracles recorded in the Gospels. Jesus did many, many more. The Bible says that if all the miracles were written down, the world would not have room for all the books (John 21:25).

The Great Storyteller

▶ **There are 40 parables in the New Testament.**

Jesus tells many stories called parables during His ministry. A parable is a story that teaches a spiritual lesson by comparing one situation with another. For example, Jesus teaches the disciples about His kingdom by comparing it to types of soil or a treasure in a field. By telling stories, Jesus can explain important truths in a way that people can easily understand.

Check out these stories Jesus tells:

The Boy Who Ran Away from Home (p. 623)

▶ Building on Sand Is Risky Business! (Matthew 7:24-27)

▶ An Expensive Pearl (p. 562)

▶ One Lamb Is Lost! (Luke 15:3-7)

▶ Hidden Treasure Found in Field (Matthew 13:44)

▶ A Widow Woman Who Wouldn't Quit (Luke 18:2-8)

▶ Mystery of the Lost Coin (Luke 15:8-10)

▶ Ten Bridesmaids Wait for Groom to Show Up for Wedding (Matthew 25:1-13)

Man Attacked on Road to Jericho (p. 617)

No Earthly Throne

FROM JOHN 6:10–15; MATTHEW 14:22–30

IT IS LATE AFTERNOON. THE CROWD THAT HAS FOLLOWED JESUS IS HUNGRY. BUT THE ONLY FOOD AVAILABLE BELONGS TO A BOY. HE EAGERLY GIVES IT TO JESUS, WHO THANKS GOD FOR IT AND HANDS IT TO HIS DISCIPLES.

DISTRIBUTE THE FOOD TO EVERYONE.

HOW FAR WILL FIVE LOAVES AND TWO FISHES GO IN FEEDING A CROWD OF OVER FIVE THOUSAND?

BUT THE DISCIPLES HAVE FAITH IN JESUS... AND THEY OBEY HIM.

LOOK! EVERYONE HERE IS GETTING ALL THE FOOD HE WANTS.

IT'S A MIRACLE!

WHEN THE PEOPLE HAVE FINISHED EATING, JESUS TURNS AGAIN TO HIS DISCIPLES.

GATHER UP THE FOOD THAT REMAINS.

TWELVE BASKETS OF FOOD ARE LEFT OVER! THE PEOPLE ARE NOW MORE AMAZED THAN EVER.

MAYBE JESUS IS THE KING THE PROPHETS TALKED ABOUT.

A KING LIKE DAVID-- WHO WILL DESTROY OUR ENEMIES AND MAKE US RICH AND POWERFUL!

UT GOD SENT JESUS TO BE THE SAVIOR, TO BRING PEOPLE INTO THE KINGDOM OF GOD--NOT TO COMMAND ARMIES AND CONQUER THRONES. WHEN JESUS SEES THAT THE CROWD WANTS TO FORCE HIM TO BE A KING, HE QUICKLY CALLS HIS DISCIPLES.

LAUNCH THE BOAT AND CROSS OVER TO THE OTHER SIDE OF THE SEA. I WILL JOIN YOU LATER.

QUICKLY--BEFORE THE EXCITEMENT OF THE PEOPLE GROWS STRONGER--JESUS DISMISSES THEM. THEN HE GOES UP ON A MOUNTAIN TO PRAY. LATER THAT NIGHT --ON THE SEA OF GALILEE...

THE WIND IS RISING! WE'RE IN FOR A STORM!

602

SOON THE STORM HITS...

SUDDENLY THEY LOOK UP TO SEE A FIGURE WALKING ON THE WATER. "A SPIRIT!" THEY CRY IN TERROR. ACROSS THE WAVES A CALM VOICE CALLS OUT: "IT IS I; DON'T BE AFRAID."

INSTANTLY PETER JUMPS FROM THE BOAT AND STARTS WALKING TOWARD JESUS. BUT WHEN HE SEES THE POWER OF THE WIND, HE LOSES FAITH-- AND BEGINS TO SINK...

Miracle on the Sea

FROM MATTHEW 14:30–36; JOHN 6:22–71; MARK 7:1–23;
MATTHEW 16:13–26; 17:1–2

A STRONG NIGHT WIND IS STIRRING UP ANGRY WAVES ON THE SEA OF GALILEE. JESUS' DISCIPLES ARE ROWING HARD AGAINST THE STORM -- WHEN SUDDENLY THEY SEE A FIGURE WALKING TOWARD THEM. THEY ARE TERRIFIED -- UNTIL THEY SEE THAT THE MAN ON THE WATER IS JESUS. PETER GETS OUT OF THE BOAT AND STARTS TOWARDS JESUS -- BUT WHEN HE SEES THE ROUGH WAVES HE LOSES FAITH...

O PETER, WHY DID YOU DOUBT?

LORD! SAVE ME!

JESUS RESCUES PETER, AND AS THEY REACH THE BOAT, THE WIND DIES, AND THE SEA IS CALM.

HE REALLY IS GOD'S SON!

AT DAYBREAK THE DISCIPLES BRING THE BOAT TO SHORE. WHEN THE PEOPLE SEE JESUS, THEY HURRY TO BRING THEIR SICK AND CRIPPLED TO HIM. PATIENTLY AND LOVINGLY HE HEALS THEM ALL.

IF ONLY I CAN TOUCH HIS GARMENT I KNOW I WILL BE HEALED.

Later THAT DAY JESUS GOES TO THE SYNAGOGUE IN CAPERNAUM. THE CROWD THAT HE FED THE DAY BEFORE IS THERE ASKING TO BE FED AGAIN. WHEN JESUS PREACHES A SERMON ABOUT THEIR SPIRITUAL NEEDS, MANY OF THEM ARE DISAPPOINTED AND TURN AWAY.

SEEING THIS, THE PHARISEES RESUME THEIR PUBLIC CRITICISM OF JESUS.

WE HAVE SEEN YOUR DISCIPLES EAT WITHOUT WASHING THEIR HANDS. WHY DO YOU LET THEM BREAK OUR LAWS AND DEFILE THEMSELVES?

NOTHING THAT GOES INTO A PERSON'S MOUTH IS DEFILING, BUT THE EVIL WORDS THAT COME OUT DO DEFILE.

605

SHOCKED BECAUSE HE DEFENDS HIS DISCIPLES, THE PHARISEES TURN AWAY, MORE DETERMINED THAN EVER TO DESTROY JESUS.

DON'T YOU KNOW THAT YOU HAVE MADE THE PHARISEES ANGRY?

THE PHARISEES ARE BLIND TO THE WILL OF GOD— AND THEY ARE LEADING THE PEOPLE TO BE AS BLIND AS THEY ARE.

BECAUSE MOST OF THE PEOPLE WILL ACCEPT HIM ONLY AS AN EARTHLY KING, JESUS LEAVES GALILEE. HE TAKES HIS DISCIPLES TO THE COUNTRY OF PHOENICIA-- AND LATER TO THE REGION OF CAESAREA PHILIPPI, WHERE HE TEACHES THEM IN PRIVACY. THERE, ONE DAY, HE ASKS THEM: "WHO DO PEOPLE SAY THAT I AM?"

JOHN THE BAPTIST... ELIJAH...

BUT WHO DO YOU SAY THAT I AM?

YOU ARE THE CHRIST, THE SON OF THE LIVING GOD.

BLESSED ARE YOU, PETER--FOR MY FATHER IN HEAVEN HAS REVEALED THIS TO YOU.

Now THAT THE DISCIPLES TRULY UNDERSTAND THAT HE IS THE PROMISED MESSIAH, JESUS TELLS THEM WHAT WILL HAPPEN WHEN HE GOES TO JERUSALEM.

THE PHARISEES AND PRIESTS DO NOT BELIEVE THAT I AM THE MESSIAH. THEY WILL HAVE ME KILLED-- BUT IN THREE DAYS I WILL RISE AGAIN.

KILLED? NEVER!

PETER, YOU DO NOT UNDERSTAND GOD'S PLAN FOR ME. LET ME WARN ALL OF YOU-- IF YOU WANT TO FOLLOW ME, YOU MUST BE PREPARED TO SUFFER AS I WILL SUFFER.

IN SPITE OF WHAT JESUS TELLS THEM, THE DISCIPLES CANNOT BELIEVE THAT HE WILL BE PUT TO DEATH. THEY BELIEVE THAT HE HAS HELPED OTHERS, AND THAT HE WILL HELP HIMSELF. SEVERAL DAYS LATER, JESUS SPEAKS TO PETER, JAMES AND JOHN.

COME WITH ME UP THE MOUNTAIN.

I WONDER WHY...

AFTER A LONG CLIMB TO THE MOUNTAINTOP, JESUS GOES ASIDE TO PRAY. THE DISCIPLES SIT DOWN TO REST, BUT SOON FALL ASLEEP. WHEN THEY AWAKEN THEY SEE SOMETHING STRANGE AND GLORIOUSLY BEAUTIFUL...

607

A Boy—And His Father's Faith

FROM MATTHEW 17:3–23; MARK 3:26, 33; LUKE 9:37–45

ALONE WITH JESUS ON THE MOUNTAIN, PETER, JAMES AND JOHN SEE HIM TRANSFIGURED. HIS FACE SHINES WITH THE BRIGHTNESS OF THE SUN--HIS CLOTHES BECOME DAZZLING WHITE. THEN TWO GREAT MEN OF THE PAST, MOSES AND ELIJAH, APPEAR TO TALK WITH HIM.

BUT AS PETER SPEAKS A BRIGHT CLOUD DESCENDS ON THE MOUNTAINTOP... AND OUT OF THE CLOUD COMES THE VOICE OF GOD:

THIS IS MY BELOVED SON, IN WHOM I AM WELL PLEASED; LISTEN TO HIM.

608

THE DISCIPLES ARE SO FRIGHTENED THAT THEY FALL TO THE GROUND BUT JESUS BENDS DOWN AND TOUCHES THEM...

DO NOT BE AFRAID.

THE NEXT MORNING-- ON THE WAY DOWN THE MOUNTAIN--JESUS WARNS HIS DISCIPLES TO TELL NO ONE OF HIS TRANS-FIGURATION UNTIL AFTER HIS RESURRECTION. AFTER WHAT THEY HAVE JUST SEEN THE DISCIPLES CANNOT BELIEVE THAT JESUS WILL DIE -- SO THEY ARE PUZZLED WHEN JESUS TALKS ABOUT RISING FROM THE DEAD.

THEY REACH THE VAL-LEY TO FIND A GREAT CROWD GATHERED AROUND THE OTHER DISCIPLES.

AT THE SIGHT OF JESUS THE PEOPLE QUICKLY SURROUND HIM.

MY SON HAS SPELLS AND OFTEN FALLS INTO THE FIRE. I BROUGHT HIM TO YOUR DISCIPLES, BUT THEY COULD NOT HEAL HIM.

BRING YOUR SON TO ME.

THE FATHER OBEYS -- BUT THE BOY HAS A SPELL AND FALLS TO THE GROUND AT JESUS' FEET.

IF YOU CAN HELP US-- PLEASE DO.

ALL THINGS ARE POSSIBLE TO ONE WHO HAS FAITH.

I BELIEVE! HELP ME, PLEASE, TO HAVE MORE FAITH.

THOU UNCLEAN SPIRIT--COME OUT OF THE BOY!

609

FOR A MOMENT THERE IS A STRUGGLE-- THEN THE BOY BECOMES SO STILL PEOPLE THINK HE IS DEAD. BUT JESUS REACHES DOWN TO TAKE HIS HAND.

ARISE!

INSTANTLY THE BOY GETS UP.

FATHER, WHAT HAPPENED?

YOU HAVE BEEN HEALED--BY THE POWER OF GOD!

WHEN THEY ARE ALONE, THE DISCIPLES TURN TO JESUS.

WHY COULDN'T **WE** HEAL THE BOY?

YOU DID NOT HAVE FAITH. IF YOU HAVE FAITH THE SIZE OF A MUSTARD SEED, NOTHING IS IMPOSSIBLE FOR YOU.

LATER ON THE WAY TO CAPERNAUM, THE DISCIPLES TALK AMONG THEMSELVES ABOUT THE KINGDOM THEY EXPECT JESUS WILL SOON ESTABLISH. ALMOST AT ONCE THEY BEGIN TO QUARREL ABOUT WHICH ONE WILL BE THE GREATEST IN THAT KINGDOM.

IF ONLY **I** COULD SIT IN THE SEAT OF HONOR NEXT TO JESUS.

Seventy Times Seven

FROM MATTHEW 18:1–14, 21–22; JOHN 7:11–52; 8:21–59

ON THE WAY TO CAPERNAUM THE DISCIPLES QUARREL ABOUT WHICH ONE OF THEM WILL BE THE MOST IMPORTANT PERSON IN THE KINGDOM THEY EXPECT JESUS TO ESTABLISH. WHEN THEY REACH THE CITY JESUS ASKS WHY THEY ARE QUARRELING AND THEY ARE ASHAMED TO SAY. HE CALLS A LITTLE CHILD TO HIM.

WHICHEVER ONE OF YOU WANTS TO BE GREATEST IN GOD'S KINGDOM MUST BE AS HUMBLE AND WILLING TO LEARN AS THIS LITTLE CHILD.

AND IF YOU HAVE ANY TROUBLE WITH ANYONE, TALK WITH HIM ABOUT IT AT ONCE. IF HE LISTENS, YOU WILL HAVE WON BACK A FRIEND.

HOW MANY TIMES SHOULD I FORGIVE SOMEONE WHO HAS MISTREATED ME? SEVEN TIMES?

NO, PETER-- SEVENTY TIMES SEVEN. OR AS LONG AS YOU WANT GOD TO FORGIVE YOU.

FROM CAPERNAUM JESUS GOES SOUTH TO PREACH IN JUDEA, AND REACHES JERUSALEM AT THE TIME OF A GREAT RELIGIOUS FEAST. AS HE TEACHES, PEOPLE BEGIN TO WONDER...

IS JESUS THE MESSIAH?

I'VE SEEN HIM DO THINGS THAT NO MAN HAS EVER DONE BEFORE.

612

WHEN THE CHIEF PRIESTS AND PHARISEES HEAR WHAT THE PEOPLE ARE SAYING, THEY QUICKLY JOIN FORCES AGAINST JESUS.

IF WE DON'T GET RID OF HIM THE PEOPLE WILL ACCEPT HIM AS THE MESSIAH.

I'LL STOP HIM. CALL THE TEMPLE GUARDS.

ARREST JESUS. BUT DO IT AT A TIME WHEN IT WILL CAUSE THE LEAST TROUBLE.

ON THE LAST DAY OF THE FEAST THE OFFICERS RETURN TO THE PRIESTS AND PHARISEES.

WHERE IS JESUS?

WE'VE NEVER HEARD ANYONE SPEAK AS THIS MAN DOES. WE COULD NOT ARREST HIM.

THE PRIESTS AND PHARISEES ARE FURIOUS -- BUT THEY ARE AFRAID TO FORCE THE ISSUE WHILE THE CITY IS FILLED WITH PEOPLE ATTENDING THE FEAST. BUT THE NEXT DAY...

JESUS RETURNS TO THE TEMPLE TO PREACH. IN THE COURSE OF HIS SERMON HE NOT ONLY POINTS OUT THE SINS OF THE PRIESTS AND PHARISEES BUT DECLARES THAT HE WAS WITH GOD EVEN BEFORE THE DAYS OF THEIR GREAT FOREFATHER, ABRAHAM.

HOW DARE HE CLAIM SUCH RELATIONSHIP WITH GOD!

STONE HIM! STONE HIM!

A Beggar Meet Jesus

FROM JOHN 9:1—10:21; LUKE 10:25

THE PRIESTS AND PHARISEES ATTEMPT TO STONE JESUS -- BUT HE ESCAPES. LATER -- ON THE SABBATH -- HE AND HIS DISCIPLES COME UPON A BLIND MAN BEGGING AT A TEMPLE GATE. JESUS MOISTENS SOME CLAY AND PLACES IT TENDERLY OVER THE MAN'S EYES.

GO, WASH IN THE POOL OF SILOAM.

THE MAN OBEYS JESUS, AND FOR THE FIRST TIME IN HIS LIFE HE CAN SEE! HE IS SO EXCITED THAT HE HURRIES HOME, WHERE HE IS MET BY HIS NEIGHBORS.

IS THIS THE BLIND MAN WHO BEGGED OUTSIDE THE TEMPLE?

IMPOSSIBLE -- BUT HE **DOES** LOOK LIKE HIM!

BUT **I AM** THE MAN WHO WAS BLIND. JESUS GAVE ME MY SIGHT!

THE NEIGHBORS ARE WORRIED BECAUSE THE MAN HAS BEEN HEALED ON THE SABBATH. THEY TAKE HIM AT ONCE TO THE PHARISEES, WHO INTERPRET THE RULES ABOUT WHAT CAN BE DONE ON THE SABBATH.

THIS JESUS YOU TALK ABOUT IS A SINNER -- HE DOESN'T OBEY THE LAWS OF THE SABBATH.

I DO NOT KNOW WHETHER HE IS A SINNER, BUT THIS I DO KNOW: I WAS BLIND AND NOW I SEE.

THE PHARISEES TRY TO MAKE THE MAN TURN AGAINST JESUS, BUT THEY CANNOT, SO THEY PUT HIM OUT OF THE SYNAGOGUE. JESUS LEARNS WHAT HAS HAPPENED, AND SEARCHES FOR THE THE MAN. WHEN HE FINDS HIM THE PHARISEES QUICKLY GATHER AROUND.

DO YOU BELIEVE IN THE SON OF GOD?

WHO IS HE -- THAT I MAY BELIEVE IN HIM?

I AM -- THE VERY ONE WHO IS SPEAKING TO YOU.

LORD, I BELIEVE!

I AM THE GOOD SHEPHERD; THE GOOD SHEPHERD GIVES HIS LIFE FOR HIS SHEEP. NO ONE CAN TAKE MY LIFE FROM ME, BUT I GIVE IT MYSELF. I HAVE THE POWER TO GIVE IT AND TO TAKE IT AGAIN, FOR I RECEIVED THIS POWER FROM GOD MY FATHER.

THIS MAN IS CRAZY AND IS POSSESSED BY AN EVIL SPIRIT. WHY LISTEN TO HIM?

BUT CAN AN EVIL SPIRIT OPEN THE EYES OF THE BLIND?

WHILE JESUS IS PREACHING IN ONE OF THE CITIES A LAWYER IN THE CROWD WAITS FOR A CHANCE TO TEST HIM.

THE PHARISEES AND PRIESTS CONTINUE TO ARGUE. SOME THINK THAT JESUS IS WORKING WITH THE DEVIL. OTHERS DECLARE THAT HE IS NOT, BUT THEY REFUSE TO BELIEVE THAT HE IS THE SON OF GOD. A FEW DAYS LATER JESUS AND HIS DISCIPLES LEAVE JERUSALEM FOR A TOUR THROUGH JUDEA.

I'LL FIND OUT FOR MYSELF HOW THIS YOUNG TEACHER HANDLES A HARD QUESTION.

Four Travelers to Jericho

FROM LUKE 10:25–40

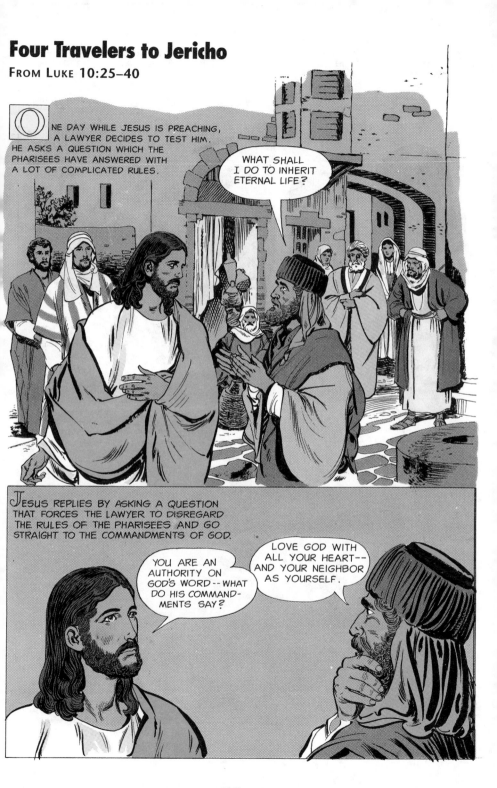

ONE DAY WHILE JESUS IS PREACHING, A LAWYER DECIDES TO TEST HIM. HE ASKS A QUESTION WHICH THE PHARISEES HAVE ANSWERED WITH A LOT OF COMPLICATED RULES.

WHAT SHALL I DO TO INHERIT ETERNAL LIFE?

JESUS REPLIES BY ASKING A QUESTION THAT FORCES THE LAWYER TO DISREGARD THE RULES OF THE PHARISEES AND GO STRAIGHT TO THE COMMANDMENTS OF GOD.

YOU ARE AN AUTHORITY ON GOD'S WORD--WHAT DO HIS COMMAND-MENTS SAY?

LOVE GOD WITH ALL YOUR HEART-- AND YOUR NEIGHBOR AS YOURSELF.

YOU ARE RIGHT-- DO THAT AND YOU WILL HAVE ETERNAL LIFE.

BUT WHO IS MY NEIGHBOR?

JESUS REPLIES WITH A STORY WHICH FORCES THE LAWYER AGAIN TO ANSWER HIS OWN QUESTION:

A MAN IS TRAVELING FROM JERUSALEM TO JERICHO. ON THE WAY HE IS ATTACKED BY BANDITS, ROBBED, AND LEFT FOR DEAD.

BY CHANCE A PRIEST COMES BY-- HE SEES THE WOUNDED MAN BUT HE QUICKLY PASSES BY.

A LITTLE LATER A LEVITE, AN ASSISTANT TO THE PRIESTS, COMES ALONG-- BUT HE, TOO, HURRIES BY.

618

BUT WHEN A SAMARITAN SEES THE INJURED MAN, HE STOPS. ALTHOUGH SAMARITANS ARE BITTER ENEMIES OF THE JEWS, HE BINDS UP THE MAN'S WOUNDS, TAKES HIM TO AN INN, AND PAYS FOR HIS CARE.

WHEN HE FINISHES THE STORY OF THE GOOD SAMARITAN, JESUS ASKS: WHICH ONE OF THE THREE WAS A NEIGHBOR TO THE MAN WHO WAS ROBBED?

THE MAN WHO HELPED HIM.

GO AND DO THE SAME.

THE LAWYER GOES AWAY-- AMAZED AT THE SKILL WITH WHICH JESUS ANSWERED HIS QUESTIONS.

NOW I SEE-- MY NEIGHBOR IS ANYONE WHO NEEDS ME.

JESUS CONTINUES ON HIS PREACHING TOUR. IN BETHANY HE STOPS TO VISIT HIS FRIENDS: MARY, MARTHA, AND LAZARUS. MARY DROPS EVERYTHING SHE IS DOING TO LISTEN TO JESUS...

BUT HER SISTER MARTHA...

IT ISN'T FAIR-- AND I WON'T STAND FOR IT ANY LONGER!

The Lord's Prayer

FROM LUKE 10:40—11:2; MATTHEW 6:9–13;
JOHN 10:22–40; LUKE 15:1–19

WHEN JESUS VISITS IN THE HOME OF HIS FRIENDS, MARY, MARTHA, AND LAZARUS, MARY STOPS HER WORK TO LISTEN TO JESUS. BUT MARTHA HURRIES TO THE KITCHEN TO PREPARE FOOD. AS SHE WORKS SHE BECOMES UPSET BECAUSE MARY DOES NOT HELP HER. AT LAST SHE COMPLAINS TO JESUS.

DON'T YOU THINK IT'S WRONG FOR MARY TO LEAVE ME WITH ALL THE WORK TO DO? TELL HER TO HELP ME.

MARTHA! MARTHA! YOU ARE WORRYING ABOUT TOO MANY THINGS. ONLY ONE THING IS IMPORTANT --TO LEARN THE WILL OF GOD, AS MARY HAS CHOSEN TO DO.

DURING THE REST OF JESUS' VISIT, MARTHA SEEKS TO LEARN MORE ABOUT GOD. THEN JESUS LEAVES HIS FRIENDS IN BETHANY AND JOINS HIS DISCIPLES FOR A TEACHING TRIP IN JUDEA.

LISTENING TO JESUS MAKES ME FEEL SO CLOSE TO GOD.

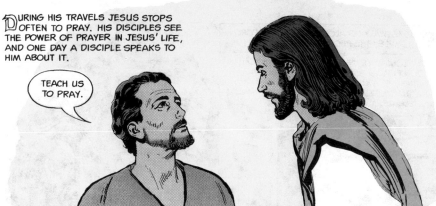

DURING HIS TRAVELS JESUS STOPS OFTEN TO PRAY. HIS DISCIPLES SEE THE POWER OF PRAYER IN JESUS' LIFE, AND ONE DAY A DISCIPLE SPEAKS TO HIM ABOUT IT.

TEACH US TO PRAY.

JESUS ANSWERS: WHEN YOU PRAY, SAY,

OUR FATHER WHO IS IN HEAVEN: LET YOUR NAME BE TREATED AS HOLY. LET YOUR KINGDOM COME. LET YOUR WILL BE DONE ON EARTH AS IT IS IN HEAVEN. GIVE US OUR FOOD FOR THIS DAY. AND FORGIVE US OUR DEBTS AS WE HAVE FORGIVEN OUR DEBTORS. AND DON'T LEAD US INTO TEMPTATION, BUT DELIVER US FROM THE EVIL ONE. FOR TO YOU BELONGS THE KINGDOM AND THE POWER AND THE SPLENDOR FOREVER, AMEN.

FOR A MOMENT NO ONE SPEAKS. THEN SOFTLY THE DISCIPLES SAY "AMEN" TO THE SIMPLE PRAYER THAT BECOMES A MODEL FOR THEIR FUTURE PRAYERS TO GOD. AFTER THIS, JESUS AND HIS HELPERS CONTINUE THROUGH JUDEA, PREACHING AND HEALING. BY THE TIME JESUS RETURNS TO JERUSALEM FOR A RELIGIOUS FEAST THE CITY IS FILLED WITH PEOPLE TALKING AND WONDERING ABOUT HIM.

AS JESUS IS WALKING ALONG SOLOMON'S PORCH OF THE TEMPLE, THE PEOPLE SURROUND HIM.

HOW LONG WILL YOU KEEP US WAITING? IF YOU ARE THE MESSIAH, TELL US.

I TOLD YOU, BUT YOU WOULD NOT BELIEVE ME. THE THINGS I HAVE DONE IN MY FATHER'S NAME SHOULD PROVE TO YOU WHO I AM.

DID YOU HEAR THAT? HE CALLED GOD HIS FATHER!

STONE HIM!

JESUS TURNS AND QUIETLY WALKS AWAY, AND--STRANGELY--NO ONE TRIES TO STOP HIM.

JESUS LEAVES JERUSALEM FOR PEREA-- WHERE HE CONTINUES TO PREACH AND HEAL THE SICK. AGAIN THE PHARISEES COMPLAIN BECAUSE HE ASSOCIATES WITH SINNERS. JESUS TELLS THEM A STORY...

A CERTAIN MAN HAS TWO SONS. ONE DAY THE YOUNGER COMES TO HIM.

FATHER, I WANT TO RUN MY OWN LIFE. PLEASE GIVE ME THE SHARE OF YOUR MONEY THAT WILL SOMEDAY BE MINE.

I HAD HOPED YOU WOULD STAY HOME AND HELP WITH THE WORK HERE-- BUT IF YOU WANT THE MONEY, YOU MAY HAVE IT.

THE YOUNG MAN GOES TO ANOTHER COUNTRY-- WHERE HE SPENDS HIS MONEY EATING AND DRINKING WITH BAD COMPANIONS. AT LAST HIS MONEY IS GONE --AND THE ONLY JOB HE CAN GET IS CARING FOR A FARMER'S PIGS.

MY FATHER'S SERVANTS LIVE BETTER THAN THIS! I'M GOING HOME AND ASK MY FATHER TO LET ME WORK FOR HIM-- NOT AS HIS SON, BUT AS A SERVANT!

The Prodigal's Return

FROM LUKE 15:20–32; JOHN 11:1–8

WHEN THE PHARISEES COMPLAIN BECAUSE JESUS ASSOCIATES WITH SINNERS, HE TELLS THEM A STORY ABOUT A YOUNG MAN WHO LEAVES HOME. THE YOUNG MAN SPENDS HIS MONEY SO FOOLISHLY THAT AT LAST HE HAS TO TAKE CARE OF A FARMER'S PIGS IN ORDER TO KEEP ALIVE. IN HIS MISERY HE DECIDES TO GO HOME AND WORK FOR HIS FATHER-- NOT AS HIS SON, BUT AS ONE OF HIS SERVANTS. WHEN HE REACHES HOME HIS FATHER RUSHES OUT TO MEET HIM.

FATHER! I HAVE SINNED AGAINST HEAVEN AND YOU. I'M NO LONGER WORTHY TO BE CALLED YOUR SON.

BRING MY SON THE BEST ROBE IN THE HOUSE. AND PREPARE A FEAST, FOR MY SON WHO WAS LOST IS FOUND!

OUT IN THE FIELD THE OLDER SON WORKS HARD TO COMPLETE HIS JOB BEFORE NIGHT.

IF MY BROTHER WERE HERE TO HELP, I WOULDN'T HAVE TO WORK SO MUCH.

THE DAY'S WORK DONE, HE GOES HOME. BUT AS HE APPROACHES THE HOUSE HE HEARS MUSIC...

WHAT'S GOING ON?

YOUR BROTHER HAS RETURNED, AND YOUR FATHER IS HAVING A FEAST FOR HIM.

IN ANGER THE OLDER SON REFUSES TO GO INTO THE HOUSE. SOON HIS FATHER COMES OUT.

YOU HAVE NEVER GIVEN A FEAST FOR ME ALTHOUGH I HAVE STAYED HOME TO HELP YOU. BUT MY BROTHER--

ALL THAT I HAVE IS YOURS, MY SON. BUT IT IS RIGHT FOR US TO BE GLAD FOR YOUR BROTHER'S RETURN. HE WAS THE SAME AS DEAD-- NOW HE IS ALIVE.

WHEN JESUS FINISHES THE STORY THE PEOPLE TURN TO ONE ANOTHER IN WONDER.

DOES HE MEAN THAT GOD IS LIKE THE FATHER IN THE STORY?

YES -- I SEE IT. GOD WANTS TO FORGIVE EVEN US SINNERS IF WE WILL COME BACK TO HIM.

WHEN THE PHARISEES SEE THE REACTION OF THE PEOPLE, THEY TURN AWAY IN ANGER. JESUS CONTINUES TO TEACH, BUT HE IS SOON INTERRUPTED...

JESUS! MARY AND MARTHA HAVE SENT ME TO TELL YOU THAT THEIR BROTHER, LAZARUS, IS ILL. THEY WANT YOU TO COME TO BETHANY--

BETHANY? THAT'S TOO CLOSE TO HIS ENEMIES IN JERUSALEM. THEY'LL KILL HIM!

Called from the Tomb

FROM JOHN 11:38–54; LUKE 18:15–23; 19:1–3

BY THE TIME JESUS AND HIS DISCIPLES REACH BETHANY LAZARUS, THE BROTHER OF MARY AND MARTHA, HAS BEEN DEAD FOUR DAYS. AT THE TOMB JESUS ASKS TO HAVE THE STONE ROLLED AWAY. HE PRAYS ALOUD TO GOD AND THEN CALLS OUT IN A STRONG VOICE...

LAZARUS, COME FORTH.

TO THE AMAZEMENT OF THE CROWD, LAZARUS APPEARS!

LAZARUS!

O JESUS, WE THANK YOU!

A MAN RAISED FROM THE DEAD! THE PEOPLE CAN SCARCELY BELIEVE WHAT THEY HAVE SEEN. MANY OF THEM TURN TO JESUS CRYING, "MESSIAH! SON OF GOD!" BUT OTHERS GO INTO JERUSALEM TO TELL THE PHARISEES WHAT JESUS HAS DONE.

IN ANGER AND DESPERATION THE PHARISEES AND CHIEF PRIESTS CALL A MEETING.

IF NEWS OF THIS GETS AROUND THE PEOPLE WILL TRY TO MAKE JESUS A KING.

AND IF THERE'S A REBELLION THE ROMANS WILL BLAME **US**. WE'LL LOSE OUR POSITIONS AND THE NATION WILL BE DESTROYED.

628

FARTHER ALONG THE WAY JESUS IS STOPPED BY A YOUNG MAN.

TEACHER, WHAT SHALL I DO TO INHERIT ETERNAL LIFE?

KEEP GOD'S COMMANDMENTS.

BUT I HAVE KEPT THE LAWS --SINCE I WAS A BOY.

YOU NEED TO DO ONE THING MORE -- SELL ALL THAT YOU HAVE, GIVE THE MONEY TO THE POOR, AND FOLLOW ME.

BUT THE YOUNG MAN THINKS TOO MUCH OF HIS RICHES...SLOWLY HE TURNS HIS BACK ON JESUS AND WALKS AWAY.

THE TRAVELERS CONTINUE ON TOWARD JERUSALEM. BY THE TIME THEY REACH JERICHO, JESUS IS IN THE MIDST OF AN EXCITED, HAPPY THRONG.

PLEASE --LET ME THROUGH!

HO--ZACCHEUS, THE CROOKED LITTLE TAX COLLECTOR, WANTS TO SEE JESUS!

I HAVE TO SEE JESUS--AND I WILL!

Man in the Tree

FROM LUKE 19:4–10; JOHN 12:1–8; LUKE 19:29–35

ZACCHEUS, THE WEALTHY TAX COLLECTOR,
IS SO SHORT THAT HE CAN'T LOOK
OVER THE HEADS OF THE PEOPLE. FRANTICALLY
HE RUNS AHEAD OF THE CROWD, CLIMBS A TREE,
AND WAITS. WHEN JESUS
SEES HIM, HE STOPS...

ZACCHEUS, COME DOWN, FOR I WANT TO STAY AT YOUR HOUSE!

ZACCHEUS IS AMAZED THAT JESUS WOULD EVEN SPEAK TO HIM, BUT HE CLIMBS DOWN AT ONCE AND LEADS THE WAY TO HIS HOUSE.

WHY WOULD A TEACHER AS GREAT AS JESUS WANT TO STAY WITH THAT CROOKED LITTLE TAX COLLECTOR?

ZACCHEUS WONDERS, TOO, BUT HE SOON DISCOVERS THAT BEING IN THE PRESENCE OF JESUS MAKES HIM ASHAMED OF EVERY WRONG THING HE HAS EVER DONE. HE WANTS TO BE FORGIVEN AND START OVER...

HALF OF MY GOODS I WILL GIVE TO THE POOR. AND IF I HAVE CHEATED ANYONE I WILL PAY HIM BACK FOUR TIMES AS MUCH.

SALVATION HAS COME TO YOU TODAY, ZACCHEUS. IT IS TO HELP PEOPLE LIKE YOU THAT I HAVE COME TO THE WORLD.

F ROM JERICHO THE CROWDS CONTINUE THEIR WAY TO JERUSALEM FOR THE GREAT PASSOVER FEAST. THE FESTIVAL IS STILL SIX DAYS AWAY, SO JESUS STOPS IN BETHANY TO VISIT HIS FRIENDS—MARY, MARTHA, AND LAZARUS. AT A SUPPER IN THE HOME OF SIMON THE LEPER, MARY KNEELS BESIDE JESUS AND ANOINTS HIS FEET WITH COSTLY OIL—THEN WIPES THEM WITH HER HAIR.

JUDAS ISCARIOT, TREASURER OF THE DISCIPLES, IS ANGERED BY WHAT HE THINKS IS A WASTE OF MONEY.

WHY WASN'T THE OIL SOLD AND THE MONEY GIVEN TO THE POOR?

I WANTED TO HONOR JESUS--

LET HER ALONE. SHE IS SHOWING HER LOVE FOR ME.

JUDAS IS ANGERED BY THIS REPRIMAND-- AND AN UGLY THOUGHT COMES TO HIS MIND.

WHEN THE TIME IS RIGHT I'LL GO TO THE PRIESTS AND PHARISEES-- **THEY'LL** BE GLAD TO LISTEN TO ME.

THE NEXT DAY JESUS AND HIS DISCIPLES JOIN THE CROWDS GOING UP TO JERUSALEM TO PREPARE FOR THE PASSOVER FEAST. ON THE WAY...

GO OVER INTO THAT VILLAGE AND AS YOU ENTER YOU WILL FIND A COLT. BRING IT TO ME. AND IF ANYONE QUESTIONS YOU, TELL HIM I NEED THE ANIMAL-- AND WILL RETURN IT.

PUZZLED, THE TWO DISCIPLES GO TO THE VILLAGE WHERE THEY FIND THE COLT. WHEN THEY START TO UNTIE THE ROPE...

WHAT DO YOU MEAN, TAKING MY ANIMAL?

JESUS SAID TO TELL YOU THAT HE NEEDED IT.

AT THE MENTION OF JESUS' NAME, THE MAN GLADLY GIVES HIS CONSENT.

I WONDER WHY JESUS WANTS MY COLT. IT HAS NEVER BEEN RIDDEN-- BESIDES, IT'S NOT A VERY NOBLE BEAST FOR ANYONE AS IMPORTANT AS JESUS TO RIDE.

Triumphal Entry

FROM LUKE 19:36–38;
MATTHEW 21:10–17; 22:15–17

IT IS THE FIRST DAY OF THE WEEK. THE ROAD TO JERUSALEM IS FILLED WITH PEOPLE ON THE WAY TO CELEBRATE THE PASSOVER FEAST OF THE JEWS. AT JESUS' REQUEST HIS DISCIPLES BRING HIM A LOWLY BEAST OF BURDEN-- HE MOUNTS IT AND JOINS THE MULTITUDE OF PILGRIMS. EAGERLY THEY MAKE WAY FOR HIM--WAVING PALM BRANCHES AND CARPETING HIS PATH WITH THEIR GARMENTS. AND, WHILE THEY ESCORT HIM-- TRIUMPHANTLY--UP THE ROAD AND INTO THE CITY, THE SOUND OF THEIR PRAISES FILLS THE AIR: "HOSANNA! BLESSED IS THE KING THAT COMETH IN THE NAME OF THE LORD!"

634

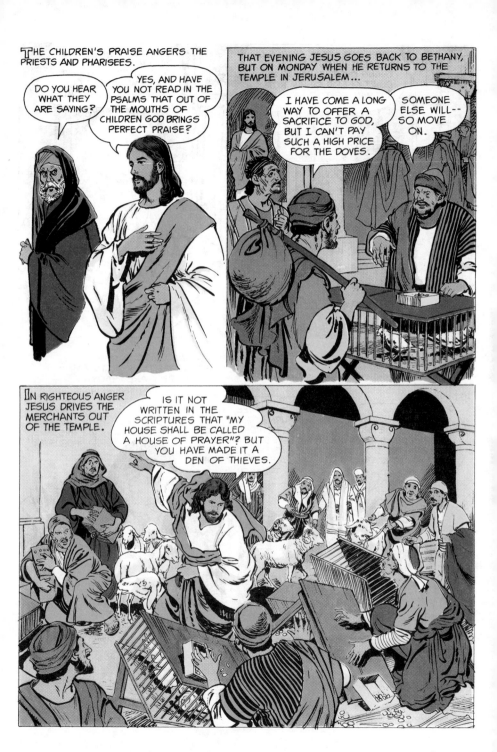

THE CHILDREN'S PRAISE ANGERS THE PRIESTS AND PHARISEES.

DO YOU HEAR WHAT THEY ARE SAYING?

YES, AND HAVE YOU NOT READ IN THE PSALMS THAT OUT OF THE MOUTHS OF CHILDREN GOD BRINGS PERFECT PRAISE?

THAT EVENING JESUS GOES BACK TO BETHANY, BUT ON MONDAY WHEN HE RETURNS TO THE TEMPLE IN JERUSALEM...

I HAVE COME A LONG WAY TO OFFER A SACRIFICE TO GOD, BUT I CAN'T PAY SUCH A HIGH PRICE FOR THE DOVES.

SOMEONE ELSE WILL-- SO MOVE ON.

IN RIGHTEOUS ANGER JESUS DRIVES THE MERCHANTS OUT OF THE TEMPLE.

IS IT NOT WRITTEN IN THE SCRIPTURES THAT "MY HOUSE SHALL BE CALLED A HOUSE OF PRAYER"? BUT YOU HAVE MADE IT A DEN OF THIEVES.

WHEN JESUS BEGINS TO PREACH, PEOPLE CROWD INTO THE TEMPLE COURTS TO HEAR HIM. BUT BEHIND CLOSED DOORS THE PRIESTS AND PHARISEES PLOT THEIR STRATEGY. BY TUESDAY THEY ARE READY...

636

The Great Commandment

FROM LUKE 20:23–26; MARK 12:28–34, 38–44; 13; MATTHEW 26:14–16

JESUS IS PREACHING IN A COURT OF THE TEMPLE, AND IN AN ATTEMPT TO GET HIM INTO TROUBLE, THE PHARISEES ASK: "IS IT RIGHT TO PAY TAXES TO CAESAR?" JESUS KNOWS THAT THIS IS A TRICK QUESTION. IF HE ANSWERS "YES," THE PEOPLE WILL TURN AGAINST HIM. IF HE SAYS "NO," THE ROMANS WILL ARREST HIM FOR TREASON. HE ASKS TO SEE A ROMAN COIN.

WHOSE IMAGE IS THIS?

CAESAR'S.

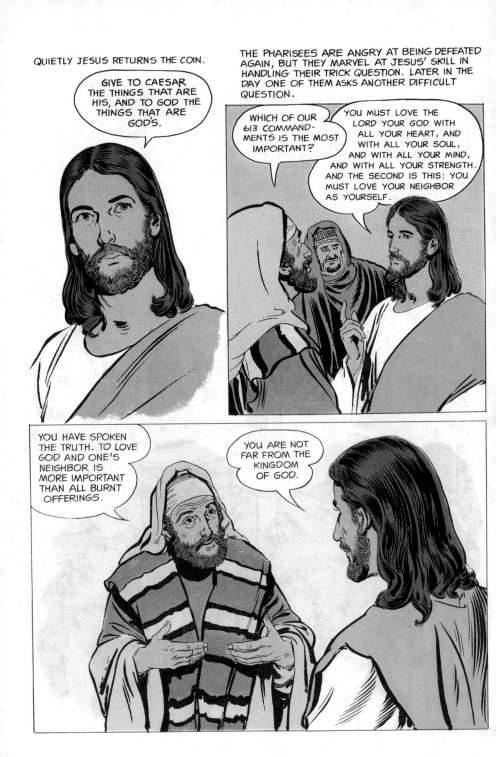

QUIETLY JESUS RETURNS THE COIN.

GIVE TO CAESAR THE THINGS THAT ARE HIS, AND TO GOD THE THINGS THAT ARE GOD'S.

THE PHARISEES ARE ANGRY AT BEING DEFEATED AGAIN, BUT THEY MARVEL AT JESUS' SKILL IN HANDLING THEIR TRICK QUESTION. LATER IN THE DAY ONE OF THEM ASKS ANOTHER DIFFICULT QUESTION.

WHICH OF OUR 613 COMMAND-MENTS IS THE MOST IMPORTANT?

YOU MUST LOVE THE LORD YOUR GOD WITH ALL YOUR HEART, AND WITH ALL YOUR SOUL, AND WITH ALL YOUR MIND, AND WITH ALL YOUR STRENGTH. AND THE SECOND IS THIS: YOU MUST LOVE YOUR NEIGHBOR AS YOURSELF.

YOU HAVE SPOKEN THE TRUTH. TO LOVE GOD AND ONE'S NEIGHBOR IS MORE IMPORTANT THAN ALL BURNT OFFERINGS.

YOU ARE NOT FAR FROM THE KINGDOM OF GOD.

638

THEN JESUS WARNS THE PEOPLE AGAINST THOSE WHO DO GOOD DEEDS JUST TO BE SEEN BY OTHERS. WHEN HE HAS FINISHED SPEAKING HE LOOKS UP TO SEE A PROUD MAN PLACE A LARGE SUM OF MONEY IN THE TEMPLE TREASURY.

THE MAN IS FOLLOWED BY A POOR WIDOW WHO HUMBLY DROPS IN TWO SMALL COINS.

THE WIDOW HAS GIVEN MORE THAN ANYONE ELSE -- FOR SHE HAS GIVEN ALL SHE HAS TO GOD.

WITH THESE WORDS JESUS LEAVES THE TEMPLE -- FOR THE LAST TIME. OUTSIDE JERUSALEM, ON THE QUIET SLOPES OF THE MOUNT OF OLIVES, SOME OF HIS DISCIPLES ASK ABOUT THE FUTURE. JESUS EXPLAINS THAT HIS GOSPEL WILL BE PREACHED THROUGHOUT THE WORLD -- AND THEN HE WILL COME AGAIN TO JUDGE THE WORLD.

639

640

Secretly—In an Upper Room

FROM LUKE 22:7–13; JOHN 13:1–20, 27–30;
MATTHEW 26:21–25

IT IS LATE TUESDAY NIGHT WHEN JUDAS BARGAINS WITH THE CHIEF PRIESTS TO BETRAY JESUS. AFTER THE AGREEMENT IS MADE HE RETURNS TO BETHANY AND SPENDS WEDNESDAY WITH JESUS AND THE DISCIPLES-- NEVER SUSPECTING THAT JESUS KNOWS WHAT HE HAS DONE. THURSDAY, JESUS CALLS PETER AND JOHN ASIDE.

GO INTO JERUSALEM AND MAKE THINGS READY FOR THE PASSOVER FEAST.

WHERE CAN WE GO SO THAT YOUR ENEMIES WILL NOT SEE US?

WHEN YOU ENTER THE CITY YOU WILL SEE A MAN CARRYING A PITCHER. FOLLOW HIM AND ASK HIS MASTER TO SHOW YOU THE ROOM THAT WE MAY USE.

PETER AND JOHN GO AT ONCE TO JERUSALEM. THEY FIND THE SERVANT CARRYING A PITCHER AND FOLLOW HIM HOME.

WHERE IS THE ROOM IN WHICH JESUS AND HIS DISCIPLES CAN EAT THE PASSOVER?

COME WITH ME.

THE MAN LEADS THEM QUICKLY UP THE STAIRS TO A BIG UPPER ROOM.

I'M HONORED TO HAVE JESUS CELEBRATE THE PASSOVER IN MY HOUSE.

PETER AND JOHN PREPARE FOR THE FEAST, AND THAT EVENING JESUS JOINS THE TWELVE IN THE UPPER ROOM. AFTER THEY ARE SEATED JESUS KNEELS, LIKE A SERVANT, TO WASH THE FEET OF HIS DISCIPLES.

NO, LORD. I'M NOT GOOD ENOUGH TO HAVE **YOU** WAIT ON ME!

IF YOU DO NOT LET ME SERVE YOU, PETER, YOU WILL HAVE NO PLACE IN MY KINGDOM.

AFTER JESUS HAS WASHED ALL OF THE DISCIPLES' FEET, HE SITS DOWN AT THE TABLE AGAIN.

IF I, YOUR LORD AND MASTER, HAVE SERVED YOU, YOU SHOULD DO THE SAME FOR ONE ANOTHER. THE SERVANT IS NOT GREATER THAN HIS MASTER.

AFTER A FEW MINUTES JESUS MAKES A STARTLING STATEMENT.

ONE OF YOU IS GOING TO BETRAY ME.

BETRAY YOU? IS IT I, LORD?

JESUS REPLIES THAT IT IS ONE WHO IS EATING WITH HIM NOW. JUDAS LEANS FORWARD.

IS IT I?

YOU HAVE SAID IT. WHAT YOU ARE GOING TO DO, JUDAS, DO QUICKLY.

AT ONCE THE TRAITOR RISES FROM THE TABLE AND HURRIES AWAY. BUT THE OTHER DISCIPLES DO NOT UNDERSTAND WHY...

The Lord's Supper

FROM LUKE 22:17–20; JOHN 13:33–38; 14;
MATTHEW 26:30, 36–56

AFTER JUDAS, THE TRAITOR, LEAVES,
JESUS PICKS UP A PIECE OF BREAD,
THANKS GOD FOR IT, BREAKS IT,
AND GIVES IT TO HIS DISCIPLES,
SAYING, "THIS IS MY BODY."
WHEN THEY HAVE EATEN THE
BREAD, HE OFFERS THEM
A CUP.

DRINK OF IT, EACH ONE
OF YOU, FOR IT IS MY
BLOOD, WHICH WILL BE
SHED TO PAY THE PRICE OF
YOUR SINS. AFTER I'M
GONE, DO THIS IN
REMEMBRANCE OF ME.

SO JESUS MAKES A NEW
COVENANT BETWEEN GOD AND
CHRISTIANS. AS WE TAKE THE
BREAD AND CUP IN THE NAME
OF JESUS WE ARE REMINDED
THAT GOD, THROUGH HIS SON,
HAS DELIVERED US FROM THE
SLAVERY OF SIN.

IN A LITTLE WHILE I MUST LEAVE YOU. YOU CANNOT FOLLOW ME, BUT BEFORE I GO, LET ME REMIND YOU: LOVE ONE ANOTHER AS I HAVE LOVED YOU.

LORD, WHY CAN'T I FOLLOW YOU? YOU KNOW I'D GIVE MY LIFE FOR YOU.

PETER, BEFORE THE COCK CROWS YOU WILL DENY ME THREE TIMES.

DENY MY LORD? NEVER! MY SWORD IS READY THIS MINUTE FOR THE FIRST PERSON WHO TRIES TO HARM HIM.

THE DISCIPLES ARE FRIGHTENED AT THE THOUGHT OF JESUS LEAVING THEM.

DO NOT BE AFRAID. BELIEVE IN GOD; BELIEVE ALSO IN ME. IF YOU LOVE ME, KEEP MY COMMANDMENTS. AND I WILL ASK GOD TO SEND YOU THE HOLY SPIRIT TO COMFORT YOU. HE WILL BE WITH YOU FOREVER. COME, IT IS TIME TO GO...

AS JESUS SPEAKS, JUDAS LEADS A BAND OF MEN INTO THE GARDEN. ACCORDING TO HIS AGREEMENT, HE IDENTIFIES JESUS WITH A KISS.

GREETINGS, MASTER!

AS THE SOLDIERS TAKE HOLD OF JESUS, PETER DRAWS HIS SWORD. SLASHING WILDLY, HE CUTS OFF THE EAR OF A SERVANT.

PETER, PUT UP YOUR SWORD. DO YOU THINK THAT I CANNOT CALL ON GOD TO SEND LEGIONS OF ANGELS TO PROTECT ME?

QUIETLY JESUS HEALS THE MAN'S EAR. WHEN THE DISCIPLES SEE THAT JESUS IS MAKING NO ATTEMPT TO SAVE HIMSELF, THEY RUN FOR THEIR LIVES. AT AN OFFICER'S COMMAND, THE SOLDIERS BIND JESUS AND TAKE HIM BACK TO JERUSALEM -- THE CITY INTO WHICH HE HAD RIDDEN SO TRIUMPHANTLY ONLY A FEW DAYS BEFORE!

WHILE JESUS IS SUFFERING THESE INSULTS, PETER -- WHO HAS SECRETLY FOLLOWED HIM INTO THE CITY--WARMS HIS HANDS BY A FIRE IN THE PALACE COURTYARD. WHILE HE IS TALKING, A MAID STOPS AND LOOKS AT HIM...

YOU WERE ONE OF THOSE WITH JESUS OF NAZARETH.

ME? I DON'T KNOW WHAT YOU'RE TALKING ABOUT.

AFRAID OF BEING QUESTIONED FURTHER, PETER GOES OUT INTO THE HALLWAY, BUT THERE...

THIS FELLOW WAS WITH JESUS.

JESUS? I DON'T EVEN KNOW THE MAN.

ABOUT AN HOUR LATER SOME MEN APPROACH PETER.

DIDN'T I SEE YOU IN THE GARDEN WHEN THE SOLDIERS TOOK JESUS?

YOU ARE A GALILEAN LIKE JESUS. I CAN TELL BY THE WAY YOU TALK.

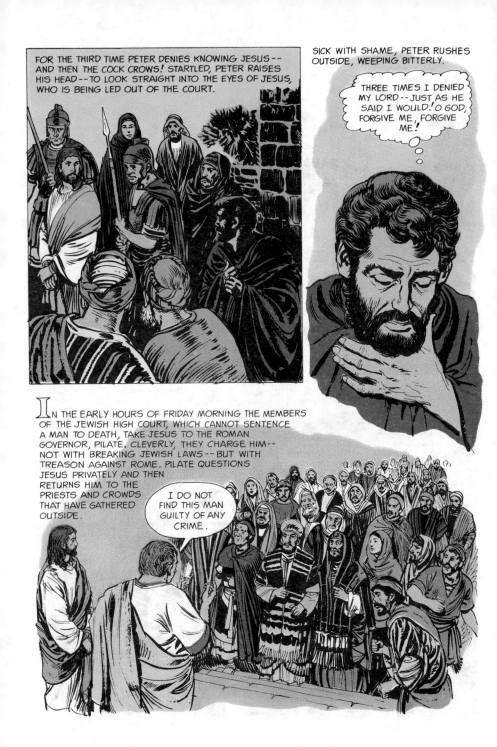

FOR THE THIRD TIME PETER DENIES KNOWING JESUS -- AND THEN THE COCK CROWS! STARTLED, PETER RAISES HIS HEAD -- TO LOOK STRAIGHT INTO THE EYES OF JESUS, WHO IS BEING LED OUT OF THE COURT.

SICK WITH SHAME, PETER RUSHES OUTSIDE, WEEPING BITTERLY.

THREE TIMES I DENIED MY LORD -- JUST AS HE SAID I WOULD.' O GOD, FORGIVE ME, FORGIVE ME.'

IN THE EARLY HOURS OF FRIDAY MORNING THE MEMBERS OF THE JEWISH HIGH COURT, WHICH CANNOT SENTENCE A MAN TO DEATH, TAKE JESUS TO THE ROMAN GOVERNOR, PILATE. CLEVERLY, THEY CHARGE HIM -- NOT WITH BREAKING JEWISH LAWS -- BUT WITH TREASON AGAINST ROME. PILATE QUESTIONS JESUS PRIVATELY AND THEN RETURNS HIM TO THE PRIESTS AND CROWDS THAT HAVE GATHERED OUTSIDE.

I DO NOT FIND THIS MAN GUILTY OF ANY CRIME.

NOT GUILTY? WHY, HE TRIED TO START REVOLTS ALL OVER JUDEA AND GALILEE!

AT THE MENTION OF GALILEE, PILATE SENDS JESUS TO HEROD, THE RULER OF GALILEE, WHO IS IN JERUSALEM FOR THE PASSOVER. HEROD IS CURIOUS AND ASKS JESUS TO PERFORM SOME MIRACLE. WHEN JESUS WILL NOT, HEROD AND HIS SOLDIERS MAKE FUN OF HIM--AND THEN RETURN HIM TO PILATE.

PILATE HESITATES TO DECLARE JESUS GUILTY OF TREASON. HE DOES NOT BELIEVE JESUS IS GUILTY. "BUT, IF I LET HIM GO," HE ARGUES TO HIMSELF, "AND THE LOCAL LEADERS MAKE TROUBLE, THE EMPEROR IN ROME WILL HOLD ME RESPONSIBLE." FINALLY HE THINKS OF A WAY TO EASE HIS CONSCIENCE AND PROTECT HIMSELF....

THE PEOPLE! I'LL LET THEM DECIDE!

Condemned to Die

FROM JOHN 18:39—19:16; MATTHEW 27:3–10

THE RELIGIOUS LEADERS HAVE CHARGED JESUS WITH TREASON AGAINST ROME. PILATE, THE ROMAN GOVERNOR, DOES NOT BELIEVE HE IS GUILTY--BUT HE IS AFRAID TO ANGER HIS OPPONENTS FOR FEAR THEY WILL STIR UP SO MUCH TROUBLE THAT THE REPORTS OF IT WILL REACH THE EMPEROR IN ROME. LOOKING AT THE CROWDS IN JERUSALEM FOR THE PASSOVER, HE SUDDENLY SEES A WAY OUT: LET THE PEOPLE DECIDE WHETHER OR NOT JESUS SHOULD DIE. BUT HE DOES NOT KNOW THAT THE PRIESTS ARE STIRRING UP THE CROWDS AGAINST JESUS.

IT IS THE CUSTOM TO RELEASE A PRISONER TO YOU DURING THE PASSOVER. WHICH SHALL I GIVE YOU-- JESUS, WHO IS CALLED THE CHRIST-- OR BARABBAS, THE MURDERER?

BARABBAS! GIVE US BARABBAS!

PILATE IS STUNNED. HE MAKES ANOTHER ATTEMPT TO SAVE JESUS.

SCOURGE HIM.

MAYBE THE PEOPLE WILL BE SATISFIED IF THE PRISONER IS PUNISHED.

SO JESUS IS WHIPPED WITH LEATHER THONGS. THEN, IN SPORT, THE SOLDIERS MAKE A CROWN OF THORNS AND PLACE IT ON HIS HEAD.

HAIL, THE KING OF THE JEWS!

HOPING THE SIGHT OF JESUS, BRUTALLY BEATEN, WILL AROUSE THE CROWD'S SYMPATHY, PILATE PRESENTS HIM TO THE MULTITUDE.

BEHOLD THE MAN!

CRUCIFY HIM!

CRUCIFY HIM!

By THIS TIME PILATE FEELS HIS PREDICAMENT. BUT, NOT WILLING TO ENDANGER HIS POSITION FURTHER, HE SURRENDERS JESUS TO BE CRUCIFIED. AS HE DOES SO, HE WRITES AN INSCRIPTION TO BE PLACED ON JESUS' CROSS.

JESUS OF NAZARETH, THE KING OF THE JEWS.

IT IS PILATE'S WAY OF SHOWING THAT HE HAS NOT BEEN COMPLETELY OUTWITTED.

NO! NO! DON'T WRITE THAT HE IS THE KING OF THE JEWS. WRITE THAT HE SAID, "I AM KING OF THE JEWS."

WHAT I HAVE WRITTEN, I HAVE WRITTEN.

TO JESUS, THE HOURS FROM THE TIME HE WAS ARRESTED UNTIL HE IS SENTENCED TO BE CRUCIFIED HAVE BEEN FILLED WITH AGONY.

SOMETIME DURING THOSE DARK HOURS THE TRAITOR, JUDAS, REALIZES WHAT HE HAS DONE AND RUSHES TO THE CHIEF PRIESTS...

A King Is Crucified

FROM LUKE 23:26–46; JOHN 19:25–27

Happy, excited pilgrims from all over Palestine have been crowding into Jerusalem for days to celebrate the Passover feast. But on Friday morning startling news sweeps across the city like a chilling wind: Jesus of Nazareth is going to be crucified -- for treason!

The street that leads to the hill of execution is soon filled with a strange mixture of people-- priests and Pharisees who demand Jesus' death; women weeping for the man who forgave sins and healed the sick; and the curious who want only to see a condemned man carry his cross...

ON THE WAY JESUS FALLS UNDER THE WEIGHT OF THE HEAVY CROSS. TO KEEP THE UGLY PROCESSION MOVING, THE ROMAN OFFICER SEIZES A BYSTANDER, SIMON FROM CYRENE.

HERE-- YOU CARRY THIS CROSS!

IT IS ABOUT NINE O'CLOCK WHEN JESUS, AND TWO ROBBERS WHO ARE TO BE CRUCIFIED WITH HIM, REACH CALVARY. AND THERE THE SON OF GOD IS NAILED TO A CROSS. ABOVE HIS HEAD IS FASTENED A SIGN: JESUS OF NAZARETH, THE KING OF THE JEWS!

FATHER, FORGIVE THEM: FOR THEY KNOW NOT WHAT THEY DO.

BUT TO THE ROMAN SOLDIERS HE IS ONLY ANOTHER CRIMINAL BEING PUT TO DEATH ACCORDING TO ROMAN LAW.

THIS ROBE IS SEAMLESS -- HOW SHALL WE DIVIDE IT?

IT'S TOO GOOD TO TEAR INTO PIECES. LET'S CAST LOTS FOR IT.

AS JESUS' FRIENDS STAND WATCHING, CURIOUS CROWDS PASS BY. THOSE WHO SCHEMED FOR HIS DEATH TAUNT HIM.

IF YOU'RE THE KING OF ISRAEL, COME DOWN FROM THE CROSS. THEN WE'LL BELIEVE YOU.

IF YOU'RE THE CHRIST, SAVE YOURSELF **AND** US.

IT IS NOW NOON. SLOWLY, A STRANGE SHADOW COVERS THE LAND. FOR THREE HOURS THERE IS DARKNESS, THEN JESUS CRIES OUT TO GOD...

The Sealed Tomb FROM MARK 15:38–39; LUKE 23:48–49; JOHN 19:38–42; MATTHEW 27:62–66

AT ABOUT NINE O'CLOCK FRIDAY MORNING JESUS OF NAZARETH IS CRUCIFIED OUTSIDE THE WALLS OF JERUSALEM. FROM NOON UNTIL THREE O'CLOCK DARKNESS COVERS THE LAND. THEN -- SUDDENLY -- AN EARTHQUAKE ROCKS THE GROUND, AND IN JERUSALEM...

THE VEIL BEFORE THE HOLIEST PLACE IN THE TEMPLE HAS BEEN RIPPED! WHAT CAN IT MEAN?

THIS IS THE ANSWER: ON A HILL CALLED CALVARY THE SON OF GOD HAS GIVEN HIS LIFE FOR THE SINS OF THE WORLD. THE VEIL IN THE TEMPLE NO LONGER SEPARATES US FROM THE PRESENCE OF GOD, FOR JESUS, THE SON, HAS OPENED THE WAY TO GOD, THE FATHER.

OUTSIDE THE CITY, EVEN THE ROMAN OFFICER WHO DIRECTED THE CRUCIFIXION IS AWED BY WHAT HAS HAPPENED. REVERENTLY, HE LOOKS UP AT THE MAN WHO FORGAVE HIS ENEMIES.

TRULY THIS MAN WAS GOD'S SON!

THE PEOPLE, TOO, ARE SHAKEN BY THE EXECUTION. AS THEY TURN BACK TO THE CITY...

I HAD HOPED THAT HE WAS THE ONE WHO WOULD DELIVER US FROM THE ROMANS.

IN JERUSALEM JOSEPH OF ARIMATHEA, A MEMBER OF THE JEWISH HIGH COURT AND SECRETLY A FOLLOWER OF JESUS, GOES BOLDLY TO PILATE.

MAY I HAVE THE BODY OF JESUS SO THAT WE MAY BURY IT BEFORE THE SABBATH?

YES...I'LL GIVE ORDERS TO MY OFFICER IN CHARGE.

REVERENTLY, JOSEPH TAKES THE BODY OF JESUS FROM THE CROSS. THEN HE AND HIS FRIEND, NICODEMUS, WRAP IT IN LINEN CLOTH, AND PLACE IT IN JOSEPH'S GARDEN TOMB.

EARLY THE NEXT DAY THE PRIESTS AND PHARISEES ALSO GO TO PILATE...

WE REMEMBER JESUS SAID THAT AFTER THREE DAYS HE WOULD RISE FROM THE DEAD. ORDER YOUR SOLDIERS TO SEAL AND GUARD THE TOMB SO THAT HIS DISCIPLES CAN'T STEAL THE BODY AND CLAIM THAT JESUS MADE GOOD ON HIS BOAST.

TAKE THE SOLDIERS YOU NEED AND SET UP A GUARD UNTIL AFTER THE THIRD DAY.

SO THE TOMB IS SEALED, AND ROMAN SOLDIERS ARE PLACED ON GUARD.

THERE-- THAT'S THE LAST WE'LL HEAR OF THIS MAN WHO CALLED HIMSELF THE SON OF GOD!

662

Arresting a King

When Jesus is arrested, His friends think their hope is gone. In a short time, Jesus is arrested, tried, and crucified. Little do they realize, that He will rise a victorious King soon. Here are some of the things that happen:

▶ Jesus is about 33 years old when He dies.

▶ When soldiers arrest Jesus, Peter cuts off an ear of the guard. Jesus heals the ear immediately (p. 647).

▶ All of Jesus' friends desert Him when He is arrested (p. 647).

▶ When Jesus dies, an earthquake occurs and the heavy veil in the temple splits in half from top to bottom. This veil is 60 feet long and 30 feet high (p. 660).

▶ Judas betrays Jesus for 30 pieces of silver, the price paid for a slave (p. 640).

▶ Soldiers mock Jesus by giving Him a robe, a crown of thorns, and a reed for a scepter (p. 653).

Be sure to turn to the other side of this page to see where Jesus went during this time.

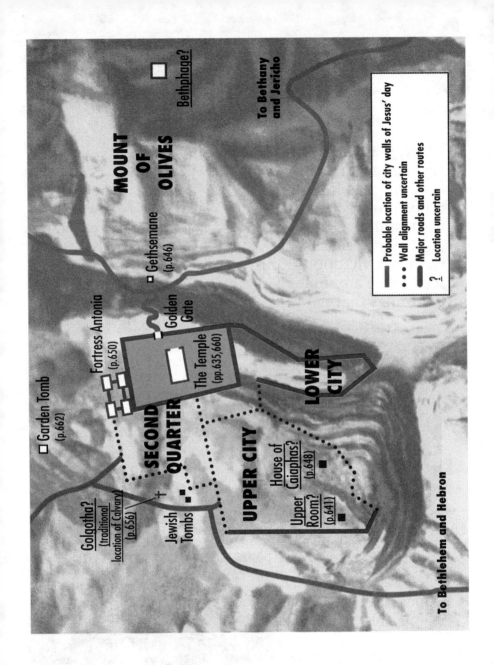

Bethphage?

MOUNT
OF
OLIVES

To Bethany
and Jericho

Gethsemane
(p.646)

Fortress Antonia
(p.650)

Golden
Gate

The Temple
(pp.635,660)

LOWER
CITY

Garden Tomb
(p.662)

SECOND
QUARTER

UPPER CITY

House of
Caiaphas?
(p.648)

Golgotha?
(traditional
location of Calvary)
(p.656)

Jewish
Tombs

Upper
Room?
(p.641)

To Bethlehem and Hebron

Probable location of city walls of Jesus' day

Wall alignment uncertain

Major roads and other routes

Location uncertain

Jerusalem
in the
First Century A.D.

The Lord Is Risen
FROM MARK 16:1–7; JOHN 20:2–18;
MATTHEW 28:11–15; LUKE 24:13–32

FRIDAY -- JUST OUTSIDE JERUSALEM -- JESUS OF NAZARETH IS CRUCIFIED AND BURIED. AT THE REQUEST OF THE PRIESTS AND PHARISEES, THE TOMB IS SEALED AND ROMAN SOLDIERS SET TO GUARD IT.

BUT ON THE MORNING OF THE THIRD DAY THE EARTH TREMBLES. AN ANGEL OF THE LORD DESCENDS -- AND ROLLS THE HEAVY STONE ASIDE. TERRIFIED, THE SOLDIERS FALL TO THE GROUND. WHEN THEY CAN GET TO THEIR FEET THEY RUSH BACK TO THE CITY.

THAT SAME MORNING MARY MAGDALENE AND OTHER FRIENDS OF JESUS HURRY TO THE TOMB WITH SPICES TO ANOINT HIS BODY. ON THE WAY, THEY WORRY ABOUT HOW THEY WILL GET THE STONE ROLLED AWAY. BUT WHEN THEY REACH THE GARDEN...

THE TOMB! IT IS OPEN!

BELIEVING THAT SOMEONE HAS STOLEN JESUS' BODY, MARY RUNS BACK TO JERUSALEM TO TELL PETER AND JOHN. BUT THE OTHERS ENTER THE TOMB-- TO FIND AN ANGEL SEATED THERE.

DON'T BE FRIGHTENED. JESUS IS RISEN. GO, TELL HIS DISCIPLES.

IN THE CITY PETER AND JOHN ARE SO STARTLED BY MARY'S NEWS THAT THEY RACE BACK AHEAD OF HER. WHEN THEY REACH THE TOMB--

ONLY HIS BURIAL CLOTHES. WHAT DO YOU MAKE OF IT?

THAT HE ROSE FROM THE DEAD-- AS HE SAID HE WOULD. OH, WHY DIDN'T WE BELIEVE HIM!

BY THE TIME MARY REACHES THE GARDEN THE OTHERS HAVE GONE. IN HER GRIEF SHE DOES NOT RECOGNIZE THE VOICE OF ONE WHO QUESTIONS HER.

WHY DO YOU WEEP?

IF YOU HAVE TAKEN JESUS' BODY, TELL ME WHERE YOU HAVE LAID IT.

SOFTLY JESUS SPEAKS HER NAME-- "MARY!" SHE TURNS--AND SEES HER RISEN LORD.

MASTER!

BUT JESUS' FRIENDS ARE NOT THE ONLY ONES WHO ARE EXCITED ABOUT WHAT HAP-PENED IN THE GARDEN. IN JERUSALEM THE ROMAN SOLDIERS REPORT TO THE PRIESTS AND PHARISEES. AFRAID OF WHAT MAY HAPPEN IF THE TRUTH IS KNOWN, THEY ACT QUICKLY.

HERE, TAKE THIS MONEY. TELL PEOPLE THAT JESUS' DISCIPLES STOLE HIS BODY.

WHILE THE SOLDIERS SPREAD THEIR LIE, JESUS JOINS TWO OF HIS DISCIPLES ON THE WAY TO EMMAUS. THEY TALK WITH HIM, BUT THEY DO NOT KNOW WHO HE IS.

THAT EVENING AS THEY DINE IN EMMAUS, JESUS BLESSES THE BREAD -- AND WHEN HE HANDS IT TO THEM THEY SUDDENLY RECOGNIZE HIM.

JESUS!

AND JUST AS SUDDENLY HE VANISHES FROM THEIR SIGHT!

Behind Locked Doors

FROM LUKE 24:33–43; JOHN 20:19—21:6

IT IS LATE SUNDAY NIGHT-- THROUGHOUT JERUSALEM PEOPLE ARE STILL TALKING ABOUT THE STRANGE REPORT OF THE ROMAN SOLDIERS.

THEY SAY JESUS' DISCIPLES STOLE HIS BODY TO MAKE US BELIEVE HE ROSE FROM THE DEAD.

I WONDER WHAT THOSE BRAVE ROMAN GUARDS WERE DOING WHILE THE TOMB WAS ROBBED. AND WHAT DO THE DISCIPLES SAY?

BUT JESUS' FRIENDS HAVE ALSO HEARD THE SOLDIERS' REPORT. THEY ARE AFRAID THEY MAY BE ARRESTED, SO THEY LOCK THE DOORS IN THE UPPER ROOM WHERE ALL-- BUT THOMAS-- HAVE GATHERED. TWO FRIENDS FIND THEM THERE.

JESUS IS ALIVE! WE WERE ON OUR WAY TO EMMAUS WHEN A STRANGER JOINED US. WE ASKED HIM TO HAVE SUPPER WITH US. AND WHEN HE BLESSED THE BREAD AND GAVE IT TO US, WE KNEW--ALL AT ONCE-- THAT THE STRANGER WAS JESUS. THEN HE DISAPPEARED.

SUDDENLY JESUS APPEARS IN THE ROOM, BUT THE DISCIPLES THINK THEY ARE SEEING A SPIRIT.

YES, WE KNOW. MARY MAGDALENE HAS SEEN HIM, AND SO HAS PETER--

YES, HE CAME EVEN TO ME-- WHO DENIED HIM.

WHY ARE YOU AFRAID? IT IS I -- SEE MY HANDS AND FEET.

O LORD, IS IT REALLY YOU?

GIVE ME SOME FOOD AND I'LL EAT IT-- TO SHOW YOU I AM REAL.

AS QUICKLY AS THEY CAN THE DISCIPLES HURRY TO FIND THOMAS.

JESUS HAS RISEN! WE HAVE SEEN HIM!

I'LL NEVER BELIEVE IT IS JESUS UNTIL I SEE THE NAILPRINTS IN HIS HANDS.

A WEEK LATER THOMAS IS WITH THE DISCIPLES WHEN THEY MEET AGAIN BEHIND LOCKED DOORS. ONCE MORE JESUS APPEARS TO THEM.

THOMAS, TOUCH MY HANDS AND MY SIDE.

MY LORD AND MY GOD!

BECAUSE YOU HAVE SEEN, THOMAS, YOU BELIEVE. BLESSED ARE THOSE WHO HAVE NOT SEEN AND YET HAVE BELIEVED.

AGAIN JESUS DISAPPEARS FROM THEIR SIGHT.

OBEYING A COMMAND THAT JESUS HAD GIVEN THEM, THE DISCIPLES GO NORTH TO GALILEE. ONE EVENING THEY GO FISHING. THEY FISH ALL NIGHT BUT CATCH NOTHING. AT DAYBREAK THEY SEE THE FIGURE OF A MAN STANDING ON THE SHORE.

CAST YOUR NET ON THE RIGHT SIDE OF THE BOAT.

THEY OBEY—AND SUDDENLY THE NET IS SO FULL OF FISH THEY CANNOT PULL IT IN.

The Last Command

FROM JOHN 21:7–18; MATTHEW 28:16–20;
LUKE 24:44–51

ALL NIGHT THE DISCIPLES OF JESUS FISH IN THE SEA OF GALILEE--AND CATCH NOTHING. AT DAYBREAK THEY SEE A MAN ON SHORE WHO TELLS THEM TO CAST THEIR NET ON THE RIGHT SIDE OF THE BOAT. THEY OBEY--AND SUDDENLY THE NET IS SO FULL THAT THE RUGGED FISHERMEN CANNOT DRAW IT UP. JOHN LOOKS AGAIN AT THE FIGURE ON THE SHORE...

LOOK, PETER, IT IS THE LORD!

PETER IS SO EAGER TO REACH JESUS THAT HE JUMPS INTO THE WATER AND SWIMS TO LAND. THE OTHERS BRING THE BOAT IN AND ANCHOR IT OFFSHORE.
AFTER THE NET IS PULLED IN, JESUS CALLS TO HIS HUNGRY DISCIPLES.

COME AND EAT.

671

DURING THE TIME BETWEEN JESUS'
RESURRECTION AND ASCENSION,
JESUS MEETS WITH HIS FOLLOWERS
AND EXPLAINS HOW--BY HIS DEATH
AND RESURRECTION--HE HAS FULFILLED
GOD'S MISSION FOR HIM TO BE THE
SAVIOR OF THE WORLD. HE CHARGES
THEM TO CARRY ON THE WORK.
"BUT WAIT IN JERUSALEM," HE
ADDS, "UNTIL THE POWER OF
GOD'S HOLY SPIRIT COMES
UPON YOU."

ON THE FORTIETH DAY
AFTER HIS RESURRECTION,
JESUS TAKES HIS DISCIPLES
TO THE MOUNT OF OLIVES
NEAR BETHANY. AND WHILE
HE IS BLESSING THEM, HE
ASCENDS INTO HEAVEN.

The Acts of the Apostles,

THE FIFTH BOOK OF THE NEW TESTAMENT TELLS HOW
JESUS' DISCIPLES OBEYED HIS COMMAND TO GO INTO
ALL THE WORLD AND PREACH THE GOSPEL.

Waiting for a Promise FROM ACTS 1:1–26

FORTY DAYS AFTER HIS RESURRECTION JESUS
TAKES HIS ELEVEN DISCIPLES TO THE MOUNT OF
OLIVES, NEAR BETHANY. WHILE HE IS GIVING
THEM HIS FINAL BLESSING, HE IS LIFTED UP OUT
OF THEIR SIGHT. IN AWE AND WONDER
THEY STAND LOOKING UP INTO HEAVEN
AS IF TO CATCH ONE MORE GLIMPSE
OF THE MASTER THEY LOVE. SUDDENLY
TWO ANGELS APPEAR.

YOU MEN OF GALILEE,
WHY DO YOU STAND HERE
LOOKING UP INTO HEAVEN?
JESUS WILL COME AGAIN-- IN
THE VERY WAY YOU HAVE
SEEN HIM GO.

THE ANGELS DISAPPEAR, AND PETER TURNS TO THE OTHERS.

LET'S DO WHAT JESUS TOLD US TO DO--GO BACK TO JERUSALEM AND WAIT FOR THE POWER HE PROMISED TO SEND US BEFORE WE BEGIN HIS WORK.

SO THE DISCIPLES, WHO HAD ONCE FLED FOR FEAR OF BEING ARRESTED AS FRIENDS OF JESUS, RETURN TO THE CITY-- KNOWING THAT JESUS IS DEPENDING ON THEM TO CARRY ON THE WORK FOR WHICH HE WAS CRUCIFIED.

IN JERUSALEM THEY TAKE LODGING IN AN UPPER ROOM WHICH SOON BECOMES A MEETING PLACE FOR OTHER FOLLOWERS OF JESUS.

JUDAS, WHO BETRAYED OUR LORD, IS DEAD. WE SHOULD APPOINT SOMEONE TO TAKE HIS PLACE.

I NOMINATE BARSABAS.

MATTHIAS.

THE DISCIPLES ASK GOD'S GUIDANCE IN THE CHOICE THEY MAKE--AND MATTHIAS IS NAMED.

THE LORD HAS BLESSED YOU, MATTHIAS.

FOR THE NEXT TEN DAYS THE DISCIPLES MEET TOGETHER IN PRAYER--WAITING FOR THE COMING OF THE HOLY SPIRIT. AT THE SAME TIME FAITHFUL JEWS FROM ALL OVER PALESTINE, AND EVEN DISTANT COUNTRIES, CROWD INTO JERUSALEM TO CELEBRATE THE FEAST OF THANKSGIVING CALLED PENTECOST.

MANY OF THE PILGRIMS PASS BY THE PLACE CALLED CALVARY, AND ARE REMINDED OF JESUS' CRUCIFIXION.

ROMAN SOLDIERS SAY JESUS' DISCIPLES STOLE HIS BODY FROM THE TOMB AND CLAIM HE ROSE FROM THE DEAD AS HE PROPHESIED HE WOULD.

BUT I'VE ALSO HEARD THAT A LOT OF PEOPLE SAW JESUS--ALIVE. I HOPE I CAN FIND SOMEONE IN JERUSALEM WHO DID.

I'M SEEKING THE TRUTH--BUT IT WILL TAKE A SIGN FROM GOD TO MAKE ME BELIEVE THAT JESUS' DISCIPLES SPEAK IT.

Like Tongues of Fire! FROM ACTS 2:1–38

WAS JESUS RAISED FROM THE DEAD? OR DID HIS DISCIPLES STEAL HIS BODY FROM THE TOMB AND CLAIM THAT HE WAS?

THESE QUESTIONS ARE STILL BEING ASKED AS JEWS COME TO JERUSALEM TO CELEBRATE THE HARVEST FEAST CALLED PENTECOST. JESUS' DISCIPLES KNOW THE TRUTH; BUT THEY ARE WAITING FOR POWER FROM GOD TO HELP THEM PREACH IT TO THE WORLD.

EARLY ON THE DAY OF PENTECOST 120 FOLLOWERS OF JESUS ARE GATHERED IN A SECRET ROOM, PRAYING. SUDDENLY THERE IS A SOUND LIKE A RUSHING, MIGHTY WIND, AND GOD'S PRESENCE FILLS THE ROOM. THEN, LIKE TONGUES OF FIRE, HIS SPIRIT RESTS ON EACH ONE.

IN THAT SACRED MOMENT JESUS' FOLLOWERS ARE FILLED WITH STRENGTH AND COURAGE THEY HAVE NEVER KNOWN. RUSHING OUT OF THE UPPER ROOM AND INTO THE STREET BELOW, THEY BEGIN TO PREACH -- EACH IN A DIFFERENT LANGUAGE AS THE SPIRIT OF GOD DIRECTS.

THE CROWDS LISTEN WITH AMAZEMENT. AS THE STORY OF THIS STRANGE EVENT SPREADS, IT REACHES TWO MEN WHO HAVE COME TO JERUSALEM SEEKING THE TRUTH ABOUT JESUS.

LET'S FIND THE DISCIPLES AND SEE FOR OURSELVES IF WHAT THE PEOPLE ARE SAYING IS TRUE.

THEY FIND THE DISCIPLES, AND AS THEY LISTEN...

IT IS TRUE! EVERYONE IN JERUSALEM -- EVEN THOSE MEN FROM ARABIA, EGYPT, ROME, CRETE -- CAN UNDERSTAND WHAT THE DISCIPLES SAY. HOW DO YOU EXPLAIN IT?

THEY'VE BEEN DRINKING TOO MUCH NEW WINE.

DRUNKEN MEN DO NOT SUDDENLY SPEAK IN FOREIGN LANGUAGES -- AND WITH SUCH WISDOM.

In answer to this insult, Peter speaks out for all the disciples.

WE ARE NOT DRUNK! WE ARE FILLED WITH THE HOLY SPIRIT AS THE PROPHET JOEL PROPHESIED. YOU MEN OF JERUSALEM, YOU CRUCIFIED JESUS, THE CHOSEN ONE OF GOD. BUT GOD RAISED HIM FROM THE DEAD, AND WE ARE WITNESSES TO THAT RESURRECTION!

This bold charge cuts deep into the hearts of the people, for they remember how they called for Jesus' crucifixion.

REPENT OF YOUR SINS, AND BE BAPTIZED IN THE NAME OF JESUS CHRIST. THEN YOU SHALL RECEIVE THE GIFT OF THE HOLY SPIRIT AS WE HAVE!

YOU SAID IT WOULD TAKE A SIGN FROM GOD TO CONVINCE YOU THAT JESUS' DISCIPLES SPEAK THE TRUTH. WHAT DO YOU SAY NOW?

Three Thousand in a Day

FROM ACTS 2:38—3:7

WHEN PETER BOLDLY TELLS THE PEOPLE IN JERUSALEM THAT THEY CONDEMNED GOD'S CHOSEN ONE TO DIE, THEY ASK, "WHAT CAN WE DO?" "REPENT AND BE BAPTIZED IN THE NAME OF THE ONE YOU CRUCIFIED," PETER REPLIES. ONE BY ONE THE PEOPLE CRY OUT...

O GOD, FORGIVE MY SINS, IN THE NAME OF YOUR SON, JESUS CHRIST, WHO CAME TO SAVE ME!

YOU SAID ONLY A SIGN FROM GOD COULD MAKE YOU BELIEVE JESUS' DISCIPLES SPOKE THE TRUTH--

YES, AND I HAVE SEEN THAT SIGN. I BELIEVE JESUS LIVES. I BELIEVE HE IS THE SON OF GOD AND THAT THROUGH HIM MY SINS CAN BE FORGIVEN. HOW GOOD GOD IS TO GIVE ME A CHANCE TO BEGIN A NEW LIFE -- WITH JESUS!

681

ONE AFTERNOON WHEN PETER AND JOHN GO TO THE TEMPLE FOR PRAYER THEY FIND A LAME MAN BEGGING AT THE BEAUTIFUL GATE.

HAVE MERCY-- A COIN FOR THE POOR.

LOOK AT US!

MAYBE **BOTH** OF THEM WILL GIVE ME SOMETHING...

I HAVE NO MONEY, BUT I'LL GIVE YOU WHAT I HAVE. IN THE NAME OF JESUS CHRIST, RISE UP AND WALK!

WALK? THE MAN WHO HAS NEVER TAKEN A STEP IN HIS LIFE CANNOT BELIEVE WHAT HE HAS HEARD. BUT AS PETER REACHES OUT HIS HAND TO HIM, THE MAN STRETCHES FORTH HIS OWN...

Miracle at the Gate

FROM ACTS 3:7—4:17

To THE LAME BEGGAR AT THE TEMPLE GATE, PETER HOLDS OUT HIS HAND AND SAYS, "IN THE NAME OF JESUS CHRIST, RISE UP AND WALK!" AT ONCE THE MAN FEELS STRENGTH COME INTO HIS LEGS AND ANKLES. HE LEAPS TO HIS FEET!

I CAN WALK! PRAISE GOD, I CAN WALK!

In his excitement the man rushes into the temple, leaping and shouting for joy.

LOOK! ISN'T THAT THE LAME MAN WHO WAS AT THE GATE?

YES, BUT--

Gratefully, the man turns to Peter and John. The crowds gather around--eager to know what has happened.

WHY DO YOU LOOK AT US AS THOUGH **WE** MADE THIS MAN WALK? THE HEALING POWER CAME FROM GOD, WHO HAS DONE THIS TO HONOR JESUS WHOM **YOU** CRUCIFIED, BUT GOD RAISED FROM THE DEAD.

Seeing that he has the attention of the crowd, Peter continues...

REPENT, AND TURN TO GOD SO THAT YOUR SINS MAY BE WIPED OUT. PREPARE YOURSELVES, FOR CHRIST WILL COME AGAIN...

AT THE BACK OF THE CROWD THE PRIESTS LISTEN. THEY ARE ANGRY—AND THEIR ANGER INCREASES AS THEY WATCH THE GROWING INTEREST OF THE PEOPLE.

HE MUST BE STOPPED AT ONCE--OR HE'LL HAVE ALL OF JERUSALEM BELIEVING THAT JESUS ROSE FROM THE DEAD.

WITH THE HELP OF THE CAPTAIN OF THE TEMPLE GUARDS, THE PRIESTS PUSH THEIR WAY THROUGH THE CROWDS.

YOU ARE UNDER ARREST!

WITHOUT ANOTHER WORD, PETER AND JOHN ARE MARCHED AWAY TO PRISON-- BUT ALREADY FIVE THOUSAND MEN HAVE DECLARED THEIR BELIEF IN JESUS.

THE NEXT MORNING THEY ARE BROUGHT BEFORE THE SANHEDRIN, THE SAME JEWISH COURT THAT CONDEMNED JESUS TO DEATH. BESIDE THEM--PERFECTLY WELL-- STANDS THE MAN WHO HAD BEEN LAME FROM BIRTH.

BY WHAT POWER AND IN WHOSE NAME HAVE YOU HEALED THIS MAN?

685

FILLED WITH THE HOLY SPIRIT, PETER SPEAKS OUT COURAGEOUSLY.

LET IT BE KNOWN TO YOU, AND ALL THE PEOPLE OF ISRAEL -- THIS MAN WAS HEALED BY THE NAME OF JESUS CHRIST OF NAZARETH, WHOM **YOU** CRUCIFIED!

THE COURT IS STUNNED. PETER AND JOHN ARE UNEDUCATED FISHERMEN, YET THEY SPEAK AND ACT WITH AUTHORITY AND POWER.

TAKE THEM AWAY --UNTIL WE CALL FOR THEM AGAIN.

THE MINUTE THE PRISONERS ARE OUT OF SIGHT, THE COURT HOLDS A MEETING.

EVERYONE KNOWS A MIRACLE HAS TAKEN PLACE. WE CANNOT DENY IT, BUT WE MUST KEEP THE NEWS FROM SPREADING. WHAT CAN WE DO?

TELL THESE "PREACHERS" THAT IF THEY SPEAK AGAIN IN THE NAME OF JESUS THEY WILL BE PUT TO DEATH AS HE WAS!

The Pretenders

FROM ACTS 4:18—5:18

687

WHETHER IT IS RIGHT IN THE EYES OF GOD FOR US TO OBEY HIM OR YOU, YOU MUST DECIDE. BUT WE HAVE TO KEEP ON PREACHING WHAT WE HAVE SEEN AND HEARD.

SUCH BOLDNESS ANGERS THE PRIESTS EVEN MORE, BUT AFTER THREATENING THE DISCIPLES AGAIN, THEY LET THEM GO. PETER AND JOHN HURRY BACK TO THEIR FRIENDS WHO IMMEDIATELY JOIN THEM IN PRAYER.

O GOD, GIVE US COURAGE TO SPEAK THY WORD FEARLESSLY.

STRENGTHENED BY THE POWER OF THE HOLY SPIRIT, THE DISCIPLES KEEP ON PREACHING. MORE AND MORE PEOPLE JOIN THEIR FELLOWSHIP. ONE DAY A MAN NAMED BARNABAS BRINGS THE DISCIPLES A LARGE BAG OF MONEY.

WHY ARE YOU GIVING ALL THIS MONEY TO US?

I SOLD MY LAND, AND I WANT THE MONEY USED TO HELP THE FOLLOWERS OF JESUS WHO ARE IN NEED.

688

THE PRAISE THAT IS SHOWERED ON BARNABAS FOR HIS GENEROUS GIFT PROMPTS A MAN NAMED ANANIAS AND HIS WIFE, SAPPHIRA, TO SEEK SUCH HONOR FOR THEMSELVES.

WE, TOO, HAVE SOLD OUR LAND AND WE WANT TO GIVE THE MONEY TO HELP THE CHURCH.

ANANIAS, THE MONEY WAS YOURS TO DO WITH AS YOU PLEASED. BUT WHY DO YOU PRETEND TO GIVE ALL, WHEN YOU KNOW THAT IS NOT TRUE? DON'T YOU SEE -- YOU ARE LYING TO GOD?

WHEN ANANIAS HEARS THESE WORDS, HE FALLS DOWN DEAD. SOME YOUNG MEN TAKE HIS BODY AWAY, AND AS THEY ARE RETURNING SAPPHIRA COMES IN. LIKE HER HUSBAND, SHE LIES ABOUT THE MONEY.

SAPPHIRA, YOUR HUSBAND IS DEAD BECAUSE HE LIED TO GOD. AND YOU WILL PAY THE SAME PENALTY.

INSTANTLY SAPPHIRA FALLS TO THE FLOOR -- AND DIES. THE FOLLOWERS OF JESUS LOOK ON THIS SEVERE PUNISHMENT AS A WARNING TO ANYONE WHO THINKS HE CAN PRETEND LOYALTY TO GOD.

IN SPITE OF THREATS, THE DISCIPLES KEEP ON HEALING IN THE NAME OF JESUS. THE PRIESTS WATCH--ANGRY BUT HELPLESS--AS FAMILIES BRING THEIR SICK ONES OUT INTO THE STREETS, WAITING FOR THE DISCIPLES TO PASS BY AND HEAL THEM.

HE IS LAME— PLEASE MAKE HIM STRONG SO THAT HE CAN RUN AND PLAY LIKE OTHER CHILDREN.

I CANNOT HEAL HIM, BUT JESUS, THE SON OF GOD, CAN. IN HIS NAME, I SAY TO YOU, YOUR SON IS HEALED.

THE FAME OF THE DISCIPLES SPREADS-- AND SOON PEOPLE FROM THE TOWNS ROUND ABOUT CROWD INTO JERUSALEM, BEGGING TO BE HEALED. AT LAST THE PRIESTS CAN STAND IT NO LONGER. IN A FIT OF RAGE THEY HAVE THE DISCIPLES ARRESTED AND THROWN INTO JAIL.

THIS TIME THERE WILL BE NO RELEASE!

Missing Prisoners

FROM ACTS 5:19—6:10

AFRAID THAT THE CROWDS MIGHT TURN AGAINST THEM, THE PRIESTS ARE FORCED TO STAND BY WHILE JESUS' DISCIPLES CONTINUE TO TEACH AND HEAL THE SICK. BUT WHEN PEOPLE FROM OTHER CITIES BEGIN TO POUR INTO JERUSALEM ASKING FOR THE DISCIPLES, THE PRIESTS CAN CONTROL THEIR JEALOUSY NO LONGER. THEY HAVE THE DISCIPLES ARRESTED AND THROWN INTO PRISON. DURING THE NIGHT AN ANGEL FROM GOD RELEASES THEM.

GO-- STAND IN THE TEMPLE AND TELL PEOPLE ABOUT THE NEW LIFE GOD HAS PROMISED THOSE WHO BELIEVE IN HIS SON, JESUS CHRIST.

THE NEXT MORNING THE HIGH PRIEST CALLS THE JEWISH COURT INTO SESSION AND ORDERS THE DISCIPLES BROUGHT BEFORE IT. WHEN THE OFFICERS RETURN...

THE PRISON IS LOCKED AND THE GUARDS ARE ON DUTY! BUT WHEN WE OPENED THE DOORS THERE WAS NO ONE THERE!

NOT THERE? WHERE ARE THEY?

AT THAT MOMENT A PRIEST ENTERS THE ROOM.

THE MEN YOU PUT IN JAIL LAST NIGHT ARE IN THE TEMPLE TEACHING ABOUT JESUS!

THE HIGH PRIEST ORDERS THE DISCIPLES BROUGHT TO THE COURT AT ONCE.

DIDN'T WE WARN YOU NOT TO PREACH ABOUT JESUS?

692

WE MUST OBEY GOD RATHER THAN MEN!

AT THIS REPLY THE COURT IS SO ANGRY THAT IT WANTS THE DISCIPLES KILLED AT ONCE. BUT GAMALIEL, A FAMOUS TEACHER, QUICKLY ORDERS THE DISCIPLES TAKEN OUTSIDE. THEN HE TURNS TO THE COURT.

BE CAREFUL OF THE ACTION YOU TAKE AGAINST THESE MEN. IF THIS TEACHING IS THEIR OWN IDEA, IT WILL FAIL. BUT IF IT IS FROM GOD YOU CANNOT DEFEAT THEM -- AND YOU WILL FIND YOURSELVES IN THE AWFUL POSITION OF FIGHTING GOD.

THE COURT IS FORCED TO ADMIT THE WISDOM OF THIS ADVICE. ANGRILY IT ORDERS THE DISCIPLES BEATEN, THEN RELEASES THEM WITH A THREAT OF MORE PUNISHMENT IF THEY CONTINUE PREACHING ABOUT JESUS.

THE DISCIPLES LEAVE...

I'M PROUD TO BE ABLE TO SUFFER FOR JESUS. WE'LL KEEP RIGHT ON WORKING FOR HIM.

IN SPITE OF THREATS THE DISCIPLES GO ON PREACHING AND HEALING. THE NUMBER OF FOLLOWERS INCREASES SO MUCH THAT THE TWELVE DISCIPLES DECIDE OTHERS MUST BE CHOSEN TO HELP WITH THE WORK. SEVEN DEACONS ARE SELECTED.

ONE OF THEM -- STEPHEN -- IS SOON RECOGNIZED AS A FINE PREACHER.

HIS FORMER FRIENDS IN THE SYNAGOGUE CHALLENGE HIM TO A DEBATE ABOUT JESUS. TO THEIR EMBARRASSMENT THEY FIND THEY ARE NO MATCH FOR STEPHEN'S WISDOM AND ABILITY TO DEFEND HIS FAITH. SECRETLY THEY PLOT THEIR REVENGE.

WE MUST BE CAREFUL NOT TO TURN THE PEOPLE AGAINST US.

RIGHT -- BUT IF WE HANDLE IT PROPERLY WE CAN USE THE PEOPLE THEMSELVES TO HELP US DESTROY STEPHEN.

Martyr for Christ

FROM ACTS 6:11—8:4

STEPHEN PREACHES SUCH POWERFUL SERMONS THAT MANY PEOPLE IN JERUSALEM BECOME FOLLOWERS OF JESUS. THE LOCAL TEACHERS CHALLENGE HIM TO DEBATES, BUT THEY ARE NO MATCH FOR HIM. THIS MAKES THEM ANGRY, AND THEY PLOT TO GET RID OF HIM.

SPREAD THE WORD AROUND JERUSALEM THAT STEPHEN IS PREACHING AGAINST THE LAW GOD GAVE TO MOSES.

THAT WILL TURN EVERY GOOD CITIZEN IN JERUSALEM AGAINST STEPHEN.

THE PLOT WORKS -- STEPHEN IS ARRESTED AND BROUGHT BEFORE THE SANHEDRIN, THE SAME COURT THAT CONDEMNED JESUS TO DEATH.

BOLDLY STEPHEN ANSWERS HIS ENEMIES...

YOUR FATHERS PERSECUTED THE PROPHETS WHO TOLD ABOUT THE COMING OF GOD'S CHOSEN ONE-- AND NOW **YOU** HAVE MURDERED **HIM. YOU** ARE THE ONES WHO RECEIVED GOD'S LAW, AND **YOU** ARE THE ONES WHO HAVE DISOBEYED IT!

THE COURT RISES UP IN RAGE, BUT STEPHEN CONTINUES.

I SEE THE HEAVENS OPEN AND JESUS STANDING AT THE RIGHT HAND OF GOD!

AT THIS THE MEMBERS OF THE COURT, LIKE A PACK OF SAVAGE BEASTS, SEIZE STEPHEN AND RUSH HIM OUTSIDE THE CITY. THERE THE PAID WITNESSES THROW THEIR OUTER GARMENTS ON THE GROUND AND ASK A YOUNG MAN NAMED PAUL TO GUARD THEM. AS STEPHEN IS STONED HE PRAYS, "LORD JESUS, RECEIVE MY SPIRIT." THEN WITH HIS LAST BREATH...

LORD, FORGIVE THEM FOR THIS SIN.

THE STONING OF STEPHEN SERVES AS A SIGNAL FOR THE ENEMIES OF JESUS TO ATTACK ALL OF HIS FOLLOWERS. BEFORE THE DAY IS OVER PAUL BEGINS RAIDING HOMES AND DRAGGING MEN AND WOMEN OFF TO PRISON.

NO! MY CHILDREN!

SOON THERE WON'T BE MANY FRIENDS OF JESUS LEFT IN JERUSALEM — THEN THE WHOLE MOVEMENT WILL DIE OUT.

REMEMBERING THE APOSTLES' STRANGE ESCAPE FROM PRISON, THE PERSECUTORS SEEM AFRAID TO ARREST THEM. BUT RAIDS AGAINST THE OTHER DISCIPLES CONTINUE, AND THEY ARE FORCED TO FLEE FOR THEIR LIVES.

WE MUST ESCAPE AT ONCE. I'M NOT A COWARD, BUT MY FAMILY--

JESUS SAID THAT IF WE WERE PERSECUTED IN ONE CITY WE SHOULD FLEE TO ANOTHER.

TWO BIG CARAVANS ARE LEAVING BY THE NORTH GATE TOMORROW MORNING. IF WE'RE CAREFUL WE CAN JOIN THEM AND NOT BE SEEN.

EARLY THE NEXT MORNING TRADERS LEAD THEIR CAMEL TRAINS OUT OF THE CITY, AND IN THEIR MIDST...

WHEREVER WE GO WE'LL TAKE OUR FAITH IN JESUS WITH US.

AND AS WE TEACH OTHERS WE'LL BE HELPING TO SPREAD THE GOSPEL AS JESUS ASKED US TO DO.

AND SO, BY DRIVING JESUS' FRIENDS OUT OF JERUSALEM, LOCAL LEADERS, UNKNOWINGLY, CAUSE HIS TEACHINGS TO BE SPREAD THROUGHOUT ALL PALESTINE--EVEN AMONG THEIR ENEMIES, THE SAMARITANS!

Simon, the Magician

FROM ACTS 8:5–26

TO ESCAPE PERSECUTION AT THE HANDS OF THE RELIGIOUS LEADERS, THOUSANDS OF JESUS' FOLLOWERS FLEE FROM JERUSALEM. PHILIP, ONE OF THE DEACONS OF THE JERUSALEM CHURCH, GOES NORTH TO SAMARIA.

SAMARITANS HATE JEWS, BUT THEY, TOO, ARE LOOKING FOR A SAVIOR, SO I MUST TELL THEM THAT HE HAS COME.

TO PHILIP'S SURPRISE THE SAMARITANS LISTEN EAGERLY AS HE TELLS THEM ABOUT JESUS, AND THEY WATCH WITH WONDER AS HE LOVINGLY HEALS THEIR SICK.

IN THE NAME OF JESUS CHRIST, STAND UP AND WALK!

I CAN STAND--ALONE! TELL ME MORE ABOUT JESUS SO THAT I CAN BECOME HIS FOLLOWER, TOO.

SOON, EVERYONE IN SAMARIA IS TALKING ABOUT PHILIP.

SIMON, THIS MAN PHILIP CAN DO GREATER THINGS THAN YOU CAN. HE CAN HEAL THE SICK, MAKE THE LAME WALK, AND--

HE CAN? WHERE CAN I FIND HIM?

SIMON, THE MOST FAMOUS MAGICIAN IN SAMARIA, HURRIES OFF TO FIND PHILIP.

I THOUGHT I KNEW ALL THE TRICKS OF MAGIC.

WHEN HE FINDS PHILIP HE WATCHES WITH AMAZEMENT THE MIRACLES OF HEALING. BUT HE ALSO LISTENS TO WHAT PHILIP SAYS, AND AFTER A WHILE...

I BELIEVE IN JESUS, TOO. BAPTIZE ME, AND LET ME GO WITH YOU TO LEARN MORE.

699

WHEN REPORTS OF PHILIP'S WORK REACH THE DISCIPLES IN JERUSALEM, PETER AND JOHN GO TO VISIT SAMARIA. AND AS THEY LAY THEIR HANDS ON THESE NEW FRIENDS OF JESUS, THE HOLY SPIRIT COMES UPON THEM.

THIS IS THE MOST WONDERFUL THING I HAVE EVER SEEN.

SELL ME THIS POWER THAT YOU HAVE.

SIMON! MONEY WILL NOT BUY THIS HOLY GIFT. YOU HAVE NO PLACE IN GOD'S WORK, FOR I CAN SEE THAT YOUR HEART IS FILLED WITH WICKEDNESS. REPENT, AND PRAY THAT GOD WILL FORGIVE YOU.

THE BIBLE DOES NOT SAY WHETHER SIMON TRULY REPENTS. HIS NAME IS NEVER MENTIONED AGAIN.

SOON AFTER THIS PETER AND JOHN RETURN TO JERUSALEM. BUT PHILIP REMAINS, AND ONE NIGHT GOD SENDS HIM NEW INSTRUCTIONS.

PHILIP! ARISE AND GO DOWN THE ROAD THAT RUNS FROM JERUSALEM TO GAZA.

WITHOUT KNOWING THE REASON FOR HIS JOURNEY, OR WHERE IT MAY TAKE HIM, PHILIP OBEYS...

On the Gaza Road

FROM ACTS 8:26–40; 9:32–35

"GO DOWN TO THE ROAD THAT LEADS TO GAZA," AN ANGEL OF GOD TELLS PHILIP. PHILIP OBEYS, AND AS HE WALKS ALONG THE HOT DESERT HIGHWAY A CHARIOT COMES UP BEHIND HIM. HE LOOKS BACK, AND AT THAT MOMENT THE HOLY SPIRIT SPEAKS UP TO HIM: "GO UP TO THE CHARIOT--AND KEEP CLOSE TO IT."

WHO COULD BE IN THAT CHARIOT THAT GOD HAS SENT ME ALL THIS WAY TO MEET?

AS THEY RIDE ALONG PHILIP EXPLAINS THAT GOD LOVED THE WORLD SO MUCH THAT HE SENT HIS SON JESUS TO DIE FOR OUR SINS, AND WHOEVER TRUSTS IN HIM WILL LIVE FOREVER WITH GOD.

I BELIEVE IN JESUS, AND I'M SORRY FOR EVERYTHING WRONG I HAVE DONE. IS THERE ANY REASON WHY I CANNOT BE BAPTIZED AND BECOME ONE OF HIS FOLLOWERS?

I'M SURE THAT'S WHAT GOD SENT ME HERE TO DO.

SO THE MAN FROM ETHIOPIA IS BAPTIZED... AND THEN HE CONTINUES HIS JOURNEY, EAGER TO TELL THE GOOD NEWS ABOUT JESUS TO HIS OWN PEOPLE.

PHILIP GOES NORTH, PREACHING IN THE TOWNS ALONG THE RIM OF THE MEDITERRANEAN SEA. IN CAESAREA, THE ROMAN CAPITAL IN PALESTINE, HE MAKES HIS HOME.

ABOUT THIS TIME A MIRACULOUS THING HAPPENS -- PAUL, WHO HAS BEEN PERSECUTING JESUS' FRIENDS, HAS A WONDERFUL EXPERIENCE. ON THE WAY TO DAMASCUS, JESUS APPEARS TO HIM. PAUL KNOWS THAT JESUS IS THE SAVIOR WHOM GOD RAISED FROM THE DEAD. SO, INSTEAD OF PERSECUTING JESUS' FOLLOWERS, PAUL BECOMES A FOLLOWER, TOO.

WHEN THE DISCIPLES HEAR THIS THEY REJOICE, FOR NOW THEY CAN TRAVEL ALL OVER PALESTINE TEACHING AND HEALING IN THE NAME OF JESUS WITH- OUT FEAR OF PAUL ARRESTING THEM.

Sea of Galilee

CAESAREA

JOPPA

LYDDA

JERUSALEM

GAZA

MEDITERRANEAN Sea

Dead Sea

WHILE PETER IS PREACHING IN LYDDA...

MY FRIEND, AENEAS, HAS BEEN PARALYZED FOR EIGHT YEARS. CAN YOU HELP HIM?

I CAN'T -- BUT THE SON OF GOD CAN. COME, LET'S GO SEE YOUR FRIEND.

IN THE HOME OF AENEAS PETER LOOKS DOWN ON THE BEDRIDDEN MAN.

JESUS CHRIST HEALS YOU. ARISE.

AENEAS STANDS UP. HE LOOKS IN AWE AT HIS STRONG ARMS AND LEGS.

JESUS MUST LOVE ME VERY MUCH TO RESTORE MY STRENGTH. TELL ME MORE ABOUT HIM SO THAT I CAN BECOME HIS FOLLOWER, TOO.

WHEN THE PEOPLE SEE AENEAS -- WELL AND STRONG -- THEY BELIEVE IN JESUS, TOO. PETER STAYS IN LYDDA, PREACHING, UNTIL ONE DAY TWO MEN FROM THE SEAPORT OF JOPPA ARRIVE IN THE CITY.

WHERE'S PETER? WE MUST FIND HIM AT ONCE!

Mission to Joppa

FROM ACTS 9:36—10:2

706

AT THE SIGHT OF DORCAS SOME OF THE WOMEN FALL ON THEIR KNEES, WEEPING FOR JOY. OTHERS RUSH OUT INTO THE STREETS TO TELL THE EXCITING NEWS.

DORCAS IS ALIVE!

SHH-- PEOPLE WILL THINK YOU'RE LOSING YOUR MIND. DORCAS IS DEAD -- AND EVERYONE KNOWS IT.

NO! NO! PETER, THE DISCIPLE OF JESUS, BROUGHT HER BACK TO LIFE. COME, SEE FOR YOURSELF!

NOT BELIEVING, BUT CURIOUS, THE WOMAN HURRIES TO DORCAS' HOME.

IT'S TRUE! IT'S TRUE! OH, GOD BE PRAISED!

THE NEWS SPREADS QUICKLY THROUGHOUT JOPPA, AND SOON GREAT CROWDS COME TO PETER, BEGGING TO BE TAUGHT ABOUT JESUS. PETER CONTINUES TO PREACH IN JOPPA UNTIL...

ONE DAY A STRANGE THING HAPPENS IN THE HOME OF CORNELIUS, A ROMAN CENTURION LIVING IN THE SEACOAST CITY OF CAESAREA, SOME THIRTY MILES NORTH. IT IS THREE O'CLOCK IN THE AFTERNOON. CORNELIUS, WHO IN HIS YEARS OF SERVICE IN PALESTINE HAS LEARNED TO WORSHIP GOD, KNEELS TO PRAY.

God, a Roman, and a Jew

FROM ACTS
10:2—11:1

ONE AFTERNOON AS CORNELIUS, AN OFFICER OF THE ROMAN ARMY, KNEELS TO PRAY, HE HAS A VISION--AN ANGEL OF GOD APPEARS AND CALLS HIM BY NAME.

WHAT IS IT?

YOUR PRAYERS AND GOOD WORKS ARE PLEASING TO GOD. SEND MEN TO JOPPA FOR A MAN NAMED PETER. HE IS STAYING WITH SIMON, THE TANNER, WHOSE HOUSE IS BY THE SEA.

WHEN THE ANGEL DISAPPEARS, CORNELIUS SENDS THREE OF HIS MOST TRUSTED MEN AT ONCE TO JOPPA. AS THEY APPROACH THE CITY, THE MAN FOR WHOM THEY ARE SEARCHING GOES TO THE ROOFTOP TO PRAY...

THE VOICE REPLIES: "YOU MUST NOT CALL WHAT GOD HAS CLEANSED UNCLEAN." ALL THIS IS REPEATED THREE TIMES; THEN THE VISION DISAPPEARS. WHILE PETER IS WONDERING WHAT IT MEANS THE HOLY SPIRIT SPEAKS TO HIM: "THREE MEN ARE HERE LOOKING FOR YOU. GO WITH THEM AND HAVE NO DOUBTS, FOR I HAVE SENT THEM TO YOU."

ACCORDING TO JEWISH LAW, GENTILES -- YOU PEOPLE OF ANOTHER NATION -- ARE UNCLEAN. THEREFORE, AS A JEW, I AM FORBIDDEN TO ASSOCIATE WITH YOU. BUT GOD HAS TOLD ME IN A VISION THAT NO MAN MUST BE CALLED UNCLEAN. SO I HAVE COME AS YOU ASKED. WHAT DO YOU WANT OF ME?

AN ANGEL OF GOD TOLD ME TO SEND FOR YOU. AND WE ARE WAITING TO LEARN WHAT THE LORD HAS COMMANDED YOU TO TELL US.

I SEE NOW THAT ANY MAN, JEW OR GENTILE, WHO LOVES GOD AND DOES WHAT IS RIGHT, IS ACCEPTABLE TO HIM.

SUCH NEWS TRAVELS FAST, AND WHEN IT REACHES THE CHURCH IN JERUSALEM...

HOW DARE PETER BREAK JEWISH LAWS AND ASSOCIATE WITH GENTILES?

THEN PETER TELLS THEM THAT JESUS WAS THE SAVIOR SENT FROM GOD TO GIVE ETERNAL LIFE TO ALL WHO BELIEVE IN HIM. WHEN PETER SEES THAT THE HOLY SPIRIT HAS COME TO THE GENTILES, HE HAS HIS CHRISTIAN FRIENDS BAPTIZE THEM.

Angel—Open Gate

FROM ACTS 11:1—12:14

THE NEWS THAT PETER HAS BEEN ASSOCIATING WITH GENTILES REACHES JERUSALEM BEFORE HE DOES--AND SEVERAL OF THE CHURCH MEMBERS ARE WAITING TO QUESTION HIM.

IS IT TRUE THAT YOU ARE BREAKING OUR JEWISH LAWS AND BEING FRIENDLY TOWARD GENTILES--EVEN EATING WITH THEM AND VISITING IN THEIR HOMES?

GOD DIRECTED A ROMAN CENTURION TO SEND FOR ME, AND GOD TOLD ME TO GO TO HIM. I OBEYED, AND WHILE I WAS TELLING THE GENTILES ABOUT JESUS, THE HOLY SPIRIT CAME TO THEM -- THE SAME AS TO US ON THE DAY OF PENTECOST. IF GOD GAVE THEM THE SAME GIFT THAT HE GAVE TO US, WHO WAS I TO STAND IN THE WAY?

THE MEMBERS AGREE WITH PETER -- AND PRAISE GOD FOR GIVING ETERNAL LIFE TO THE GENTILES. THE CHURCH CON-TINUES TO GROW...

711

AND AS IT DOES, THE ANGER OF THE LOCAL LEADERS GROWS. TO WIN THEIR FAVOR, KING HEROD AGRIPPA BEGINS TO PERSECUTE JESUS' FOLLOWERS.

ARREST THE DISCIPLE CALLED JAMES. CHARGE HIM WITH STIRRING UP TROUBLE AND PUT HIM TO DEATH-- AT ONCE!

So JAMES, ONE OF THE FOUR FISHERMEN WHO LEFT THEIR NETS TO FOLLOW JESUS, IS SLAIN TO SATISFY A WICKED KING'S STRUGGLE FOR POWER.

THIS PLEASES THE RELIGIOUS LEADERS WHO CONDEMNED JESUS TO DEATH. EAGER TO GAIN MORE OF THEIR FAVOR, HEROD ORDERS PETER ARRESTED AND PUT IN PRISON--TO BE EXECUTED AFTER THE FEAST OF THE PASSOVER.

CHAIN EACH HAND TO A GUARD. KEEP FOUR SOLDIERS ON WATCH AT ALL TIMES. THIS PRISONER **MUST NOT** ESCAPE!

BUT ON THE NIGHT BEFORE HEROD PLANS TO SENTENCE PETER, AN ANGEL OF GOD ENTERS THE PRISON CELL...

GET UP! PUT ON YOUR SANDALS, WRAP YOUR CLOAK AROUND YOU, AND FOLLOW ME.

AS PETER OBEYS THE CHAINS FALL FROM HIS WRISTS -- AND THE ANGEL LEADS HIM OUT OF THE PRISON CELL.

WHEN THEY APPROACH THE GREAT IRON GATE IN THE PRISON WALL, IT OPENS! THEY GO OUT INTO THE CITY STREETS, AND -- SUDDENLY -- THE ANGEL VANISHES!

SCARCELY BELIEVING WHAT HAS HAPPENED, PETER HURRIES TO THE HOME OF MARY, THE MOTHER OF HIS YOUNG FRIEND, MARK. THERE HE POUNDS ON THE DOOR OF THE GATE UNTIL RHODA, A SERVANT GIRL, ANSWERS.

IT'S PETER!

BUT INSTEAD OF LETTING HIM IN, RHODA TURNS AND RUNS BACK INTO THE HOUSE...

Fall of a Tyrant

FROM ACTS 12:14–24

IT IS NIGHT IN JERUSALEM. PETER HAS JUST BEEN RESCUED FROM PRISON BY AN ANGEL AND IS SEEKING ADMITTANCE AT THE HOME OF A FRIEND. WHEN THE SERVANT GIRL RECOGNIZES HIS VOICE, SHE RUSHES BACK INTO THE HOUSE.

IT'S PETER!

PETER? O RHODA, YOU'RE SO UPSET THAT YOU'RE IMAGINING THINGS.

THE GIRL INSISTS. FINALLY SOME OF THE GROUP, WHO HAVE GATHERED TO PRAY FOR PETER, ACCOMPANY HER TO THE GATE.

IF YOU KNEW IT WAS PETER, WHY DIDN'T YOU LET HIM IN?

I WAS SO EXCITED-- I HAD TO TELL YOU.

CAUTIOUSLY THEY OPEN THE DOOR...

PETER! IT **IS** YOU! COME IN--QUICKLY!

DID HEROD RELEASE YOU?

NO--BUT GOD DID. AN ANGEL AWAKENED ME AND TOLD ME TO FOLLOW. I DID--AND THE PRISON GATES OPENED BEFORE US. IN THE STREET, THE ANGEL DISAPPEARED. TELL THE OTHERS THAT I AM FREE. AND NOW I MUST GET OUT OF JERUSALEM BEFORE HEROD LEARNS WHAT HAS HAPPENED.

THE FRIENDS OF PETER REJOICE AND THANK GOD FOR HIS ESCAPE, BUT THE NEXT MORNING WHEN HEROD DISCOVERS THAT HIS PRISONER IS GONE--

YOU SAY HE WAS CHAINED TO TWO GUARDS, AND OTHERS WERE GUARDING THE DOOR, YET YOU EXPECT ME TO BELIEVE THAT HE JUST DISAPPEARED? WHAT WERE THE GUARDS DOING? SEARCH THE CITY. FIND PETER OR THOSE TRAITORS WILL PAY FOR THIS WITH THEIR LIVES!

BUT THE SEARCH FAILS.

A FEW DAYS LATER HEROD APPEARS AT A PUBLIC CELEBRATION IN CAESAREA. THERE, DRESSED IN A DAZZLING ROBE OF SILVER, HE GOES OUT AND SPEAKS TO THE PEOPLE. TO FLATTER HIM, THEY SHOUT:

IT IS THE VOICE OF A GOD--NOT A MAN!

HEROD ACCEPTS THE PRAISE WHICH SHOULD HAVE BEEN GIVEN ONLY TO GOD. SUDDENLY GOD STRIKES HIM DOWN, AND A FEW DAYS LATER HE DIES.

WITH THE DEATH OF HEROD, THE PERSECUTION OF THE CHURCH STOPS FOR A TIME. THE GOOD NEWS OF JESUS CHRIST CONTINUES TO SPREAD THROUGHOUT THE LAND OF THE JEWS...

The Story of Paul

FROM ACTS 7:58—8:4; 9:1–3A; 22:3

Adventurer for Christ

BOLDLY HE FACES ANGRY MOBS... CROSSES MOUNTAINS... AND SAILS THE STORMY SEAS TO PREACH THE GOOD NEWS THAT JESUS IS THE SON OF GOD AND SAVIOR OF THE WORLD.

THE EXCITING STORY OF THIS GREAT MISSIONARY BEGINS LONG AGO...

A FEW YEARS AFTER THE BIRTH OF JESUS PAUL* IS BORN IN TARSUS. THE SON OF GOOD JEWISH PARENTS, HE IS BROUGHT UP TO WORSHIP AND OBEY GOD.

WHAT WILL YOU DO WHEN YOU GROW UP, PAUL?

I DON'T KNOW YET. BUT WHATEVER I DO, IT WILL BE FOR GOD, AND IT WILL BE EXCITING.

*HIS JEWISH NAME IS SAUL.

HE TAKES THE FIRST STEP TOWARD MAKING HIS DREAM COME TRUE WHEN HE GOES TO JERUSALEM TO STUDY. THERE HE MEETS SOME OF THE SAME TEACHERS THAT JESUS TALKED WITH ONLY A FEW YEARS BEFORE.

IN TIME PAUL BECOMES THE MOST BRILLIANT PUPIL OF THE FAMOUS TEACHER, GAMALIEL. TOGETHER THEY DISCUSS THE SCRIPTURES-- ESPECIALLY THE PARTS THAT TELL ABOUT THE COMING OF THE SAVIOR.

LIKE KING DAVID, HE WILL MAKE OUR COUNTRY STRONG AND POWERFUL. IF ONLY HE WOULD COME NOW-- I'D SPEND MY LIFE SERVING HIM.

With some strong-armed men, Paul sets out on a 190-mile journey to Damascus. His excitement mounts with every mile, for he believes with all his heart that in destroying Jesus' followers he is serving God...

A Light and a Voice

FROM ACTS 9:3–22

PAUL RIDES TOWARD DAMASCUS WITH THE EAGERNESS OF A HUNTER ON THE TRACK OF HIS PREY. AT THE SIGHT OF THE CITY IN THE DISTANCE, HE URGES HIS HORSE ON -- AS IF EVERY MINUTE COUNTED IN HIS SEARCH TO DESTROY JESUS' FOLLOWERS.

SUDDENLY HE IS SURROUNDED BY A LIGHT BRIGHTER THAN THE NOONDAY SUN. HE FALLS TO THE GROUND -- AND A VOICE CALLS HIM BY HIS JEWISH NAME: "SAUL! SAUL, WHY ARE YOU PERSECUTING ME?"

WHO ARE YOU?

I AM JESUS OF NAZARETH, WHOM YOU ARE PERSECUTING.

WHAT DO YOU WANT ME TO DO?

"GO INTO THE CITY," JESUS ANSWERS, "AND YOU WILL BE TOLD WHAT TO DO."

THE MEN WITH PAUL ARE TERRIFIED BY WHAT HAS HAPPENED.

PAUL, WHAT'S THE MATTER?

MY EYES—I CAN'T SEE! HELP ME INTO THE CITY.

SO, BLIND, AND AWED BY HIS EXPERIENCE, THE ONCE-PROUD PAUL IS LED INTO DAMASCUS— DOWN A STREET CALLED STRAIGHT.

WHERE ARE YOU TAKING ME?

TO THE HOME OF JUDAS, A FRIEND OF MINE.

IN DARKNESS PAUL PRAYS AND WAITS. ON THE THIRD DAY HE CALLS TO HIS HOST.

HAS A MAN NAMED ANANIAS ASKED TO SEE ME?

NO. WHAT MAKES YOU EXPECT HIM?

I HAVE BEEN PRAYING, AND IN A VISION I HAVE SEEN A MAN BY THAT NAME COMING TO RESTORE MY SIGHT.

IF HE COMES I'LL BRING HIM TO YOU AT ONCE.

723

Man with a Mission

FROM ACTS 9:27–30; 11:22–25

PAUL RETURNS TO JERUSALEM ONLY TO FIND THAT JESUS' FRIENDS BELIEVE HE IS STILL THEIR ENEMY. AT THE SIGHT OF HIM THEY HIDE. BUT BARNABAS, THE MAN WHO SOLD HIS FARM AND GAVE THE MONEY FOR THE POOR, IS NOT AFRAID. HE LISTENS TO PAUL-- AND TAKES HIM TO PETER.

PAUL SAYS HE IS NOW A FOLLOWER OF JESUS--AND I BELIEVE HIM.

BRING HIM IN.

FOR DAYS AND NIGHTS PAUL, THE BRILLIANT STUDENT OF JEWISH LAW, AND PETER, THE RUGGED FISHERMAN FROM GALILEE, TALK ABOUT THEIR LORD AND SAVIOR.

JESUS' LAST COMMAND DIRECTED US TO GO INTO ALL THE WORLD AND PREACH THE GOSPEL.

I'M GLAD HE TRUSTS ME TO HELP CARRY OUT THAT COMMAND.

725

BUT JESUS' FOLLOWERS AGAIN LEARN OF THE PLOT AGAINST PAUL'S LIFE, AND WARN HIM.

YOUR ENEMIES ARE POWERFUL MEN, PAUL, AND THEY WILL NOT STOP UNTIL THEY HAVE PUT AN END TO YOUR WORK IN JERUSALEM. LET US HELP YOU ESCAPE.

YOU ARE RIGHT! I CAN SERVE MY LORD ELSEWHERE.

WITH THE HELP OF FRIENDS, PAUL ESCAPES TO THE SEACOAST. THEN HE SAILS NORTH TO HIS BOYHOOD HOME OF TARSUS. THERE HE EARNS HIS LIVING BY MAKING TENTS -- AND DEVOTES THE REST OF HIS TIME TO TELLING PEOPLE THAT JESUS IS THE PROMISED SAVIOR.

ONE DAY A SHIP DOCKS AT TARSUS... A PASSENGER HURRIES DOWN THE PLANK.

NOW TO FIND PAUL!

Foreign Assignment

FROM ACTS 11:25–30; 12:25—13:7

IN ANTIOCH, THE THIRD LARGEST CITY OF THE ROMAN EMPIRE, PAUL AND BARNABAS WIN BOTH JEWS AND GENTILES TO FAITH IN CHRIST. HERE THE FOLLOWERS OF JESUS ARE GIVEN THE NAME OF CHRISTIANS!

AFTER A TIME TEACHERS FROM JERUSALEM COME TO VISIT THE GROWING CHURCH. ONE OF THEM, AGABUS, MAKES A TRAGIC PROPHECY.

I HAVE RECEIVED A WARNING FROM GOD THAT A GREAT FAMINE IS COMING. MANY OF OUR PEOPLE IN JERUSALEM ARE POOR. THEY WILL STARVE UNLESS--

PAUL INTERRUPTS EXCITEDLY.

LET US ALL GIVE WHAT MONEY WE CAN. I'LL HELP DELIVER IT!

BUT YOU HAVE ENEMIES IN JERUSALEM!

AND OUR LORD HAS FOLLOWERS THERE! WE MUST HELP THEM IN SPITE OF THE DANGER.

Their mission over, Paul and Barnabas prepare to leave Jerusalem.

PAUL, THIS IS MY COUSIN, MARK. HE WOULD LIKE TO GO WITH US.

GOOD! WE CAN USE YOU, MARK.

In Antioch they meet with others for prayer. God tells the leaders of the church that he wants Paul and Barnabas to take the good news of Jesus to other lands. The two men accept the call -- and set out with Mark.

THERE'S CYPRUS -- THE ISLAND WHERE I WAS BORN!

AND THAT'S WHERE OUR MISSIONARY WORK BEGINS.

After preaching in several cities of the island, the missionaries reach the capital, Paphos.

HOW EAGER THE PEOPLE ARE TO HEAR ABOUT JESUS.

YES, AND SO FAR THERE'S NO TROUBLE FROM ANYONE.

BY ORDER OF SERGIUS PAULUS, THE ROMAN GOVERNOR, COME WITH ME!

The Enemy Strikes

FROM ACTS 13:7–50

AFTER A TOUR ACROSS THE ISLAND OF CYPRUS, PAUL, BARNABAS, AND YOUNG MARK REACH THE CAPITAL. TO THEIR SURPRISE, THE ROMAN GOVERNOR CALLS THEM BEFORE HIM AND ASKS TO HEAR ABOUT JESUS. EAGERLY PAUL TELLS ABOUT JESUS AND HOW GOD RAISED HIM FROM THE DEAD. AT THIS THE COURT MAGICIAN RISES UP IN ANGER...

LIES! ALL LIES! NO MAN CAN DIE AND LIVE AGAIN!

YOU CHILD OF THE DEVIL! IT IS TIME YOU STOPPED TRYING TO TURN PEOPLE FROM THE RIGHT WAYS OF THE LORD. NOW HIS HAND IS UPON YOU-- AND FOR A TIME YOU WILL BE BLIND!

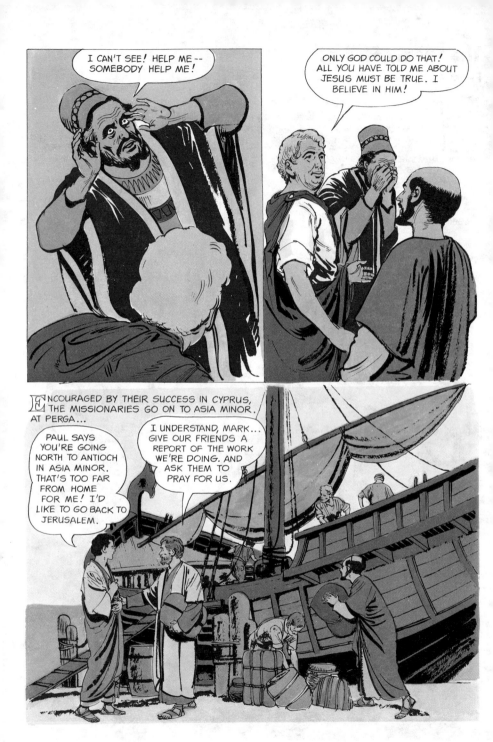

732

THIS MAN IS A LIAR—AND A TRAITOR TO THE FAITH OF OUR FATHERS.

WE FELT IT OUR DUTY TO GIVE GOD'S MESSAGE OF EVERLASTING LIFE TO YOU JEWS FIRST, BUT IF YOU DO NOT WANT THE MESSAGE, WE'LL TAKE IT TO THE GENTILES!

THE GENTILES REACT WITH JOY AND THANKSGIVING.

THANK GOD FOR SENDING PAUL WITH SUCH GOOD NEWS!

ETERNAL LIFE WITH GOD— I MUST TELL MY FRIENDS AT ONCE!

BUT CERTAIN LOCAL JEWS ARE SO ANGRY THAT THEY CARRY THEIR CAMPAIGN OF LIES AGAINST PAUL TO THE LEADING CITIZENS OF ANTIOCH.

DON'T YOU SEE? PAUL IS TRYING TO CAUSE TROUBLE BETWEEN JEWS AND GENTILES. IF IT LEADS TO BLOODSHED THE GOVERNMENT IN ROME WILL SEND SOLDIERS TO INVESTIGATE--

WE KNOW HOW TO HANDLE TROUBLEMAKERS! PAUL AND HIS FRIEND MUST LEAVE AT ONCE --OR BE PUNISHED!

734

Paul, A Champion Who Switches Sides!

Paul is a great man of God who first kills Christians because he honestly believes they are going against God. Then when Jesus speaks to him directly on the road to Damascus, Paul realizes he has been on the wrong side. He becomes a great champion for the Gospel.

Here are some other interesting facts about him:

▶ He has two names—Paul (Roman) and Saul (Hebrew).

▶ Paul is a Jew and a Roman citizen (Acts 22:27).

▶ As a boy, he learns to make tents (Acts 18:3).

▶ At his conversion, he is blind for three days (p. 722).

▶ He writes 13 letters called the Pauline Epistles, which become part of the Bible.

▶ Paul and Barnabas are the first Christian missionaries (p. 730).

▶ When Paul and Silas are thrown in jail for disturbing the peace, they sing praises to God and God sends an earthquake (page 752).

▶ He faces danger and hardship as a missionary . . .
5 times whipped
3 times beaten with rods
1 time stoned with rocks
3 times shipwrecked
plus bandits, hunger, thirst, cold.
From 2 Corinthians 11:23-27

But he later said . . .
I have kept the faith . . . a crown of righteousness awaits me.
From 2 Timothy 4:7-8

Spreading the Good News . . .

Many people throughout history have chosen to follow Jesus' command to take the Gospel to all nations (see p. 672). Here are just a few:

▶ **William Carey** (1761-1834) went to India from England. Besides preaching the Gospel, Carey set up mission stations, schools, translated the Bible into several languages, and brought agricultural improvements to the Indian people.

▶ **Adoniram Judson** (1788-1850) was an American who went to Burma. After years of struggle and imprisonment, he translated the entire Bible into Burmese.

▶ **James Hudson Taylor** (1832-1905) was an English medical missionary to China. Unlike other missionaries, he ate and dressed like the Chinese people he served. Under his leadership, 800 missionaries served the China Inland Mission from several church denominations.

▶ **Mary Slessor** (1848-1915) left Scotland to help the people of Nigeria, Africa. She taught the people to read the Bible and became a peacemaker among tribal chiefs. She wanted to reach tribes that had never heard of Jesus.

▶ **Amy Carmichael** (1867-1951) grew up teaching Sunday classes to mill workers in Northern Ireland. In 1895, she went to India. As well as preaching the Gospel, she rescued many children from evil temple practices.

Miracle in Lystra

FROM ACTS 13:51—14:19

TO ESCAPE PERSECUTION, PAUL AND BARNABAS ARE FORCED TO LEAVE ANTIOCH. THEY GO SOUTHEAST ABOUT 80 MILES TO ICONIUM, ANOTHER CITY IN THE PROVINCE OF GALATIA. THERE JEWS AND GENTILES ALIKE ACCEPT THE GOOD NEWS OF JESUS. THIS UPSETS PAUL'S ENEMIES.

PAUL! BARNABAS! YOU MUST LEAVE AT ONCE! THERE'S A PLOT UNDER WAY TO STONE YOU!

DON'T WORRY -- YOU HAVE FRIENDS HERE WHO WILL FIGHT TO PROTECT YOU.

WE CANNOT LET YOU RISK YOUR LIVES FOR US. WE MUST LEAVE -- BUT KEEP STRONG IN YOUR FAITH, AND HELP THE OTHERS.

BUT YOU ARE LIKE THE GODS JUPITER AND MERCURY.

JUPITER AND MERCURY ARE FALSE GODS. WORSHIP THE TRUE GOD WHO HAS SENT YOU RAIN FROM HEAVEN AND FRUIT IN ITS SEASON.

THE PEOPLE LISTEN EAGERLY. BUT, UNKNOWN TO PAUL AND BARNABAS, THEIR ENEMIES FROM ANTIOCH AND ICONIUM FOLLOW THEM TO LYSTRA. THEY SPREAD THEIR LIES AMONG THE SIMPLE PEOPLE.

PAUL AND BARNABAS CAUSE TROUBLE WHEREVER THEY GO. GET RID OF THEM AS WE DID!

THERE'LL BE NO TROUBLE IN LYSTRA. I'LL SEE TO THAT!

SO A MOB IS WHIPPED INTO ACTION!

THERE'S PAUL! STONE HIM!

Storm Warning

FROM ACTS 14:19—15:1

WHIPPED INTO A RAGE BY MEN FROM ANTIOCH AND ICONIUM, THE PEOPLE OF LYSTRA TURN AGAINST PAUL AND STONE HIM.

WHEN THE STONING IS FINISHED, THE ANGRY MOB DRAGS PAUL'S BODY OUT OF THE CITY.

QUICKLY BARNABAS AND CHRISTIANS OF LYSTRA GATHER AROUND PAUL'S MOTIONLESS FORM. BUT AS THEY STAND WEEPING...

HE'S GETTING UP! THANK GOD, HE LIVES! HE LIVES!

PAUL! WE THOUGHT THEY HAD KILLED YOU!

THEY MEANT TO, BUT GOD HAS SAVED MY LIFE FOR A PURPOSE. COME, LET'S GO BACK INTO THE CITY.

BACK TO LYSTRA? THAT MOB WILL NEVER LET YOU OUT ALIVE!

GOD WILL PROTECT ME.

THE NEXT MORNING PAUL AND BARNABAS SET OUT FOR DERBE WHERE THEY WIN MANY FOLLOWERS TO JESUS. ONE DAY PAUL STATES THAT IT IS TIME TO START THEIR HOMEWARD JOURNEY.

I AGREE. THE SHORTEST ROUTE IS THROUGH THE MOUNTAINS BY THE WAY OF YOUR BOYHOOD HOME OF TARSUS.

NO-- WE MUST GO BACK THE WAY WE CAME. OUR CHRISTIAN FRIENDS MAY NEED OUR HELP.

SO, IN SPITE OF THE DANGERS, PAUL AND BARNABAS RETRACE THEIR STEPS, VISITING THE CITIES OF GALATIA AND ORGANIZING THE CHURCHES THEY STARTED BEFORE. AT LAST THEY SAIL TOWARD THEIR HOME BASE-- ANTIOCH IN SYRIA.

ON THEIR FIRST MISSIONARY JOURNEY TO THE GENTILES, PAUL AND BARNABAS TRAVELED SOME 1400 MILES BY LAND AND SEA, AND WERE GONE FROM HOME ABOUT TWO YEARS.

ANTIOCH
Galatia
ICONIUM
LYSTRA
DERBE
TARSUS
ANTIOCH
ATTALIA
PERGA
Syria
Cyprus
SALAMIS
PAPHOS
Mediterranean Sea

IN ANTIOCH THEY RECEIVE A ROYAL WELCOME. THE CHURCH IS PROUD OF ITS MISSIONARIES AND THANKFUL TO HAVE A PART IN HELPING OTHERS KNOW JESUS.

I AM GLAD SO MANY GENTILES HERE IN ANTIOCH HAVE BECOME CHRISTIANS.

YES, AND THEY ARE LOYAL, TOO.!

Council in Jerusalem

FROM ACTS 15:1–13; GALATIONS

LIKE A VIOLENT WIND, A DISAGREEMENT BETWEEN THE JEWISH AND GENTILE CHRISTIANS RIPS THROUGH THE ANTIOCH CHURCH, DIVIDING THE MEMBERS. UNKNOWN TO PAUL AND BARNABAS, WHO ARE STRUGGLING TO KEEP THE CHURCH UNITED, ANOTHER STORM IS BUILDING UP IN THE AREA OF THEIR FIRST MISSIONARY JOURNEY...

INSIDE THE CITY THE MEN FIND PAUL AND GIVE HIM THEIR MESSAGE.

THE CHURCHES YOU STARTED IN GALATIA ARE IN TROUBLE. SOME JEWISH CHRISTIANS CLAIM THAT GOD SENT JESUS TO BE **THEIR** SAVIOR, AND IF WE GENTILES WANT TO BECOME CHRISTIANS WE MUST FIRST BECOME JEWS.

THEY ALSO QUESTION YOUR RIGHT TO PREACH THE GOSPEL BECAUSE YOU WERE NOT ONE OF JESUS' DISCIPLES. YOUR KNOWLEDGE, THEY SAY, IS SECONDHAND.

THE SAME PROBLEM HAS DIVIDED OUR CHURCH HERE. BUT THE ISSUE IS BIGGER THAN THE CHURCHES IN GALATIA AND ANTIOCH. THE WHOLE CHURCH OF CHRIST IS THREATENED.

THEN YOU CAN'T GO BACK WITH US?

NOT NOW. THE ELDERS HERE HAVE ASKED BARNABAS AND ME TO GO TO JERUSALEM TO TALK THIS PROBLEM OVER WITH JESUS' DISCIPLES. BUT I'LL WRITE A LETTER WHICH YOU CAN TAKE BACK WITH YOU.

Second Journey

FROM ACTS 15:13—16:8

THE JERUSALEM COUNCIL FACES A PROBLEM THAT IS DIVIDING THE CHURCH: MUST GENTILES BECOME JEWS AND OBEY ALL THEIR RULES BEFORE THEY CAN BECOME CHRISTIANS? THE ARGUMENTS ARE PRESENTED. THE COUNCIL TURNS TO JAMES, BROTHER OF JESUS AND HEAD OF THE COUNCIL.

BROTHERS, LET US NOT MAKE IT HARD FOR GENTILES TO BECOME CHRISTIANS. WE SHOULD ASK ONLY THAT THEY OBEY A FEW NECESSARY RULES. THEY MUST AVOID EATING FOOD THAT HAS BEEN OFFERED TO IDOLS, AND THEY MUST LEAD PURE LIVES.

THE COUNCIL AGREES, AND TWO OF ITS MEMBERS, JUDAS BARSABAS AND SILAS, JOIN PAUL AND BARNABAS IN TAKING THE DECISION TO ANTIOCH.

THE NEWS IS RECEIVED WITH JOY IN ANTIOCH THAT JEWS AND GENTILES CAN GO ON WORKING TOGETHER FOR JESUS. WITH THIS SETTLED, PAUL IS FREE TO CONTINUE HIS MISSIONARY WORK IN GENTILE COUNTRIES.

BARNABAS, LET'S MAKE A TRIP TO VISIT THE CHURCHES WE STARTED.

GOOD IDEA-- I'D LIKE TO ASK MARK TO GO WITH US AGAIN.

NO -- MARK LEFT US BEFORE.

I KNOW, BUT WE SHOULD GIVE HIM ANOTHER CHANCE.

PAUL DISAGREES, SO BARNABAS TAKES MARK AND SAILS TO THE ISLAND OF CYPRUS. PAUL TAKES SILAS WITH HIM BY LAND TO VISIT THE CHURCHES HE STARTED.

IN LYSTRA, THE CITY IN WHICH HE HAD BEEN STONED, PAUL FINDS A GROWING CHURCH.

PAUL, I WANT YOU TO MEET TIMOTHY. HE'S BECOME ONE OF OUR BEST YOUNG LEADERS.

I'VE HEARD MANY FINE REPORTS OF YOU, TIMOTHY. WOULD YOU LIKE TO GO WITH SILAS AND ME?

THERE GOOD FORTUNE AWAITS THE TRAVELERS.

TIMOTHY EAGERLY ACCEPTS, AND THE CHURCH GIVES ITS BLESSING. SOON THE THREE TRAVELERS ARE ON THEIR WAY. GOD TELLS THEM NOT TO FOLLOW THE TRADE ROUTE TO EPHESUS, SO THEY GO NORTH AND WEST UNTIL THEY REACH TROAS ON THE AEGEAN SEA.

DR. LUKE! THE LORD MUST HAVE LED YOU TO JOIN US HERE.

PAUL! I WILL TRAVEL WITH YOU.

AS THE FOUR MISSIONARIES WALK THROUGH THE STREETS OF THE GREAT SEAPORT...

ONE HUNDRED AND FIFTY MILES ACROSS THE SEA LIES MACEDONIA, THE LAND FROM WHICH ALEXANDER THE GREAT BEGAN HIS CONQUEST OF THE WORLD.

I WONDER WHERE GOD WANTS ME TO PREACH NEXT...

Call from across the Sea

FROM ACTS 16:9–19

A GOOD WIND SPEEDS THE FOUR MISSIONARIES ACROSS THE AEGEAN SEA TO THE PORT OF NEAPOLIS. FROM THERE THEY WALK EIGHT MILES TO THE CITY OF PHILIPPI.

MACEDONIA

Black Sea

PHILIPPI   NEAPOLIS

THESSALONICA

SAMOTHRACE

TROAS

Aegean Sea

ATHENS

ASIA

THE CITY HAS NO SYNAGOGUE, SO ON THE SABBATH THEY WORSHIP BY A RIVERSIDE.

DO YOU HEAR THOSE WOMEN? THEY ARE PRAYING TO GOD.

THE MISSIONARIES JOIN THE WORSHIPERS--AND SOON PAUL IS TELLING THEM ABOUT JESUS. A BUSINESSWOMAN, NAMED LYDIA, SPEAKS FIRST.

GOD HAS OPENED MY HEART TO BELIEVE IN HIS SON, JESUS. MAY I BE BAPTIZED?

OF COURSE, LYDIA.

750

Earthquake

FROM ACTS 16:20–37

PAUL REMOVES AN EVIL SPIRIT FROM A GIRL WHO WAS A FORTUNETELLER FOR SOME GREEDY MEN. ANGRY BECAUSE THEIR BUSINESS HAS BEEN RUINED, THE MEN DRAG PAUL AND SILAS BEFORE THE JUDGES IN THE PUBLIC SQUARE. A CROWD GATHERS.

THESE MEN ARE JEWS. THEY ARE TRYING TO MAKE TROUBLE BY TEACHING THINGS AGAINST ROMAN LAW.

YES! WE ALL HEARD HIM!

BUT I--

SILENCE! THERE'LL BE NO TROUBLE IN THIS CITY. GIVE THESE MEN A BEATING AND THROW THEM IN JAIL, AND SEE THAT THEY DON'T ESCAPE.

AFTER A SEVERE BEATING, PAUL AND SILAS ARE TAKEN TO PRISON AND PUT IN STOCKS.

IN SPITE OF THEIR SUFFERING, THE CHRISTIAN MISSIONARIES PRAY AND SING THEIR PRAISES TO GOD.

SUDDENLY— AT MIDNIGHT— THE PRISON FOUNDATION TREMBLES. THE WALLS TWIST AND CRACK-- SNAPPING CHAINS AND HINGES FROM THE HEAVY DOORS.

WHEN THE QUAKE IS OVER THE JAILER RUSHES DOWN INTO THE DUNGEON, AFRAID THAT HIS PRISONERS HAVE ESCAPED.

THEY'RE GONE! I MIGHT AS WELL KILL MYSELF.

NO! NO! WE'RE ALL HERE!

BELIEVING THAT PAUL AND SILAS HAD SOMETHING TO DO WITH THE EARTHQUAKE THE JAILER FALLS ON HIS KNEES BEFORE THEM.

WHAT MUST I DO TO BE SAVED?

BELIEVE ON THE LORD JESUS CHRIST.

THE JAILER QUICKLY TAKES THE TWO PRISONERS TO HIS HOUSE AND TREATS THEIR WOUNDED BODIES. HE AND HIS FAMILY LISTEN EAGERLY AS PAUL TELLS THEM ABOUT JESUS -- AND ALL ARE BAPTIZED.

EARLY IN THE MORNING ROMAN OFFICERS COME TO THE PRISON.

THE JUDGES HAVE ORDERED YOUR RELEASE.

WE ARE ROMAN CITIZENS, YET WE HAD NO TRIAL. NOW THE JUDGES THINK THEY CAN GET RID OF US QUIETLY. TELL THE JUDGES THEMSELVES TO COME AND MAKE OUR RELEASE AS PUBLIC AS OUR BEATING.

Out of Trouble . . . Into Trouble

FROM ACTS 16:38—17:13

THE ROMAN JUDGES, WHO ORDERED PAUL AND SILAS RELEASED FROM PRISON, ARE SURPRISED WHEN THE OFFICER RETURNS WITH A MESSAGE FROM THE PRISONERS.

THOSE MEN ARE ROMAN CITIZENS. THEY DEMAND THAT YOU COME TO THE PRISON AND RELEASE THEM AS PUBLICLY AS YOU PUNISHED THEM.

ROMAN CITIZENS? AND WE SENTENCED THEM WITHOUT A TRIAL! THIS COULD MEAN TROUBLE FOR US.

FORGETTING THEIR DIGNITY THE JUDGES GO IMMEDIATELY TO THE PRISON.

WE ARE TRULY SORRY FOR THE WAY WE TREATED YOU. NOW PLEASE LEAVE THE CITY TO AVOID FURTHER TROUBLE.

WE FORGIVE YOU-- AND WE WILL LEAVE TODAY.

755

AT THE HOUSE OF LYDIA, PAUL, SILAS, AND TIMOTHY BID THEIR FRIENDS GOOD-BYE.

THANK YOU FOR LEAVING DR. LUKE HERE TO LEAD OUR CHURCH.

WE WILL RETURN SOMEDAY. HOLD FAST TO YOUR FAITH IN JESUS AND HELP OTHERS TO KNOW HIM.

TRAVELING ON SOME 90 MILES, THE MISSIONARIES REACH THESSALONICA ON THE AEGEAN SEA. PAUL GOES AT ONCE TO THE SYNAGOGUE TO PREACH.

THE SCRIPTURES PROMISED THAT A SAVIOR WOULD COME. JESUS, WHO DIED ON THE CROSS AND ROSE FROM THE DEAD, IS THAT SAVIOR.

MANY PEOPLE LISTEN AND BELIEVE -- BUT SOME OF THE JEWISH LEADERS DO NOT.

WE'VE GOT TO GET RID OF HIM BEFORE HE HAS THE WHOLE CITY BELIEVING WHAT HE SAYS.

HE'S STAYING AT JASON'S HOUSE. LET'S GET HIM THERE.

GATHERING A STRONG-ARMED MOB, THE RELIGIOUS LEADERS CALL ON JASON.

IF YOU'RE LOOKING FOR PAUL, HE'S NOT HERE.

YOU'RE HIDING HIM. IF YOU WON'T LET US HAVE HIM, WE'LL TAKE YOU.

Paul Explains the "Unknown God"

FROM ACTS 17:13—18:12; 1 AND 2 THESSALONIANS

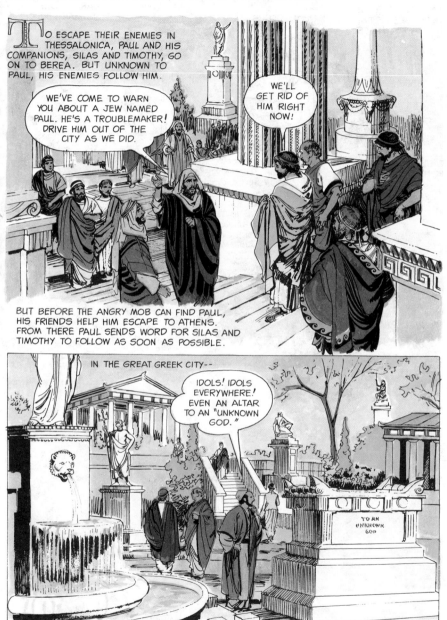

TO ESCAPE THEIR ENEMIES IN THESSALONICA, PAUL AND HIS COMPANIONS, SILAS AND TIMOTHY, GO ON TO BEREA. BUT UNKNOWN TO PAUL, HIS ENEMIES FOLLOW HIM.

WE'VE COME TO WARN YOU ABOUT A JEW NAMED PAUL. HE'S A TROUBLEMAKER! DRIVE HIM OUT OF THE CITY AS WE DID.

WE'LL GET RID OF HIM RIGHT NOW!

BUT BEFORE THE ANGRY MOB CAN FIND PAUL, HIS FRIENDS HELP HIM ESCAPE TO ATHENS. FROM THERE PAUL SENDS WORD FOR SILAS AND TIMOTHY TO FOLLOW AS SOON AS POSSIBLE.

IN THE GREAT GREEK CITY--

IDOLS! IDOLS EVERYWHERE! EVEN AN ALTAR TO AN "UNKNOWN GOD."

TO AN UNKNOWN GOD

ON THE SABBATH PAUL PREACHES TO THE JEWS, BUT DURING THE WEEK HE CARRIES HIS MESSAGE OF JESUS TO THE GREEKS IN THE MARKET PLACE.

HE SAYS THERE IS ONLY ONE GOD, AND THAT HE SENT HIS ONLY SON, JESUS, TO SAVE US.

I'D LIKE TO HEAR MORE ABOUT A GOD WHO CARES FOR PEOPLE. LET'S ASK THIS MAN TO SPEAK BEFORE THE COURT OF MARS' HILL.

PAUL ACCEPTS THE INVITATION EAGERLY.

GENTLEMEN OF ATHENS, SINCE YOU WORSHIP A GOD YOU DO NOT KNOW, I'LL TELL YOU WHO HE IS -- THE TRUE GOD, WHO MADE ALL THINGS. HE DOES NOT LIVE IN TEMPLES MADE BY HUMAN HANDS. HE IS NOT FAR FROM EACH ONE OF US, FOR IN HIM WE LIVE, AND MOVE, AND HAVE OUR BEING.

THE MEN OF ATHENS LISTEN EAGERLY -- UNTIL PAUL SAYS THAT JESUS ROSE FROM THE DEAD.

NOBODY CAN BE RAISED FROM THE DEAD. WHAT A SILLY IDEA!

I'M NOT SO SURE...

759

IT IS DOING WELL, BUT THE PEOPLE ARE HAVING A HARD TIME.

I'LL WRITE TO THEM AT ONCE.

PAUL'S **First Letter to the Thessalonians,** WHICH IS A BOOK OF THE NEW TESTAMENT.

To the church of the Thessalonians-- from Paul, Silas, and Timothy

We remember how joyfully you turned from idols to serve the true God. Though we had to leave, it was good to receive news that you are standing true to your faith, even though people have been making it hard for you.

As we urged you when we were with you, live in the way that will please God, who invited you to have a place in His Kingdom. Keep on praying, and love one another more and more. I know you have worried about Christians who have died, but you need not. For Jesus promised that when He comes back from Heaven these will meet Him.

Be sure this letter is read to all the members of the church.

PAUL GETS FURTHER WORD FROM HIS FRIENDS IN THESSALONICA. HE WRITES A **Second Letter to the Thessalonians.** THIS ALSO IS A BOOK OF THE NEW TESTAMENT.

To the church of the Thessalonians-- from Paul, Silas, and Timothy

Don't get a mistaken idea of what I told you. No one should quit working because he thinks Jesus will return right away. If anyone will not work, he should not be fed. Before Jesus comes, there will be a time when an evil man tries to rule the world, taking the place of God. But God will keep you from evil. Don't get discouraged in doing what is right.

In any letter that I send to you, I write a few words at the close in my own handwriting-- like this-- so that you will be sure the letter is from me. May Christ's love be with you all.

FOR A YEAR AND A HALF PAUL PREACHES IN CORINTH. A STRONG CHRISTIAN CHURCH IS STARTED. BUT THE JEWISH LEADERS ARE ANGRY AT PAUL AND LOOK UPON HIM AS A TRAITOR TO HIS RELIGION.

GALLIO IS A NEW GOVERNOR. HE WON'T RISK HAVING TROUBLE BREAK OUT RIGHT AWAY. I THINK WE CAN WORK THINGS SO THAT **HE** WILL GET RID OF PAUL FOR US!

Talk of the Town

FROM ACTS 18:13—19:16

JEWISH LEADERS IN CORINTH ARE ANGRY BECAUSE PAUL IS WINNING SO MANY PEOPLE TO JESUS. THEY TAKE HIM BEFORE THE NEW ROMAN GOVERNOR.

MOST EXCELLENT GALLIO-- THIS MAN IS TELLING PEOPLE TO WORSHIP GOD IN WAYS THAT ARE AGAINST THE LAW. HE IS CHANGING THE JEWISH CUSTOMS WHICH THE ROMANS PERMIT.

PAUL IS ABOUT TO DEFEND HIMSELF, BUT TO EVERYONE'S SURPRISE GALLIO TURNS ON PAUL'S ENEMIES.

I WILL TAKE NO PART IN QUARRELS ABOUT THE JEWISH RELIGION. THIS HAS NOTHING TO DO WITH ROMAN LAW. NOW, GET OUT OF COURT!

761

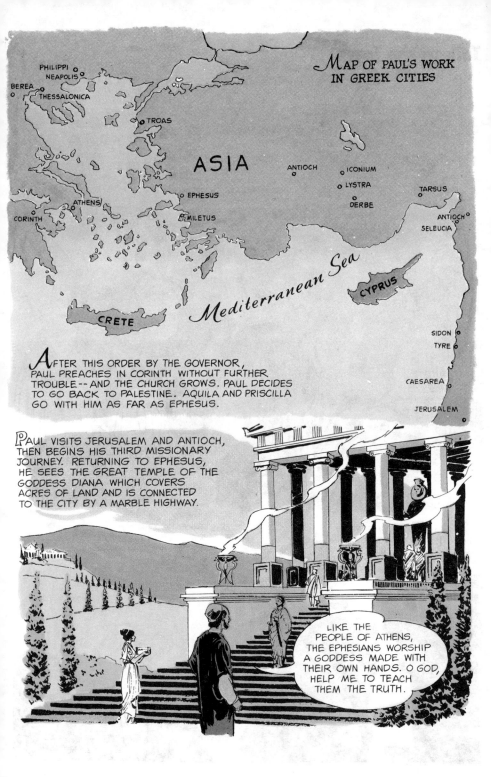

MAP OF PAUL'S WORK IN GREEK CITIES

ASIA

Mediterranean Sea

AFTER THIS ORDER BY THE GOVERNOR, PAUL PREACHES IN CORINTH WITHOUT FURTHER TROUBLE -- AND THE CHURCH GROWS. PAUL DECIDES TO GO BACK TO PALESTINE. AQUILA AND PRISCILLA GO WITH HIM AS FAR AS EPHESUS.

PAUL VISITS JERUSALEM AND ANTIOCH, THEN BEGINS HIS THIRD MISSIONARY JOURNEY. RETURNING TO EPHESUS, HE SEES THE GREAT TEMPLE OF THE GODDESS DIANA WHICH COVERS ACRES OF LAND AND IS CONNECTED TO THE CITY BY A MARBLE HIGHWAY.

LIKE THE PEOPLE OF ATHENS, THE EPHESIANS WORSHIP A GODDESS MADE WITH THEIR OWN HANDS. O GOD, HELP ME TO TEACH THEM THE TRUTH.

The Angry Mob
FROM ACTS 19:17—20; 1 CORINTHIANS

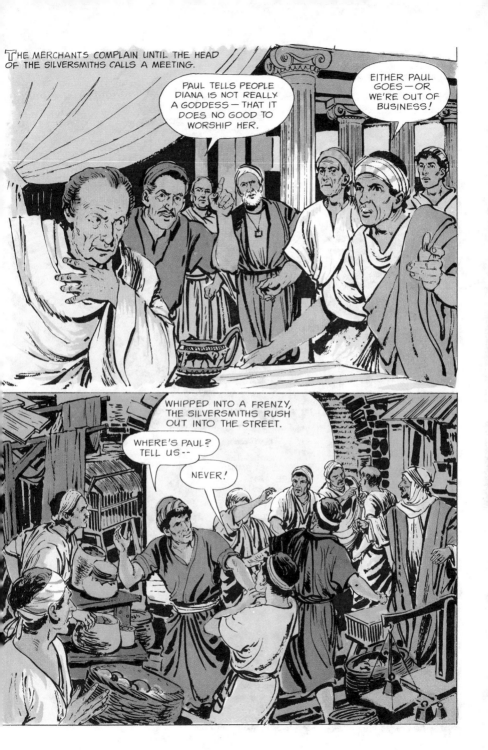

765

Riot in Ephesus

FROM ACTS 19:31—20:3; 2 CORINTHIANS; ROMANS

CITY OFFICIALS BEG PAUL TO STAY AWAY FROM THE MOB. FOR TWO HOURS THE RIOTERS SHOUT, "GREAT IS DIANA OF THE EPHESIANS." FINALLY THE TOWN CLERK MAKES HIMSELF HEARD...

GENTLEMEN OF EPHESUS -- IF THE SILVERSMITHS HAVE A COMPLAINT, LET THEM BRING IT BEFORE THE COURTS. I WARN YOU -- IF THE ROMAN GOVERNMENT ASKS THE REASON FOR THIS RIOTING, THERE IS NO EXCUSE WE CAN GIVE FOR IT.

IN FACE OF THIS THREAT, THE RIOT BREAKS UP. PAUL SENDS FOR HIS FRIENDS.

THE MOB WAS REALLY AFTER ME -- SO TO PREVENT TROUBLE FOR ALL OF YOU, I WILL GO TO PHILIPPI.

OUR PRAYERS WILL GO WITH YOU.

SOON AFTER PAUL REACHES PHILIPPI, TITUS JOINS HIM WITH NEWS FROM CORINTH.

PAUL, YOUR LETTER TO THE CHRISTIANS AT CORINTH MADE THEM CORRECT THEIR WRONG-DOING. BUT NOW SOME PEOPLE HAVE COME TO CORINTH WHO CLAIM YOU ARE NOT A TRUE APOSTLE OF JESUS.

ONCE AGAIN PAUL WRITES TO THE CHURCH IN CORINTH. THE LETTER -- KNOWN AS II Corinthians -- IS A BOOK OF THE NEW TESTAMENT.

I can see that my letter upset you, but I am glad I sent it. Not because I want to hurt you, but to make you sorry as God would have you sorry for the things that were wrong.

We are taking a collection for poor Christians in Jerusalem. Other churches have given large sums. I trust you will be able to do the same. Let everyone give what he has decided in his own heart to give, for God loves a cheerful giver.

And now, for those who question whether or not I am a true minister of Christ. I have been imprisoned, I have been beaten many times, I have often faced death. I have been stoned, I have been shipwrecked three times -- all to carry out the work of Christ. When I visit you again, I hope it will be a happy meeting. Good-bye till then.

THIS MONEY WILL SHOW THE CHRISTIANS IN JERUSALEM THAT YOU'RE CONCERNED FOR THEM.

WHILE TITUS TAKES THE LETTER TO CORINTH, PAUL CONTINUES VISITING CHURCHES IN MACEDONIA, COLLECTING MONEY FOR THE POOR IN JERUSALEM. MONTHS LATER HE REACHES CORINTH WHERE HE IS GREETED BY FRIENDS WHO HAVE GIVEN EAGERLY TO HIS COLLECTION.

Bound Hand and Foot

FROM ACTS 20:3—21:14

THANK GOD!

HE WAS DEAD -- I'M SURE HE WAS. WHAT POWER GOD HAS GIVEN PAUL!

AFTER PREACHING UNTIL DAYBREAK, PAUL SAYS GOOD-BY TO HIS FRIENDS.

MUST YOU GO, PAUL?

YES, I HAD PLANNED TO BE IN JERUSALEM FOR THE FEAST OF THE PASSOVER, BUT I COULD NOT. NOW I WANT TO REACH THERE FOR THE FEAST OF PENTECOST.

AT MILETUS, PAUL SENDS WORD FOR THE ELDERS OF EPHESUS TO MEET HIM. EAGERLY THEY TRAVEL THE 35 MILES TO SEE HIM.

I MUST GO TO JERUSALEM -- EVEN IF MY LIFE IS IN DANGER. I DO NOT CONSIDER MY LIFE IMPORTANT SO LONG AS I COMPLETE THE MINISTRY WHICH THE LORD GAVE ME. YOU ARE NOW SHEPHERDS OF THE CHURCH OF CHRIST -- WHICH HE BOUGHT WITH HIS OWN LIFE. HELP THE WEAK -- AND REMEMBER THE WORDS OF JESUS: TO GIVE IS BETTER THAN TO RECEIVE.

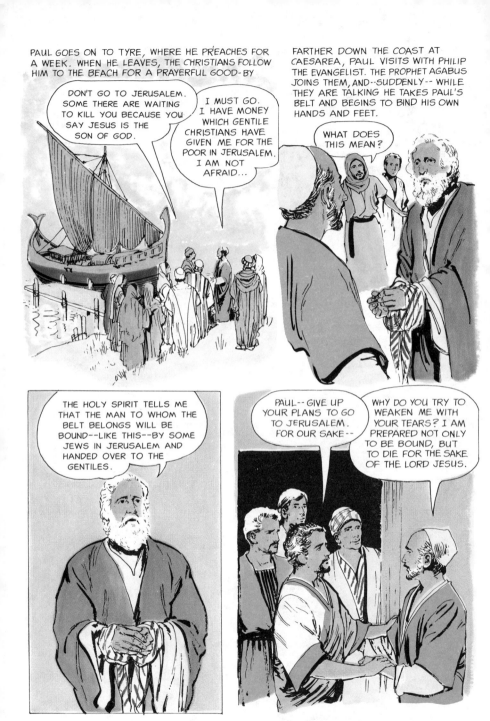

PAUL GOES ON TO TYRE, WHERE HE PREACHES FOR A WEEK. WHEN HE LEAVES, THE CHRISTIANS FOLLOW HIM TO THE BEACH FOR A PRAYERFUL GOOD-BY

DON'T GO TO JERUSALEM. SOME THERE ARE WAITING TO KILL YOU BECAUSE YOU SAY JESUS IS THE SON OF GOD.

I MUST GO. I HAVE MONEY WHICH GENTILE CHRISTIANS HAVE GIVEN ME FOR THE POOR IN JERUSALEM. I AM NOT AFRAID...

FARTHER DOWN THE COAST AT CAESAREA, PAUL VISITS WITH PHILIP THE EVANGELIST. THE PROPHET AGABUS JOINS THEM, AND--SUDDENLY-- WHILE THEY ARE TALKING HE TAKES PAUL'S BELT AND BEGINS TO BIND HIS OWN HANDS AND FEET.

WHAT DOES THIS MEAN?

THE HOLY SPIRIT TELLS ME THAT THE MAN TO WHOM THE BELT BELONGS WILL BE BOUND--LIKE THIS--BY SOME JEWS IN JERUSALEM AND HANDED OVER TO THE GENTILES.

PAUL-- GIVE UP YOUR PLANS TO GO TO JERUSALEM. FOR OUR SAKE--

WHY DO YOU TRY TO WEAKEN ME WITH YOUR TEARS? I AM PREPARED NOT ONLY TO BE BOUND, BUT TO DIE FOR THE SAKE OF THE LORD JESUS.

A Boy and a Secret

FROM ACTS 21:15—23:24

THE DAY AFTER PAUL REACHES JERUSALEM, HE MEETS WITH JAMES AND OTHER LEADERS OF THE JERUSALEM CHURCH. HE DELIVERS THE MONEY FOR THE POOR AND TELLS WHAT GOD HAS DONE IN OTHER LANDS.

I MUST WARN YOU, PAUL, YOU HAVE ENEMIES HERE WHO THINK YOU ARE A TRAITOR. EVEN THE CHRISTIAN JEWS HAVE QUESTIONS BECAUSE OF YOUR WORK AMONG THE GENTILES.

I'LL WORSHIP WITH THEM IN THE TEMPLE TO SHOW THAT I AM TRUE TO THE FAITH OF OUR FATHERS.

JAMES' WARNING COMES TRUE WITHIN THE WEEK. WHILE PAUL IS WORSHIPING IN THE TEMPLE HIS ENEMIES ACCUSE HIM, FALSELY, OF BRINGING GENTILES INTO GOD'S HOUSE WHERE ONLY JEWS ARE ALLOWED.

THERE HE IS -- THE TRAITOR!

HE HAS DEFILED THIS HOLY PLACE OF GOD!

IN ANGER THE PEOPLE TURN AGAINST PAUL. A MOB DRAGS HIM FROM THE TEMPLE AND STARTS TO BEAT HIM.

LOOK OUT-- ROMAN SOLDIERS ARE COMING!

NOW, TELL US WHAT THIS MAN HAS DONE.

TAKE HIM AWAY-- KILL HIM!

THE SOLDIERS CARRY PAUL TO THE PRISON. ON ITS STEPS PAUL STOPS AND TELLS THE PEOPLE HOW HE BECAME A CHRISTIAN, BUT WHEN HE MENTIONS PREACHING TO THE GENTILES, THE MOB GOES WILD.

HE IS NOT FIT TO LIVE!

KILL HIM!

KILL HIM!

Paul Pleads His Case

FROM ACTS 23:25—28:4

TO PROTECT PAUL'S LIFE, THE ROMAN COMMANDER AT JERUSALEM SENDS HIM TO CAESAREA, WHERE PAUL IS KEPT IN PRISON. AFTER TWO YEARS PAUL APPEARS BEFORE FESTUS, THE ROMAN GOVERNOR, AND DEMANDS HIS RIGHT TO BE TRIED BY THE EMPEROR NERO AT ROME. BUT FIRST FESTUS BRINGS PAUL BEFORE A NEIGHBORING RULER, KING AGRIPPA, WHO IS VISITING THE CITY.

I ONCE THOUGHT IT MY DUTY TO OPPOSE JESUS. I HAD MANY OF HIS FOLLOWERS IMPRISONED. BUT ON MY WAY TO DAMASCUS I SAW A LIGHT FROM HEAVEN... AND JESUS SAID TO ME, "I SEND YOU TO TURN PEOPLE OF ALL NATIONS FROM THE POWER OF SATAN TO GOD... O KING AGRIPPA, I COULD NOT DISOBEY THE HEAVENLY VISION.

YOU'RE TRYING TO PERSUADE ME TO BE A CHRISTIAN.

FESTUS AND AGRIPPA WOULD HAVE SET PAUL FREE IF HE HAD NOT DEMANDED A TRIAL IN ROME. SO -- UNDER ROMAN GUARD AND ACCOMPANIED BY LUKE -- PAUL IS TAKEN ABOARD A SHIP BOUND FOR ROME. AT THE ISLAND OF CRETE...

THE WINTER STORMS WILL SOON BE HERE. IT WILL BE DANGEROUS TO GO ON UNTIL SPRING.

THE HARBOR AT PHOENIX IS NOT FAR AWAY -- WE'LL SPEND THE WINTER THERE.

THE SHIP SETS SAIL -- ONLY TO BE STRUCK BY A RAGING "NORTHEASTER."

TAKE DOWN THE MAINSAIL!

ON THE 14TH NIGHT OF THE STORM THE SAILORS TRY TO DESERT THE SHIP.

UNLESS THOSE MEN STAY WITH THE SHIP, YOU CANNOT BE SAVED!

THE SOLDIERS CUT THE SMALL BOAT LOOSE --AND THE SAILORS ARE FORCED TO STAY WITH THE SHIP. AT DAYBREAK...

LAND AHEAD!

HEADING TOWARD A BAY, THE SHIP RUNS AGROUND. THE BOW STICKS FAST, BUT THE STERN BEGINS TO BREAK UNDER THE POUNDING OF THE HEAVY WAVES.

ABANDON SHIP!

KILL THE PRISONERS -- IF THEY REACH SHORE THEY'LL ESCAPE.

BECAUSE OF HIS FRIENDSHIP FOR PAUL, THE ROMAN OFFICER SPARES THE PRISONERS. SOLDIERS, SAILORS, PASSENGERS, AND PRISONERS STRUGGLE FOR THEIR LIVES IN THE RAGING SEA.

Apostle on the March

FROM PHILIPPIANS; 1 TIMOTHY; TITUS

As soon as he is well, Epaphroditus goes to see Paul.

"THE CHURCH IN ROME IS GROWING RAPIDLY. UNLESS YOU NEED ME HERE, I WOULD LIKE TO GO BACK HOME."

"YES, THAT'S WHAT YOU SHOULD DO. I HAVE WRITTEN A LETTER TO MY FRIENDS IN PHILIPPI. YOU CAN TAKE IT BACK WITH YOU."

Paul's letter to the *Philippians* is a book of the New Testament.

To the church at Philippi,

I don't know yet how my trial will come out, but I believe God will let me visit you again. Make me happy by living in harmony among yourselves. Think as Christ did. Though divine, He was willing to humble Himself and become a Man— willing even to die on the cross.

Thank you for your gift which Epaphroditus brought. You have been generous. God will also supply all that you need. Always be glad, since you are Christians, and think about the things that are good. The Christians here send greetings, especially the ones who are working in Caesar's palace.

Two years—and finally Paul's case is brought to court.* Before Nero, the most powerful ruler in the world, Paul makes his defense, and in a few days...

"THANK GOD! NOW I CAN CARRY OUT MY DREAM TO TAKE THE GOSPEL OF CHRIST TO THE FARTHEST CORNERS OF THE EMPIRE!"

"PAUL! PAUL! THE COURT HAS SET YOU FREE!"

*ALTHOUGH THE BIBLE DOES NOT TELL ABOUT PAUL'S RELEASE, THE LETTERS HE WROTE AFTERWARD SHOW THAT IT MUST HAVE TAKEN PLACE.

The Burning of Rome

FROM 2 TIMOTHY; HEBREWS 13:23

HISTORICAL BACKGROUND . . .

IT IS THE YEAR 64. NERO, THE CRUEL EMPEROR OF ROME, HAS MANY ENEMIES AMONG HIS OWN PEOPLE. THERE ARE RUMORS OF PLOTS AGAINST HIS LIFE. THEN, STRANGELY, A FIRE SWEEPS ACROSS THE CITY. FOR NINE DAYS IT RAGES--BURNING GREAT SECTIONS OF THE CITY AND DRIVING THOUSANDS FROM THEIR HOMES. FROM HIS PALACE, NERO WATCHES....

EVEN WHILE THE CITY IS STILL IN FLAMES NEW RUMORS SPREAD.

NERO! THE PEOPLE ARE SAYING **YOU** STARTED THE FIRE. THERE ARE UGLY THREATS--

AND I SAY THE CHRISTIANS STARTED THE FIRE. ARREST THEM-- TORTURE THEM-- KILL THEM!

THIS WILL TURN PEOPLE'S ATTENTION AWAY FROM ME.

ARMED WITH ORDERS FROM THE EMPEROR, SOLDIERS KILL HUNDREDS OF CHRISTIANS IN ROME. THE ORDER REACHES OUT ACROSS THE SEA FROM ITALY-- AND ONCE AGAIN PAUL IS ARRESTED!

BY ORDER OF THE EMPEROR, YOU ARE UNDER ARREST!

ONCE AGAIN PAUL COMES TO ROME-- A PRISONER. THIS TIME HE IS CHAINED TO THE WALL OF THE MAMERTINE PRISON. LUKE COMES TO COMFORT HIM.

I'M SURE I HAVE ONLY A FEW MONTHS TO LIVE. BRING SOME PAPER AND **A** PEN AND WRITE WHAT I TELL YOU TO TIMOTHY.

I'LL BRING THE MATERIAL ON MY NEXT VISIT.

WHEN LUKE RETURNS, PAUL TELLS HIM WHAT TO WRITE. THE LETTER, **II Timothy**, IS A BOOK OF THE NEW TESTAMENT.

WHEN TIMOTHY RECEIVES THE LETTER, HE SAILS AT ONCE TO ROME. THERE HE FINDS LUKE, WHO TAKES HIM TO THE PRISON. BUT AS TIMOTHY GREETS PAUL...

Dear Timothy,

Be strong, like a good soldier for Christ. Remember the truth as you learned from me and from the Holy Scriptures. Keep preaching it, even though the time will come when people don't want to hear the truth.

I want to see you very much. Do your best to come before winter. Bring the coat I left at Troas, and the books. I have almost reached the end of my life. Soon I will be with the Lord and He will give me a place in His heavenly Kingdom. Try to come soon.

Paul

> I HAVE JUST RECEIVED ORDERS -- YOU ARE UNDER ARREST!

SO TIMOTHY, TOO, IS ARRESTED FOR TEACHING ABOUT JESUS. IN THEIR PRISON CELLS THE TWO MISSIONARIES WAIT FOR ROMAN LAW TO BRING THEM TO TRIAL. IN TIME PAUL'S CASE IS CALLED. ALONE, HE IS MARCHED TO THE COURT OF NERO.

Soldier Victorious

FROM 2 TIMOTHY 4:6–8

IN ROME, PAUL IS ON TRIAL FOR HIS LIFE BEFORE THE CRUEL EMPEROR, NERO.

I FIND YOU GUILTY OF STIRRING UP TROUBLE IN THE EMPIRE. THE SENTENCE IS DEATH-- BY THE SWORD.

The End of an Era

HEBREWS THROUGH REVELATION

JESUS' DISCIPLES WHO WERE STILL ALIVE WERE GROWING OLD IN THE LATTER HALF OF THE FIRST CENTURY AFTER HIS BIRTH. THEY COULD NOT TRAVEL TO ALL THE CHURCHES, SO THEY TURNED TO WRITING LETTERS TO JESUS' FOLLOWERS.

THE LAST NINE BOOKS OF THE NEW TESTAMENT, HEBREWS THROUGH REVELATION, ARE MESSAGES THESE MEN WROTE TO GIVE ADVICE, COURAGE, AND COMFORT TO THE EARLY CHRISTIANS.

The Book of Hebrews

THE LETTER TO THE HEBREWS WAS WRITTEN AT A TIME WHEN JEWISH CHRISTIANS WERE BEING PRESSURED BY THE ROMANS AND JEWS TO GIVE UP THEIR FAITH IN JESUS.

THEY ASKED THEMSELVES: WHICH IS RIGHT, FAITH IN JESUS OR FAITH IN THE RELIGION OF OUR FOREFATHERS ABRAHAM, MOSES, AND DAVID?

"GOD HAS SPOKEN TO US THROUGH HIS SON, JESUS," THE LETTER SAID. "ABRAHAM, MOSES, AND DAVID WERE GREAT MEN WHO LIVED BY FAITH. THEY DIED; BUT JESUS CHRIST WILL LIVE FOREVER. HOLD FAST TO YOUR FAITH IN HIM."

THE LETTER ALSO BROUGHT THE GOOD NEWS THAT TIMOTHY HAD BEEN RELEASED FROM PRISON.

The Book of James

AS LEADER OF THE CHURCH IN JERU-SALEM, JAMES, THE BROTHER OF JESUS, WROTE A LETTER OF ADVICE TO CHRISTIANS LIVING IN OTHER COUNTRIES.

"True religion is shown by what you do. Help those who need help. Be fair to all people. Ask God for wisdom, and keep your lives pure."

THUS THE BROTHER OF JESUS, WHO WAS KNOWN AS JAMES THE JUST, CONTINUED TO SPREAD THE GOSPEL.

The Book of I Peter

PETER WAS NOW AN OLD MAN. HE COULD SEE THAT THE ROMANS WERE TURNING AGAINST THE CHRISTIANS AND THAT JESUS' FOLLOWERS WOULD BE IN GREAT DANGER. HE HAD SILAS WRITE A LETTER FOR HIM.

"Face your hardships bravely," Peter told the people. "There is one thing no one can take from you -- the hope of living in Heaven with Christ. Trust in Him; He will reward those who follow Him faithfully."

The Book of II Peter

PETER KNEW THAT HE DID NOT HAVE MANY YEARS TO LIVE. HE WANTED TO HELP THE FOLLOWERS OF JESUS TO BE TRUE TO HIM, SO HE SENT THEM THIS LETTER.

"You believe in Jesus," he wrote, "Then act the way His followers should." Then he warned the Christians not to be upset by people who laughed at them because they believed that Jesus would return. "When the time is right," Peter wrote, "Christ will return. "God is giving people a chance to repent. He has promised a new world for those who love and obey Him. "See how important it is for you to live for God!"

THESE ARE THE LAST WORDS WE HEAR FROM THE FISHERMAN WHO GAVE UP HIS NETS TO FOLLOW JESUS.

The Book of I John

JOHN, WHO HAD BEEN SO CLOSE TO JESUS IN EARLIER YEARS, WAS NOW THE LEADER OF THE CHRISTIANS AROUND EPHESUS.

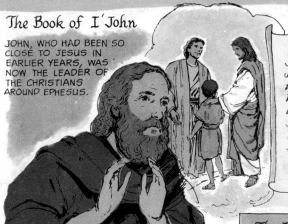

"I have been with Jesus," John wrote to his people, "and I want you to have the same joy in knowing Him that I have. Don't believe anyone who says that God's Son did not come to the world as a real Person. God loved us and sent His Son to be our Savior. As He loved us, we should love one another."

The Book of III John

"Dear Gaius," John wrote to his Christian friend, "I have heard good things about you. You are doing right in receiving Christians into your home, especially traveling preachers. Your kindness helps in their work. Don't pay attention to anyone who tries to stop you from doing this."

The Book of II John

"I was very glad," John wrote, "to find some of your children living by the truth and obeying God's command to love one another. If any enemies of the truth come to you teaching that Christ was not a real man, do not receive them into your house. If you do, you will be helping in this evil work."

The Book of Jude

JUDE, ANOTHER BROTHER OF JESUS, DID NOT BELIEVE THAT JESUS WAS THE SON OF GOD--UNTIL HE ROSE FROM THE DEAD. THEN JUDE BECAME A CHRISTIAN AND AFTER THAT HE WAS A STRONG WORKER FOR CHRIST.

ONE DAY HE RECEIVED BAD NEWS--THAT PEOPLE IN SOME OF THE CHURCHES WERE TEACHING THINGS THAT WERE NOT TRUE.

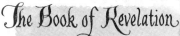

JUDE WROTE THE CHURCHES A LETTER:

"You must defend our Christian faith. You have been warned that people would try to turn you away from Christ. I understand some of these false teachers are with you now. Pray that God will keep you strong, and that He will help you strengthen others."

The Book of Revelation

JOHN, WHO WROTE THE BEST-LOVED GOSPEL AND THREE LETTERS TO THE FOLLOWERS OF JESUS, ALSO WROTE THE BOOK OF REVELATION--TO HELP CHRISTIANS FACE THE ANGRY POWER OF ROME.

THE ROMANS HAD ARRESTED JOHN AND SENT HIM AS A PRISONER TO THE ISLAND OF PATMOS. THERE HE SAW A VISION OF HEAVEN, AND HE HEARD JESUS SAY:

"BEHOLD, I STAND AT THE DOOR, AND KNOCK: IF ANYONE HEARS MY VOICE, AND OPENS THE DOOR, I WILL COME INSIDE."

IN HEAVEN, JOHN SAW THE BOOK OF LIFE--IN WHICH WERE WRITTEN THE NAMES OF THOSE WHO LOVE CHRIST. AND FINALLY, THE OLD DISCIPLE SAW THE HOLY CITY, WHERE THERE IS NO SICKNESS, NO SORROW, NO DEATH. THOSE WHOSE NAMES ARE IN THE BOOK OF LIFE WILL ENTER THE GLORIOUS CITY AND LIVE FOREVER WITH CHRIST!

AND WITH JOHN'S VISION ENDS THE GREATEST STORY EVER TOLD, THE STORY OF THE BIBLE.

Life in Bible Times

It's easy to take some of our modern-day conveniences for granted, isn't it? Have you ever wondered what it would have been like to live when Jesus did? If you wanted a drink, a trip to the local well was in order.

In this section, you'll see what life was like two thousand years ago in Palestine.

When it's time for bed and the fire has died down to a few glowing coals, a board will be laid over it and then a carpet. This keeps the room warm for hours. The family sleeps on mattresses spread on the floor.

AT HOME IN PALESTINE

The lower floor of the average house was used as a stable for animals when they couldn't be left outdoors. At other times it served as a workshop or a playroom.

MOST HOMES IN PALESTINE
[HA]D TWO FLOORS. THE PEOPLE
[U]SED THEIR FLAT ROOFS
[FO]R MANY ACTIVITIES, BUT
[T]HE SECOND FLOOR WAS
[TH]EIR MAIN LIVING QUARTERS.
[H]ERE THEY SLEPT AT
[NI]GHT, DID THEIR COOKING
[AND] STORED THEIR BELONGINGS.
[IN T]HIS PICTURE WE SEE A TYPICAL
[FAMILY IN THE SECOND
[FLOOR OF THEIR HOME.

[F]ATHER IS BRINGING HOME
[A] SACK OF WHEAT. THE GIRL
[AN]D BOY ARE GRINDING FLOUR.
[MO]THER IS TAKING SOMETHING
OUT OF ONE OF THE
[CLO]SETS" (THEIR CLOSETS WERE
[JU]ST "PIGEON HOLES" IN THE
[MU]D WALLS). THE FIRE IS
[A L]ARGE HOLE IN THE FLOOR,
FILLED WITH BURNING
CHARCOAL.

ONE THING TO BE SAID IN FAVOR OF THE
CLOTHING STYLES IN JESUS' TIME IS THAT
THEY DIDN'T CHANGE FROM YEAR TO YEAR
AS OURS DO TODAY. SOME PEOPLE LIVING
IN THAT PART OF THE WORLD TODAY
DRESS ALMOST THE SAME AS THEY
DID IN BIBLE TIMES.

LABORERS USUALLY
WORE ONLY THE
UNDERGARMENT—
WITH OR WITHOUT
SLEEVES—OR
MERELY A WAIST-
CLOTH WHICH REACHED
TO THEIR KNEES.

A WIDE GIRDLE
AROUND THEIR
WAIST SERVED AS
"POCKETS" IN WHICH
THEY CARRIED MONEY,
FOOD, A SWORD OR
DAGGER, ETC.

"FAMILY FASHIONS in the FIRST CENTURY

SOME WORE A PLAIN
SHEET WOUND AROUND
THE BODY WITH ONE
END FLUNG OVER
THE SHOULDER. JESUS
IS USUALLY
PICTURED DRESSED
THAT WAY.

GIRLS WORE THE SAME
KIND OF CLOTHING AS
THEIR MOTHERS WORE...
WHICH, BY THE WAY, WAS
PRACTICALLY THE SAME AS
THE MEN WORE. IN FACT,
SOME OF THE GARMENTS
WERE SO MUCH ALIKE THAT
THEY COULD BE WORN BY
EITHER MEN OR WOMEN,
AND NO ONE WOULD KNOW
THE DIFFERENCE, EXCEPT
FOR THE HEADDRESS. WOMEN
AND GIRLS WORE LONG
HEAD SCARFS.

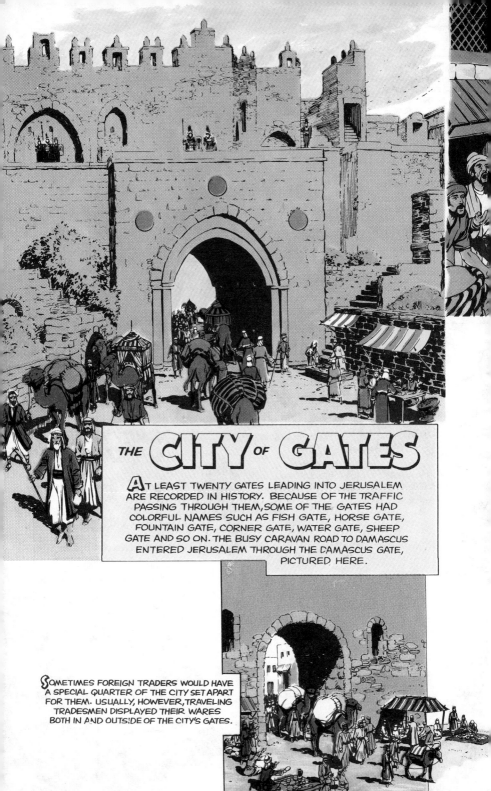

THE CITY OF GATES

AT LEAST TWENTY GATES LEADING INTO JERUSALEM ARE RECORDED IN HISTORY. BECAUSE OF THE TRAFFIC PASSING THROUGH THEM, SOME OF THE GATES HAD COLORFUL NAMES SUCH AS FISH GATE, HORSE GATE, FOUNTAIN GATE, CORNER GATE, WATER GATE, SHEEP GATE AND SO ON. THE BUSY CARAVAN ROAD TO DAMASCUS ENTERED JERUSALEM THROUGH THE DAMASCUS GATE, PICTURED HERE.

SOMETIMES FOREIGN TRADERS WOULD HAVE A SPECIAL QUARTER OF THE CITY SET APART FOR THEM. USUALLY, HOWEVER, TRAVELING TRADESMEN DISPLAYED THEIR WARES BOTH IN AND OUTSIDE OF THE CITY'S GATES.

WHEN YOU GO TO A SUPERMARKET TODAY, YOU GO TO THE RIGHT SECTION AND CHOOSE THE FOOD YOU WANT. BUT IN BIBLE DAYS ALL THE SHOPS THAT SOLD BREAD WOULD BE ON "BAKER'S STREET," ... ALL THE MEAT SHOPS ON "BUTCHER'S ROW," ... CANDY SHOPS ON "THE STREET OF SWEETS."

SO SHOPPING IN THOSE DAYS MEANT A LOT OF WALKING FROM STREET TO STREET.

STREETS OF BIBLE-TIME TOWNS WERE USUALLY NARROW, CROWDED AND NOISY. THEY WOUND THEIR WAY THROUGH THE CITY, TWISTING AND TURNING UPHILL AND DOWN. THROUGH THESE STREETS WENT MERCHANTS WITH THEIR HEAVILY LOADED CAMELS, HORSES AND DONKEYS ... PORTERS CARRYING HEAVY BUNDLES ON THEIR BACKS ... WOMEN BALANCING WATER JARS ON THEIR HEADS ... BEGGARS ... PEDDLERS — ALL PUSHING, BUMPING AND JOSTLING.

THERE WERE NO PRICE TAGS. WHAT YOU PAID WAS DETERMINED BY HOW GOOD YOU WERE AT BARGAINING AND HOW ANXIOUS THE MERCHANT WAS TO MAKE A SALE.

A SHEKEL COINED ABOUT 140 B.C.

THE SHEKEL WAS THE MOST COMMON COIN USED IN PALESTINE IN BIBLE DAYS. A GOLD SHEKEL WAS WORTH ABOUT FIFTEEN SILVER SHEKELS. A SILVER SHEKEL WAS EQUAL TO A DAY'S WORKER'S PAY FOR FOUR DAYS. ONE HALF AND ONE QUARTER SILVER SHEKELS WERE ALSO USED.

OCCUPATIONS IN BIBLE TIMES

FARMERS IN JESUS' TIME DIDN'T LIVE ON THEIR FARMS. THEY LIVED IN THE VILLAGES FOR MUTUAL PROTECTION FROM WILD ANIMALS AND BANDITS. EACH MORNING THE FARMERS WOULD DRIVE THEIR ANIMALS TO THEIR FIELDS FOR THE DAY'S WORK, WHICH BEGAN AT SUNRISE AND ENDED AT SUNSET.

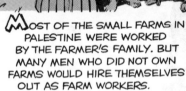

MOST OF THE SMALL FARMS IN PALESTINE WERE WORKED BY THE FARMER'S FAMILY. BUT MANY MEN WHO DID NOT OWN FARMS WOULD HIRE THEMSELVES OUT AS FARM WORKERS.

A SHEPHERD'S LIFE IN BIBLE TIMES WAS FILLED WITH DANGER AND HARDSHIP. HE WAS ON GUARD DAY AND NIGHT PROTECTING HIS SHEEP FROM RUSTLERS AND WILD ANIMALS. HIS DEFENSES AGAINST THESE LURKING DANGERS WERE HIS STAFF, HIS SLING AND HIS COURAGE.

SHEPHERDS USED A SLING WITH AMAZING ACCURACY. THE SMALL STONES THEY HURLED STRUCK WITH TERRIFIC FORCE. DAVID SLEW THE GIANT GOLIATH WITH A SHEPHERD'S SLING. (I SAMUEL 17:32–51)

THE SLING WAS A SHORT STRIP OF LEATHER. A WIDE PIECE IN THE CENTER HELD THE SMALL STONE. AFTER WHIRLING THE SLING AROUND HIS HEAD A FEW TIMES, THE SHEPHERD LET GO OF ONE END, SENDING THE STONE SPEEDING LIKE A BULLET TOWARD THE TARGET.

AT NIGHT FLOCKS WERE BROUGHT INTO A SHEEPFOLD FOR PROTECTION. AS EACH SHEEP ENTERED, IT WAS COUNTED – EVEN CALLED BY NAME. THROUGHOUT THE NIGHT THE SHEPHERD SLEPT AT THE OPENING OF THE FOLD, ACTING AS THE VERY GATE ITSELF.

LIFE IN BIBLE TIMES WAS QUITE DIFFERENT FROM TODAY. BUT THE WORDS JESUS PREACHED IN THE NEW TESTAMENT APPLY TO US AS MUCH AS THEY DID TO THESE PEOPLE WHO LIVED 2,000 YEARS AGO.

Scripture Index

Look for each of these *Picture Bible*
products from Chariot Victor . . .

PAPERBACK

DELUXE HARDCOVER

HARDCOVER

THE PICTURE BIBLE

NEW TESTAMENT

The Picture Bible makes a good first Bible for young readers,
though this classic best-seller is loved by people of all ages.
The full-text version contains 233 Bible stories in full-color comic
format that makes Bible stories exciting for kids. Newly revised,
the new information pages, maps, and an improved index give
this classic Bible storybook fresh significance for today!

DELUXE HARDCOVER
ISBN: 0-78143-057-7
PAPERBACK
ISBN: 0-78143-058-5
HARDCOVER
ISBN: 0-78143-055-0
THE NEW TESTAMENT
ISBN: 0-78143-056-9

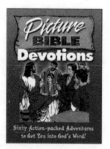

PICTURE BIBLE DEVOTIONS

ISBN: 0-78143-067-4

Interactive activities and full-color pictures
from *The Picture Bible* make this an innovative
approach to devotions. Kids learn to apply
Bible knowledge to their lives through 30 Old
Testament and 30 New Testament stories.